New Visions for Market Governance

I0882110

The financial crisis of 2008–09 and the "Great Recession" that it precipitated highlight a number of important questions about the governance of contemporary capitalism. How do shortcomings in existing market governance institutions help to account for trends of rising economic inequality and financial instability? What new forms of market governance would better embody norms of stability, equality and justice? And how do present political conditions both constrain and enable possibilities for reform?

This volume brings together an array of leading thinkers to consider these pressing questions about market governance and its potential reform. Contributors combine in-depth empirical analysis with innovative explorations of alternative arrangements to consider challenges of market governance in advanced and developing countries, as well as global and regional organizations.

New Visions for Market Governance will be of interest to students and scholars in a wide range of areas including international and comparative political economy, public and social policy, and normative social theory.

Kate Macdonald is Lecturer in Politics, University of Melbourne, Australia.

Shelley Marshall is Senior Lecturer in Business Law and Taxation, Monash University, Australia.

Sanjay Pinto is a Ph.D. Candidate in Sociology and Social Policy, Harvard University, USA.

Routledge/challenges of globalisation

Edited by Charles Sampford

Griffith University, Australia

This series seeks to make systematic contributions to international debates over two intimately related issues:

- The values that should inform the governance of modern states and the globalizing world in which they are increasingly enmeshed, in particular whether the liberal democratic values that sought to civilize the sovereign state need to be reconceived as global values.
- The institutions that are needed to realize those values, be they local, national, regional, international, transnational or global.

1 **Globalisation and Equality**
Edited by Keith Horton and Haig Patapan

2 **Globalisation and the Rule of Law**
Edited by Spencer Zifcak

3 **Environmental Values in a Globalising World**
Nature, justice and governance
Edited by Jouni Paavola and Ian Lowe

4 **Globalisation and Citizenship**
The transnational challenge
Edited by Wayne Hudson and Steven Slaughter

5 **Global Democracy and its Difficulties**
Edited by Anthony J. Langlois and Karol Edward Sołtan

6 **New Visions for Market Governance**
Crisis and renewal
Edited by Kate Macdonald, Shelley Marshall and Sanjay Pinto

New Visions for Market Governance

Crisis and renewal

Edited by Kate Macdonald, Shelley Marshall and Sanjay Pinto

Routledge
Taylor & Francis Group
LONDON AND NEW YORK

First published 2012
by Routledge
2 Park Square, Milton Park, Abingdon, Oxon OX14 4RN

Simultaneously published in the USA and Canada
by Routledge
711 Third Avenue, New York, NY 10017

First issued in paperback 2017

Routledge is an imprint of the Taylor & Francis Group, an informa business.

British Library Cataloguing in Publication Data
A catalogue record for this book is available from the British Library

Library of Congress Cataloging in Publication Data
A catalog record has been requested for this book

ISBN 13: 978-1-138-11037-3 (pbk)
ISBN 13: 978-0-415-69111-6 (hbk)

Typeset in Times New Roman
By Wearset Ltd, Boldon, Tyne and Wear

In memory of Alice Amsden, who forged new pathways for thinking about the challenges of economic development, and whose deeply committed and independent scholarship will continue to inspire.

Contents

Figures and tables

Figures

Tables

Contributors

Alice Amsden was the Barton L. Weller Professor of Political Economy in the Department of Urban Studies and Planning at MIT. Her books include *Asia's Next Giant: South Korea and Late Industrialization* and *The Rise of "the Rest": Challenges to the West from Late Industrializing Economies.*

Jason Beckfield is Professor of Sociology at Harvard University. His articles include "Inequality in the World Polity: The Structure of International Organization" and "European Integration and Income Inequality", both in the *American Sociological Review.*

Fred Block is Research Professor of Sociology at the University of California-Davis. His books include *The Vampire State and Other Myths and Fallacies About The U.S. Economy*, *Postindustrial Possibilities: A Critique of Economic Discourse*, and *Revising State Theory: Essays in Politics and Postindustrialism.*

Ross P. Buckley is Professor of Law at the University of New South Wales. His publications include *The International Financial System: Policy & Regulation*, and "Debt-for-development Exchanges: The Origins of a Financial Technique" in *The Law and Development Review.*

Damien Cahill is Lecturer in the department of Political Economy at the University of Sydney. His writings include "Business Mobilisation, the New Right and Australian Labor Governments in the 1980s" in the journal *Labour History*, and "Regulating the power shift: the state, capital and electricity privatization in Australia" in the *Journal of Australian Political Economy.*

John D. Conroy is a special consultant at the Foundation for Development Cooperation. His books include *Banking with the Poor*, *Getting the Framework Right: Policy and Regulation for Microfinance in Asia*, and *The Role of Central Banks in Microfinance.*

Marina Durano is a Post-Doctoral Fellow at the Women's Development Research Centre or KANITA of the Universiti Sains Malaysia, where she coordinates DAWN's research on the political economy of globalization. She is also a fellow of the GEM-IWG Gender and Macroeconomics Summer School in Salt Lake City.

Shaun Fitzgerald holds a Masters of International Politics from the University of Melbourne, having studied both there and at the University of London. He was part of a team at the University of Melbourne that taught a graduate subject on the United Nations, with Professor John Langmore. His research interests include the G20, U.S.–UN relations and UN Security Council reform. He is currently based in New York City, where he works with the United Nations.

Kevin P. Gallagher is Associate Professor of International Relations at Boston University. His books include *Free Trade and Environment: Mexico, NATFA, and Beyond*, and (with Roberto Porzecanski) *The Dragon in the Room: China and the future of Latin American Industrialization.*

John Howe is Director of the Centre for Employment and Labour Relations Law at the Melbourne Law School. John is the author of *Regulation for Job Creation*, and co-editor of the volume *Labour Law and Labour Market Regulation.*

John Langmore is Professor in the School of Social and Political Sciences at the University of Melbourne. He is the author of *Work for All: Full Employment in the Nineties* and *Dealing with America: The UN, the US, and Australia.*

Kate Macdonald is Lecturer at the University of Melbourne, Australia. Her research examines emerging systems of global economic governance, with a particular focus on social, labor, and human rights governance arrangements and their implications for developing countries. Before taking up her current job in Melbourne she held positions as Fellow of Government (Global Politics) at the London School of Economics and Political Science, Research Fellow at the Centre for Applied Philosophy and Public Ethics at the Australian National University and Research Officer at the Department of Politics and International Relations at Oxford University. She has carried out research and consultancy work for a range of development and human rights organizations, including Amnesty International, ActionAid Australia, and the U.K.'s Corporate Responsibility Coalition.

Shelley Marshall is Senior Lecturer in the Department of Business Law and Taxation at Monash University, Australia. She is a graduate in Arts and Law, and in Development Studies from the University of Melbourne and the London School of Economics and Political Science respectively. She has published widely on comparative "varieties" of capitalism, corporate accountability, and labor market regulation in industrialized and developing and transitional contexts. Her recent publications include *Fair Trade and Corporate Accountability: Experiments in Globalising Social Justice*, co-edited with Kate Macdonald and *Law, Corporate Governance and the Management of Labour: A Study of Australian Regulatory Style and Business Practice.*

José Antonio Ocampo is Professor of Professional Practice in International and Public Affairs at Columbia University. His recent publications include *Stability with Growth: Macroeconomics, Liberalization and Development*, with Joseph E. Stiglitz, Shari Spiegel, Ricardo French-Davis and Deepak Nayyar.

Sanjay Pinto is a Ph.D. Candidate in Sociology and Social Policy at Harvard University. Previously, he worked as a political canvasser, a writer for a civil rights non-profit, and a researcher for U.S. unions. His main areas of academic interest are economic sociology, political economy, and social stratification, and his dissertation project aims to promote a more multi-dimensional approach to the macrocomparative study of labor market institutions, one that addresses how they vary along national as well as sectoral lines. He is also currently doing work that looks at increases in flexible employment and declines in union organization in the economically advanced world. During his doctoral studies, Sanjay has been a visiting researcher at the Institute for International Integration Studies at Trinity College Dublin, and the Max Planck Institute for the Study of Societies in Cologne.

John Quiggin is Professor of Economics at the University of Queensland, and an Australian Research Council Federation Fellow. He is the author of *Zombie Economics: How Dead Ideas Still Walk Among Us* and "A Theory of Anticipated Utility", published in the *Journal of Economic Behavior and Organization.*

Joel Rogers is Professor of Law, Political Science, Public Affairs, and Sociology at the University of Wisconsin-Madison. He also directs COWS, the national think-and-do tank on high road development. His books include (with Richard Freeman) *What Workers Want* and (with Erik Olin Wright) *American Society: How it Really Works.*

Sandy Ross is an Honorary Fellow, School of Social and Political Sciences, University of Melbourne. Recent publications include *The World Food Programme in Global Politics* and "The World Food Programme: A Case of Benign U.S. Policy?" in *Australian Journal of International Affairs.*

Charles Sampford is Professor of Law and Ethics at United Nations University and Griffith University, and Director of the Institute for Ethics, Governance and Law at Griffith University. His publications include *Measuring Corruption* and "Future of Business Ethics-Legal Regulation, Ethical Standard Setting and Institutional Design" in *Griffith Law Review.*

Frances Stewart is Emeritus Professor of Development Economics at the University of Oxford. Her books include *Technology and Underdevelopment, Planning to Meet Basic Needs, War and Underdevelopment*, and *Horizontal Inequalities and Conflict: Understanding Group Violence in Multiethnic Societies.*

Robert H. Wade is Professor of Political Economy and Development at the London School of Economics and Political Science. His publications include: *Governing the Market: Economic Theory and the Role of Government in East Asia's Industrialization* and *Village Republics: Economic Conditions for Collective Action in South India.*

Min Zhou is a Ph.D. Candidate in Sociology at Harvard University. Zhou's publications include "Multidimensionality and Gravity in Global Trade, 1950–2000", in *Social Forces*; and "Intensification of Geo-Cultural Homophily in Global Trade: Evidence from the Model", forthcoming in *Social Science Research.*

Foreword

Fred Block

The appearance of *New Visions of Market Governance* is very good news: it is an indicator that a serious conversation about structural economic reform – at the national, regional, and global levels – might finally be under way. To be sure, this conversation should have occurred back in the 1990s in time to provoke actions that could have averted the global financial crisis of 2007–09. Or even better, the conversation should have begun in the 1970s when the Bretton Woods system slid into crisis, and government leaders adopted a series of misguided patches to the international monetary system that set us on the path to a global financial meltdown.

At a certain level, the absence of such a conversation at these earlier moments is puzzling; economic arrangements at the national, regional, and global levels are of obvious importance because they set limits on what is possible to achieve within societies. Social scientists and other intellectuals should have been examining the defects in the rules of the game governing the global economy and proposing bold reform ideas for the global economy, for supra-national regions, and for national economies – changes that would make possible more stable, sustainable and just patterns of economic growth.

That this did not happen earlier is important and tells us a great deal about the evolution of the social sciences over the decades since World War II. The production of knowledge is supposed to be a progressive process; we should see further because we stand on the shoulder of previous generations of intellectuals. But in this particular case, the social sciences regressed because we lost touch with the lessons that our predecessors of the 1930s and 1940s had learned. It is important to understand how this happened.

Forgetting the lessons of the interwar period

As part of the peace agreement after World War I, the leaders of the world's major powers agreed to restore the international gold standard that had been in place before the war. As Karl Polanyi (1944: 26) memorably states:

> Indeed, the essentiality of the gold standard to the functioning of the international economic system of the time was the one and only tenet common to men of all nations and all classes, religious denominations, and social philosophies.

However, this blind faith in the gold standard was ultimately undermined by the severity of the Great Depression of the 1930s. A number of important thinkers came to recognize that the restoration of the gold standard had been a disastrous mistake that contributed both to the severity of the economic downturn and to the collapse of democratic regimes across Europe. Constructing a different global economic regime that would make greater space for domestic economic policies became a central goal for the United States and the United Kingdom in planning for the post World War II world. Their intention was to create an international regime that would be consistent with domestic reforms such as full employment policies and an expanded welfare state.

To be sure, the conversation in the 1930s and 1940s about reforming the global economic system was almost entirely an elite conversation. The average citizen in the U.S. or Europe understood little about global payment systems, exchange rates, or reserve currencies. Nevertheless, popular opinion was an important consideration for those engaged in the elite conversation; they understood the public's strong desire for post-war societies that assured full employment and generous social provision. In replacing the gold standard they sought to create arrangements that would be consistent with projects of domestic reform.

But how did this elite consensus in favor of replacing the gold standard emerge? Much of the credit goes to John Maynard Keynes, who had been campaigning against the gold standard since the early 1920s. As a consequence of his growing intellectual prestige following the publication of *The General Theory* in 1936, his critique of the gold standard moved from the margins of economics into the mainstream. But Keynes' insights did not emerge in a vacuum; they were a response to the intensifying debates in Europe that erupted in the aftermath of the revolutionary upheavals at the end of World War I, especially the triumph of the Bolsheviks in Russia.

It is true that growing socialist movements had been challenging existing institutions in Europe for decades, but the success of the Bolsheviks in Russia meant that intellectuals could no longer ignore the possibility of radical discontinuities in historical development. They had to address the possibility that the future would be very different from the past. Some intellectuals went over to the side of the Bolsheviks, others were drawn to the new movements of European fascism, others sought to revive the model of laissez-faire capitalism, and still others pursued social democracy as yet another pathway to a different future. After the Russian Revolution, in other words, intellectuals were questioning every aspect of modern Western societies. It was in the midst of this broader theoretical ferment that Keynes challenged the inevitability and the desirability of the gold standard.

But another aspect of this intellectual ferment is also important. In this period after World War I, economics had not yet walled itself off from other academic fields. Important economists of the 1920s and 1930s continued to read widely so that discussions of appropriate international monetary regimes encompassed insights from history, political science, law and sociology. While Keynes was broad in his intellectual interests, he was hardly unique. Central Europeans of this period such as Joseph Schumpeter, Karl Polanyi, and Friedrich Hayek were also wide-ranging intellectuals who roamed across disciplinary lines with ease.

In short, the agreement at Bretton Woods in 1944 to reconstruct the global economic order with new rules was the culmination of decades of debate that cut across disciplinary lines and that seriously questioned *all* existing institutions. But once World War II came to an end the conditions that had sustained the earlier debate disappeared. Even though the arrangements agreed to at Bretton Woods were not fully implemented until the late 1950s, the return of economic prosperity against the backdrop of a Cold War between the U.S. and the Soviet Union ended the previous discussions. For the most part, intellectuals lined up on one side or the other; either they embraced the institutions of the U.S. economic model or they favored the Soviet Union. Either way, they saw little reason to pay attention to the rules governing the global economy or spend time envisioning broad new reforms within national societies.

Moreover, the experts left in charge of global economic arrangements were overwhelmingly professional economists who followed the post World War II trajectory of their discipline. As economics became both more prestigious and more mathematical, the connections between economics and the other social sciences atrophied. Economists were decreasingly likely to have a broad intellectual formation and citations of work in other fields became rarer in their publications. The space for deep interrogation of the international monetary regime within the subfield of international economics became progressively narrower. But even more seriously, as the practitioners of international economics lacked grounding in history, political science, and sociology, they increasingly became prisoners of abstract models in which outcomes would be optimal if capital were allowed to move freely across the globe in response to market signals.

To be sure, this brief sketch overstates the case. As a result of the social movements of the 1960s, there was a revival within some intellectual circles of the broad-ranging and critical conversation of the interwar years and some powerful critiques of the organization of the global economy were developed. Intellectuals and political leaders in the developing world placed on the agenda in the 1970s the demand for a "New International Economic Order" that would bring about a more equitable distribution of global resources. And even among economists, there were important exceptions to the pattern described here; some scholars did build on Keynes' insights and analyze global economic institutions from a less complacent intellectual perspective.

But the point remains that these efforts did not reach the critical mass required to influence the highest level policy debates. Even the project of a New International Economic Order that achieved some significant victories within UN institutions was effectively demolished in the early 1980s when the debt crisis increased the leverage of rich nations over poorer nations.

And in the 1990s when social movements opposing "free market globalization" culminated in the Seattle demonstration against the World Trade Organization, they still had only a limited number of legitimate and influential allies within the social sciences. Especially among economists, the prevailing view continued to be that "free market globalization" was both a desirable and an inevitable process; they could see no real alternative.

Has the tide turned?

It is still too early to assert that reform of global and domestic economic institutions is now firmly on the world's agenda. There are still powerful forces that block the way, including the political and economic influence of large financial institutions and transnational corporations, ongoing political stalemate within the U.S., and the continuing insularity of mainstream economists. But as the contributions to this volume make clear, there are significant new factors:

- The severity of the 2007–09 crisis, and its disastrous impact in both rich and poor countries, deeply delegitimated the proponents of "business-as-usual". The claims to expert knowledge by bankers, financial economists, and free market theorists increasingly ring hollow.
- The growing economic power and influence of China, India, Brazil, and other rising nations has destabilized the institutional basis of the old order and significantly expanded the openings for new ideas about the organization of global governance institutions, regional economies, and national economies.
- At the same time it is increasingly obvious that many nations have been left behind during this long period of market liberal globalization. Some have experienced de-development or declining standards of living, and others have seen the collapse of states and civil order. These experiences increase the pressures for a more just global order that is responsive to the poorest of the world's people.
- Even within economics there are expanding efforts to study the lessons of the 2007–09 crisis and a growing number of scholars are beginning to reconsider some of the assumptions that proved untrustworthy.

It will, however, take a daunting combination of sustained intellectual work, widespread efforts to popularize reform ideas and extensive political mobilization in different parts of the global economy to launch a true project of global economic reform. But the urgency of returning to the task that was begun in the 1940s could not be greater.

Acknowledgments

The "Re-Embedding the Market" workshops were made possible by the generous financial and organizational support of a number of institutions. We thank the Australian Research Council funded Governance Research Network and the Institute for Ethics, Governance and Law at Griffith University; the Max Planck Institute for the Study of Societies, Cologne; the Department of Business Law and Taxation at Monash University; the Social Justice Initiative at the University of Melbourne; the Tobin Project; the United Nations Association, Australia; and, at Harvard University, the Committee on Australian Studies, the David Rockefeller Center for Latin American Studies, the Minda de Gunzburg Center for European Studies, the Project on Justice, Welfare and Economics, the Multidisciplinary Program in Inequality and Social Policy, and the Weatherhead Center for International Affairs.

We would like to thank all the participants in the workshops at Harvard University, the Max Planck Institute for the Study of Societies, Cologne, and the University of Melbourne, as well as the many people who graciously provided logistical support.

A special note of gratitude goes out to Fred Block for his advice and encouragement throughout the project, and to Kamillea Aghtan for her truly exceptional editorial assistance.

1 Re-thinking market governance

Kate Macdonald, Shelley Marshall and Sanjay Pinto

The financial crisis of 2008–09 and the "Great Recession" that it precipitated highlighted a number of troubling dynamics in contemporary capitalism. Rising financial instability has received particular attention (Obstfeld and Rogoff, 2009), as have other social problems such as trends of increased economic inequality (Manning, 2011). For many observers these problems have revealed serious weaknesses in systems of national, regional and global market governance that are linked to the rise of market liberal ideology and a set of associated policies and practices (Abdelal and Ruggie, 2009). The crisis has been heralded as an opportunity for change that would "embed" markets in public control, establishing new institutional forms that better embody norms of stability, equality, and justice (Sen, 2009).

In late 2009, to consider such possibilities for institutional change, we convened a series of workshops at Harvard University, the University of Melbourne, and the Max Planck Institute for the Study of Societies, Cologne, with the title of "Re-embedding the Market: Crisis and Reinvention?" Contributors to these workshops came from a variety of geographical and disciplinary locations, and considered topics ranging from financial reform to industrial policy to labour market regulation. All were oriented to addressing a common set of questions. What social problems and related shortcomings in existing market governance institutions has the crisis revealed? How might these institutions be reformed in ways that better address the abiding challenges underscored by the crisis? And what are the prospects of realizing possible reform trajectories in light of current political conditions?

In this introduction we consider how the contributions in this volume address these key questions. The first section focuses on the transformations in market governance – defined here as "the institutions, governmental and non-governmental, that constrain market activity" (Gereffi and Mayer, 2006) – which helped to produce the crisis, and that the crisis spotlighted in turn. Authors consider the institutional changes that have occurred in the financial sphere and other market domains, and the shifting state-society and international relationships that have been entailed in these transformations. We draw out a recurring theme that appears in many of the contributions, which is that market governance has become "disembedded" from broad-based democratic control, both within societies and in the international arena.

The second section highlights authors' visions of reform. We asked contributors to propose new ideas for institutional reform without limiting their imagination to proposals that appear politically viable in the current environment. Political conditions quickly shift from right to left and back again. In the meantime it is the job of visionary thinkers to consider how markets might be more fairly and effectively governed, without the process of imagining alternatives being suffocated by the weight of established practice (see Unger, 1998). Contributors to this volume do just this, formulating a wide range of reform ideas and agendas that would "re-embed" markets in new ways.

There is no shortage of ideas for reforming market governance institutions, as this volume demonstrates. But the ability of these ideas to find institutional expression is another matter. Even though one key motivation for this project was to encourage the articulation of ideas that transcend the politics of the moment, contributors also take seriously questions of feasibility and transformative agency, analyzing the political struggles through which reform agendas are contested. In the third section we turn attention to current political dynamics and how they shape the conditions of possibility for new forms of market governance.

The disembedding of markets

Among observers of the financial crisis, much commentary identifies trends of market liberalization and deregulation as helping to lay the conditions under which the crisis emerged. Polanyi, in his classic account, described the rise of the "free market" in the nineteenth century as a process by which markets became "disembedded" from the kinds of norms and control mechanisms by which they had previously been governed (Polanyi, 1944). Shifts in recent decades have often been cast in a similar light. Drawing on this Polanyian conception, the free market logic of "neoliberalism" has been contrasted to a postwar era of "embedded liberalism" that placed greater emphasis on stabilizing markets within national contexts (Abdelal and Ruggie, 2009; Ruggie, 1982).

Especially in the wake of the crisis, criticisms of market liberalism have often been expressed in hotly ideological terms, and it is useful to break down the substantive claims that lie behind them. Contributors to this volume have analyzed three main dimensions of market disembedding. First, many authors have detailed institutional transformations within the financial sector, and a variety of interlinked market domains. Second, contributors have highlighted shifts in the role of the state in governing markets, and related changes in the power and influence exerted by a range of competing social interests. Third, authors have shown how processes of change play out at the local, national, regional, and global levels, and analyzed how dynamics at these different geographic levels interact.

Disembedding within and across policy domains

Processes of liberalization have been observed across a range of market arenas in recent decades. The crisis of 2008–09 placed particular focus on how these processes occurred in the financial arena, generating remarkable instability. As Quiggin argues in this volume, the appearance of spectacular panics and crashes in the financial arena due to processes of market disembedding is a long-standing historical phenomenon. However, recent decades have seen the frequency of major financial crises that spill across national borders rise to historically unprecedented levels (Kindleberger, 2000).

In Chapter 16, Sampford describes how free market thinking found expression in the financial arena. Based on assumptions of rationality and perfect information, the "efficient market hypothesis" postulated that individuals acting freely in the market would produce the most efficient and desirable outcomes possible (see also Fox, 2009). This view helped to provide the rationale for financial market deregulation in the United States and other countries. Moreover, as Quiggin argues, the relatively unconstrained development of financial innovations has meant that even the regulatory frameworks that do remain in place are increasingly unable to detect and contain new forms of risk taking.

Through the creation of sub-prime asset-backed securities, financial innovations have created opportunities for lower-income groups to access cheap credit. Yet, as Conroy suggests in his chapter comparing microcredit in India with sub-prime mortgage lending in the U.S., the explosion of cheap credit has also led lower-income groups across a range of national contexts to take on unsustainably high amounts of debt. When asset bubbles have burst these vulnerable populations often have been hardest hit in relative terms, with their ability to fulfil basic needs thrown in jeopardy.

The growth and liberalization of the financial sector has had far reaching consequences that permeate through a variety of other sectors. Ross notes in his chapter that financial speculation in agricultural markets has contributed to problems of food insecurity in many parts of the world. Food commodities and finance have become increasingly intermeshed due to rapidly growing markets in commodity-based derivative financial instruments. As the price of food has become subject to financial speculation, it has alternately become too expensive for the poor and even middle class consumers, or so cheap as to rob producers of a living wage.

Such links between finance and other sectors can also flow in the other direction. While financial innovation – enabled by supportive government policies – helps to account for the increased supply of cheap credit in the U.S., rising economic inequality has been a key factor in increased demand. Gains from economic growth in recent decades have gone largely to the top 1 per cent (Piketty and Saez, 2006), while real wages have been relatively stagnant for most U.S. workers, apart from an uptick in the 1990s (Bernstein and Mishel, 2007). As noted by Goodman (2009), a contributor to the Harvard "Re-embedding the Market" workshop, this stagnation helps to account for the increased demand for cheap credit. It is in this sense that rising inequality within the U.S. labour market (and society more broadly) helped to fuel the conditions for heightened risk and instability within the financial market.

Disembedding from state and society

A crucial feature of neoliberalism has been the shifting role of the state (Harvey, 2005). In the wake of the crisis much attention has been focused on the failure of national governments to effectively address problems such as economic inequality and financial instability. As suggested by Gereffi and Mayer (2006), the role of states in "facilitating the operation of markets" has remained strong or even grown in prominence, especially in many newly industrialized and transitional countries, while their role in "regulat[ing] the negative externalities of market transactions" and "limiting and mitigating the[ir] unequal impacts" has been thrown into question (Gereffi and Mayer, 2006: 42). To be sure, state regimes still vary substantially across countries (Hall and Soskice, 2001; Esping-Anderson, 1990), but these broad trends are observable even in countries that have been historically characterized by less free market-oriented forms of organization (Streeck, 2009).

Another broad set of shifts with important implications for market governance has to do with changes in the power and mobilization of different interest groups within national societies. As Stewart discusses in her Concluding Note, large corporations have grown in power and influence during recent decades, especially in the Anglo-American world. And, as Quiggin aptly captures in Chapter 2, large financial firms have become particularly ascendant, asserting increased power over what happens in the "real" economy.

An important dimension of this rise in corporate power is that countervailing pressures exerted by other groups have declined in many ways. In the economically advanced world this is especially true in the case of organized labour. To be sure, there are important differences across different sectors and countries. In Nordic countries, for example, unions and collective bargaining institutions remain quite strong. In other economically advanced countries, however, the trend has been one of steeply declining rates of union density (Pinto and Beckfield, 2011). And, as Rogers notes in Chapter 14, these developments have profoundly altered dynamics of power within labour markets. Whereas the capital–labour accord in place under embedded liberalism helped to ensure a mode of governance in which gains from growth were more evenly shared, the erosion of this accord has been an important factor in trends of rising inequality under neoliberalism.

Several contributors to this volume discuss the ways in which these shifts within state and society are related. Sampford notes in Chapter 16 that strong actions were taken by Margaret Thatcher in the early 1980s to undercut the power of organized labour in Britain. Certainly broader structural shifts including deindustrialization have been important drivers of union decline in economically advanced countries, but actions by conservative governments have accelerated this decline, and countervailing measures by Left or center-Left governments have generally amounted to rearguard efforts.

Conversely, the increasing power of corporate interests has extended deep into the formal political arena (Hacker and Pierson, 2010). As Quiggin suggests, the continued power wielded by financial interests can help to explain the relatively limited nature of financial reform following the recent crisis, despite widespread criticism of big banks, ratings agencies and other key actors.

There is thus a strong mutually reinforcing dynamic to these developments in state and society. The growing power of large financial firms and other corporate interests of various stripes goes hand-in-hand with a curtailment of many of the regulatory and redistributive functions of states. As Cahill suggests, the development of "free markets" is not, then, a process in which state and society no longer have a role in market governance (see also Block, 2008). Instead, as Polanyi argues, it is one in which markets become disembedded from broader-based public control.

Disembedding at the national and international levels

In addition to looking at changes in governance within societies, several authors consider how the relationship between market governance at the national and international levels has evolved in recent decades. Under embedded liberalism, the International Monetary Fund (IMF), the World Bank, and the General Agreement on Tariffs and Trade (GATT) promoted a balance between international integration and the national embedding of markets. But, in recent decades, these organizations have more intently promoted liberal agendas and a shrinking of policy space at the national level. Moreover, these and other global governance organizations have proved inadequate in addressing developments such as the increased organization of production on a multinational scale (Gereffi and Mayer, 2006), and, as discussed by Buckley, Langmore and Fitzgerald, and Ocampo, the rising volume of international financial flows.[1] It is in this sense that markets have become more "disembedded" at both the national and international levels.

As shown by Beckfield and Zhou, liberalization has also been promoted by regional organizations. For example, in the European Union (E.U.), the world's most tightly integrated regional entity, legal and legislative measures concerning labour mobility and other issues have contributed importantly to an increased commodification of labour (see also Höpner and Schäfer, 2010). They also note that, overall, economic and political integration within the E.U. has been associated with welfare state retrenchment and rising income inequality (see also Beckfield, 2006).

While nearly all countries have negotiated increased regional and global economic integration during recent decades, a number of contributors to the volume also underscore the manner in which more powerful countries have been able to dictate the terms of this integration – for themselves and for other countries. For example, Amsden shows that advanced countries and major newly industrialized countries have been able to use "subterfuge" to deploy policies aimed at promoting key industries, finding creative ways to work within and around bilateral, regional, and global trade agreements. Even in the context of broad liberalizing trends, these countries have been able to work – and work around – the rules of the game in ways that suit their interests.

At the same time major global governance organizations, controlled by economically advanced countries, have played an important role in promoting liberalization in developing countries.[2] Under the regime of "embedded liberalism", the GATT, the IMF and the World Bank were far less relevant to the prospects of developing countries than they are today. Moreover, as Block notes in his Foreword, there was a period during the 1960s and 1970s when developing countries were able to advance their agendas within more inclusive fora such as the United Nations General Assembly.

Since the Third World debt crisis of the early 1980s, however, the centre of gravity in global economic decision making has shifted decisively to the Bretton Woods organizations and the GATT/WTO. Amsden, Buckley and Durano note how these organizations have intruded ever more deeply into the governance regimes of developing countries, pushing liberalization and deregulation across a range of areas (see also Toye, 1993; Chang, 2002). Indeed, Durano points out that IMF dictates on fiscal discipline have played a role in constraining how developing country governments have responded to the recent crisis, even as advanced countries have implemented large bailout packages.

While there is often a tendency to focus on the distinction between advanced and developing countries when characterizing inequalities in the global arena, a number of authors also highlight the importance of addressing the ways in which inequalities within societies intersect with this North–South divide. Buckley notes in his chapter that IMF loan conditions following the 1997–98 Asian Financial Crisis effectively entailed a redistribution from ordinary Indonesians to Northern creditors for transactions over which the former had negligible responsibility. In some such cases, engagement with the IMF has actually provided willing developing country governments with political cover in pushing through unpopular austerity measures (see Vreeland, 2003).

Visions of re-embedding

Given these processes of dis-embedding, contributors to this volume present a rich and varied set of ideas on how markets might be re-embedded. Many draw inspiration from currently or previously existing forms of practice, considering, for example, how principles or features of institutional design in place under embedded liberalism might be restored.

Many also contemplate hitherto unrealized institutional and social arrangements. For Polanyi a key aspect of embedding was that broad social participation should shape market institutions, and a number of contributions consider market governance arrangements that would break new ground in their social inclusiveness.

Most contributors combine these two impulses in some fashion, considering how currently or previously existing forms of practice might be reworked so that they are more inclusive of different interests, and more attentive to key contemporary problems. Having looked at different dimensions of dis-embedding, we now consider how these same dimensions are reflected in contributors' visions of reform.

Reform in different policy domains

Responding to the pressing need to promote greater stability in the financial arena, a number of contributors to this volume, including Buckley, Quiggin, Langmore and Fitzgerald, Ocampo, Ross, and Wade, discuss possible reforms of existing institutions and the development of new ones. In doing so, many harken back to the greater financial discipline of the post-war era.

Quiggin, as well as Langmore and Fitzgerald, discusses the possibility of a "Tobin tax" on financial transactions, which could dampen destabilizing financial speculation and constrain the size of the financial sector, while helping to fund important development objectives (and, as others have suggested, to insure against future crises). Like many others, Langmore and Fitzgerald suggest that such a tax should be levied on international financial transactions, but Quiggin argues that it should apply to domestic transactions as well.

For Amsden, Howe and Gallagher, industrial policy has a prominent place in the landscape of possible reforms. In the early 1990s two contributors to this volume, Amsden and Wade, were central figures arguing against a dominant narrative which suggested that the rapid and sustained growth of several East Asian newly industrialized countries could be explained by international market integration (World Bank, 1989). Both pointed to the important role of carefully tailored industrial policy (Amsden, 1989; Wade, 2004).

Now, in her chapter excavating "underground" practices of industrial policy in today's environment, Amsden updates her earlier work. As before her analysis is geared largely towards characterizing in empirical terms the nature of contemporary industrial policy. But, again, she identifies models that leaders in the least developed countries might look to as they try to design policies for promoting economic development.

More far-reaching transformation of the way that markets are governed is envisaged by Rogers, in Chapter 14. Posing "productive democracy" as an alternative to both neoliberalism and currently and previously existing forms of social democracy, Rogers sets forth a reform program that covers a range of areas including education, social insurance and tax policy. A unifying theme is that whereas social democracy has promoted equality largely through compensatory redistribution, productive democracy would establish a more equitable distribution of productive assets that fosters broader based contributions towards socioeconomic output.

State and non-state actors as agents of reform

Explicitly or implicitly, many of the contributions in this volume assign the state an important role in embedding and re-embedding markets. The financial and industrial policy reforms endorsed by several authors would entail, in important respects, shifts in the regulatory powers exerted by states, and their role in redistributing economic resources. Howe and Ocampo also affirm the importance of countercyclical Keynesian macroeconomic management, both in responding to crises and helping to prevent their emergence in the first place.

In addition to asserting the importance of states in embedding markets, many authors focus on the potential for market embedding to take on a more decisively democratic flavour via the involvement of a wider array of social interests and groups in shaping regimes of governance. Indeed, while there is an important role for state actors in applying Keynesian-style technocratic expertise to address key problems of governance, several contributions advocate reform trajectories that embody Polanyi's more participatory normative conception of embeddedness (see Rahman, 2011).

In this vein, given the prevalence of gender inequality within labour markets (Fraser, 1997), Durano suggests that deliberative procedures which afford women a greater voice in decision making processes will be crucial to advancing the kinds of gender-equitable public policies that she advocates. This includes policies to ensure that industrialization strategies in developing countries counteract rather than reinforce gender segregation within labour markets, partly by increasing women's access to technology and opportunities for upgrading their skills.

Similarly, Howe cites the Textile, Clothing and Footwear (TCF) Industry Innovation Council, Australia to consider how the formation of industrial policy can be more broadly embedded in deliberative processes. He notes that, while unions have had a voice in workplace issues under traditional corporatist models, the TCF Council affords unions and NGOs a more expansive role in shaping the industry's economic strategy. Such engagement is important not only in influencing the content of the policies, but in conferring legitimacy and facilitating effective policy implementation.

Rogers' vision of productive democracy also features a strong state–society nexus, forged through public deliberation and associational activity. In his conception, these state–society linkages are pursued not just nationally, but through experimentation at a sub-national level. Moreover, he suggests that new arrangements might emerge outside the immediate orbit of the state, perhaps addressing limits in the capacity of local, state or national governments to address key public concerns.

National and international dimensions of reform

As the global economy has become more integrated, national and international dimensions of reform have become inseparable. Authors approach this from two angles. First, several contributors argue that policymakers and other actors within individual countries require greater autonomy with respect to the international environment, including global and regional governance organizations. For example, Rogers argues that international organizations are too often bent upon pushing aggressively for market integration, and that the international rules of the game should be revised to permit greater diversity in national development strategies.

The question of how to ensure that the poorest countries are granted ample room for manoeuvre is one that preoccupies a number of authors. Amsden argues that, in order for these countries to successfully make use of "new industrial policy" strategies, their policy rights vis-à-vis the World Bank and the WTO must be substantially enlarged. Buckley, for his part, is not optimistic that the IMF will stop intruding on the policy rights of the poorest countries. Given its history of imposing free market-oriented structural adjustment policies even after professing that it would do otherwise, he argues that an important reform imperative is to substantially scale back its mandate.

Second, in contrast to Buckley others argue that the mandate of the major economic organizations should be enhanced in concert with increased country participation. Ocampo suggests that a more broadly inclusive IMF should take up a central role in macroeconomic policy coordination. Wade recommends reforming the International Bank for Reconstruction and Development (IBRD), which is part of the World Bank Group, so that poor and middle income countries that have already undergone substantial industrial development can use it as a sort of banking cooperative. These countries would play a more active role in guaranteeing IBRD bonds and running the organization, and they would also be able to draw more resources from the Bank to finance long term projects (e.g., infrastructure development) for which it is otherwise difficult to find funding.

At the same time, Ocampo and Langmore and Fitzgerald suggest that efforts should be made to make decisions about economic governance in more fully representative fora. Ocampo argues for the establishment of a "Global Economic Coordination Council" under the auspices of the UN, which he envisions as a "democratically legitimate forum for discussion of the principal issues of global political economy". Langmore and Fitzgerald agree with this in principle, although they suggest that it would be difficult to establish, possibly involving a change in the UN Charter. As a "next best" option, they recommend the creation of a mechanism through which the Group of 20 (G20) would consult with the full UN membership prior to its meetings.

While many of the reform proposals revolve around the issue of country participation in inter-governmental organizations, another important question has to do with the role of different non-state actors in international governance. Given the association that they observe between E.U. regional integration and rising inequality in member countries, Beckfield and Zhou argue that strengthening of union organization at the regional level might help to counteract this trend. Specifically, they regard cross-nationally portable union-run unemployment insurance as one potentially promising idea, even though they do not foresee such participation by organized labour in E.U. level governance as likely given the current direction of change.

In certain regards there are tensions between these calls for greater autonomy vis-à-vis international economic governance organizations, on the one hand, and greater participation, on the other. At least in part these tensions stem from tactical disagreements concerning, for example, the likely timeline on substantially expanding participation within organizations such as the IMF, which contribute to differing views on the near term plausibility of significantly changing their agendas.

Still, the various authors who address these matters would likely agree that there is an important sense in which these two principles can be mutually reinforcing. Wider participation in international organizations could play an important role in helping to ensure that these bodies afford greater autonomy in policy and institutional design to different countries, including the least developed countries. And greater autonomy does not imply a retreat from the global economy. Rather, as Rogers suggests, it can ensure that different countries (and localities) are able to engage on their own terms, enhancing the democratic quality of this participation.

The politics of reform

Politics and power are central to many of the underlying reform ideas discussed above. In suggesting that finance should be placed in the service of the real economy, that market governance should be more inclusive of different social actors, and that international organizations need to give voice to all countries, authors argue that there is an important relationship between what market governance institutions do and the configurations of power and interest in which they themselves are embedded. There is no one-to-one correspondence between the presence of certain groups and the substantive agendas that are pursued in a given institutional context, but patterns of representation do help to demarcate the boundaries of what is possible (Phillips, 1995).

In this section we consider how the political conditions related to reform of market governance institutions have evolved since the crisis. On the one hand entrenched structures of power and interest have thwarted the realization of many reform ideas such as those discussed in this book. Even if market liberalism as an ideology seemed to be in tatters following the crisis, we returned, for the most part, to business-as-usual. On the other hand this crisis, like others, has not only challenged dominant ideas; it has unsettled prevailing alliances and power relations in ways that are still unfolding.

The politics of reform in different policy domains

The financial crisis of 2008–09 provoked widespread criticism of existing financial regulations and seemed to generate substantial momentum for reform. One of the more significant developments in the financial arena has been increasing political support for the “Robin Hood” or Tobin tax idea discussed above. For many years conversations about the Tobin tax have largely been the preserve of academics such as those writing in this volume, or activist organizations such as the Paris-based Association for the Taxation of Financial Transactions and for Citizens’ Action (ATTAC). Following the crisis, however, French President Nicolas Sarkozy and several other government leaders have endorsed the idea.

On June 29, 2011, the European Commission proposed the introduction of a Tobin style tax on the E.U.’s financial sector to generate direct revenue – starting from 2014 (European Commission, 2011). The proposal was presented to the

G20 Summit in Cannes in November 2011, with the backing of 1,000 economists (Stewart, 2011) as well as high profile supporters such as Bill Gates. Although the tax was not endorsed at the Cannes meeting of the G20 it was backed by a number of countries, and Sarkozy vowed to continue pursuing the initiative (Wroughton, 2011).

Other reforms implemented in the financial arena have so far been limited. For example, Quiggin and Ocampo note that the increased capital adequacy requirements in the Basel III guidelines are a significant advancement over Basel II, but both agree that these and other improvements still fall far short of developing the kind of new financial architecture that is needed. As Quiggin suggests, the Basel guidelines still do not fundamentally challenge the mastery of the financial sector over decisions in other arenas. Many have also pointed to limits in how well these guidelines stand to accomplish even their stated objectives, criticizing their low and imprecise requirements for bank equity holdings (Admati *et al.*, 2010) and suggesting that the aim of implementing them by late 2012 is simply unrealistic (*The Economist*, 2011).

As Ross demonstrates in his chapter, reforms to address the food crisis have also been very slow to materialize. In June 2008 the 180 governments that met in Rome for the UN's Food Summit had difficulty even agreeing to an agenda. The November 2009 Food Security Summit had a greater sense of urgency and coherence, but, while 60 world leaders were present, notably absent from the summit were the leaders of the G8 countries (AFP, 2009b).

Perhaps most alarmingly in light of Ross' identification of financialization as an important factor contributing to the food crisis, the primary response to the food crisis by the World Bank – the Agriculture Price Risk Management (APRM) facility – actually involves deepening the financialization of food commodity markets (BWI, 2011). Such initiatives by the World Bank and other top economic governance organizations suggest that, despite the outpouring of public criticism of financial liberalization following the crisis, the political appetite for deeper paradigm shifts within these organizations remains limited.

In the areas of social and labour policy there have actually been serious cutbacks in spending in many countries during recent times. A number of European countries have pursued particularly drastic austerity measures. For instance, in 2011, Silvio Berlusconi's government in Italy passed two measures worth a total of €134 billion that entailed, among many other consequences, increased healthcare fees, pay freezes and salary cuts in the public sector. And in October 2010 David Cameron's government in the U.K. passed spending cuts – including especially large reductions in social service spending – that were the largest seen since World War II (BBC, 2011).

Fiscal austerity measures have also been undertaken in many developing countries. In September 2011 the United Nations Children's Fund (UNICEF) released a report showing that government spending cutbacks in areas including food subsidies, old age pensions and public employment were having a particularly noticeable effect on vulnerable populations across the developing world (Ortiz *et al.*, 2011).

Social mobilization and the politics of state action

While the implementation of austerity measures was a significant trend in many countries during 2010 and 2011, it is worth recalling just how much political conditions have shifted back and forth in the short span of time since the crisis began. Initially, of course, the crisis and the economic dislocations that it set in motion led to widespread criticism of free market ideology, even among many mainstream politicians. Then-Australian Prime Minister Kevin Rudd blamed the crisis on a "political and economic ideology of extreme capitalism" and "a fundamental failure of values" (Kirchner, 2008). As discussed by Howe, governments in Australia and elsewhere implemented significant Keynesian style stimulus packages. With the crisis relatively contained it seemed as if the stage might be set for a significant expansion in the redistributive and regulatory powers exerted by states in various market domains.

When bailouts and Keynesian style stimulus packages in many OECD countries were not followed by quick economic recoveries, however, a view that increased state spending and involvement in resource allocation was in fact the problem rather than the solution gained significant political traction. A "pincer movement" of elite and grassroots mobilizations – the latter exemplified by the rise of the Tea Party in the U.S. – contributed to electoral gains for right and center-right parties in several countries. Conservative governments proceeded to implement austerity programs, joined in some cases and to varying degrees by more cent or Left governments in a number of countries.[3]

By 2011 there were signs that yet another pendulum swing was gathering momentum, galvanized in no small way by the unfolding events of the "Arab Spring" (El-Din Haseeb, 2011). As noted by Quiggin, austerity measures implemented in response to the European sovereign debt crisis have been felt disproportionately by those without significant economic means. In turn, protests against the distributional implications of austerity measures have swept across many European capitals (see, e.g., Hewitt, 2011; Rainsford, 2011), and there have been similar protests again public sector cutbacks in a number of U.S. states (Ariosto, 2011), with organized labour playing a central role in many of these mobilizations.

In September of 2011 the "Occupy Wall Street" movement erupted in New York before spreading to many other cities around the world. Initiated largely by tech-savvy, left-of-center young people, local Occupy sites have generally been organized according to principles of direct democracy, encouraging wide participation in conversations about how society might be reorganized.[4]

Whereas the Tea Party criticized "big government", the Occupy movement has advanced a critique of plutocracy: the undue influence of a wealthy few – the so-called "1 per cent" – in ways that, as Stewart puts it, "distort 'democratic' politics". This movement has contributed in some way to challenging the prevailing political discourse, directing greater attention toward economic inequality and related issues. It remains to be seen, at the time of writing, how this movement might shape the next round of elections in the U.S. and other countries.

Developing and middle income countries have not experienced the same general rightward turn as their economically advanced counterparts in recent years. Indeed, as Stewart discusses, Latin America in particular has moved in the opposite direction. There, many countries have taken a "Left Turn" that entails forms of market governance vastly different from those seen in the 1980s era of structural adjustment, including some far-reaching policies aimed at reducing poverty and inequality (Levitsky and Roberts, 2011). Following the recent crisis, a number of Left parties in Latin America have suffered losses at the polls, but most have managed to hold on to power.

It also warrants noting that many developing and middle income countries have seen significant social mobilizations of their own in the years since the crisis. In China, where exports dipped significantly following the crisis, factory workers responded to ensuing layoffs and wage freezes by unleashing a large wave of protests in the summer of 2010. Many condemned not only their employers but the state-run unions, enunciating a desire for greater workplace democracy (Hui and Chen, 2011). Indeed, demands for more deeply and broadly embedded forms of democratic control seem to be driving many of the recent citizen movements around the world.

The shifting international politics of reform

With respect to the intergovernmental arena, a number of authors suggest that the crisis has served to reinforce existing configurations of power in important respects. Durano argues that the financial crisis has expanded the legitimacy of the Bretton Woods organizations, while undermining the United Nations as a body for economic coordination. As Langmore and Fitzgerald point out, the UN's broad membership of nation states would afford it greater legitimacy as a more fully representative forum, and yet it has not emerged from the crisis with any significant role.

Despite a consolidation of the power of these organizations, several contributors to this volume also suggest that the growing multipolarity is reshaping the balance of power in the global economy and the organizations that govern it. Gallagher uses World Bank data to show that developing countries have grown faster than industrialized countries since 2000. Moreover, this trend has only been hastened by the crisis, with developing countries posting an average 5.5 per cent annual growth versus just 0.46 per cent for their industrialized counterparts.

In turn the rising economic power of the BRIC countries (Brazil, Russia, India and China), and other major developing and middle income countries, is being reflected even within the Bretton Woods organizations. As discussed by Ocampo and Wade, the BRIC countries and other major developing and middle income countries have seen small but notable increases in their voting shares within the IMF and World Bank in the time since the crisis. There is also growing political agreement across the North–South divide that the U.S.–Europe monopoly over the leadership of these organizations should and will be broken in the foreseeable future.[5]

Outside the Bretton Woods organizations, the G20 (established in 1999) officially supplanted the G8 as the main international forum for economic consultation on international issues in 2009, taking up a central role in discussions about global recovery. Ocampo suggests that this is an important development, even though he would like to see the establishment of a more formal and fully representative forum for economic consultation under the auspices of the UN. In the WTO, Gallagher notes that large developing and middle income countries have gained increasing confidence to reject the proposals of economically advanced countries. The resulting stalemate has prevented a further constriction of policy space during the 2000s, including the period since the crisis.

Other contributors to this volume are less sanguine about this mounting self-assurance. Wade, for instance, observes that middle income and large developing countries have not so far exercised their new voting clout to push for alternative policy visions in the G20. Such dynamics may be evidence of an increasing tension confronting decision makers within these countries. On the one hand they desire greater democratic control over international institutions. Yet they also want to avoid restricted policy autonomy that often results from tighter economic coordination at the international level. According to Wade these emerging powers wish to be "*at* the top table, *in* global governance, but are wary of *more* global governance (which might curb their sovereignty) and of proposing initiatives which would put more responsibilities on their shoulders".

In addition to questions about how the BRIC countries and other major developing and middle income countries assert their views and interests in the international arena, it is also far from assured that these countries will continue to exert this power to advance interests of "developing countries" as a group. Gallagher argues that as these countries become capital exporters they may start to have more in common in many respects with countries of the economic North. This development has serious implications for the least developed countries, which may find themselves ever-more-isolated as they attempt to advance their interests within the major intergovernmental organizations.

Another important set of questions has to do with the degree to which labour, environmental, and other social movement actors are able to exert power in the international arena. While Polanyi envisioned processes of embedding playing out in national spaces, what are the possibilities that more broadly participatory forms of governance might extend across national boundaries (Evans, 2008)? Here, some of the more significant efforts in recent years have not been aimed at intergovernmental organizations or even national governments, but at pressing multinational corporations (MNCs) to improve environmental and labour standards throughout their supply networks, including in the developing world (Gereffi and Mayer, 2006).

To be sure there are limits to what these initiatives have been able to achieve. Moreover, the mobilizations around labour standards face challenges to their legitimacy, in part because the participation of developing country workers has often been low. However, developments such as the wave of labour protests in China could begin to alter these dynamics, creating new conditions for cross-border labour solidarity.[6]

What next?

Despite great expectations in many quarters, reform of market governance institutions has been limited in the period following the crisis. Nevertheless, the political dynamics noted above suggest that there may be a more substantial re-embedding of markets still to come, even if such dynamics do not unfold right away. Many countries have experienced a dizzying succession of political shifts in the short time that has elapsed since the crisis, with a recent surge of activism pushing for broadly democratic forms of market embedding. In the international arena a changing balance of power among nations, together with strengthening cross-border ties among social movement actors, is beginning to create new conditions of possibility for change, despite the barriers and contradictions that emerge at every turn.

Moreover, while entrenched interests and institutions are difficult to dislodge, it is important to remember that ideas can wield power, too (Blyth, 2002). Fresh or newly resonant reform ideas can mobilize new coalitions and movements, which can transform institutions. And, on a shifting political terrain marked by significant uncertainty, it is ill advised to hazard predictions about the exact parameters of which reforms might be feasible. As Erik Olin Wright (2010: 28) observes, "robust projects of emancipatory social transformation must be formulated with relatively thin knowledge of the likely conditions to be faced in the future". It is precisely this indeterminacy that lends an abiding importance to the kinds of ideas discussed by contributors to this book.

Notes

1 Of course, as noted by Quiggin, shifts within the IMF played an important role in promoting increased financial instability – particularly the end of fixed exchanges rates in early 1971.
2 Since their foundation, these countries have held the bulk of voting shares in the IMF and World Bank, and the presidents of these organizations have always been chosen, respectively, by Europe and the United States. The WTO is formally more democratic than the Bretton Woods organizations to the extent that it operates on the principle of "one member, one vote", though advanced countries have wielded de facto control based on factors such as technical expertise and the sheer size of their negotiating contingents (Narlikar, 2003).
3 It is important to note, though, that austerity measures have also been passed by Left and center-Left governments in many countries.
4 See the Meerkat Media Collective website http://meerkatmedia.org/.
5 Even through French lawyer Christine Lagarde was named the new IMF Managing Director in July 2011, there had been a wide chorus of voices calling for the appointment of someone from a developing country.
6 To the extent that macroeconomic imbalances were a key background condition to the emergence of the crisis, the demand of Chinese workers to consume a larger share of their country's burgeoning economic output is tied in no small way to the possibility of a more stable economy.

2 Financial markets

Masters or servants?

John Quiggin

Trade and markets of one form or another have always been part of human society. Borrowing and lending are similarly ancient and ubiquitous. On the other hand, markets for trade in financial obligations such as debts and future sales and purchases are specific to capitalism. The key financial institutions of capitalism such as fractional reserve banking, joint stock companies and regular markets for trade in government bonds date, in their modern form, from the eighteenth century, although precursors can be found as early as the fifteenth century in Italy and the Netherlands.

Throughout the history of capitalism there have been tensions between financial institutions and the state, and between financial capital and the firms and households engaged in the production and consumption of physical goods and services. In some periods, most notably in the decades after World War II, financial markets were reduced to a subordinate role, channelling household savings into credit for business investment and (relatively constrained) consumer credit, under tight public regulation. In other periods, including the decades since the 1970s, financial markets became, or at least seemed to become, all-powerful "Masters of the Universe".

Periods of financial sector dominance have regularly ended in spectacular panics and crashes, often resulting in the liquidation of large numbers of financial institutions and the reimposition of regulatory controls previously dismissed as outmoded and unnecessary. These panics have typically precipitated lengthy periods of recession or depression, with high unemployment and slow or negative economic growth.

The financial crisis that engulfed the global economy in 2008 has been, so far, an archetypal example of this process. The power, and pretensions, of financial markets in the decades leading up to the crisis exceeded anything that had been seen in the past. The magnitude of the crisis was similarly impressive, with losses of billions or tens of billions of dollars becoming routine daily events and talk of trillions becoming commonplace. At several points it appeared likely that the entire global financial system might collapse, and this danger has not passed at the time of writing (August 2010). The aim of this paper is to consider measures to restore financial markets to their proper role as servants rather than masters of the market economy and the society within which it is embedded.

The paper is organized as follows. The first section provides a background to the crisis, showing how the Bretton Woods system restricted financial activity and the potential for financial panics. The breakdown of Bretton Woods was followed by a massive expansion in the scale, scope and speculative nature of financial activity. I next describe the global financial crisis that began in 2008 and shows how it was driven by the complex, interlinked and uncontrolled nature of the financial system. The European "sovereign debt crisis" of 2010 is a continuation of the global crisis, but has been used by financial markets in an attempt to reassert their power. Section 3 deals with the reform of the international financial system. The central argument is that the idea of a "global financial architecture" is misconceived. The necessary system is one of national (or E.U. level) financial regulation, coordinated through international institutions. It is argued, in Section 4, that the central goal of national financial regulation should be to constrain the size and power of the financial system to levels appropriate to its role as a provider of services, ultimately dependent on the backing of the state. Finally, some concluding comments are offered.

Background

Periodic financial crises and panics have been a feature of capitalism ever since the South Sea Bubble, which brought an end to the first great experiment with joint-stock corporations. By the nineteenth century financial crises replaced crop failures as the primary cause of economic distress. Some notable examples include the "Long Depression" following the Panic of 1873 in the United States, and the 1890s Depression in Australia (Kindleberger 2000).

None of these crises, however, were comparable in their effects to the Crash of 1929 and the subsequent Great Depression. As well as producing a decade of misery and deprivation, the Great Depression helped bring Hitler to power in Germany and was therefore a major cause of World War II.

Meeting in Bretton Woods, New Hampshire, in 1944, to plan a post-war economic order, the Allied governments were determined to avoid a repetition of the disasters of the interwar years. Although the most radical proposals for financial reform, put forward by John Maynard Keynes, were rejected by the U.S. Government, the financial system that emerged from Bretton Woods was far more tightly restricted than any in the past.

The Bretton Woods system supported, and was supported by, Keynesian macroeconomic policies, operating at the national level with the aim (largely achieved for several decades) of maintaining full employment, price stability and fiscal balance.

Even during this post-war boom, the financial sector sought and found ways to undermine and avoid controls and regulations. The emergence of the "Eurodollar" market in the 1960s, which facilitated trade in U.S. dollar-denominated financial instruments outside the control of the U.S. Federal Reserve, was a crucial step in this respect (Robinson and Quiggin, 1985).

After Bretton Woods

The inflationary upsurge of the late 1960s rendered untenable key aspects of the Bretton Woods system, most notably the fixed U.S. dollar price for gold. Although a variety of responses might have been possible, the gradual erosion of financial controls in the 1960s paved the way for a complete breakdown in the 1970s. Fixed exchange rates were replaced by attempts at flexible management, and then to freely floating rates. Controls on international financial flows were relaxed and ultimately abandoned. National financial systems were deregulated.

By the 1980s almost nothing was left of the Bretton Woods system. Governments had little option but to obey the dictates of global financial markets, expressed most notably through the judgements of ratings agencies such as Standard & Poor's and Moody's. The volume of international financial flows grew to levels that had previously been unimaginable, and kept on growing even faster. By some measures, when the bubble burst in 2008, the total outstanding volume of financial assets was more than a quadrillion dollars.

By 2007 financial corporations accounted for 40 per cent of U.S. corporate profits. The bulk of income growth in the U.S. over the period since the 1970s accrued to high income earners, an increasing proportion of whom derived their income directly or indirectly from the financial sector. In particular, those in the top 1 per cent of the income distribution approximately doubled their share of income. Within that group, the top 0.1 per cent did disproportionately well (Piketty and Saez, 2003). Similar, though less extreme, developments took place throughout the developed world (Atkinson and Leigh, 2007; Piketty and Saez, 2006).

Nevertheless, by the mid-1990s, the beneficence of financial sector dominance seemed evident to all, particularly in the U.S. Booming stock markets encouraged an atmosphere of triumphalism epitomized by such writers as Thomas Friedman (1999) and Edward Luttwak (1999).

But the first signs of failure were becoming apparent. The global financial system was threatened in 1998 by the failure of Long Term Capital Management, a hedge fund with leveraged borrowings in the trillions. The danger was averted by a bailout, hastily organized by the U.S. Federal Reserve. The bubble and bust in dotcom stocks in the late 1990s repeated the pattern on a larger scale.

Bubble, bust and bailout

Although no-one predicted the exact course of the global financial crisis that began in 2008, a substantial minority of economists pointed to the unsustainability of the imbalances in the U.S. and global economy that developed from the late 1990s onwards, and predicted that the resolution of those imbalances would require a painful adjustment, and probably a recession, followed by more restrictive regulation of the financial system (Bell and Quiggin, 2006).

By contrast, the dominant market liberal ideology encouraged the view that booming asset markets were benign. The massive growth in the volume of international financial transactions was seen as reflecting the (presumptively rational) voluntary choices of borrowers and lenders, and as a way of diversifying risk internationally.

Like other aspects of the financial system that developed during the bubble era, this reasoning was reminiscent of the deacon in Oliver Wendell Holmes' poem who tried to build a carriage (the "wonderful one-hoss shay") that could never break down, on the theory that a system always fails at its weakest spot: "The way t' fix it, uz I maintain, Is only jest T' make that place uz strong uz the rest." As applied to the global financial system, the "one-hoss shay" theory provided two systems of protection against failure. First, risks were widely dispersed throughout the global financial system, so that a localized failure in any one economy could not cause significant loss to investors with highly diversified portfolios. Second, central banks extended "too big to fail" protection to any institution large enough to be critical of the sustainability of the system as a whole.

The only way a system of this kind could fail was through a total global collapse. Holmes' poem, written in 1858, described the end of the one-hoss shay thus: "[It] went to pieces all at once, All at once, and nothing first, Just as bubbles do when they burst." And that, more or less, is what happened.

In scale and scope the crisis was larger than any financial failure since the Great Depression. The estimated losses from financial failures amounted to $4 trillion or about 10 per cent of the world's annual income. Losses in output from the global recession have also amounted to trillions, and recovery has barely begun.

Unlike the Great Depression this crisis was entirely the product of financial markets. All of the checks and balances in the system failed comprehensively. The ratings agencies offered AAA ratings to assets that turned out to be worthless, on the basis of models that assumed that asset prices could never fall. The entire ratings agency model, in which issuers pay for ratings, proved to be fundamentally unsound, but these very ratings were embedded in official systems of regulation. Crucial public policy decisions were, in effect, outsourced to for-profit firms that had a strong incentive to get the answers wrong.

The bailouts undertaken by the U.S. and European governments in late 2008 only reinforced the bad incentives in the system. Financial sector participants kept most of the rich rewards they had reaped during the bubble years, when their activities had massively distorted the allocation of investment capital and thereby reduced the sustainable growth rate of the economy. The terms on which public credit was extended for worthless assets were so generous that the financial sector has led the way in the recovery of corporate profits. Unsurprisingly, given these incentives, the behaviour of the financial sector has changed hardly at all as a result of the crisis.

The European debt crisis

The role of financial markets in the European "sovereign debt crisis" provides a good illustration of the extent to which the financial sector has reasserted its claims to mastery over the economy. In nearly all respects the crisis is the result of the financial excesses of the bubble era and of the costly misallocation of resources it created.

Many of the European governments most severely affected by the crisis were in fiscal balance or surplus in 2007. The slide into deficit can be attributed to:

- The direct and indirect costs of financial sector bailouts (most notable in Ireland);
- The loss of revenue from the financial sector and from housing following the bursting of the bubble (most notable in Spain); and
- The fiscal impact of the general economic downturn and the cost of stimulus and relief measures.

Even in Greece, where fiscal profligacy was a primary cause of the crisis, financial enterprises were both leading accomplices in the evasion of eurozone fiscal targets and leading beneficiaries of the E.U. bailout.

Yet the financial sector has presented itself as the guardian of fiscal probity, with ratings agencies downgrading public debt and bond markets demanding cuts in public expenditure which are invariably targeted at those who benefited least from the bubble.[1] The most striking examples include the United Kingdom, where the cost of the bank bailout is being used to justify ever-harsher treatment of the homeless and unemployed, and Ireland where the government plans to sell most of the assets of the National Pension Reserve Fund (created to finance public service and social welfare pensions) to pay off creditors of failed private banks. Elsewhere in Europe, "austerity" proposals have generally been more reasonable, with a primary focus on proposals to enhance tax revenue and measures to reduce the cost of retirement incomes policies, mostly by increasing the age of retirement.

Budgets must balance in the long run and policies of this kind are, to some extent, a necessary response to a real reduction in the net worth of governments as a result of the financial crisis. Nevertheless, the demands of the financial sector for austerity have produced an undesirable focus on measures to reduce budget deficits in the short term, at a time when the depressed state of the European economy implies the need for stimulus.

A striking example is that of the increases in value added tax rates adopted in Spain, Portugal and other European countries. A far more sensible policy would have been to announce an increase in the VAT rate, deferred for two to three years. The effect on long-term fiscal balance would be only marginally smaller than that of an immediate increase. On the other hand, a deferred increase would stimulate demand in the short-term, as consumers seek to beat the tax increase. Such a temporary stimulus is exactly what is needed.

Reforming the international financial system

The aftermath of the crisis has produced a range of efforts to improve upon the systems of financial regulation that failed so spectacularly in 2007 and 2008. The most important instance is that of the proposed Basel III Accords on banking supervision. The draft rules reverse many of the presumptions that informed the "light-handed" approach of the Basel II system, which failed spectacularly in the global crisis. Basel III involves a substantial increase in bank capital requirements. More importantly, the "risk-based" framework of Basel II, in which banks were largely free to make their own judgements about the riskiness of their capital base, has been replaced by more prescriptive requirements to hold specific capital assets.

These efforts have not, however, been informed by any rethinking of the role of the financial sector. As a result, they amount to an attempt to repair and recreate the pre-crisis system, fixing the obvious defects while maintaining the status of the financial sector as the core of economic activity. Ideally, in this view, the financial sector would retain its role of mastery over investment decisions and public policy, while avoiding the excesses of the past.

Such an approach is doomed to failure. Even while the crisis was at its worst, there were regular examples of excess, such as massive payouts and lavish junkets for executives of bailed-out banks. Now that, for the financial sector at least, the crisis is effectively over, the return to pre-crisis attitudes and behaviour is gathering pace.

Starting from the view of the financial sector as a servant of the broader economy and society, rather than as a master, would produce a radically different approach to its regulation. A whole series of presumptions that have characterized the failed regulatory approaches of recent decades would be reversed. Most notably:

- The financial sector should be regarded as the biggest single source of economic risk rather than being the pre-eminent social institution for risk management;
- Financial innovation should be regarded as harmful unless it can be shown to be beneficial, rather than *vice versa*;
- Growth in the financial sector share of the economy should be regarded with concern rather than celebration; and
- Financial markets must be regulated as interlinked national markets rather than as a global market transcending national boundaries.

A successful approach to global financial regulation must rely primarily on cooperation between the U.S. Federal Reserve and the European Central Bank, which between them account for more than 90 per cent of currency reserves, and cover economies that produce around a third of global output. Although the U.K. and Japan remain as significant financial centres, the severe fiscal and regulatory problems they face suggests that they are unlikely to be in a position to play an independent role in the restructuring of the global financial system for some time to come. Other members of the G20 are similarly constrained.

Financial innovation

The process of financial innovation, involving either the creation of new financial instruments or the design of new financial strategies for firms (often termed "financial engineering") was a central feature of the era of market liberalism. The growth of finance has been almost unstoppable. Seemingly major financial crises like the stock market crash of 1987, or the NASDAQ crash of 2000, stimulated the development of yet more innovative responses. Even the exposure of spectacular fraud at the Enron Corporation, which had been nominated by *Fortune* magazine as "America's most innovative" for six years in succession, did little to dent faith in the desirability of innovation.

It is now clear that unrestricted financial innovation played a major role in the advent of the financial crisis by facilitating the growth of unsound lending and by undermining systems of regulation. There is an inherent inconsistency between unrestricted financial innovation and a regulatory system aimed at preventing the failure of financial systems or at insuring market participants against such failures. Guarantees create "moral hazard" by allowing financial institutions to capture the benefits of risky investments, while shifting some or all of the losses to government-backed insurance pools.

Moral hazard can only be offset by the design of regulatory mechanisms that discourage excessive risk-taking. But, as the literature on mechanism design has shown, the effectiveness of such mechanisms depends on the existence of stable relationships between the observable variables that are the subject of regulation and the risk allocation that generates these observables. Financial innovation changes the relationship. In the presence of moral hazard, therefore, there is an incentive to introduce innovations that increase the underlying level of risk while leaving regulatory measures of risk unchanged.

It follows that the only sustainable approach to financial innovation is one in which proposed innovations are introduced only after the implementation of necessary changes to regulatory requirements and risk measures. If reliable risk measures cannot be computed, the associated innovations should not be permitted.

Obviously, this approach is directly opposed to the Basel II system which sought to control the total risk exposure of regulated banks, while maximizing the freedom of financial institutions to benefit from financial innovation. The failure of that system is reflected in the substantially more prescriptive approach of Basel III. However, despite the substantial tightening of restrictions in Basel III, the underlying presumption in favour of financial innovation remains. It is this presumption that needs to be reversed if financial regulation is to be effective.

Controlling risk in the financial sector

Given an unlimited public guarantee for the liabilities of these institutions, a permissive attitude to innovation is a guaranteed and proven recipe for disaster, offering huge rewards to any innovation that increases both risks (ultimately borne by the public) and returns (captured by the innovators).

Post-crisis financial regulation must begin with a clearly defined set of institutions (such as banks and insurance companies) offering a set of well-tested financial instruments with explicit public guarantees for clients, and a public guarantee of solvency, with nationalization as a last-resort option. Financial innovations must be treated with caution, and allowed only on the basis of a clear understanding of their effects on systemic risk.

In this context it is crucial to maintain sharp boundaries between publicly guaranteed institutions and unprotected financial institutions such as hedge-funds, finance companies, stockbroking firms and mutual funds. Institutions in the latter category must not be allowed to present a threat of systemic failure that might precipitate a public sector rescue, whether direct (as in the recent crisis) or indirect (as in the 1998 bailout of Long Term Capital Management). A number of measures are required to ensure this.

First, ownership links between protected and unprotected financial institutions must be absolutely prohibited, to avoid the risk that failure of an unregulated subsidiary will necessitate a rescue of the parent, or that an unregulated parent could seek to expose a bank subsidiary to excessive risk. Long before the current crisis these dangers were illustrated by Australian experience with bank-owned finance companies, most notably the rescue of the Bank of Adelaide by the Reserve Bank of Australia in the 1970s.

Second, banks should not deal in unregulated financial products such as share investments and hedge funds.

Third, the provision of bank credit to unregulated financial enterprises should be limited to levels that ensure that even large scale failure in this sector cannot threaten the solvency of the regulated system.

In the resulting system of "narrow banking" the financial sector would become, in effect, an infrastructure service, like electricity or telecommunications. While the provision of financial services might be undertaken by either public or private enterprises, governments would accept a clear responsibility for the stability of the financial infrastructure.

Another important regulatory adjustment will be the end of the system by which prudential regulation has been, in effect, outsourced to ratings agencies such as Standard & Poor's and Moody's. Agency ratings have been enshrined in regulation, for example through official investment guidelines that require regulated entities to invest in assets with a high rating (AAA in some cases, investment grade in others) or provide those responsible for making bad investment decisions with a "safe harbour" against claims of negligence if the assets in question carried a high rating. For these purposes at least, an international, publicly backed non-profit system for the assessment and rating of investments is required.

Constraining the size of the financial sector

The first objective must be to ensure that exchange rate movements reflect the economic fundamentals of trade and long-term capital flows rather than the vicissitudes of financial markets. The most promising candidate here is the idea, long-advocated and long-resisted, of a small tax on financial transactions commonly called a Tobin tax.[2]

A tax at a rate of 0.1 per cent would be insignificant in relation to the transactions costs associated with international trade or long term investments. On the other hand daily transactions of $3 trillion would yield revenue of $30 billion per day, or nearly $1 trillion per year. Since this amount exceeds the total profits of the financial sector an effective Tobin tax would imply a drastic reduction in the volume of short-term financial flows. It follows that the revenue from a Tobin tax, while significant, would not be sufficient to replace the main existing sources of taxation such as income tax.

The large literature on the Tobin tax has identified some problems with the simple proposal for a tax on international financial transactions. First, it is possible to replicate spot transactions on foreign exchange markets with combinations of forward, futures and swap transactions. To make a Tobin tax effective it would have to be applied to all financial transactions, including domestic transactions. During the bubble era, when the few remaining taxes on domestic financial transactions were being scrapped to facilitate the growth of the financial sector, this was seen as a fatal objection. It has become apparent, however, that the destabilizing effects of explosive growth in the volume of financial transactions are much the same, whether the transactions are domestic or international.

The fact that a Tobin tax on international financial transactions would be integrated with taxes on domestic transactions suggests that, in all probability, revenue would be collected and retained by national governments. However, suggestions that at least some of the revenue could be used to fund global projects such as the international development goals of the UN Conference on Trade and Development remains worthy of consideration.

The second problem is that the tax would require global cooperation to prevent financial market activity from migrating to jurisdictions that did not apply the tax. Although this will remain a problem in the post-crisis world, it is likely to be much less severe than indicated by earlier discussions. The number of separate jurisdictions that would need to agree has been substantially diminished by the emergence of the euro.

As part of the resolution of the crisis it seems inevitable that most remaining European currencies, with the possible exception of the British pound, will disappear, and that a Europe-wide regulatory system will emerge. The number of separate jurisdictions with well-developed financial systems is therefore likely to be very small, with the E.U. and the U.S. being overwhelmingly dominant. Furthermore, successful resolution of the sovereign debt crisis will involve a substantial and growing role for fiscal transfers within the eurozone, beginning with the European Financial Stability Facility. Thus, the E.U. will be more and more comparable to the U.S. in economic terms.

As in the case of tax evasion the problem of "offshore" financial centres, such as Caribbean island states, is unlikely to be a serious stumbling block. The free market dogmas that prevented action to preserve the effectiveness of financial regulation in the late twentieth century have lost much of their force. A Tobin tax on transactions among complying jurisdictions may have to be supplemented by a punitive tax at a rate of, say, 10 per cent, on transactions with non-compliant jurisdictions. This would ensure that non-compliant jurisdictions were excluded from global financial markets though the penalty would be modest as regards trade and long-term investment flows.

The new financial architecture: global or international?

The first step towards a sustainable financial architecture is the recognition that the idea of a "global financial architecture" is both misleading and unattainable. The starting point for any financial architecture must be the institution that acts as lender of last resort for others. This function is, and is likely to remain, one undertaken by national governments and their central banks.[3] It follows that there can be no global financial architecture. Rather, national systems of financial regulation must be linked and integrated to produce a sustainable international financial architecture. Here I do not differ significantly from other contributors to this volume, who have addressed the reform of international financial architecture, including Ocampo, Wade and Buckley. However, my emphasis on inter-*national* rather than global markets is significant.

The first requirement for a sustainable international architecture is that there should be no "offshore" financial system, outside the agreements that govern the international financial architecture but nevertheless allowed to transact with institutions inside the system.

This issue has already arisen in relation to international tax avoidance and evasion, and will arise in an even more acute form in relation to the Tobin tax, as discussed below. Fortunately the OECD has already made substantial progress on tax avoidance and the approach here will serve as a model for financial regulation.

The OECD prepared an internationally agreed tax standard allowing countries to choose their own tax rates but requiring exchange of information to prevent avoidance and evasion. Jurisdictions which implemented the standard were placed on a white list, while those that refused were placed on a black list. Countries that promised to implement the standard but had not yet done so were placed on a grey list. Blacklisted jurisdictions were threatened with sanctions, largely unspecified but sufficiently effective that by October 2009 no jurisdictions surveyed by the OECD global forum remained on the blacklist.

The tax standard is inadequate in many respects and open to the evasive tactics for which tax havens are famous. Nevertheless, it seems clear that standards will be tightened progressively, and that no jurisdiction will be willing to risk the consequences of refusal to implement them.

The Financial Stability Board, established after the 2009 G20 London Summit to strengthen prudential oversight of capital, liquidity and risk management, provides the potential to apply the tax haven model that will be applied to "regulatory havens" offering lax financial regulation. As with taxation the process will undoubtedly be slow. Nevertheless, the powers of the G20 financial regulators are sufficient to ensure that evasion of financial regulation through the use of offshore transactions can be prevented. It remains to be seen whether, in the absence of immediate crisis, governments will find the political will required to resist the demands of financial institutions for light-handed regulation.

These new developments raise fundamental questions about the role of existing international organizations, most importantly the IMF. As Buckley (in this volume) notes, the IMF has historically acted to preserve the interests and power of the global financial sector. IMF interventions, presented as "bailouts" of indebted countries, have typically imposed terms only marginally more favourable to the country concerned than the outcomes they would incur through default. The real beneficiaries have been lenders. After a brief conversion to policies of Keynesian stimulus, in the deepest phase of the global financial crisis, the IMF is again acting as an advocate of "austerity" in the interests of bondholders.

As Ocampo (in this volume) observes, the World Bank and the regional development banks also have an important role to play in countercyclical responses to financial crises. The experience of the recent crisis showed the need for more rapid and flexible responses.

Conclusion

Like previous episodes of finance-dominated capitalism, the bubble economy that emerged in the 1990s has ended in disaster and depression. Despite the support of sophisticated economic theories, "best practice" national and international regulation and the almost unbounded information flows made possible by technological advances in computing and telecommunications, the global financial sector has proved just as vulnerable to fraud and failure as in the days of the South Sea Bubble.

Economically and socially sustainable growth will be possible only if the financial sector is forced back into the role of servant rather than master. This will not be easy to achieve. Despite their spectacular collective failure and evident dependence on government handouts for survival, the leaders of the financial sector remain both wealthy and powerful. So far they have successfully resisted all but the most limited encroachments upon their power and freedom.

They have, however, lost their most important asset: the aura of infallibility that surrounded "the markets". While ordinary citizens may find it difficult to conceive an alternative to financial market dominance, they no longer believe that a finance-dominated economy ultimately works for the benefit of all. Given a properly articulated programme of reform it should be possible to mobilize sufficient public support, and anger, to overwhelm the defences raised by these twenty-first century "malefactors of great wealth".

Notes

1 A particularly striking example of financial sector unwillingness to learn from experience was that of Timothy Ash, of the Royal Bank of Scotland. Speaking about the IMF rescue package for Ukraine, Ash observed: "We hope the fund is maintaining its push for a more flexible exchange rate, far-reaching reforms in the banking sector, and more privatization." (quoted in Krasnolutska and Martens, 2008). A few weeks before this comment was made, RBS had been nationalized as a result of failed speculation and catastrophic mismanagement.

2 The idea was first put forward by James Tobin (1988) and discussed further in Mahbub ul Haq, Inge Kaul and Isabelle Grunberg (1996).

3 The eurozone, where national governments run their own prudential policies but share a common central bank, raises some interesting questions but is unlikely to serve as a model for the rest of the world.

3 A development-friendly reform of the international financial architecture

José Antonio Ocampo[1]

The financial crisis showed how dysfunctional the current international macroeconomic and financial architecture (financial architecture, for short) is for managing today's global economy. The need to govern globalization has never been clearer but at the same time the institutional arrangements to do so have never been so inadequate. The calls for and steps taken to reform the financial architecture are, therefore, welcome. Similar calls for reform were made after the Asian and Russian crises of 1997 and 1998, which engulfed most of the developing world (including the so-called "emerging economies") in deep recessions, but led at best to marginal reforms. The fact that this time the industrial countries have been at the centre of the storm has led to greater action, but has also implied that some measures of direct interest to developing countries have been marginalized from the agenda.

There are two fundamental problems with the reforms that are under way. The first is that they constitute an incomplete agenda. Most of the action has concentrated on macroeconomic policies to counter the world recession (significantly weakened since mid-2010), on regulation of domestic financial systems, and on countercyclical financing from the International Monetary Fund (IMF) and the multilateral development banks. Other issues have been prominently absent including the regulation of cross-border capital flows, the design of adequate debt workout mechanisms at the international level, and global monetary reform. Second, the reform process has been led by an ad hoc arrangement: the G20. There is no doubt that this represents an improvement over the G7. However, no fundamental reform can take place if the process does not lead to the design of *inclusive*, representative, institutions. In short, global institutions, not ad hoc groupings of countries, should be at the helm of the international financial architecture – and of global governance in general.

Given these problems with existing reform efforts, this paper argues for an international financial architecture that meets two basic criteria. First, it should be comprehensive in its scope. Second, it must be based on representative institutions, structured as a multilayered network of global, regional and national financial institutions.

The first five sections of this paper look at substantive elements of the reform agenda. The next two address the institutional structure of the desirable architecture. The last briefly presents some conclusions. There is an extensive literature on the issues covered here that I cannot fully survey. So, references are kept to a bare minimum.

Improving global macroeconomic policy coordination

The recent Great Recession called for a strong macroeconomic policy response through expansionary monetary and fiscal policies in industrial countries. This countercyclical response was crucial to avoid the recurrence of a Great Depression similar to that of the 1930s. However, it was uneven among industrial countries and, as recovery took place, it led to growing disagreement. The controversies that erupted over the speed of fiscal consolidation at the G20 meeting in Toronto in June 2010 may be seen, in this light, as a step back in this process. They reflect, in particular, the growing reluctance of European countries to prioritize the countercyclical role of macroeconomic policy under the current circumstances. Also, much more limited progress has been made on global imbalances and exchange rate management. Global imbalances fell as a result of the crisis, but the risk of their reappearance is evident. China announced the reintroduction of some exchange rate flexibility before the Toronto G20 Summit, but the broader issue of the global exchange rate system has been absent from the agenda until it erupted in the form of the "currency war" in the run up to the October 2010 IMF meetings and the November 2010 Seoul G20 Summit.

An additional step forward was the broader acceptance of the principle that developing countries should be part of the solution, by adopting equally expansionary policies, facilitated by expanding countercyclical financing (see below). The fact that many of them had accumulated large amounts of foreign exchange reserves after the Asian crisis – largely as a "self-insurance" policy against an international financial architecture they perceived to be inadequate – and had lower external and public sector debts and stronger financial systems than during previous crises, implied that they *did* have more room for maneuver and were better placed to adopt expansionary policies than in the past. Indeed a key difference between the recent Great Recession and the Great Depression of the 1930s was that at that time there was no "China": that its to say a substantial economy without a financial sector in crisis and with the foreign exchange and fiscal room to pursue the most aggressive Keynesian policies in the world. Most Asian countries adopted expansionary policies and this was also true of several Latin American and African countries, though the story in these continents is mixed in this regard.

One of the major lessons of history is that a desirable coordinated macroeconomic policy reform should lead to more aggressive expansionary policies by countries enjoying external surpluses. Relying excessively on the expansionary policies of deficit countries – and, in particular, in this case, on the major deficit country, the United States – runs the risk of igniting (or, rather, reigniting) fears of disorderly adjustment to global imbalances. More generally, relying on an export-led recovery was highly undesirable in the face of the collapse of international trade, except perhaps for smaller countries with large external deficits. In both senses the response was suboptimal. Several surplus economies lagged behind in their expansionary policies and relied to a large extent on an export recovery – notably Germany and Japan, though in the latter case the response was constrained by very high levels of public sector debt.

Another major deficiency of the response effort was that no international organization – with the IMF being the obvious candidate – was placed at the centre of global macroeconomic policy coordination. Instead, an ad hoc body, the G20, assumed the role, following the pattern for managing major world economic shocks that has prevailed since the breakdown of the original Bretton Woods arrangements in the early 1970s. This was a suboptimal solution, as the only way to provide a clear institutional structure for such macroeconomic policy coordination at the world level is to put the IMF at its centre, as the original design of the Fund envisioned. The basic advantages of the Fund are that it can provide a Secretariat with some level of independence from individual countries (which no doubt operates imperfectly, especially in relation to the U.S.) and an ability to make an overall outside evaluation of how countries are meeting or failing to meet their commitments.

This should obviously be accompanied by a reform of voice, and participation of developing countries in the IMF: a point to which I return below. It must be emphasized, however, that despite the significant problems of representation that characterizes it, the IMF does provide an indirect representation to *all* members through its system of constituencies used to elect Board members, which is certainly better than the ad hoc selection (or, more precisely, self-selection) that is used by the G7 and the G20. Giving global macroeconomic policy coordination to the IMF – or, to be precise, to a more representative IMF – should therefore be the way forward.

Correcting the regulatory deficit of global finance

The severity of the recent global financial crisis was clearly associated with inadequate regulation and supervision of financial activities. Since the Asian crisis it had become an established principle that financial liberalization must be accompanied by stronger prudential regulation and supervision. This principle was applied in many parts of the developing world, which thus had stronger domestic financial systems at the onset of the crisis. But it was entirely disregarded in the U.S., where further liberalization was accompanied by deregulation and weak supervision of financial intermediation. European banking also suffered major problems associated with investments in high-risk assets issued in the U.S., real estate euphoria in a number of countries, and the lending booms in several Central and Eastern European countries, among other factors.

The discussion that took place in the G20 led to agreement on basic regulatory principles, all of which could be said to be necessary to make the financial sector the servant, not the master of the market economy and the society within which it is embedded (to use Quiggin's terminology in his contribution to this volume; see also Jane D'Arista and Griffith-Jones, 2010). However, the full adoption and implementation of these regulatory principles is still unfinished business.

The first principle is that regulations should have a strong *countercyclical* focus, thus avoiding excessive indebtedness (leverage) and forcing financial institutions to accumulate increasing cushions during booms to be better able to withstand the crises; these cushions should be made of variable mixes of higher capital, provisions for loan losses (reserves) and liquidity. Absolute limits on leverage should be part of the solution. This also implies that, when pricing assets according to their market value in the balance sheets of financial agents to maintain transparency (rather than at the historical or purchase value), the system must have other mechanisms (such as increased provisions or reserves, or countercyclical loan-to-value ratios) to prevent asset price bubbles from feeding into the credit expansion, and asset price busts from reinforcing the credit squeeze.

A second agreed principle is that regulations must be as *comprehensive* as possible, both in terms of agents and financial instruments. This is necessary to avoid the massive loopholes that allowed non-banking intermediation to increase systemic leverage during the previous boom. This also includes regulating the types of assets that led to the current crises, particularly asset-backed (e.g., mortgage-backed) securities and derivatives, and forcing all the markets to be open and transparent, thereby limiting over-the-counter operations. In this regard, it has also been agreed that systemically important financial intermediaries must be subject to particularly stringent supervision and perhaps to stronger regulatory standards. Excessive reliance on the internal risk evaluation models of financial institutions (the major focus of Basel II) should be avoided. It has already been shown how perilous this can be and how the use of similar risk models by financial institutions can lead to greater instability.

In addition to these principles a high level of consensus also formed around a third one, particularly in U.S. debates: *consumer protection*. This was essential to avoid supplying toxic mortgages and highly risky investment vehicles offered to unsophisticated agents during the recent boom. A fourth and traditional objective of regulation, *restricting monopoly power*, has been generally absent from the agenda. It will be a major issue looking forward, as private finance has experienced rapid concentration worldwide.

The U.S. has already approved an important financial reform (the Dodd–Frank Bill), but the scope of reforms is still subject to debate in Europe as this paper goes to press. Prior to the November 2010 Seoul G20 Summit, the Basel Committee on Banking Supervision approved an important set of reforms (referred to as Basel III), including increases in capital requirements, a stricter definition of capital, strengthened liquidity requirements, and a new maximum leverage that limits banks' total assets as a multiple of the basic regulatory capital (named Tier 1 in regulatory standards). The reform remains incomplete, as the rules for countercyclical capital or provisions and the mechanisms to prevent and manage crisis of systemically important institutions remain to be fully agreed. Equally important, responding to pressures from major private financial institutions, the timetable for implementation of the agreed rules is excessively long.

In institutional terms an important G20 decision was to give all its members access to international regulatory bodies, especially to the Financial Stability Board (FSB), which has now been assigned the task of coordinating world financial reform.[2] Similar steps were taken by the Basel Committee and other global regulatory bodies. However, these positive steps are not without problems. The first is the very uneven number of representatives from different countries. More fundamental are the institutional issues that are analyzed below: the total lack of representation of small and medium-sized countries; the ad hoc nature of the arrangement; the lack of a formal secretariat; and the absence of accountability to a representative political body.

To solve some of these problems a desirable transition would be to formally adapt one of the existing international organizations to play the role that the FSB plays today. The most appropriate one among existing institutions would be the Bank for International Settlements (BIS). This would give the new global regulatory structures an independent secretariat with technical capacity; in fact, the BIS has been operating for some time as the effective secretariat of the Basel Committee. However, an essential prerequisite for this institution becoming the world financial authority would be a considerable enlargement of its membership to transform it into a truly global institution and to make it more politically accountable to governments rather than merely to Central Bank governors. Accountability is also essential to avoid one major problem that the Basel Committee has faced in recent years: the capture of regulation by large multinational banks. Clear accountability mechanisms should therefore be introduced in all regulatory bodies, both national and international.

In any case creating a single world financial regulator is probably not viable or, for that matter, desirable, given different regulatory traditions around the world. So the system that is designed in this area should be based on a well functioning *network* of national and regional authorities (which is still missing even in the E.U.) and include truly international supervision of financial institutions that are global in their scope and impact (here, a college of supervisors such as that proposed by the G20 is a possibility).[3]

Aside from problems of institutional structure the most important gap in the debate on regulation is the absence of cross-border capital flows from the agenda. This is important given the destabilizing effect that procyclical capital flows can have on global financial stability, including carry trade.[4] Developing countries have been severely hit by procyclical capital flows in the past, and some European countries have been equally affected by this factor during the current crisis. This means that capital account regulations – including generalized reserve requirements on cross-border flows, minimum stay periods, and even the prohibition of certain transactions – can be as important for maintaining global financial stability as domestic prudential regulations. The latter should also take into account some aspects that are related to cross-border flows, such as currency mismatches in portfolios – prohibiting, for example, lending in foreign currencies to economic agents that do not have revenues in those currencies. The IMF has played a positive role in this regard by launching a still incipient discussion on the role of prudential capital account regulations (or "capital controls" as they are usually called). This issue should be at the core of the discussion of the development dimensions of any global financial safety net.

It should be recalled in this regard that, despite attempts made in 1997 to include capital account convertibility into the IMF agreement, the original rules on which the Fund was designed continue to be in place in this area. Countries thus have full autonomy to adopt capital account regulations, either to restrict excessive capital inflows during booms or to control capital flight during crises. The evidence of strong linkages through which both financial euphoria and panic are transmitted worldwide indicates that it would be wise to make more active use of these regulations. So the Fund should probably be encouraged to advise countries on what regulations to adopt under given circumstances, while fully respecting the full autonomy they have to regulate cross-border flows.

Countercyclical financing for developing countries

The strong retrenchment of private capital from developing countries during crises implies that one of the major roles of multilateral financial institutions (the IMF and multilateral development banks) and bilateral development cooperation is to facilitate financing during crises, which should also allow these countries to put in place countercyclical macroeconomic policies. Furthermore, based on the debates that took place during previous crises, it is essential that such financing should have a preventative focus, particularly with regard to rapid reversals of capital flows and the avoidance of the overburdening conditionalities of the past that forced developing countries to adopt procyclical (contractionary) macroeconomic policies during crises.

Improvements in this area can be seen as an important area of progress during the recent crisis. In March 2009 the IMF created a preventative facility, the Flexible Credit Line (FCL), for countries with "strong macroeconomic fundamentals" but a risk of facing problems in their capital account (IMF 2009). Other credit lines were doubled, and a broader use of the ordinary Fund facilities (the standby agreements) for preventative purposes was authorized (the so-called "high-access precautionary arrangements") (IMF, 2009). In turn, in December 2009, the IMF reformed its concessional credit lines by offering a menu of options according to different situations facing low-income countries in relation to their debt vulnerability and their macroeconomic and public finance management capacity. In 2010 further actions were adopted to expand the FCL and create a new Precautionary Credit Line (PCL), which was made available to a broader set of countries.

Advances in the application of conditionality have been somewhat frustrating, however. Although structural conditions can still be required from borrowing countries, a major step forward (adopted in March 2009) was elimination of the link between loan disbursements and structural conditionality. However, fiscal conditionality seems to have gone back to old procyclical practices in recent European programs, including requirements adopted to access the new European Financial Stability Facility created by the European Union in June 2010.

Past crises have also shown that multilateral development banks (MDBs) can play an essential role when private financing dries up. The capitalization of the World Bank and all regional development banks in the aftermath of the crisis, to enhance their capacity to support developing countries, can thus be regarded as an additional area of progress. Indeed, the recognition that MDBs have a countercyclical role should be seen as an advance in itself, as it had not been openly recognized before the crisis. However, capitalization as well as disbursements of new loans came with a lag. As a result MDBs played a somewhat passive role at the peak of the crisis, though they responded dynamically later on. Automatic rules must therefore be introduced to speed up the capitalization of banks and loan disbursements during global shocks of the future.

Crises, including the current one, have also shown that one particularly problematic issue that developing countries face is the curtailment of commercial credit available to exporters. This then becomes an additional mechanism of crisis transmission and severely limits an essential mechanism through which deficit countries can recover. Thus, the initiative by the MDBs to launch several credit facilities to increase commercial lending was also a step forward during the recent turmoil.

The major drawback has been the performance of Official Development Assistance (ODA), which is essential for low-income countries to also adopt countercyclical policies. This is crucial to avoid debt accumulation in poor countries, an area in which there has been progress in recent decades through a sequence of debt relief initiatives. Low-income countries can also play a role in generating aggregate demand at the global level. So, the reduction of ODA and uncertainty regarding the fulfillment of existing ODA commitments in the face of strong competing fiscal demands in industrial countries, are significant areas of concern. Indeed, the major deficiency of the countercyclical financing response was its bias towards middle-income countries.

Global monetary reform

The IMF was created on the basis of the dual gold-dollar system. This arrangement collapsed in the early 1970s and was replaced by a system based on fiduciary dollars (i.e., on the use of a *national* currency as a global currency). It is secondarily a system of competing fiduciary reserve currencies, but the dollar continues to be dominant, both as the currency used for international transactions and as a reserve asset, due to the "network externalities" associated with the use of a common monetary unit and the limitations of alternative currencies. The euro in particular, backed by a heterogeneous group of countries and lacking a unified Eurobond market, has proved to be an imperfect substitute.

This system is inequitable and unstable (see Ocampo, 2010a). It is inequitable because it forces a transfer of resources from developing countries to the industrial nations that provide reserve currencies. This transfer has sharply increased over the past two decades due to the realization by developing countries that "self-insurance" in the form of large foreign exchange reserves is the only defense they have in a world marked by acute financial instability and an inadequate financial safety net.

The system is also unstable because it is plagued by cyclical shifts determined by U.S. macroeconomic conditions and policies, which are reflected in strong cycles in the real dollar exchange rate and in the evolution of U.S. current account deficits. During the expansionary phase the U.S. swamps the world with liquidity, leading to rising current account deficits and a depreciation of the dollar – indicating, in fact, that the system does not impose macroeconomic discipline on the reserve issuing country. In turn, almost invariably, corrections of U.S. current account deficits take place in the midst of, and indeed contribute to, global recessions or strong slowdowns. During both phases of these cycles the world becomes hostage to the macroeconomic policies of the reserve currency country, which are generally adopted without any consideration as to their international impact.

It is important to emphasize that a system based on competing reserve currencies would not solve the inequities and instability of the current arrangement and may not be viable, given the revealed deficiencies of the major alternative currencies (particularly the euro, the yen and the British pound, with the renminbi as a future alternative). It could actually add another problem: the instability of exchange rates among major reserve currencies. Indeed this problem is already partly present in the current system.

The inequities and instability of the current set of arrangements are why the world monetary system should be based on a truly global reserve currency: a fiduciary currency backed by the central banks of the world. This is what was hoped for when the Special Drawing Rights (SDRs) were created in the 1960s.[5] This process must therefore be completed by transforming the SDRs into the major global reserve asset, as the IMF Articles of Agreement already state. Among other advantages, this system would provide a mechanism for the IMF to play a more active role during crises, by issuing SDRs in a countercyclical way and using them to finance its countercyclical lending. This would be the global equivalent of how central banks operate, and was evident on a massive scale during the recent crisis.

An important step was, therefore, the G20 decision adopted in London in April 2009 to revive this dormant mechanism of international cooperation by issuing SDRs equivalent to $250 billion, together with the U.S. decision to complete the Congressional approval process for the smaller 1997 allocation. The IMF decision of July 2009 to allow the issuance of securities denominated in SDRs to draw in resources from some emerging economies (Brazil, China and Russia) can also be considered a step in the direction of creating a "substitution account" to manage the varying demands for reserve currencies.

These areas constitute, however, only the beginning of a debate concerning reform of the global monetary system. The major proposals in this area were made by the Governor of the People's Bank of China in March 2009, and by the

Commission of Experts convened in 2009 by the President of the UN General Assembly on Reforms of the International Monetary and Financial System, which was chaired by Joseph Stiglitz (Zhou, 2009; United Nations, 2009).[6] The issues associated with global monetary reform have been entirely absent from the G20 agenda so far, but France has expressed its intention to place them at the centre of the agenda of the Group at the meeting that it will host in 2011.

Creating an international debt workout mechanism

The lack of a regular institutional framework to manage debt overhangs at the international level – i.e., a court similar to those created to manage bankruptcies in national economies, the decisions of which are legally binding – is one of the major deficiencies of the current international financial architecture. The only regular institutional mechanism in place is the Paris Club, which deals exclusively with official financing. The system has relied in the past on ad hoc mechanisms, such as the Baker and Brady Plans of the 1980s and the Heavily Indebted Poor Countries (HIPC) and the Multilateral Debt Relief (MDRI) Initiatives since the mid-1990s, or on traumatic individual debt renegotiations.

The problem with all these mechanisms has been that they generally come too late, after high indebtedness has had devastating effects on countries. This is also true of the Paris Club, due to its traditional reliance on sequential debt rescheduling, which again means that countries are left with debt overhangs for excessively long periods. The system is also horizontally inequitable as it does not treat all debtors or all creditors with uniform rules. Even Paris Club creditors regularly complain that private lenders do not follow their agreements. Unilateral renegotiations can also lead to an unfair treatment of borrowers depending on their weight and influence.

The discussion of the new international financial architecture should solve this problem by creating an international debt court that would serve both as mediator and eventual arbitrator of both public and private sector international loans. Privately run restructuring mechanisms, based on the use of collective action clauses, are clearly insufficient in this regard. Debtors may in fact delay using the mechanism to avoid antagonizing creditors. It is also unlikely to generate a uniform treatment of creditors, and fails to treat official and private lending with a unique set of rules, therefore maintaining the horizontal inequalities of the current system.

Any debt workout mechanism that is developed at the global level would have to start with defaults by debtor countries, which would then trigger off the negotiations. The system must be based on the principle that, after renegotiations, the debt ratio is sustainable, thus allowing borrowers a "fresh start" and even a (relatively) swift return to private capital markets. Furthermore, active support by MDB lending during and after renegotiations is essential, and these institutions should also support countries' return to markets.

The major initiative to create a multilateral mechanism of this sort was the 2001 IMF proposal to create a sovereign debt restructuring mechanism (SDRM).

This failed due to opposition by both the United States and some major developing countries. Although no global initiative has been launched in this area during the current crisis, the European Union has agreed, under German pressure, to put in place a debt restructuring mechanism in the future. This may be the door to broader discussions of this issue, as it is difficult to launch a mechanism of this sort as a merely regional framework.

Building an inclusive international financial architecture

Important, though incomplete, steps have been taken in the direction of improving global financial governance. The most important have been the decision to extend the membership of global financial regulatory institutions to the G20 members, and the inclusion of major developing countries in the G20 itself, which self-designated itself in the September 2009 meeting in Pittsburgh as "the premier forum for our international economic cooperation" (G20, 2009: [19]). But, as already noted, such advances are also a major problem, as ad hoc bodies cannot replace inclusive, representative institutions in a well-structured international financial architecture.

The reforms of "voice and representation" for developing countries in the Bretton Woods Institutions (BWIs) predate the creation of the G20 at the leaders' level, and have continued to take place partly on a parallel track. There is a clear consensus that one of the signals of success or failure of the G20 would be its capacity to complete this process, including solving the problems of both significant underrepresentation (Asia) and overrepresentation (Western Europe). In April 2008 a modest agreement was adopted on reforming quotas and votes on the IMF Board, which entailed a redistribution of the quotas and a tripling of the basic votes to increase the voting rights of developing countries by 2.7 percentage points. At the meetings of the BWIs in the spring of 2010 the ministers of the developing and transition countries called for a more ambitious realignment of quotas. In the run up to the Seoul meeting of the G20, finance ministers agreed to additional reform in this area. Together with the 2008 agreement, this led to an increase of 3.9 percentage points in the quota shares of emerging and developing countries, and an increase of 5.3 percentage points in their voting power. Some countries saw significant gains (particularly China, the Republic of Korea, Brazil, India, Mexico and Turkey, in that order), but there were also other developing countries that experienced large losses. It was also agreed that the number of European seats on the board would be reduced by two, while at the same time the number of executive directors from underrepresented countries would be increased. This reform was later ratified by the IMF Board.

To these we must add other important proposals made on various occasions, including those made by the 2009 Commission for IMF Governance Reform, headed by Trevor Manuel. These include proposals for a reduction in the threshold of votes needed to approve important IMF reforms from the current 85 per cent to, for example, 70–75 per cent; the creation of a Council of Ministers with effective powers to adopt the most important political decisions, thus replacing the International Monetary and Financial Committee; and a clear redefinition of the relations between this Council, the Board and the administration (CIMFGR, 2009). There has been no action in this area.

For its part, in the spring 2010 meetings, the World Bank approved a transfer of 3.13 per cent of voting power from the developed economies to the developing and transition economies, which will now hold 47.19 per cent of voting power and a promise that they will reach parity in the near future. The increases were mainly concentrated in middle-income countries, especially in Asia, which were underrepresented, while low-income countries saw limited change. This change was achieved through an ad hoc capital increase, not through agreement on a formula for dynamic revision of capital based on clear principles. There was agreement that this would be done by 2015, but developing countries expressed their clear preference for a more ambitious calendar.

The G20 has also agreed that the senior management of these organizations should be chosen on the basis of transparent and open processes, based on the merit of the candidates, without their nationality being an issue. It would also be useful for the personnel of these institutions to be more diverse, not just in terms of nationality but also educational and professional experience, as well as gender. We wait to see how these principles will be applied in practice.

The broader issues on global financial governance relate, however, to the G20 itself. The creation of this "G" at a leaders' level was, of course, a step forward compared to the G7, in terms of representation of developing countries. But this solution also created problems because of the ad hoc nature of the cooperation mechanism adopted, including the way in which the membership was defined, which implies the exclusion of some large countries (Nigeria is the case that stands out) and (once again) the overrepresentation of Western Europe. This reflects the strong revealed preference by industrial countries for "Gs" over which they can exercise greater influence – as well as perhaps a similar preference by large developing countries.

This preference for "Gs" over representative international institutions reflects the perceived challenge of overcoming the tension between representativeness and the legitimacy associated with it, on the one hand, and existing power structures, on the other. This issue is sometimes expressed as the tension between inclusiveness and effectiveness, but this is clearly a wrong way to pose it, as national democracies have shown that representative institutions can be effective. At the international level, although the record is mixed, it is unclear whether the G7 has proven in the past more "effective" than the BWIs or, for that matter, the United Nations. In this regard it can be argued that the United Nations has proved to be an effective mechanism for consensus building, the generation of new ideas, and as the framework for international cooperation (see, for example, the Millennium Development Goals in recent years), even though its effectiveness has been limited by the tendency of industrial countries to constrain its resources and the role it plays in implementing these agreements. The record of the G7 in terms of effectiveness is probably no better than that of these representative institutions and, in any case, both the G7 and now the G20 must act through these institutions.

Therefore, although "Gs" can play an important role in placing new issues on the agenda and facilitating consensus among major powers, no structure of governance can generate legitimacy when decision-making processes are not inclusive. For this reason, the G20 should be seen as a transition to a more representative, and thereby legitimate, mechanism of international economic cooperation. One such mechanism would be the Global Economic Coordination Council proposal by the previously mentioned Commission of Experts that was convened by the President of the UN General Assembly (or, for that matter, previous proposals to create an "Economic Security Council"). According to this proposal the Coordination Council would be set in the framework of the UN *system*, to which the BWIs belong and the WTO would become a member (see Ocampo, 2010b). It would be formed on the basis of constituencies elected through weighted votes (based, for example, on population and economic power, with an element of basic votes that are given to all members independently of size), thus following the model by which the boards of the BWIs are constituted, though with formulae for representation that overcome the problems that those institutions face.

In short the G20 should see itself as a transitional arrangement to a more representative and formal governance structure. This should in a sense be its major concern, but it is clearly not (or at least not yet) on its agenda.

The political economy dynamics of the G20 and the reforms of the BWIs are scrutinized in Robert Wade's contribution to this volume. I agree with his conclusion that, although developing countries have raised their presence in these fora, this has resulted so far in only small changes in international economic reform, thus contributing little to transform the rising economic multipolarity into a better multilateral order. Rather, in his terms, the G20 and the Bretton Woods organizations continue to show more "hegemonic incorporation" and "Westphalian assertion" than "multilateral cooperation" (Wade, 2011a). The gap between economic globalization and multipolarity, on the one hand, and political globalization and multilateralism, on the other, has thus remained wide open. In this context, as in my analysis, a new Global Economic Council is essential to reduce this gap.

Enhancing the role of regional institutions

In all of the areas of reform the global architecture should rely more broadly on regional institutions. Indeed, in a heterogeneous international community, the creation of *networks* of global, regional and national institutions will provide a better system of governance than arrangements based on a single global organization. This is based on old federalist principles: regional and sub-regional institutions give a stronger voice and sense of ownership to smaller countries. These institutions are, therefore, more likely to respond to their demands. This has already been recognized in some areas, such as the system of multilateral development banks, where the World Bank is complemented by regional development banks and, in some parts of the world, by sub-regional banks (in particular, in

Latin America and the Caribbean) and inter-regional banks (such as the Islamic Development Bank).

The creation of such an institutional network is particularly urgent in the monetary arena, where the IMF should make more active use of regional institutions such as the Chiang Mai Initiative and the Latin American Reserve Fund, and support their creation in other parts of the developing world. The 2010 debate on a possible European Monetary Fund and the creation of the European Financial Stability Facility has also been an important step in that direction. Indeed the IMF of the future should be positioned at the apex of a network of regional reserve funds – closer in design to the European Central Bank or the Federal Reserve System than to the unique global institution it currently is.[7] As already noted a similar institutional design could be adopted for prudential regulation and supervision.

Given their large foreign exchange reserves developing countries are in an excellent position to contribute to this task. Using those reserves more actively for swap arrangements among central banks, pooling them in reserve funds, or using them to support the development of regional bond markets are all mechanisms to expand the room for maneuver that they provide. These reserves and existing sovereign wealth funds could also be used to create or capitalize multilateral development banks owned by developing countries and to invest in bonds issued by such organizations. The multiplication and growth of sub-regional development banks and inter-regional banks owned by developing countries represents fertile ground for South-South cooperation, but these possibilities still remain largely underexploited.

Conclusions

This paper argues that the recent global financial crisis demonstrated, once again, the need for deep reforms of the international monetary and financial architecture. Current reforms, though welcome, are insufficient as they are partial in scope and rely excessively on an ad hoc body, the G20. Given these problems, the paper calls for an international architecture that meets two basic criteria.

First, it should be comprehensive in its scope. This means that a broad range of reforms should be on the agenda: better macroeconomic policy coordination; regulatory reform, including reform of cross-border capital flows; ample countercyclical IMF and development financing with limited conditionality; global monetary reform; and the creation of an international debt court.

Second, *inclusive*, representative institutions should stand at the centre of the new international financial architecture, not ad hoc groupings of countries. Furthermore, the paper argues that the structure that is developed should be based on a multilayered framework comprising a network of global, regional and national financial institutions. Given the large foreign exchange reserves and resources accumulated in sovereign wealth funds, developing countries are particularly well placed to contribute to the regional component of this architecture.

The political economy dynamics that have been at the centre of ongoing reforms, and could facilitate further action, include several elements. The fact that industrial countries have been at the centre of the crisis, and that several European countries have required exceptional financing needs, have been central to their willingness to adopt certain reforms (such as global reforms of financial regulation and creating preventive credit lines), some of which had been proposed by developing countries in the past to no avail. In turn, new emerging powers are clearly reshaping the power structure of global economic governance and demanding both a stronger voice as well as a financial architecture that responds to their own needs (for example, building an appropriate financial safety net, including regional institutions, aimed at avoiding the repetition of events such as the Asian crisis).

As a result of growing economic multipolarity, major industrial countries have also recognized that no global decision-making structure would make sense without the participation of the emerging powers. The U.S. has been more inclined to rethink governance structures, as it would not be a loser under any foreseeable arrangement (although it may lose its veto power in the IMF and the guarantee that it would head the World Bank). This is more difficult for European countries, and particularly smaller European countries, which are clear losers in any arrangement that takes into account today's, and not early post World War II, power structures. However, a full exploration of these political and political economy issues is beyond the scope of this paper. The contribution of Robert Wade to this volume goes a long way in understanding these dynamics.

Notes

1 Professor and Fellow of the Committee on Global Thought at Columbia University. Former Under-Secretary General of the United Nations for Economic and Social Affairs and former Minister of Finance of Colombia. This paper draws on two previous short essays by the author: "A 7-point plan for development-friendly reform" (2009) and "G-20 and Global Financial Governance", prepared with Stephany Griffith-Jones (2010). Financial support from the Ford Foundation is kindly acknowledged. I thank Sanjay Pinto and the editors of *Politics & Society* for their extensive comments and editorial support.

2 The Financial Stability Forum was created by the G7 after the Asian Crisis, to identify systemic risks that could arise in the global financial system. It clearly did a very poor job at that. With the recent decision, its successor, the FSB, became the apex of the network of financial regulators of the G20 and a few other countries.

3 This proposal differs from that of Quiggin in his contribution to this volume, which would rely on national institutions, with one regional institution (the European Central Bank) playing also a fundamental role. However, an *international* multilayered structure, such as that suggested here, is fundamental to guarantee the coherence of the different national frameworks, and to protect the weaker members of the international community (e.g., most developing countries) from financial mismanagement in the most systemically important economies.

4 This is the name given to short term capital movements that are financed by borrowing in countries with low interest rates, to profit from higher interest rates or expectations of exchange rate appreciation in other countries.

5 The SDRs are an asset issued by the IMF to central banks of member countries which, as its name indicates, takes the form of the right of countries to draw upon (as they draw from their quota contributions) and sell it to other countries in exchange for their currencies. Despite its name it is a truly global reserve asset (global money) backed by all Fund members.

6 For a broader debate on this issue, see the 2010 *Journal of Globalization and Development* 1(2).

7 This proposal was made by a 1999 United Nations Task Force that I chaired (see United Nations, 1999).

4 Reforming international financial governance

Ross P. Buckley[1]

The principal criticisms of the International Financial Institutions (IFIs) such as the International Monetary Fund (IMF) and the World Bank centre on their addiction to neoliberalism and insistence on smaller government and an increased allocative role for markets (Vines and Gilbert, 2004; Meltzer, 2000). It is therefore reasonable to assume that markets have figured prominently in the policies and practices of the IFIs and that the Global Financial Crisis (GFC) has potentially shaken the extent to which market disciplines and practices are embedded in the IFIs. It is a reasonable assumption but a wrong one.

One of the principal challenges in reforming the IFIs is to embed, not re-embed, important market principles and practices; specifically, to let the market allocate losses among borrowers and lenders when loans go sour. This market discipline has been notably absent from our system of global financial governance since at least 1982. When analyzing the re-embedding of markets it is vital to understand the areas in which the World Bank, and particularly the IMF, have never allowed market principles to govern.

How the IMF has consistently abrogated market principles

The multilateral system of international financial governance, with the IMF at its centre, works to reward the international commercial banks and the elites in developing countries at the expense of the common people in the debtor countries. It does this by only selectively applying market principles and disciplines. The market is allowed to operate unimpeded when it delivers profits to the international banks and the elites in the developing countries, and its operation is interfered with, grossly, when market forces impose massive losses on the banks and/or the developing country elites.

A few examples will suffice to demonstrate this dynamic.

After the 1982 debt crisis struck, a mechanism was needed to allow hundreds of creditors to negotiate with hundreds of debtors in each nation. The commercial banks appointed steering committees of six to eight banks to represent all creditors, and persuaded the sovereign to represent all debtors within its jurisdiction (including state governments, state-owned industries and private corporations). This was sensible. The banks, however, went further, and persuaded debtor nations to bring all debt incurred by all entities within their jurisdiction under their sovereign guarantee. This was unnecessary and, for the people of the debtor nations, deeply unjust. The inevitable, massive shortfall between what the sovereign now owed the bank creditors and what it could recover from the original debtors was added to the nation's debt. The people paid in reduced services or higher taxes so that the foreign banks could receive a free credit upgrade on their assets (Marichal, 1989; Buckley, 1999).

Likewise, after the Asian economic crisis, the IMF and foreign commercial banks insisted Indonesia assume the obligations of the local banks to foreign lenders and then recover the funds from the local banks. Recovery of such sums from insolvent Indonesian banks was always going to be problematic, and eventually only about 28 per cent of the total liabilities assumed were recovered (ADB, 2009). Accordingly, almost three-quarters of the costs of repaying these foreign loans was borne by the Indonesian people, and without good reason. The market mechanism, if left to work, would have seen many Indonesian banks made bankrupt by their Western creditors who would have recovered a portion of their claims in the bankruptcy. Instead insolvent local banks were put into bankruptcy by Indonesia, the creditors were repaid in full, and the Indonesian people bore most of the cost. The funds to repay the creditors came from the long-term loans organized by the IMF, contributed by the Pacific Rim developed countries (except the U.S.), and invariably described as bailouts of the debtor nations. Yet the terms of these loans required they be used to repay outstanding indebtedness, so the bailouts were of the foreign banks. In Indonesia, the IMF coordinated a restructuring that socialized massive amounts of private sector debt (Buckley, 2002).

Similarly, the centrepiece of the G20 response to the GFC in April 2009 was a US$500 billion additional credit facility for debtor nations. However, the eligibility conditions required for these loans exclude virtually all African and most Latin American nations. While it is not apparent on the face of the conditions, they are carefully crafted so that most of these loans will go to East European countries, where German banks are heavily overexposed. So this additional credit facility, in large measure, is designed to bail out the German banks. The funds will be repaid. Official credit always is. The loss will fall on the people of Eastern Europe, who will carry massive debt burdens for decades to come. Once again normal market processes, which in Eastern Europe would have led to German banks incurring large losses on their ill-judged lending, are abrogated to favour foreign banks over the people of debtor nations (Arner, 2010).

The benefits of the current system of global financial governance to the commercial banks are thus manifestly clear. The market is given full rein when yielding large profits to the banks, but is interfered with when it would yield large losses. The benefits to the elites in developing countries are less obvious, but nonetheless substantial, and explains why voices well placed to argue against the current system are rarely raised against it.

Consider the situation in Indonesia after the Asian crisis. When the assets of insolvent local banks were sold, who was best placed to bid for them? Who knew everything about the assets and their precise value? The families that had owned them as the principal shareholders of the banks – that is who. So these families were able to regain control of the assets they had owned before the crisis, with their foreign debts discharged by their government, for an average cost of 28 per cent. Who would speak out against such largesse? Our system of financial governance transferred the real cost of the crisis, which should have been borne by Indonesian and foreign banks that had engaged in imprudent borrowing and lending, onto the innocent people of the debtor nation. These debts, foisted in this way upon the Indonesian people, now represent almost 30 per cent of the total sovereign indebtedness of Indonesia (CIA, 2009; Soesastro *et al.*, 2003).

Sadly, after Argentina's economic implosion in 2000, the international financial community, with the assistance of a compliant Argentine government and the IMF, found two ways to socialize private indebtedness. The first is the familiar IMF bailout, in this case a US$40 billion loan to Argentina in late 2000 that was required to be used to repay a mix of public and corporate debt (Hershberg, 2002). The second was a new way to achieve an old end: having the people repay corporate debts. This technique was known as "pesofication".

Under pesofication, banks were required to convert their assets (such as loans) into pesos at a one-for-one rate and their liabilities (such as deposits) into pesos at a rate of 1.4 to one. This generated huge losses for the banks, for which the government sought to compensate them by a massive issue of government bonds (Gaudin, 2002).

Thus the circle was completed in the usual way – the ultimate burden fell on the public purse. In the words of Pedro Pou, President of the Central Bank of Argentina until mid-2001, "[t]he government has transferred about 40% of private debt to workers .... We are experiencing a mega-redistribution of wealth and income unprecedented in the history of the capitalist world" (Gaudin, 2002).

To require the common people to repay corporations' debts, through increased taxes and reduced services, is immoral. It is a massive interference with the market mechanism that the IMF professes to support. In each of these crises the market, through the mechanism of bankruptcy, would have allocated the costs of the poor lending and borrowing decisions onto the lenders and borrowers. The IMF, either as architect or complicit partner, in each case allocated the costs of poor decisions to parties who had nothing to do with them: the common people of the debtor nations (Buckley, 2002).

Yet the system was not designed to do this. Its architects were Keynes and White at Bretton Woods in 1944. Their primary goal was the promotion of global trade. Fixed exchange rates were to facilitate that trade. The IMF was established to provide short-term loans and technical advice to nations to facilitate their management of these fixed rates. This fixed exchange rate system ended in the 1970s as the U.S. went off the gold standard and floated its currency, and other developed nations followed suit. During the 1970s the IMF's core mission ended.

Yet global institutions are notoriously hard to kill. Witness the Bank for International Settlements, which Keynes and White had intended be closed, but which lived on to become the most significant global banking regulatory institution.

So the IMF continued on until the debt crisis of 1982 gave it a new role. The commercial banks needed to keep lending to the sovereign debtors so they could service their debts, but didn't want to advance more funds without changes to the policies that had led these nations to the brink of insolvency. Yet it was politically impossible for a U.S. commercial bank to be dictating economic policy to Brazil or Argentina. The IMF stepped in. As a supposedly independent IFI it was well positioned to play the role of crisis manager of nations in trouble. It was well positioned for the role, but not staffed or equipped to discharge it. So the IMF performed poorly, with disastrous consequences for the human rights of poor people in poor nations. Yet it has continued to fulfill this function, with substantially unchanged policies, ever since. Over time, as its litany of policy failures began to mount, the IMF attracted unrelenting criticism from both sides of politics in the U.S. and from developing countries, and it was allowed to shrink in size (Vines and Gilbert, 2004; Stiglitz 2002; Meltzer, 2000).

Yet in 2009 another crisis rescued the Fund. The GFC meant the G20 needed an organization through which it could channel most of its US$1.1 trillion funding package. And so, the credibility of the IMF has been somewhat restored by having a new role, and its staffing levels are again climbing.

So why do the normal checks and balances of democratic systems not rein in and redirect the system of global financial governance if it so often implements ends that serve the rich and hurt the poor? Part of the answer is that voters in rich countries cannot understand how international finance works, and care far less about the problems of people in poor countries than they do about their own back yards. This lack of understanding is promoted by the poor job done by the media in covering global financial governance. The media typically focuses on the most recent development, and reports it shorn of context. Its coverage is often inaccurate, promoted by the closeness with which information is guarded in this sector. The poverty of the media coverage means the powerful can continue to exploit the system free from countervailing pressures from civil society and democratic voters.

Two examples will suffice. In late 1997 the IMF-organized bailouts of Indonesia, Korea and Thailand were reported widely as if they were grants, not loans. Furthermore, the purpose for which the bailout funds could be applied was not reported at all, because that information was not made available. Yet, as we later learned, the loans could only be applied to debt then due, which was mostly short-term debt. So the bailouts were essentially bailouts of Western banks, not East Asian nations, and the bailouts rewarded the lenders who advanced the most destabilizing form of loans, short-term ones, at the expense of those who had advanced less volatile, longer term debt (Sachs, 1997). Thus was perpetrated a disastrous policy which received no critical media coverage until it was old news, years later.

In 2009 the G20's principal response to the GFC was a US$1.1 trillion funding package. US$100 billion was concessional financing for poor nations. US$250 billion was to support trade finance. Another US$250 billion was an increase in Special Drawing Rights, the IMF quasi-reserve-capital. And the final US$500 billion was the additional credit facility we have already considered (Arner, 2010).

The first two tranches are readily understandable, the latter two are not. Special Drawing Rights (SDRs) are based on a basket of four currencies, the U.S. dollar, Pound sterling, Euro and Yen, and are the mechanism through which nations make their contributions to the IMF. They are an excellent source of funding for poorer nations and the increase in them is a laudable response to the GFC. However, SDRs can only be drawn down in proportion to a nation's quota. Accordingly, nearly two-thirds of the increase in SDRs is available to OECD nations, leaving only US$100 billion for developing countries of which only US$19 billion is available for low-income nations (Oxfam International, 2009; IMF, 2009c). So reporting the US$250 billion increase in SDRs as principally a measure to assist poor countries was quite misleading.

The most frequent criticisms of the IMF focus upon its applying market disciplines and policies too rigidly, and in institutional settings its inability to support efficiently operating markets. There is no paradox here. The IMF is consistent – not in its commitment to the allocative efficiency of markets, but in its commitment to furthering the interests of the international commercial banks and the elites in some debtor countries. For when it suits the international commercial banks and the elites in the debtor countries, the Fund turns its back on market principles and engineers massive interventions in the market, and at other times when it suits the international commercial banks and elites in debtor countries, the IMF applies market principles with extreme rigour.

How the IMF has consistently applied inappropriate market doctrines: the rise of market fundamentalism

The basket of IMF policies has come to be known as the Washington Consensus. The criticisms of these policies have become legion, and rather than repeating them, I'll simply analyse one recent instance.

Throughout the late 1980s and 1990s, IMF Structural Adjustment Policies (SAPs) were decried by critics for their failure to reduce poverty significantly (Sanchez and Cash, 2003). Poverty Reduction Strategy Papers (PRSPs) were introduced in 1999 in response to this global outcry and were to contain policies negotiated between debtor nations and the IMF that would lead to poverty reduction, and provide the basis for debt relief and access to new funding.

According to the IMF, "PRSPs are prepared by the member countries through a participatory process involving domestic stakeholders" (IMF, 2007). PRSPs are to outline the economic, social, and structural programmes to be used to reduce poverty (Steward and Wang, 2003). Instead of focusing on macroeconomic stability and growth like SAPs, PRSPs were to put poverty reduction at the core of the nation's economic policies.

The IMF has its own internal evaluation division, the Independent Evaluation Office, and in March 2007 it released *The IMF and Aid to Sub-Saharan Africa*

(IEO, 2007), which evaluated the IMF's performance in Africa. The report noted the differences of views among the Executive Board of the Fund about its role and policies in poor countries, and concluded that:

> lacking clarity on what they should do on the mobilization of aid ... and the application of poverty and social impact analysis, IMF staff tended to focus on macroeconomic stability, in line with the institution's core mandate and their deeply ingrained professional culture.
>
> (IEO, 2007: vii)

In other words, more than seven years after the replacement of SAPs with PRSPs and the establishment of the Poverty Reduction and Growth Facility, IMF staff were unclear on the priority to be given to poverty reduction and how to achieve it, and so sought to attain that which they knew how to attain: macroeconomic stability. This is ridiculous. For an institution that had maintained steadfastly since 2000 that poverty reduction was its highest priority, to still be trying to bed down poverty reduction initiatives in 2007 is utterly unacceptable.

The Report also found the IMF's policies accommodated increased aid "in countries whose recent policies have led to high stocks of reserves and low inflation", but "in other countries additional aid was programmed to be saved to increase reserves or to retire domestic debt" (IEO, 2007: 2). Very few African countries have high reserves and low inflation. Accordingly, across sub-Saharan Africa, the IMF channelled extra aid into foreign exchange reserves or into debt repayment. Such an approach has two flaws:

1 It diverts extra aid away from healthcare, education and other social welfare expenditures; and
2 It risks being a "self-fulfilling prophecy" as diverting aid flows into reserves and debt reduction is likely to dissuade donors from giving more aid. Most donors want to give aid to assist suffering people directly, not to improve a nation's macroeconomic profile.

On the basis of the report by the IMF evaluation office, it would appear that while the rhetoric of the IMF has changed, in practice its officers still give primacy to macroeconomic stability at the expense of assisting the poor and investing in the human capital of a nation.

So the pressing issue is: how can the IMF apply sensible economic policies with moderation, insight and appropriate allowance for the institutional fragility of the recipient countries, rather than as doctrinaire rules?

How to reform the IMF

Seven steps are required to reform global financial governance. The initial step is to applaud the move from the G7 to the G20. Such a move was decades overdue. I agree with Jose Antonio Ocampo that the role of an institution for financial decision making needs to be given to a more representative body than any "G-club", such as a body of the United Nations (Ocampo, 2011). But if this is not achieveable, and it may well not be, then at the least the G20 could be made more representative by the inclusion of more regional representatives. The E.U. is currently the only regional member. The addition of regional representation of North Africa and the Middle East, sub-Saharan African, South Asia, East Asia and Latin America would result in a G25 that directly or indirectly represents virtually all nations. While it will be extremely difficult to remove the seat of any current nation politically, logically Italy should lose its seat, Saudi Arabia's seat should go to the regional grouping for North Africa and the Middle East, and Argentina's seat to the regional grouping for Latin America. This would result in a G22, a grouping of manageable size (Bergsten, 2004; Helleiner, 2001).

The next step is to reform the governance of the IFIs. There have been tiny reforms in the past two years, but, essentially, most votes are in the hands of the U.S. and the leading European countries. So the IMF and World Bank, whose clients are the world's poorer countries, do the bidding of the richest countries. This is absurd.

The communiqués of the World Bank and IMF at Istanbul in October 2009 promised for the IMF "a shift in quota share to dynamic emerging market and developing countries of at least 5 per cent from over-represented countries" (IMF, 2009a). Likewise, the World Bank committed to increase by at least 3 per cent "voting power for developing and transition countries" (World Bank, 2009). The need for reform of the IMF voting rights has been widely recognized (Thimann, 2009; Leech, 2009).

Yet these tiny changes won't shift the fundamental balance of power in the World Bank and the IMF. The European nations, in particular, are grossly over-represented on the IFIs, as they are in the G20. Fully one quarter of the seats on the G20 go to Europe: those of Britain, France, Germany, Italy and the E.U. Europe needs to provide real leadership on these issues.

In addition to reforming IMF governance, we need to return it to its original mandate. It is only on this issue that I part company significantly from Professor Ocampo. He argues that we need to place the IMF at the centre of global macroeconomic policy coordination. Yet, as I see it, the IMF has become a fundamentalist organization and unless the Fund can be so fundamentally reformed that it sees the world through an entirely new lens, its policy prescriptions will routinely be flawed.

The skills required to turn around poorly performing economies are utterly different from those typically held by central bankers and Ph.D. graduates in macroeconomics: the two most common backgrounds of IMF staffers. The IMF is the wrong organization to set economic policy for nations in crisis and it should be removed from this role. If an IFI is required to play this role, a new one, with the right skillset, attitudes and culture needs to be established. This change would limit the IMF to data collection, technical surveillance and advice-giving roles.

Next we need to make three fundamental changes to the international financial architecture: (i) new financial mechanisms to mitigate risk, including international institutions lending in local currencies; (ii) a moratorium or partial cancellation of debt for a much wider range of countries than currently are eligible; and (iii) new mechanisms for handling sovereign debt restructuring, such as a sovereign bankruptcy regime (Stiglitz, 2009).

There are strong reasons why all reschedulings of rich-country-to-poor-country loans should be in local currency, as should all lending by IFIs such as the IMF and World Bank (Buckley and Dirou, 2006). Our current system places the currency risk on the party least able to bear it, the borrower. Lending in local currency puts the currency risk on those best able to bear it and hedge against it, the lenders.

Likewise there are strong arguments for debt relief, or at least a moratoria on interest repayments, for far more countries than currently qualify under the Highly Indebted Poor Country Initiative and the Multilateral Debt Relief Initiative. A repayment moratoria would assist poorer nations hurt by the GFC far more than saddling them with yet more debt.

Likewise, as Professor Ocampo has stressed, there is a pressing need for an orderly, rules-based approach to sovereign insolvencies (Buckley, 2009). The prospect of substantial losses in a debtor's bankruptcy focuses a bank's mind when making credit decisions. No national financial system is able to operate without this discipline. Its absence in the international system explains much of the overlending we have seen across the world in the past 35 years. Why shouldn't banks overlend when they can expect borrowers to increase taxes, reduce services and reborrow from the IMF so as to service the loans (Bolton and Jeanne, 2007; Sachs, 1995)?

Finally, we need a new global reserve currency, and I agree with all Professor Ocampo has written in this regard. Whenever one nation's currency serves as the global reserve currency, the extra liquidity required in order to meet the global liquidity needs inevitably puts downward pressure on the currency's value and thereby makes it more volatile and less attractive as a reserve currency. In addition, financial markets don't impose fiscal discipline on the reserve issuing country. Our system will remain unstable for as long as any one nation's currency serves as the global reserve currency.

China is concerned about holding most of its reserves in dollars. Twice in 2009 the Governor of China's central bank called for a new reserve currency regime focused on special drawing rights (Bergsten, 2009; Xiaochuan, 2009). China is hard at work researching alternatives, such as denominating and settling its trade with Brazil in real and renminbis, not dollars (Wheatley, 2009).

Today, when it comes to currencies, China and the U.S. are in the same boat, and it has one inch of freeboard. There are better vessels available: vessels that are a mix of currencies, that offer far more stability and fewer problems for the treasuries of the currencies in the basket. But to move from the current inadequate vessel to a better one requires cooperation. No one can afford to rock a boat with one inch of freeboard. China cannot – most of its foreign exchange reserves are in U.S. dollars, and it stands to lose massively if it triggers a collapse in the value of the U.S. dollar. The U.S. cannot, for if China precipitately places its reserves in other currencies, and uses other currencies to price and pay for all its foreign trade, the demand for dollars will drop dramatically. So, for now, China keeps saying it wants out of this unstable boat and the U.S. keeps replying, "No, please stay in here with us." This is simply not a long-term answer.

Europe's difficult challenge is to work towards only having the number of seats in the G20 and the number of votes in the IFIs that its size and population warrants.

America's difficult challenge is to accept its currency can no longer serve as the global reserve currency and to cooperate with China, Japan and Europe in managing the orderly transition to a more stable regime.

The IFIs' difficult challenge is to embed market principles in their approaches to crisis resolution. Whenever a crisis hits, the commercial banks will work hard to transfer the losses onto the common people of the debtor nations. The IFIs must be vigilant to prevent this happening. During crises markets must be allowed to allocate losses upon creditors as well as debtors.

Note

1 Professor of Law, University of New South Wales; Fellow, Asian Institute for International Finance Law, University of Hong Kong. Sincere thanks to the Australian Research Council for the Discovery Grant that has helped support this research, and to Lara K. Hall for her invaluable research assistance. All responsibility is mine.

5 Sub-prime lending and microcredit

An uncomfortable analogy

John D. Conroy[1]

Introduction: microcredit, microfinance and financialization

If the global crisis from 2007 reflected a disembedding of market economies (as well as demonstrating their incapacity to self-regulate) perhaps we should consider how market processes might become re-embedded in our societies and cultures (Polanyi, 1944).[2] Negative outcomes of the crisis are now evident in many aspects of economic life. This is nowhere more so than in disruptions associated with the growth in global reach and pervasiveness of financial markets. As Quiggin observes in his contribution to this volume, periods of financial sector dominance have regularly ended in spectacular panics and crashes and the liquidation of large numbers of financial institutions. This financial growth has been fuelled by many factors, but not least by "financialization", defined with disarming simplicity as "the act of making something sellable or tradable that didn't use to be" (Welsh, 2006).

This paper looks at some emerging consequences of financialization in one small and rather arcane corner of the financial markets, the microcredit "industry". Contemporary developments in microcredit give evidence of economic processes that have become disembedded in the Polanyian sense. As these processes unfold observers may be led to ask whether microcredit in developing economies will come to provide an uncomfortable analogy with "sub-prime" home mortgage lending in the United States.

Microcredit is the provision of very small loans to poor people, usually without physical collateral. In the popular imagination microcredit is associated with Muhammad Yunus of Bangladesh, and with the Grameen Bank (GB) he founded. In 2006 the man and his bank shared the Nobel Peace Prize for which the citation said, in part, that:

> From modest beginnings three decades ago, Yunus has, first and foremost through Grameen Bank, developed microcredit into an ever more important instrument in the struggle against poverty. Grameen Bank has been a source of ideas and models for the many institutions in the field of microcredit that have sprung up around the world.
>
> (Nobel Committee, 2006)

This tribute, and others, reflect the fact that microcredit is regarded by some as the greatest innovation in "development" over the past quarter century. Thus Senator Dick Durbin, nominating Muhammad Yunus for the U.S. Congressional Gold Medal in 2009, states:

> Dr. Yunus has given hope to millions through his Grameen Bank. Over the last thirty years, his theory of microenterprise has become a phenomenon – touching the lives of more than 100 million people around the world. It is hard to think of any single idea in our lifetime which has lifted so many people out of the deepest depths of poverty.

The international donor community, led by the World Bank, endorsed such judgements by establishing the Consultative Group to Assist the Poor (CGAP) in 1995. This body, bringing together multi- and bilateral donor agencies with microfinance practitioners, adopted microfinance as the primary policy instrument to be employed against poverty.

Yunus successfully challenged the conventional wisdom that the poor are not bankable. His group-based methods have been widely influential and replicated in many countries. Grameen Bank was criticized for lacking transparency and relying on donor subsidies while neglecting client savings in favour of providing credit. Nonetheless, GB and other microcredit models made many important innovations. GB subsequently modified its approach to reflect more recent advances in "microfinance". A new "Grameen2" model now offers a wider range of financial services, at least in Bangladesh. Around the world, however, many Grameen-inspired micro-lending institutions continue to flourish, and to attract the attention of commercial investors, not least because of the high interest rates micro-borrowers seem willing to pay and the generally good repayment performance of well managed microcredit programs.

The term "microfinance" represents a broader approach to the financial service needs of the poor than that of "microcredit". By the 1990s approaches with greater focus on other financial services had moved to the centre of professional discourse, supplanting microcredit. This occurred even as microcredit and the Grameen Bank began to exert a stranglehold on the popular and political imaginations that has endured to the present. The newer microfinance approach emphasized the value to the poor of a range of services, including savings, payments and remittances, and micro-insurance, in addition to credit.[3] The experience of microfinance service providers has been that, just as the poor are "bankable" borrowers, they also have the capacity to save, if offered safe, liquid, inexpensive and convenient deposit services. Moreover, deposit-taking opens the road for microfinance institutions (MFIs) to become financial intermediaries within the broader financial system. It is now acknowledged that any financial institution can "do" microfinance, if it is prepared to make the necessary investments and adopt appropriate organizational and procedural changes. This applies whether institutions are publicly or privately owned, whether operated for profit or not-for-profit, and whether regulated or informal. The term "MFI", which originally connoted a voluntary sector entity (or "NGO/MFI"), now has much wider application. For example, many commercial banks now have microfinance divisions which can be regarded as MFIs in this broader sense.

From early in the twenty-first century further "micro-financial" insights have emerged, having to do with the value to the poor of their being financially "included". "Financial inclusion" as an approach to poverty alleviation (which means giving people access to formal financial services) will be discussed in detail below. Suffice to say, for the moment, that the current discussion of inclusion represents a clarification or a refocussing of attention among microfinance practitioners. It is not an abrupt change of emphasis, such as occurred when microcredit was supplanted by microfinance in the professional debate. In the meantime, however, microcredit has continued to grow in the marketplace, as the vulgar face of microfinance. Since 2000 the proportion of private, for-profit, investors in microcredit has grown quite markedly. Some of these new commercial investors are misappropriating the microfinance "label" to describe their ventures. Their failure to offer products other than microcredit, thus rejecting a central insight of the microfinance movement, is particularly egregious under the circumstances.

The misappropriation of microfinance and the neglect of savings

Microcredit, masquerading as microfinance, is the primary target of a new surge in investment. Why investors who focus exclusively on lending should choose to label their product as microfinance is not entirely clear. It could be they appreciate that the newer term carries positive connotations not attached to microcredit. It is not surprising that commercially focussed investors might shy away from deposit taking. Any attempt to mobilize deposits, especially the small balances of the poor, will present difficulties for new and rapidly growing institutions. Many MFIs lack the systems, human resources and other capacities needed to mobilize deposits in amounts sufficient to finance a significant proportion of their lending. Also, many MFIs are barred by law or regulation from taking deposits without changing their legal form and/or making costly and demanding changes to their operations. But microcredit has succeeded, historically, in finding technical solutions to the daunting problems of uncollateralized lending to poor people. Why then should it be impossible for microfinance (and its financial regulators) to find innovative solutions for deposit mobilization among the poor?

In terms of regulatory responses to the challenge, *The Economist* offers encouragement:

> Some countries are addressing these challenges by adopting legal and regulatory frameworks that explicitly allow and govern microfinance deposit-taking and mobilisation.... For those countries that have adapted adequate policies to promote such activities, the rewards of success can be significant.

> For example, in 2008 Bangladesh's Grameen Bank, perhaps the world's most famous MFI, generated almost half of its US$934m in deposits from non-borrowers.
>
> (Economist Intelligence Unit, 2009)

The community of financial regulators has begun to give attention to issues arising from "depository microfinance". In 2010 the Basel Committee for Banking Supervision issued a consultative paper, *Microfinance Activities and the Core Principles for Effective Banking Supervision.* While concluding that the "Basel Core Principles" are generally applicable to microfinance, the paper identifies particular principles that require a "tailored approach" to it (Basel Committee for Banking Supervision, 2010: 12). The document emphasizes "the need for specialised knowledge of supervisors to identify and measure risks that are specific to microfinance" as well as "a proportional regulatory and supervisory framework suitable for small microfinance institutions" (ibid.: 2–3). Basel's willingness to study microfinance is encouraging. Unintended regulatory barriers may become less common in future and the creative energies of regulators may be directed to assisting the industry to grow to maturity.

Despite such encouraging signs the unfortunate reality remains; that access to investment funding often appears to disincline MFIs from seeking deposit-taking status, or from exploiting that status fully even if authorized to do so. Certainly many institutions find it easier and cheaper to rely on external resources (donor funds, loans, investors) than to mobilize the savings of the poor. This has unfortunate consequences at both the systemic and the personal (or household) levels. At the systemic level, when financial institutions are ineffective in savings mobilization, the processes of financial intermediation are hobbled. Resources are not channelled efficiently from savers to borrowers and scarce capital is used inefficiently. Even within a minor sub-system of the whole, such as microfinance, more effective financial intermediation contributes to aggregate financial deepening and supports domestic financial development. Indeed deposit mobilization by MFIs among their low-income clients is the basis for autonomous grassroots financial development. Greater reliance on domestic funding resources, and especially deposits, reduces the vulnerability of MFIs (and, by extension, the broader system) to external shocks. Conversely, growing reliance on external capital increases the vulnerability of MFIs to such shocks.

At the micro level, the domain of individuals and households, negative consequences also flow from ineffective savings mobilization. The absence of deposit facilities denies important benefits to low-income and poor people. For example, discipline gained from the experience of saving prepares the poor to engage in micro-enterprise activities and self-employment, as well as providing them opportunities to establish "financial identity". With savings in reserve they are able to smooth consumption expenditures in the face of uncertain income streams. Savings give households a shield against catastrophic events, whether affecting individuals or entire communities. Misfortunes such as illness or bereavement, or destruction due to natural disasters, might otherwise force the vulnerable to divest productive assets, tipping them over the divide between meagre sufficiency and poverty. Access to deposit services also assists the recipients of "lumpy" income flows, such as remittances or periodic crop receipts, to manage these more efficiently and prudently. To the extent that it neglects or even represses domestic savings mobilization, the surge of commercial investment in micro-lending does nothing to meet this complex bundle of needs, so important to the welfare of poor and low-income people.

That the growth of microcredit lending, in the aggregate, has been proceeding without corresponding growth in domestic savings mobilized by MFIs is suggested by data reported by USAID (2009). Citing data for 2003–07, USAID concluded that:

> in 2004, the breakdown of MFI liabilities was approximately 92 per cent deposits and 8 per cent debt, by 2007 the breakdown was only 45 per cent deposits and 55 per cent debt funding despite an increase in the number of institutions authorized to mobilize savings since 2004.

This increased level of gearing suggests the growing influence of financialized micro-lending.

The "financialization" of microcredit

The financialization of microcredit is evident in a range of financial technologies familiar from the mainstream capital markets. These include the creation of special purpose vehicles to acquire microcredit assets (microfinance investment vehicles, or MIVs) and the use of securitization, collateralized debt obligations and structured finance among other risk-management tools. Examples abound of credit wraps or guarantees, loan syndications and hedging mechanisms, while specialized services, including ratings agencies, support the industry. A small number of initial public offerings (IPOs) have occurred. These are seen as pointing the way to "exit" opportunities for private equity investors, thereby increasing the allure of for-profit investment in microcredit. Financialized microcredit stems from activities of the investment arms of multi- and bilateral development agencies. Commencing in the 1990s, entities such as the International Finance Corporation (IFC) and the German agency KfW began to extend finance to MFIs on a "near-commercial" basis. Supplemented by private foundations and "social" investors, this funding was intended to encourage borrowing MFIs to operate at higher levels of commerciality and professionalism, as well as to augment their resources. Some international commercial banks made experimental investments during this period, though usually through their in-house charitable foundations.

A CGAP review of foreign capital flows to microfinance to end-2004 noted that, while most funding still consisted of grants or highly subsidized loans, "since 2000 there has been a rapid growth in foreign investment by various agencies and funds that tend to be more commercially oriented" (CGAP, 2005: 1). However, genuine private investment (loans and equity) still accounted for less than a quarter of flows during 2004, while fully commercial investments were very few. Indeed the availability of such funds appeared to CGAP to exceed the demand. It predicted that "as MFIs continue to grow and absorb more funding ... domestic sources seem likely to become more prevalent, particularly for regulated MFIs" (ibid.: 2)

The next few years, however, would see great changes in the foreign funding landscape, illustrating the pitfalls of prediction in a global economy where international savings imbalances were precipitating increasing cross-border capital flows. Even such an obscure corner of the capital markets as microcredit could not be wholly exempt from this influence. Another CGAP review carried the story forward to end-2006. It reported excitedly:

> Microfinance is experiencing an unprecedented investment boom. The past five years have seen remarkable increases in the volume of global microfinance investments. Between 2004 and 2006, the stock of foreign capital investment – covering both debt and equity – more than tripled to US$4 billion.... The entry of private investors is the most notable change in the microfinance investment marketplace. New players arrive on the scene every month. Forty specialized microfinance investment funds have been established in the past three years alone. Individuals and institutional investors –including international retail banks, investment banks, pension funds, and private equity funds – are all looking for ways to channel capital into microfinance, and investment banking techniques are being introduced to create investment vehicle alternatives that appeal to an increasingly broad range of investors.
>
> (CGAP, 2008)

Yet another CGAP review (CGAP, 2009) brought the story forward to end-2008. It noted evidence that MFI profitability had stimulated surging investment, since in many countries the return on assets for MFIs appeared higher than for commercial banks. In relation to the rapid growth of MIVs, the review noted that some 75 per cent of these vehicles dealt entirely or mainly in fixed interest investments. While some were "socially focussed" and accepted lower returns, others offered "structured" products with a range of risk/return options. Overall the average gross yield on debt held by MIVs was 9.5 per cent in 2008. Other MIVs were private equity funds and took equity stakes in microcredit operators. This newest class of profit-seeking investors had the highest rate of asset growth among MIVs. More than 100 MIVs in operation at end-2008 held total funds under management of some $6.6 billion. These vehicles recorded asset growth of 72 per cent in 2007 and 31 per cent in 2008, while an industry survey projected 29 per cent growth for 2009. Equity holdings of MIVs were growing even more rapidly (by 47 per cent in 2008). In aggregate, foreign capital commitments to MFIs from all sources were estimated to total $14.8 billion at end-2008, divided almost equally between donors (48 per cent) and investors (52 per cent). In terms of the instruments employed, grants made up 17 per cent, debt 63 per cent and equity 11 per cent (up from 9 per cent in the previous year). Total disbursements in 2008 were about $3 billion (two-thirds by investors) (CGAP, 2009). Almost all of these flows supported retail MFIs directly or indirectly, marking the growing engagement of micro-lending institutions with corporate funding sources and the financialization process.

Commercialization and foreign investment: pros and cons

Some clarifications are necessary at this point. The writer has no objection either to the commercialization of microfinance or to foreign investment in it, per se. It is not obvious that either commercialization or for-profit foreign investment is *necessarily* liable to "disembed" microfinancial services from the social or cultural milieu in which they arise. Indeed commercialization is a necessary condition for building sustainable grassroots financial services. Further, some level of investment in MFIs by foreign financial institutions should be welcome, since capital shortage is a defining feature of underdevelopment. Foreign investment may bring positive technology "spill-overs", to the benefit of domestic MFIs. It is possible that foreign investment may discourage domestic investment in MFIs, but it might on the other hand prove complementary to it. It is probably too early to come to a conclusion on these matters; no doubt there are lessons to be drawn from experience of foreign investment elsewhere in the financial sector.

The most telling objections to foreign investment are based upon negative consequences for the domestic financial system, as described above. The availability of foreign funding represses domestic savings because it reduces the incentive for regulated financial institutions to mobilize deposits among the poor, while non-regulated MFIs have less incentive to upgrade to deposit-taking status. When domestic savings mobilization is inhibited domestic financial intermediation and financial deepening are retarded. Autonomous financial development at the grassroots is repressed and the poor continue to be excluded from the financial services of most value to them. This is not "embedded" finance. Further, MFIs receiving foreign commercial funds will often experience the phenomenon known as "mission drift". They will come under pressure to meet performance benchmarks set by investors. They may tend to switch focus away from the poor to middle-income (albeit also "excluded") clients and towards consumer durable lending, because these yield higher returns. The poor will continue to be excluded.

Turning to *domestic* investment in microcredit, some level of funding from domestic financial institutions should benefit MFIs, especially in terms of technology spill-overs and the potential for mutually beneficial operating linkages. As the USAID study cited above comments:

> The advantages of local bank lending are many. Loans are typically in local currency and represent banking relationships that can grow deeper over time. Alliances with commercial banks in some cases promise the possibility of offering MFI clients financial services that MFIs often cannot, including savings or ATMs.
>
> (Magnoni and Powers 2009)

Domestic, or cross-sectoral, investment flows might also provide some solution to problems of capital shortage in the regions where the poor are found (although experience suggests that in developing countries deposits usually flow in the opposite direction, from periphery to centre). However, if domestic for-profit investment causes mission drift in MFIs, or if it represses personal savings in particular sectors or social strata (for example, in rural areas or among the poor), there are again strong reasons for objection. If locally based institutions become excessively dependent on access to resources through enmeshment in national and international capital flows their communities may be excluded from the intermediation process other than as passive recipients of consumer finance.

Some cautionary tales

Early experience of the microcredit boom has provided a fund of cautionary tales concerning foreign investment in microcredit, whether direct or with domestic financial partners. Examples are presented here from just two countries: Mexico and India. Observing the rush by corporates and international banks to invest, *Time Magazine* reported that:

> The pinstripes are chasing the poor. Microfinance, once a relative cottage industry … is on the verge of a revolution, with billions of dollars from big banks, private-equity shops and pension funds pouring in, driving growth of 30% to 40% a year. Financiers are convinced that there's huge money to be made in microfinance. [Among the results are that] as lending to poor people has gone mainstream, certain markets, like Mexico, have been flooded with loans that have nothing to do with providing capital to aspiring entrepreneurs—just racking up household debt.
>
> (Kiviat, 2008)

While the experience of Mexico is not unique, that country occupies a special place in the narrative due to an infamously successful IPO in 2007, reported by *The Times* (Blakely, 2008) in the following terms:

> When *Banco Compartamos*, Mexico's largest microlender with more than 840,000 customers, went public last year, it raised $450 million for a group of backers that had originally invested just $6 million. It emerged that the bank routinely charges annual percentage rates (APR) of interest of more than 100 per cent – about treble the global microfinance average. Its return on equity is more than three times the 15 per cent delivered by Mexico's conventional lenders.

Proceeds of the float represented 12 times book value, yielding an internal rate of return for the initial investors of about 100 per cent per year, compounded over eight years. Those profiting included directors and managers of Compartamos, other Mexican private investors and a U.S.-based NGO. Particularly piquant was the fact that Compartamos had previously benefited from grants, loans, technical assistance and guarantees from public international agencies, including CGAP, and social investors. With some understatement, CGAP (2007) suggested that "the transaction will probably give a significant boost to the credibility of microfinance[4] in commercial capital markets and accelerate the mobilization of private capital for the business of providing financial services to poor and low-income people".

Turning to India, in 2008 and 2009 it experienced booming investment in micro-lending, both foreign and domestic. An Indian journalist recorded that:

> Recently, three micro finance institutions (MFIs) of varying sizes collectively received private equity (PE) investments of around Rs550 crore [more than $110 million].... Till recently, such investments went into retail or real estate.... What's noteworthy now is the arrival of pure-play venture capital funds that are sensing opportunity at the bottom of the pyramid. Sequoia Capital, Sandstone and JM Financial are among those that have bet on this sector.
>
> (Chakravarty, 2009)

The funds named are all non-Indian entities. An industry report speculated that:

> 2009 may go down as the watershed year for the Indian microfinance industry. Marked by strong growth and pioneering deals the industry is riding high, growing at a rapid pace of 100%–200% year-on-year. There were 11 PE [private equity] deals worth $178 million during the financial year 2009, compared to three deals worth $52 million in 2008.
>
> (Azmi 2009).

Domestic entities broke new ground for the sector with innovative capital raisings. SKS Microfinance issued the "first ever" listed non-convertible debentures to a foreign investor, while it and other MFIs carried out credit-rated securitizations of microcredit loans in which the investors included domestic banks and mutual funds (Azmi, 2009). SKS was reported to be preparing an IPO that could challenge the success of the Compartamos float.

In this fevered atmosphere speculation arose that a microcredit investment bubble was forming. The *Wall Street Journal* (Gokhale, 2009) reported that traditional village moneylenders, far from being driven out of business by the proliferation of microcredit, appeared to be thriving. The *WSJ* attributed this paradox to overindebtedness among MFI clients who had been persuaded to take out multiple loans. Another analyst judged microcredit investment in the South Indian state of Andhra Pradesh, with a population of 80 million, to be very close to bubble conditions by the end of 2008. This state had a very high incidence of multiple borrowings by microcredit clients, with the "immediate risk" that "some of these borrowers may be falling into a debt spiral, borrowing from one MFI to repay another". There was also a greater risk, "that increasingly many clients are carrying debts that leave little room for absorbing even relatively moderate economic shocks" (Rozas, 2009). Investment professionals were reassessing the Indian microcredit sector, wary of overheated valuations demanded of PE investors, and concerned by the evidence of overextended lending. Perhaps 2010, rather than the previous year, may prove to have been the "watershed" for Indian micro-lending, because in that year the debt crisis became impossible to ignore (*The Economist*, 2010). It will be instructive to learn how far this situation bears similarities with circumstances in a more "advanced" credit market.

Sub-prime mortgage lending and microcredit: some curious parallels

In the United States sub-prime mortgage financing can be traced back to the *Community Re-investment Act* (the *CRA*) of 1977. And while microcredit in developing countries originated in voluntary "self-help" activities, it was given a transformative boost by the official development assistance (ODA) expenditures of "Northern" governments from the late 1980s. Both forms of lending flourished due to apparently laudable government efforts to provide credit for the "unbankable". Federal Reserve Chair Ben Bernanke (2007) has explained the *CRA* as intended to reduce "credit-related discrimination" and to expand access to credit. It was "an attempt to rectify market failures – for example, by inducing banks to invest in building the knowledge and expertise necessary to lend profitably in lower-income neighborhoods". While the *CRA* introduced the process, the Clinton administration accelerated it. In 1999, the *New York Times* reported that:

> The Fannie Mae Corporation is easing the credit requirements on loans that it will purchase from banks and other lenders.... [Fannie Mae] has been under increasing pressure from the Clinton Administration to expand mortgage loans among low and moderate income people. With some prescience, *The Times* warned that "Fannie Mae is taking on significantly more risk, which may not pose any difficulties during flush economic times. But the government-subsidized corporation may run into trouble in an economic downturn".
>
> (Holmes, 1999)

International action by governments was crucial to launching microcredit. Official development assistance (ODA) promulgated and funded the industry from the second half of the 1990s, with CGAP as the driving force. Muhammad Yunus was taken up as the "darling" of the donors and an enthusiastic cheer squad, centred on the World Bank, CGAP and the "Microcredit Summit", pursued an extraordinarily effective campaign to raise awareness and secure funding commitments for micro-lending.

In both cases, sub-prime and microcredit, financial innovation was crucial to their growth. Concerning the former, Chairman Bernanke has described how "during the 1980s and 1990s, technological progress significantly improved data collection and information processing, which led to the development and widespread use of credit-scoring models and the availability of generic credit history scores" while "securitization of affordable housing loans expanded, as did the secondary market for those loans" (Bernanke, 2007). In the case of microcredit the success of Grameen and other MFIs depended initially on successful innovations in non-collateralized lending to the poor. More recently the adoption of financial technologies from "Northern" capital markets has underpinned commercial investment and growth.

To turn to other parallels, both sub-prime mortgages and microcredit loans came to be seen as new "asset classes", attracting the attention of aggressive, "non-traditional" lenders and intermediaries. In consequence both experienced some degree of malpractice and excess. Like microcredit, sub-prime lending appears to have suffered from "mission drift". Again, cross-border capital flows were a major funding source for sub-prime lending, while they are a rapidly growing source of support for microcredit. Finally, the collapse of sub-prime mortgage lending has had destructive consequences for financial systems outside the U.S. (Iceland, Ireland and the U.K., to mention three early cases). This paper poses the question: how far will growing reliance on external funding of microcredit prove to have negative consequences for developing country financial systems? Will the negative effects of financialization diminish the possibility of their developing embedded systems of grassroots finance, capable of providing the full suite of financial services needed by the poor?

How microcredit became a new "asset class"

Foreign philanthropy and "socially responsible" investment directed to NGO/MFIs helped build the microcredit industry from the 1980s, with a surge in ODA from the 1990s. In the twenty-first century, however, new forces were at work transforming the funding landscape, including that of microcredit. The global financial crisis has been attributed to "imbalances" between trading nations. The U.S. has been able to sustain a low, or even negative, gross savings rate by virtue of being the issuer of the world's de facto reserve currency. "Surplus" economies with favourable trade balances vis-à-vis the United States have been willing to hold dollars, or dollar-denominated financial assets, as a large proportion of their foreign currency reserves. Major surplus countries have been unable, or unwilling, to deploy more than a minor proportion of their external dollar reserves for domestic investment. In the particular case of China, a very high rate of aggregate domestic savings presents the mirror-reverse image of American overconsumption. In these circumstances the U.S. was confronted by a "wall of money", directed into its financial markets by the governments and monetary authorities of the trade surplus economies, and spilling over into European and other developed economy financial markets. Absorbing the flood of capital to "Northern" financial markets required financial innovation to identify new investments (including the sub-prime housing market) and to devise new financial instruments (including collateralized debt obligations).

The imperative of finding new outlets for investment drove the search for new asset classes that could be presented to fund managers and other institutional investors and in turn recommended to retail investors. This search coincided with growing interest in "bottom of the pyramid" investment opportunities, and with the rise of "socially-responsible" or "ethical" investment criteria for portfolio allocation. What, then, could be more intriguing than a new asset class offering gilt-edged ethical credentials, with "benchmark" returns, tapped from the bottom of the pyramid? This new investment opportunity was found in a novel and exotic "sub-prime" finance opportunity, the microcredit lending market.

The financialization of microcredit is ironic in the extreme because Muhammad Yunus has been famously antagonistic to formal financial systems. He was appalled by developments described in this paper, including the Compartamos IPO (Burgis, 2008) and the crisis in Andhra Pradesh (AFP, 2010). Grameen Bank had been his reaction to market failure in the formal banking sector of Bangladesh, which was unable to serve the great majority of its population. GB might be seen as an instance of Polanyi's "*double movement*" (Polanyi, 1944). Its creation was a protective response, or counter-reaction, against a "disembedded" and dysfunctional financial system. In its original form GB was an attempt to ameliorate these problems by embedding a functional credit mechanism, whereas the reformed "Grameen2" model now aims to provide a range of financial services. It offers a vision of "embedded" microfinance, applicable to the particular circumstances of Bangladesh and perhaps certain other countries as well.

Financial inclusion and "distributed" finance

The difference between financial inclusion and microfinance is the same as that between ends and means, goals and instruments. "Financial inclusion" simply means having access to formal financial services. Observed rates of financial inclusion differ enormously between countries. They range, at one extreme, from 98 per cent of the adult population in Singapore, to less than 20 per cent in parts of sub-Saharan Africa and the Pacific (World Bank, 2008). In policy terms financial inclusion is a goal, while microfinance is currently the most appropriate policy instrument for achieving that goal. In future, as rates of financial inclusion improve and other conditions change, microfinance will become less relevant to the goal of universal provision of formal financial services. Between 30 and 40 million people in the USA still lack access to formal banking services, indicating the long-term nature of the task.

Achieving high levels of financial inclusion is important because, *inter alia*, it supports distributional equity and social cohesion. Growing levels of financial inclusion are a necessary condition for creating an embedded financial system, functional in terms of societal and cultural values. Another way of looking at this is to say that a financial system capable of serving grassroots populations is likely also to be a “distributed” system. Elizabeth Rhyne (2009) has likened the global financial system to “an overly centralized energy grid that crashes when overloaded”. She contended that:

> a more durable approach could resemble a financial microgrid, with self-sufficient local power centers, drawing capital from local communities. These *distributed* financial centers would not be walled off from each other, but neither would they depend on the mainline current. Microfinance institutions would feature prominently in a financial microgrid.

Writing in 2009, Rhyne suggested that:

> institutions like MFIs that grow through savings accounts and domestic capital markets while offering responsible lending could be the basis for a distributed, diversified and durable financial system. Community banking in developed countries offers another illustration of such a model.[5]

Distributed systems are also likely to be embedded systems, and they are very likely to support growing levels of financial inclusion. Moreover, rapid technological change and managerial innovation offer new possibilities to expand the frontiers of financial inclusion. But will “distributed” service providers, many of which are relatively small, be able to benefit from such changes, when economies of scale might appear to favour larger operators?

The modern “drivers” of financial inclusion

Innovations supporting increased financial inclusion are likely to have both technological and managerial elements and will often require regulatory change. A set of “policy solutions”, drawn from studies of successful innovations in a number of developing countries, has been proposed for widespread adoption.[6] Briefly, the proposed solutions are:

- **Agent banking**, which involves non-bank agents partnering with banks to provide decentralized distribution of services
- **Mobile phone banking**, which draws on the rapid growth in volume and scope of financial services delivered via mobile telephony
- **Greater diversity of microfinance service providers**, requiring regulatory reform to facilitate the adoption of new institutional models and products
- **Governance and management of state banks**, reforming and rehabilitating public sector banks and reversing long-term disinvestment in them
- **Financial identity regulations**, creating financial identities for a growing proportion of national populations, thereby easing access to financial services
- **Protection of consumer and creditor rights**, instituting policies for fair treatment, privacy, transparency and dispute settlement, together with financial literacy

The list is diverse and includes requirements for private and public investment and regulatory change. In a financial environment subject to such initiatives, it is not inevitable that small and agile local institutions in close touch with their communities will be outmanoeuvred by larger and better-capitalized competitors. Deregulation and competition in national markets for telephony and internet services, together with innovative software providers, might help small operators maintain their competitive positions, capturing a share of the billion people in emerging markets who have mobile phones but still lack access to banking services (Beshouri and Gravråk, 2010). Regulatory frameworks will play an important role in determining how far distributed systems of finance can maintain and extend their influence.

Conclusion

We should be concerned about excessive preoccupation with microcredit at the expense of microfinance, and about the potentially distorting influence of foreign investment. Good policy will aim to achieve progressive improvements in financial inclusion. Adoption of financially inclusive policy frameworks may offer poor societies an escape from the contradictions posed by foreign-funded microcredit, as will efforts to create financial institutions more in tune with (and embedded in) local social and cultural norms.

A striking feature of the microcredit industry is its internationalization, especially in terms of diffusion of ideas and technology. More problematic is its internationalization in terms of capital flows if microcredit becomes merely a vent for foreign capital in search of higher returns. To the extent that financialization tends, first, to diminish the incentive to mobilize domestic resources in countries where many are denied access to deposit services and, second, to cause mission drift in funded institutions, there is strong cause for objection. Domestic commercial investment in microcredit may be somewhat less problematic. To the extent that it also results in mission drift, however, and/or the repression of personal savings in particular domestic sectors or social strata, it too is subject to reservations. Such trends in investment jeopardize the financial inclusion of the poor, who would otherwise benefit greatly from a financial development strategy founded on extending deposit and other services to low-income households via distributed and embedded financial institutions.

Notes

1 Visiting Fellow, Crawford School of Economics and Government, Australian National University.

2 Karl Polanyi's argument in *The Great Transformation* turns on notions of "embeddedness" and "disembeddedness" in economic systems. These terms reflect a qualitative distinction, calibrating the extent to which a given set of market processes is appropriate and constructive (that is, embedded) in a particular social and cultural context. Market processes are regarded as disembedded when they have become inappropriate or disruptive to the context in which they occur.

3 This brief account does not do justice to those, especially scholars associated with the "Ohio School", who had long championed savings and observed the rise of the micro-credit phenomenon with some scepticism. A seminal work in this tradition is Vogel (1984).

4 Most published accounts of Compartamos (and other microcredit providers benefiting from the boom) bear out the writer's contention that the term "microfinance" is commonly misused to describe pure lending operations. Even CGAP is guilty of this, despite also reporting that Compartamos had not offered deposit services prior to the IPO, although it was licensed to do so.

5 Member institutions of the World Savings Bank Institute include many such community banks, particularly in Europe. See www.wsbi.org/

6 An international network, the Alliance for Financial Inclusion, commenced campaigning for the adoption of these initiatives in 2008. See www.afi-global.org/

6 GFC[2]

The global food and financial crises

Sandy Ross[1]

We regulate finance over and above the way we regulate other industries because finance exhibits market failures that can have devastating consequences.

(The Warwick Commission)

Introduction

During 2007 and 2008, peaking a few months before the collapse of Lehman Brothers confirmed the existence of a global financial crisis, the price of food – in particular the staple food grains of wheat, corn and rice – rose steeply enough to create a "global food crisis". Consequently, after some years hovering around 820–850 million, the Food and Agriculture Organization (FAO) estimated that by early 2009 the number of hungry people went past the one billion mark (Blas, 2009). Since these price peaks, prices have dropped but remain relatively high, especially in many poor countries (Demeke *et al.*, 2008), and the FAO predicts they will remain at high levels for some years to come, with concomitant increases in hunger and poverty for millions of people around the world. Yet despite the dire consequences of this global food crisis, the World Food Programme reported a significant drop in food aid donations from national governments in 2009 (Vidal, 2009), and there has been relatively little attention given to the issue from heads of state or the world media since the global financial crisis arose. In fact, by the second half of 2008, the food crisis appeared to be largely displaced from the central concerns of the most powerful states by the global financial crisis. This paper compares the global level responses to the two crises, and argues that they should be thought of, and responded to, in a complementary rather than competitive way.

A complementary approach is also consistent with the fact that it is not easy to disentangle the way the food crisis has interacted with the global financial crisis and consequent economic downturn, although the increase in numbers of people suffering from malnutrition began in conjunction with increasing food prices in 2007, and well before the global financial crisis. The recessions prompted by the global financial crisis are having effects in conjunction with elevated food prices. For example, the number of food insecure people in the

United States has also hit record levels in this context; amongst Americans, according to a late 2009 report by the U.S. Department of Agriculture (USDA), "more than 16 per cent – or 49 million people – sometimes ran short of nutritious food, compared with 12 per cent the year before" (Goldstein, 2009).

The chapter is structured in three sections. Section One is a necessarily brief consideration of the factors contributing to the global food crisis. While these are multifarious and complex, of particular interest are the different levels of market failure that have operated to magnify and exacerbate problems with food supply in many parts of the world. In the second section, the global political responses to the financial and food crises are compared. While the United Nations has been sidelined by the Group of Eight (G8) and Group of Twenty (G20) in the response to the global financial crisis, it has remained important to the global food crisis response. This pattern of response is linked to the scant regard of the most powerful states for the UN as a central coordinating and legitimating institution for global governance, as well as the relatively low priority given by them to the food crisis, and continuing resistance to meaningful reform of food and agricultural markets at the global level.

In the concluding section I argue that the coincident crises have created some potential for effective change by combining the responses to them into a coherent program of institutional renovation of sufficient breadth to encompass both agricultural and financial markets. However, powerful agricultural market actors, interlinked with state interests and free market norms they work so hard to construct as identical to their own, will be extremely resistant to change, even in the face of likely repeated food crises and consequent human suffering – in ways that echo the problems of financial market reform. The food sovereignty movement acting as a counter to transnational corporations and Western states remains marginal, with little high level political impact. This is emphasized by their continuing focus on attempting to influence global governance through the UN Yet, as a number of contributors to this volume show, the UN is effectively sidelined when it comes to many areas of economic coordination, with organizations such as the G20, the International Monetary Fund (IMF) and the World Bank playing much more prominent roles despite their less democratic character. Nevertheless, increasing political instability is likely to increase the chances of a change to this situation. Moreover, the growth in power and presence within the G20 of less wealthy nations with large, food insecure populations, may help create the political space for more effective reform efforts.

The global food crisis: contributory factors

In late 2009 the Food and Agriculture Organization (FAO) estimated that the global food crisis had added something like 150 million people to the 850 million or so who were already suffering from chronic hunger (Blas, 2009). There is no doubt that as people desperate for food sell productive assets, deplete scarce capital or flee their homes, the crisis has also increased poverty and rendered not only vastly expanded malnourishment, but far wider and deeper food insecurity. It has also destabilized a range of governments and contributed to political violence (Adam, 2008; Doyle, 2008).[2]

In a crisis the temptation is to look narrowly at the proximate causes and place relatively little weight on the broader context which allowed these to combine to generate the crisis. Thus much of the public discussion of the food crisis has focused on a range of causal factors, many of which are linked to perceived problems with the supply of food. Loss of supply, in this analysis, has led to insufficient food and/or increased prices. This generated a global food crisis when prices peaked in the first half of 2008, following steady and significant rises in the previous couple of years.

The food crisis is a large and complex phenomenon, and supply side factors have undoubtedly been important proximate causes of some aspects of it. These factors include: the diversion of grain production in the U.S. and Europe from food use to biofuels as a result government subsidies (ENS, 2008; Elliott, 2009; Freidrich, 2009; Monbiot, 2009); shifts in consumption patterns leading to diversion of grains and pulses into relatively expensive and inefficient meat production and away from direct human consumption (Bittman, 2008); the impacts of climate change on food production (Gregory, 2009); the increases in the price of oil increasing the costs of production and transport (ENS, 2008; Headey and Fan, 2008); the failure of the Doha Round to reform agricultural trade; and the stalling of agricultural development, especially in Africa (Geminder, 2008; Bertini and Glickman, 2009; WSFS, 2009: 7).[3] Of these various factors, the biofuels subsidies are generally regarded as the most significant (Headey and Fan, 2008).

Apart from these proximate causes that relate to shifts in demand and supply,[4] there are other causal factors that are more systemic in relation to the operation of agricultural and food markets at the global level. At the risk of oversimplifying these are most easily described in terms of the market effects of structural changes in agricultural production and market speculation.

These factors have been given little recognition by much (though not all – see Clapp, 2009a) of the mainstream analysis of the food crisis, so will be examined in more detail here, though it is important not to underestimate the importance of the proximate causal factors listed above.

Since at least the 1960s agricultural production has increasingly been subject to industrial style intensification and globalization (Coleman *et al.*, 2004: Chapter 2). This has led in developed countries to the increasing displacement of smallholder family farms by large agribusiness concerns able to achieve economies of scale and deploy capital intensive production technologies, and capable of market integration with upstream processing and supply corporations. Similar processes are also taking place in developing countries, albeit via foreign capital inflows and through the agency of multinational agribusiness corporations, and with more devastating effects on the relatively large rural populations in those countries.

Advocates for developing country farmers have criticized the pressures on them to adopt capital intensive agricultural technologies, along with the use of debt for finance. These processes have led to the impoverishment of smallholder farmers not able to generate industrial style economies of scale (Patel, 2007). They also link to phenomena such as the high rates of farmer suicides in India (Shiva, 2000: 10). A small number of agribusiness corporations increasingly dominate commodity production and transportation (Patel, 2007: Chapter 5; Clapp and Fuchs, 2009).

These structural developments in agricultural production are resulting in globally integrated agricultural production chains, driven by supermarkets and food processors (Josling, 2009: 2). These chains are capable of significant commodity production but are also vulnerable to failures and bottlenecks; moreover, they tend to allocate resources according to a market logic often quite divorced from human needs. In the context of wealth disparities this market logic tends to intensify distributional inequities. For example, people in Peru suffer malnutrition because their fisheries produce is exported to feed North American pets, with whose owners they cannot compete on capacity to pay (McGovern, 2001: pp. 150–1); in Brazil the Amazonian deforestation has been driven by the establishment of large scale soybean production to supply feed to intensive chicken production facilities in Europe, even while malnutrition remains a significant problem within Brazil (Wagenhofer, 2005). The power of large agribusinesses also operates to influence political decision making in favour of a narrow group of interests; at the global level, powerful corporate interests in food production exert influence in ways that distort the political economy of food and exacerbate inequalities in food security.

At the same time food commodities and finance have become increasingly intermeshed due to the potential significance of the rapidly growing markets in commodity-based derivative financial instruments and associated speculation. Integrated and interlinked production chains have contributed to good information flows about production, but this has also resulted in problems with the functioning of markets, as speculative capital looks for opportunities to leverage information on commodity production into profits. Thus, in the context of loosened regulation of derivative trading and debt financed capital flows leading to a financial services bubble, commodity price fluctuations were intensified by processes of market speculation. The U.S. Commodity Futures Trading Commission has been loosening the rules governing agricultural futures trading since the early 2000s. This has enabled a significant increase in the trading of agricultural derivatives as more and more financial players outside the agricultural sector look for profit making opportunities (Irwin *et al.*, 2007). This change has been linked to changes in price movements in grains at the Chicago Board of Trade (since 2005) that have defied standard economic explanation (Henriques, 2008).

The then UN Special Rapporteur on the Right to Food, Jean Ziegler, stated in April 2008 at the height of the food crisis that speculation on international markets was behind 30 per cent of the increase in food prices (ENS, 2008; see also Aguiar, 2009), however there was little evidential basis for this claim. It does seem likely that speculation did affect agricultural commodity prices in the lead up to the food crisis – just as it affects many other markets. However it is very difficult to quantify those effects. The problems posed by hedge funds and derivatives did not exist to nearly the same extent in the early 1970s, yet there were still large price fluctuations in commodity prices causing a global food crisis at that time (see Horton, 2009).

So, although speculators undoubtedly make things worse, the operation of markets, even without rampant speculation, can intensify supply and demand imbalances into larger price fluctuations than would seem warranted on the "fundamentals". Economists and financial analysts often seek to explain commodity price shifts by pointing to proximate causes such as the biofuels subsidies and climate change (or, in the case of oil, regime change and uncertainty in the Middle East). However, such explanations are cast in a manner that smacks of post-facto rationalizations of market behaviour, when systemic problems with markets themselves can also be at issue (see Soros, 2009).

Overall none of the causal factors listed above worked in isolation; rather we need to recognize their confluence in what the head of the World Food Programme, Josette Sheeran, called a "Perfect Storm". Nevertheless it is important to recall that the food crisis has been primarily identified and defined as a *market* phenomenon – based on sudden and dramatic price rises at the global level. Attention has tended to focus on discovering a rational basis for these price rises. Analysts have asked what are the supply failings or demand shifts that have caused the price rises, rather than also considering what role might have been played by systemic or structural market deficiencies. In part this reflects who has been doing the mainstream analysis: predominantly organizations and experts concerned with technical problems hampering agricultural production. There is only a much smaller literature concerned with other questions about the functioning of agricultural commodity markets, and, in particular, the functioning of price volatility within them. Yet these issues need to be examined in far more detail than orthodox economics tends to allow (Clapp, 2009b).

Responses to the crises

> We resolve … to use all means to alleviate the suffering caused by the current crisis, to stimulate food production and to increase investment in agriculture, to address obstacles to food access, and the use of the planet's resources sustainably, for present and future generations.… We commit to eliminating hunger and to securing good for all today and tomorrow.
>
> (Declaration of the High Level Conference on World Food Security Rome, June 2008)

The advent of the global financial crisis has seen a relatively strong and focused response from the most powerful governments in the world. This response has involved an apparent resurgence of Keynesian economic policies, endorsing the role of governments in boosting Western economies through stimulus spending. Yet neoliberal policies hostile to government "intervention" in markets still hold significant influence. There is considerable evidence that the IMF has continued to apply contractionary economic policies to debtor states in many cases (Weisbrot *et al.*, 2009). Moreover, after initial stimulus spending by Western governments, many states (including the U.K., the U.S., Ireland and Germany) have begun to engage in "austerity" measures amounting to serious fiscal contraction, even in the midst of recession. There has also been serious resistance to the development of international regulation over financial markets, leading to a great emphasis instead on coordination of national level responses. However, for the first time in several decades there seems to be the possibility of a shift from the neoliberal "Washington Consensus" concerning the primacy of unfettered markets (Nesvetailova and Palan, 2010). The dominance of the G8 in coordinating policy between the most powerful nations has also lost legitimacy and the G20, for all its faults a more inclusive group of nations, is playing a central role in developing coordination and cooperation between nations as they deal with the international aspects of the crisis, with direct involvement from key government leaders (Beeson and Bell, 2009).

Precedent has played an important role in responses to the financial crisis. Since the early days of the crisis, policymakers have had their attention focused by public concerns in Western nations about the possibility of a repeat of the Great Depression of the early 1930s. It seems fairly well accepted that inadequate government responses both domestically and internationally deepened and lengthened the Depression, and contributed to the advent of World War II. This perception has helped to validate much more interventionist approaches to dealing with the global financial crisis (Quiggin, 2010b).

Of course it is important not to be sanguine about the prospects for some real change in the political economy of financial markets, let alone other market sectors. The powerful people and institutions that have benefited and continue to benefit from neo-liberalized markets are mounting a vigorous resistance to any deep or structural changes. But there are at least some prospects for change in this area.

In contrast to the global financial crisis, the response to the global food crisis has been quite different: precedent has been largely ignored, and while there has been some short-term response with emergency aid and pledges to improve agricultural development, there has been a singular lack of interest or leadership from Western nations compared to their response to the financial crisis. This no doubt reflects the perspective of Western leaders, for whom the mix of human and electoral costs from serious recession in Western countries will tend to trump concern about an increase in food insecurity amongst the global poor. The food crisis has also failed to draw the attention of a wide range of scholars. The tomes that have been generated as a response to the Great Recession rarely address this urgent matter, despite its inter-relatedness with other aspects of the crisis.

The global food crisis is not unprecedented – a similar world food crisis occurred between 1972 and 1974, with similar triggers related to market forces, production disruptions and increased costs linked to a rise in the price of oil (Headey and Fan, 2008; Horton, 2009; see Figure 6.1). However there has been little or no discussion or thought given to the lessons that could have beeen learned from this precedent. This is disturbing at two levels.

First, the absence of consideration of the precedent seems to me to reflect a normalization of widespread food insecurity and of associated malnutrition and hunger. In the sequence of country-based or regional food crises since the 1970s (Somalia, Ethiopia, Zambia, Mali, Zimbabwe and North Korea to name just a few) it is difficult to escape the impression that the global food crisis is just more of the same, on a slightly larger scale. Such a view, understandable as it might be, represents not only a profound failure of moral imagination but also the political limitations of the humanitarian and right-to-food campaigns which have dominated activist responses to hunger issues.

Second, the very fact that a similar crisis took place some decades ago implies there might be structural causes linking the two events that it would be useful to examine in the interests of preventing such crises from occurring in future. Such an examination would be useful, for example, in developing early warning systems identifying the confluence of factors triggering catastrophic food price rises along with appropriate remedial action in terms of international and national level responses. The absence of such considerations creates the potential for major flaws and limitations in the global response to the food crisis.

In contrast to the current global food crisis, the response of governments to the 1970s world food crisis was one of shock. The post-war script had been of steady progress to eliminating hunger, thanks to the Green Revolution that proposed to export to the rest of the world the massive increases in agricultural production

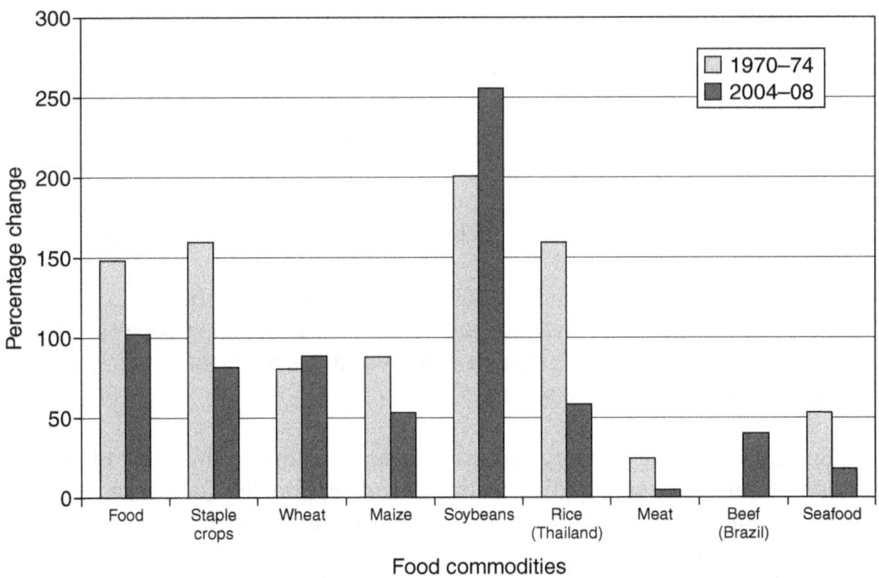

Figure 6.1 Food price percentage changes (source: Data from Headey and Fan 2008: 376, Table 1 (derived from IMF International Financial Statistics)).

enjoyed by the U.S. since the 1940s. UN economists such as Hans Singer confidently expected in the early 1960s that the deployment of development funds and food aid would be necessary for less than 20 years (Shaw, 2001: 26). The world food crisis tore up this script, with the implication that despite the promises of the Green Revolution the world was going backwards in the area of hunger. The crisis was perceived, like the latter day global financial crisis, as *systemic* in nature, and requiring a systemic response. A large, high level World Food Conference was held at the behest of the U.S. in 1974, despite a confused and split U.S. position. This resulted in significant reforms to international institutions leading ultimately to today's relatively effective, albeit underfunded, emergency food relief structures – though, as is now obvious, it was not to prove an adequate response to the structural factors making global level famine possible.

Almost 40 years later, despite attempts to organize a similar response by the UN system, there has been a decided lack of galvanization; the leading member states have been much less engaged, and the UN system has appeared a great deal more bureaucratic. While the response to the financial crisis was organized by the powerful states through the G8 and G20, it was left to the UN bureaucracy to lead the global response to the food crisis. The Secretary-General's creation in April 2008 of a High Level Task Force on the Global Food Security Crisis involved a list of 13 different UN system organizations as participants. However, in contrast to the deep involvement of UN system components, UN member states seem much more sceptical about the capacity of international cooperation to change the systems of poverty and malnutrition that clearly underpin the food crisis – at least without unacceptable political costs to their own position.

FAO Director-General Jacques Diouf began lobbying publicly in January 2009 for engagement with an FAO convened high level summit on food security in Rome in November 2009 (Drago, 2009). The G8 meeting at L'Aquila in July 2009 issued a statement on food security acknowledging the crisis with a vague pledge to "aim at substantially increasing aid to agriculture and food security including through multiyear resource commitments" in the context of commitments by states "towards a goal of mobilizing $20 billion over three years" (G8, 2009: 12).

The G20 meeting in September 2009 in response to the global financial crisis focused mainly on lending and access to finance for developing countries in the context of the financial crisis, though there was a statement of general support for measures to improve food security:

> Sustained funding and targeted investments are urgently needed to improve long-term food security. We welcome and support the food security initiative announced in L'Aquila and efforts to further implement the Global Partnership for Agriculture and Food Security and to address excessive price volatility. We call on the World Bank to work with interested donors and organizations to develop a multilateral trust fund to scale-up agricultural assistance to low-income countries.

Despite the brief reference to "addressing price volatility" in the second sentence, this statement focuses on funding and coordinating aid for development rather than any process for examining the market institutions which are deeply implicated in the volatility of food prices.

The FAO World Summit on Food Security was held on 16–18 November 2009 in Rome. State representations at the Summit told the story of the relative marginalization of the global food crisis. The Summit did involve 60 government leaders, but almost all were from poor and developing nations where the food crisis had great and immediate human and political significance. The only G8 leader in attendance was the host country's Prime Minister and Summit Chairperson, Silvio Berlusconi; only two other G20 member heads of state (Brazil and Turkey) attended. The U.K. and U.S. were represented by relatively junior government ministers, below cabinet level (Squires, 2009; IATP, 2009; Ross, 2011).

Only three paragraphs (out of 41) in the Declaration of the World Summit on Food Security relate explicitly to markets and trade. These place an emphasis on not "distorting" markets, and a vague reference to requesting other international organizations to examine possible links between speculation and agricultural price volatility. They are broadly consistent with the G8's views on markets and the food crisis as set out in Paragraph 7 of its L'Aquila Statement in July 2009:

> Open trade flows and efficient markets have a positive role in strengthening food security. National and regional strategies should promote the participation of farmers, especially smallholders and women, into community, domestic, regional and international markets. Markets must remain open, protectionism rejected and factors potentially affecting commodity price volatility, including speculation, monitored and analysed further. We are therefore committed to reduce trade distortions and refrain from raising new barriers to trade and investment and from implementing WTO-inconsistent measures to stimulate exports.[5]

Basically these statements continue to show faith in the WTO nostrums about (implicitly neo-liberal) markets and emphasize the extent to which a fundamental rethinking of agricultural markets as socio-political structures is not on the agenda of global actors responding to the food crisis.[6]

A tale of two crises

It should be clear from the discussion of contributory factors that significant spikes in global level hunger result from complex interactions between failure of supply/production due to technical factors, and the flawed functioning of global markets.[7]

Aggregate global production has arguably been sufficient to feed the world for some decades (Fogel, 2004: 54), largely due to the long-term linear increases in grain production yields linked to the Green Revolution (Gregory, 2009).

However, the industrialized production model connected to the Green Revolution is highly capital intensive and heavily dependent on fossil fuels for production of fertilizer and transportation. It has favoured large industrial producers over small farm holders (George, 1979; Patel, 2007), and has had significant and growing social and environmental costs. The recent International Assessment of Agricultural Knowledge, Science and Technology for Development report (McIntyre *et al.*, 2009) focused squarely on options for shifting agriculture onto a more socially and environmentally sustainable footing, and was notable for its scepticism about the Genetically Modified (GM) crops as a silver bullet, though the large U.S. agribusinesses which have invested heavily in the technology continue to push it as the centrepiece of American policy, with some support from American policy commentators and the American government (see, for example: Collier, 2008; McGovern, 2001; Clapp, 2009b; Zerbe, 2009; Vidal, 2011).

Moreover, a range of environmental factors, land use changes and social processes such as urbanization are resulting in loss of land to food production, while population growth requires food production to grow as well – the FAO estimates it will need to grow by 70 per cent to meet world needs in 2050 (WSFS, 2009: 2). At the same time there is some alarming evidence that yield increases are tailing off, at least in Asia (Gregory, 2009).

Apart from these significant challenges to production levels, however, the structure of global agricultural markets is deeply implicated in the problem of global hunger. Moreover, the structural problems with these markets, as has happened with global financial markets, are more likely to be worsened than improved by the standard prescription of liberalization. The advocates of liberalization argue that free markets will increase production to meet demand, but this argument all too often ignores the "externalities" imposed by the costs of intensifying industrialized fossil fuel production, and the distortions created by inequalities such as the purchasing power of Western pet owners. It also ignores the history of Western production gains that have come from extensive public investment in research and development, not market mechanisms.

Rather, if, as seems likely, the quantum of aggregate production capacity that is surplus to aggregate demand declines, there will be an increasing need for food markets to be structured in socially responsible ways, as well as re-establishment of public investment in research and development, and extension services to work with rural producers on improving sustainable production. As food production chains increasingly become global, the political processes around the structuring of food systems, including markets, will also need to become more conducive to forms of global coordination.

The central proposition of this paper is that the re-examination of governance of markets brought on by the Global Financial Crisis should be linked with a similar process examining the governance of food markets at the global level, together with some consideration of the problems posed for food security by speculation on commodities in financial markets. It is important that the efforts to increase production and supply, important as they are, do not excuse the need to rethink the structuring of agricultural commodity markets at global (as well as regional and local) levels so that chronic food insecurity is addressed more effectively.

Power, structures and the food crisis

At present the crucial political debates about the political economy of food lie between two camps. On the one hand is the mainstream intergovernmental position, strongly influenced by agribusiness interests via the U.S., which advocates high-tech improvements in production, continued globalization of industrialized production chains, and the operation of minimally regulated markets (see, for example: Collier, 2008). The other camp is the activist position, focused on defending and advocating small landholders against big agribusiness, local rather than transnational supply chains, equity in land distribution, and support for food sovereignty and "progressive" development (Patel, 2007; Shiva, 2000).

Yet this debate does not seem likely to be resolved any time soon; for all the merits of the activist critique, the challenges of sustainably producing sufficient food to feed the world's population, and distributing that food through functional, accountable and sustainable markets, are going to need to work with the reality of a mix of industrial and traditional production regimes.

The interests of powerful agribusiness firms are entwined with the definition of the national interest of the U.S. in a manner that leads to an apparent stranglehold over advanced economy views in global fora such as the G20. The entrenched nature of the mainstream position goes deeper than just an effective corporate lobby, however: it goes to the heart of the identity of the rich, agriculture exporting countries – their national success is built in many ways on their capacity to feed themselves cheaply (and export food to hungry others in the world), as much as their manufacturing expertise, or well-endowed military. The institutions governing global food production and distribution may incorporate the flaws that make future food crises inevitable, but they also have worked well for many Western countries for decades and are well supported and entrenched.

What is needed is a process of reconceptualizing and re-embedding food markets at the global level. Such a process may provide a means to move beyond the current David and Goliath standoff between post-industrial and industrial food production systems, if only by beginning to shift some of the structural power away from the status quo advocates – not that this will be easy. One logical move that might enhance the prospects of such a power shift would be to make more explicit the close links between food and energy markets, and join together the impetus for dealing with climate change and the impetus for improving food security.

This proposition is ambitious and difficult. There is not the space here to explore in much detail what a useful reconceptualization of food markets would look like. Suffice to say such a reconceptualization must start by rejecting an atomistic view of markets as ontologically prior to government – as abstract "natural" structures distorted or constrained to varying degrees by regulation. Instead, markets should be conceived of as organically derived from the interaction of economic, social and political actors and structures. As such, they can be differently structured through the influence of norms, laws and regulations interacting with technological processes and various types of economic decision making in a mix of individual, small, medium and large collective contexts.

Conclusion

Current OECD and FAO forecasts are for food prices to remain at historically high levels for the medium to long-term (Friedrich, 2009). The implications of this are broad and complex in terms of the wider economy. For example, the economics of production will change with sustained higher prices for agricultural commodities. It may lead to an intensification of production techniques such as monoculture with significant question marks over sustainability; the windfall increases in profits for agribusiness may lead to concomitant increases in their political influence. Another impact is on the price of land, which is starting to reflect increased demand in African and some Asian countries as wealthier food importing countries embark on significant land acquisitions, motivated by food security concerns (Cotula and Vermeulen, 2009).

These trends are all associated with the possibility of significantly increased political instability. For example, apart from widespread riots connected to the food crisis in 2008 destabilizing a number of governments, a foreign land acquisition deal brought down the government of Madagascar in 2009 (Cotula and Vermeulen, 2009: 1245). Commentary on this is replete with unease as to the political effects of foreign governments exporting food from countries suffering from food shortages. Another political concern associated with the food crisis is its effects on the movement of people, in particular migration to developed countries from the poorest countries. These political facts on the ground, along with more abstract appeals to humanitarianism or justice, may help focus the minds of G20 leaders and other governments on systemic reforms to food systems that will enhance their stability (and implicitly their sustainability and equity).

The tale of the two crises has tended to portray them as in competition for the limited attention of global leaders and the world's media (see, for example: Ghosh, 2009). The financial crisis has clearly displaced the food crisis from prominent consideration, despite the fact that the latter has been more immediate and direct in its life and death effects, and continues to ensure recession derived poverty will lead to malnutrition on a large scale. However, this competitive depiction, apart from pointing to the privileging of the interests of the wealthy, is of limited value. The crucial question should really be how to integrate the consideration of both crises as different aspects of the same issue – the deficiencies in the current structuring of markets at the global level when it comes to human, social and economic necessities.

The structure of food and agricultural markets lies in at least as much need of overhaul as that of financial markets, for much the same reason – repeated failures of those structures have led, and will continue to lead, to mass suffering, illness and death on an enormous scale. Indeed, reform of food and agricultural markets is arguably an "easier" proposition. Compared to financial markets, food markets have the virtue of concreteness – relatively direct and immediate human and political consequences when their flaws overcome their benefits. While there is a concentration of financial resources and concomitant political power in the hands of the main agribusinesses (Clapp and Fuchs, 2009), such companies are arguably negotiable obstacles in comparison to the enormous wealth, political influence and capacity for widespread market disruption in the hands of major banks, hedge funds and related organizations.

The Warwick Commission on international financial regulation begins with a statement on the importance of a systemic grasp of the global financial crisis:

> This is not the first international financial crisis the world has seen.... [I]n trying to prevent or dampen future crises, we must not focus too heavily on the specific character of the present crisis. We must focus on those factors that are common across financial crises. There will be a different financial innovation or product at the centre of the next crisis.... While we doubt that financial crises can be prevented, we do believe strongly that policymakers, regulators and supervisors have the power to make them less frequent, shallower and with less spill over onto the welfare of ordinary households.
>
> (Warwick Commission 2009: 2)

These sentiments are surely of equivalent relevance to the food crisis. Just as there are serious arguments for limiting excessive movement of capital, or speculative risk taking using abstract financial instruments, so are there similar arguments for limiting excessive price movements (up or down) in basic foodstuffs, or for otherwise protecting the poor (consumers and producers) from the effects of price shocks. This points to the food crisis as a relevant issue for consideration by the G20 as it considers reforms to the global financial infrastructure. Ultimately, if the response to either crisis is to get beyond the piecemeal and ad hoc, a reform agenda needs to be developed that can bridge the range of state interests in the G20, and find common ground for reconceptualizing financial and food markets at the global level.

Notes

1 School of Social and Political Sciences, University of Melbourne, email: rossda@unimelb.edu.au. This paper has benefited from comments received from participants at the University of Melbourne/Harvard University workshop "Re-embedding Markets and the Global Financial Crisis" held in December 2009, where it was presented in an early form. I am also grateful to Kate Macdonald for her considered comments on a draft.

2 By mid-2010 FAO estimates of the number of hungry people had dropped from one billion at the peak of the crisis to 925 million (FAO, 2010). However, further climatic events during the latter half of 2010 in Russia, Pakistan, India, and Australia have placed food prices again on an upward trajectory. At the time of writing we seem to be at substantial risk of a repeat of 2008, with the FAO index of food prices in January 2011 at higher level than the June 2008 peak at the height of the global food crisis (Treanor, 2011).

3 Headey and Fan (2008) also note that there is an historical relationship between the value of the U.S. dollar (US$), functioning both as the international reserve currency and the currency of the world's largest agricultural exporter, and commodity prices. Because of this association they consider it is possible that the long-term decline in the value of the US$ since the mid-2000s may have also contributed to long run increases in commodity prices, although it will have also had complex macroeconomic impacts on the balance of trade of other countries too.
4 Some additional factors, such as the run down in global stocks of grain, have also been raised, but for the most part discredited as causal factors (Dawe, 2009; Headey and Fan, 2008).
5 This statement was also endorsed by a range of U.N. agencies and organizations and another 19 countries, including all the G20 bar Argentina, Russia and Saudi Arabia.
6 See Clapp (2009b) for a nuanced analysis of the differences between G8 and U.N. responses to some key recent reports on agricultural production and development in the context of the food crisis, although she was writing before the World Summit on Food Security.
7 Another important layer of complexity comes from poorly functioning local, domestic and regional markets in the poorest parts of the world. At this level of analysis, domestic government responses to the 2007–08 food price spike were varying and important in their effects, not only on domestic access to food, but on other countries – for example, export restrictions on commodities such as rice led to increases in its price for countries needing to import it (see Jones and Kwiecinski, 2010). Examining this sub-global level of food markets is beyond the scope of this paper, however.

7 Embedded regionalism

Jason Beckfield and Min Zhou[1]

Polanyi's central insight is that markets are "always embedded" (Block, 2003a). Markets are also everywhere embedded. With this as a point of departure, and in the context of the economic crisis that began in 2008, the central questions for positive and normative analysis become *how* and *where* markets are embedded. In this essay we consider what lessons might be drawn for the "re-" embedding of markets through the lens of regional integration. We begin by offering a conceptualization of regional integration as a particular form of embeddedness. We then present evidence on the regionalization of markets, using data on international trade for 1948–2008. Next, we review some consequences of regional integration for income inequality and the welfare state in Europe, with the aim of demonstrating that some of the recent "dis-embedding" of markets is due to regional actions. Finally, we offer three scenarios for the future of market re-embedding in Europe. Our most general thesis is that regional integration presents particular opportunities for, and challenges to, the visions for market re-embedding that are discussed in this volume and elsewhere.

Regional integration can be conceptualized as the formation of transnational political economies through the increasing density of international market exchange and the development of international political institutions within geographically bounded, politically negotiated, and historically specific transnational regions. Most generally, attention to regional integration suggests that we should consider scale and scope in developing approaches to market embeddedness. Regional integration is a near-global phenomenon, with formal intergovernmental organizations pursuing integration in Africa (e.g., the African Union), Asia (e.g., the Association of Southeast Asian Nations), Europe (e.g., the European Union), Latin America (e.g., the Central American Common Market and MERCOSUR), and North America (e.g., the North American Free Trade Agreement). Indeed, Zhou (2010) demonstrates that the effects of cultural similarity and geographical proximity on trade are growing, as a general matter, in the international trade network.

Thus, markets are realized differently in different regions. In much the same way as the world-systems/dependency approach to economic development highlighted the broader context of relations among nation states in the world system, attention to the regional political-economic context can yield insights into the sociology of markets by adding a scale of social relations. Indeed, regional integration can itself be conceptualized as a form of embeddedness distinct from urban, national, and global embeddedness. Markets are embedded in social relations that take place at the regional scale. Arguably, there are consequential social relations at the regional level that contribute to contemporary political and economic changes. Moreover, in some regions, regional integration is an increasingly consequential form of embeddedness.

The European market is just such a case. The European Union has broadened its scale and expanded its scope dramatically since its founding as the European Economic Community in 1957. As of 2011, the E.U. has grown from six to 27 member states, with a population of more than 500 million European citizens. Several member states now use the common Euro currency, and the E.U. has developed a governance structure that includes the Council of Ministers, European Commission, European Parliament, and European Court of Justice. Indeed, European integration now occupies a large proportion of the total volume of legislation in many E.U. countries, especially the newer members, as national legislators work to bring their legal regimes into compliance with the body of E.U. law, the *acquis communautaire*. The E.U. is also pursuing a European Constitution.

The expansion and institutionalization of the European Union has shifted the scale of social relations in Europe, by establishing frameworks for regional social orders that structure fields of interaction (Fligstein, 2008). Our argument is that this regional integration has had important consequences for income inequality and European welfare states in a way that differs from global embeddedness (Beckfield, 2005 and 2006). In disentangling regional integration from globalization, the embeddedness concept helps by drawing attention to the specification of social relations. The key difference between the two forms is scale: globalization is the increasing density of intercontinental forms of interaction, whereas regionalization is the increasing density of forms of cross-national interaction that are nonetheless bounded within particular places. It can be argued that regional integration and globalization can be mutually exclusive, reinforcing, or orthogonal. Market interaction can be embedded in social relations at several different scales simultaneously. A challenge for research, and for activists who would like to see new forms of embeddedness, is to consider how regional embedding is accomplished across regions and over time.

Consider the European market. A straightforward way of measuring the regional integration of (product) markets is to consider the intra-regional trade share, or what proportion of exports is directed toward the regional economy. Using data from the *Direction of Trade Statistics* and *International Financial Statistics* from the International Monetary Fund (IMF, 2010a and 2010b), Figure 7.1 shows that, from 1948 through 2008, exports in the European region have grown more regionalized (where "Europe" is defined as the United Nations' macro-region). The pace of regionalization has slowed in the last decade, but this may be a ceiling effect, as more than 75 per cent of exports from European nations are now directed toward other nations in the European region. We note

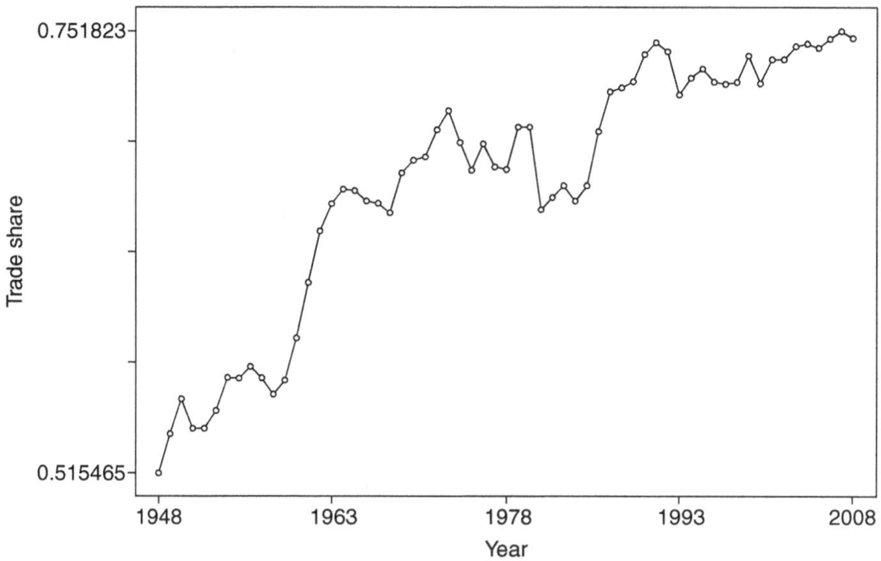

Figure 7.1 The regional trade share in Europe, 1948–2008 (source: Data from the IMF *Direction of Trade Statistics* and *International Financial Statistics*).

Notes
The regional trade share is the proportion of total exports from nation states in the region that are directed to other nation states in the region. Trade is in constant U.S. dollars, with 1982–84 as the base year.

that similar trends hold for the E.U.-15, as well as the E.U.-27; these results are available from the authors upon request. Of course, the extent of regionalization of other markets – including labour markets – is an open empirical question. The trade data are suggestive of the growing regionalization of European markets, but we view our analysis as just a first step toward assessing regional integration. The growing regionalization of trade in Europe is significant in itself, considering that trade in open markets can, under strong assumptions, substitute for factor mobility.

Regionalization is not limited to Europe. Below, we use the same data sources and the same analytical techniques to evaluate the regionalization of international trade in North America, Asia, Africa, Latin America, and Oceania. As above, we vary the definition of region by using both the largely geographical boundaries provided by the United Nations' "macro-regions", and the political boundaries defined by membership in prominent intergovernmental organizations (NAFTA, ASEAN, and MERCOSUR).

Figure 7.2 shows that the trend in North America is toward deeper regional integration, with a peak in 2002 of more than 57 per cent of North American exports directed within the boundaries defined by NAFTA. This peak capped a wave of integration that accelerated after the NAFTA took effect in 1994, and although there has been a decline since 2002, the long-term trend is clearly

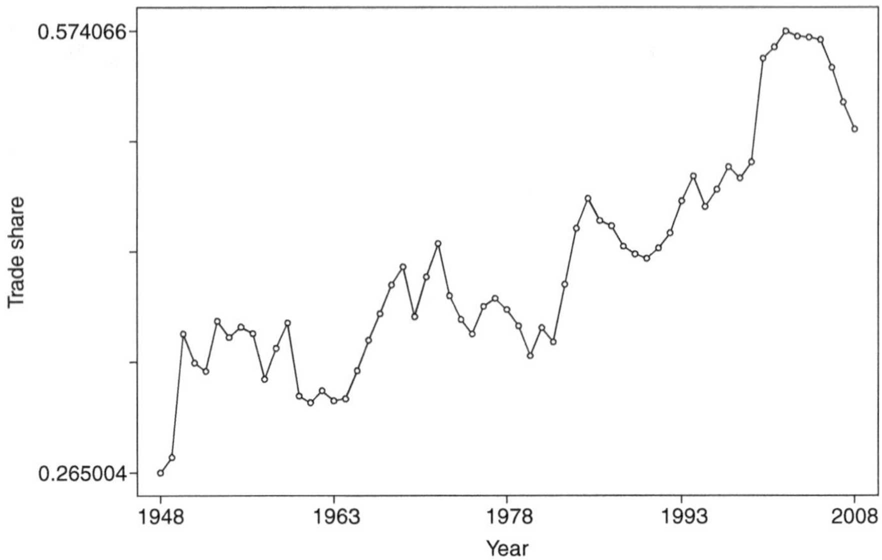

Figure 7.2 The regional trade share in North America (NAFTA), 1948–2008 (source: Data from the IMF *Direction of Trade Statistics* and *International Financial Statistics).*

Notes
The regional trade share is the proportion of total exports from nation states in the region that are directed to other nation states in the region. Trade is in constant U.S. dollars, with 1982–84 as the base year.

toward more regional integration (and less globalization, if globalization is defined as inter-continental trade).

Figure 7.3 shows a steady increase in the regionalization of Asian trade since 1959, when the regional trade share reached a low of 26 per cent after a decade of decline. Currently, more than 50 per cent of exports from Asian nations are directed toward other Asian nations, after a decades-long steady upward trajectory. This trend is interesting in light of Northeast Asia's "stunted regionalism" (Rozman, 2004). In contrast, Southeast Asia is relatively advanced in the formation of regional institutions, led by the Association of Southeast Asian Nations. Figure 7.4 shows evidence of increasing trade regionalization among the ASEAN nations: the intra-ASEAN trade share increases steadily throughout the period, to a recent peak of more than 26 per cent of exports. Following the institutionalist approach of Fligstein and Stone Sweet (2002), this increasing regionalization might represent an increasing demand for regional institutions to order markets, which suggests a political opportunity for influencing the quality of market embeddedness in the Asian region.

Figure 7.5 shows evidence of regional disintegration in Africa through 1980, when the intra-African trade share reached a low of 3 per cent, followed by a sharp increase in regional economic integration through the end of the period.

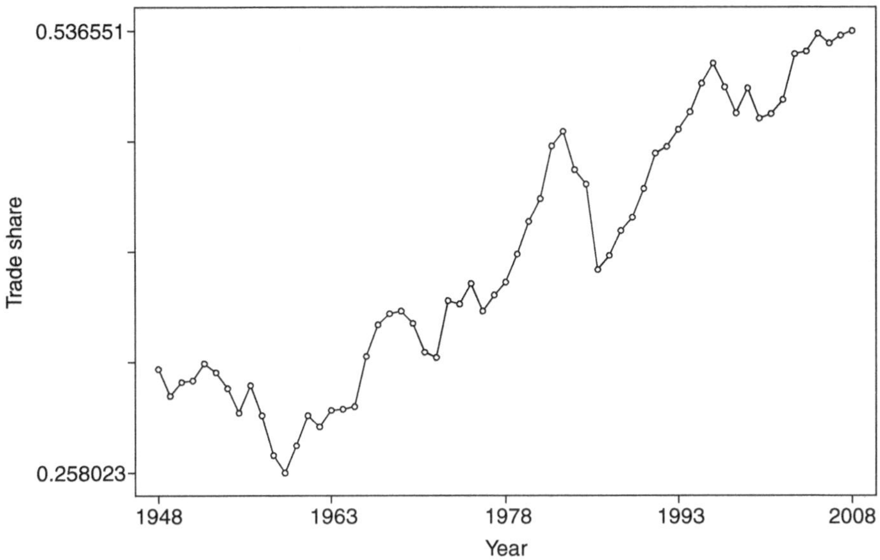

Figure 7.3 The regional trade share in Asia, 1948–2008 (source: Data from the IMF *Direction of Trade Statistics* and *International Financial Statistics*).

Notes
The regional trade share is the proportion of total exports from nation states in the region that are directed to other nation states in the region. Trade is in constant U.S. dollars, with 1982–84 as the base year.

While the current level of economic integration – about 13 per cent – is low relative to the other world regions, the trend is clear. The same recent trend toward greater regional integration also holds for the region's primary intergovernmental organizations (IGOs): the League of Arab States, the Common Market for Eastern and Southern Africa (COMESA), and the Economic Community of West African States (ECOWAS); these analyses are available from the authors upon request. Again, these findings suggest that international market exchanges are increasingly regionalized, such that the scale of embeddedness is shifting to the regional level. As observers and critics of international markets we would do well to consider regional institutions and political opportunities.

Figure 7.6 shows no evidence of a clear trend toward regional integration in Latin America. At most, we can say that there has been a very recent uptick in regional integration, to a peak (for the 1948–2008 period) of 23 per cent. But, in light of the large fluctuations in trade integration in the region over this period, future decreases seem as likely as an ongoing increase, and it should be noted that the UN includes Mexico, a NAFTA signatory, in the group of Latin American nations.

Similar inferences can be made from the intraregional trade share for the MERCOSUR nations, shown in Figure 7.7: a recent uptick in regional integration, after trendless fluctuations. The difference between Latin American

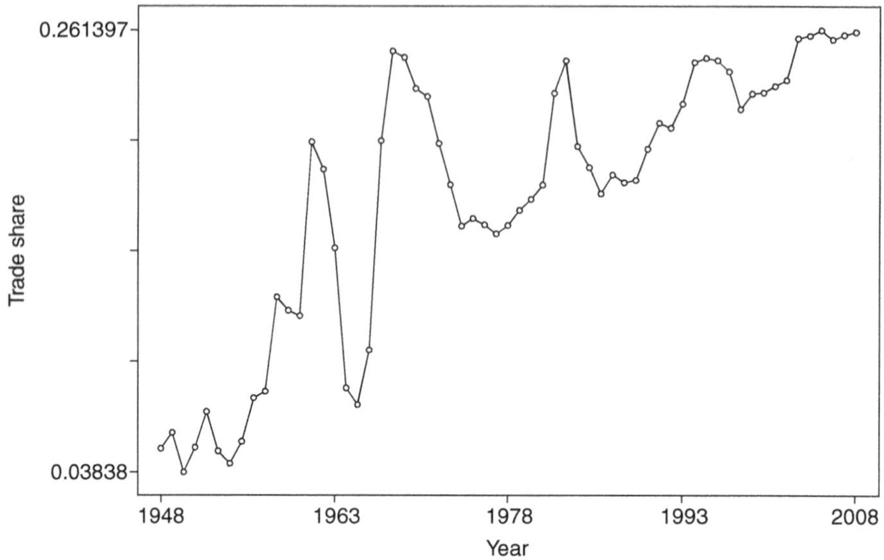

Figure 7.4 The regional trade share in Southeast Asia (ASEAN), 1948–2008 (source: Data from the IMF *Direction of Trade Statistics* and *International Financial Statistics*).

Notes
The regional trade share is the proportion of total exports from nation states in the region that are directed to other nation states in the region. Trade is in constant U.S. dollars, with 1982–84 as the base year.

integration and MERCOSUR integration is that among the MERCOSUR nations, one can detect a relatively clear U-shaped trend in the regional trade share for this period, with a significantly higher average trade share for the post-1990 period (17 per cent) than for the pre-1990 period (9 per cent). This again suggests evidence of demands and opportunities for embedding markets at the regional scale, although these demands and opportunities are certainly less pronounced in the Southern Cone than in Europe or North America.

Finally, Figure 7.8 suggests growing regionalization in the Oceania region, up to a regional trade share of nearly 15 per cent over the last decade. This increase in regionalization of Oceanic trade was fastest in the 1950s and 1960s, but it has continued increasing since then. Like the African region, regional trade integration is at a low level relative to other world regions, but we find it interesting that the trend toward increasing regional integration is widely shared.

What does this broad-based trend toward increasing regional integration around the world mean for the embeddedness of markets? More specifically, considering the labour–capital balance of power as one dimension of social relations that embeds markets, what does regional integration mean for that balance of power? Before we consider these questions, two caveats are in order: (1) trends in the regional integration of other markets (such as labour markets and

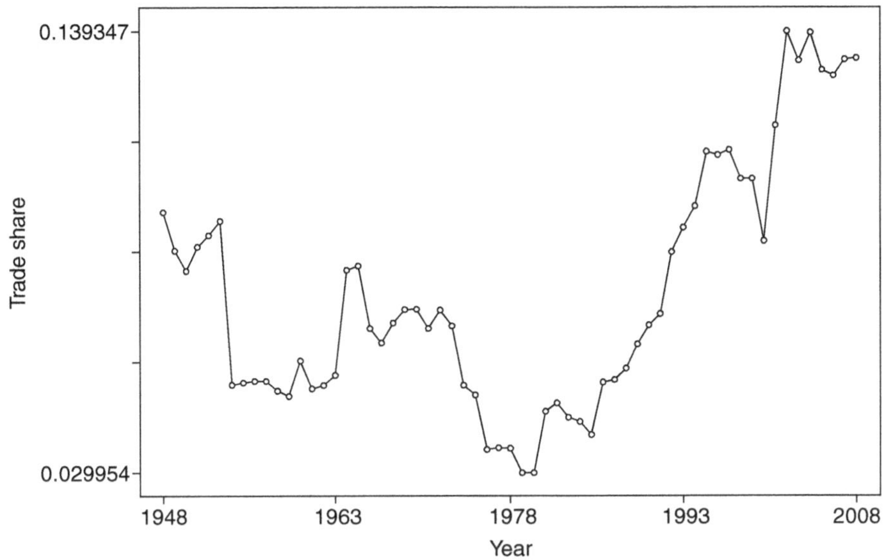

Figure 7.5 The regional trade share in Africa, 1948–2008 (source: Data from the IMF *Direction of Trade Statistics* and *International Financial Statistics*).

Notes
The regional trade share is the proportion of total exports from nation states in the region that are directed to other nation states in the region. Trade is in constant U.S. dollars, with 1982–84 as the base year.

financial markets) may or may not match the trends we have shown in the regional integration of international trade; and (2) the sociology of regional integration is still a nascent field, and most scholarly attention has focused on Europe (Beckfield, 2005; Duina, 2006; Favell and Guiraudon, 2010; Fligstein, 2008). Nevertheless, we think it is possible to read regional trade integration as part of a complex of economic liberalization that has taken different forms in different places, and we think that the lessons of European integration can be placed into a broader comparative framework of embedded regionalisms.

In Europe, as the Single Market Program accelerated through the introduction of the single Euro currency in the late 1990s, regional integration was associated with welfare state retrenchment and rising income inequality in many E.U. member states (Beckfield 2005 and 2006). These trends toward more inequality and retrenchment have continued over the past decade, punctuated by major changes in regimes of embeddedness such as the Hartz reforms in Germany (OECD, 2010; LIS, 2010). European integration is argued to have such consequences through several political and economic mechanisms: (1) weakening labour unions by exposing labour to more intense international competition, (2) diffusing and enforcing market-liberal policy scripts, and (3) facilitating a "politics of blame avoidance" (Pierson, 1996) that eases welfare state retrenchment by shifting blame for unpopular welfare cutbacks to the E.U. Interestingly, while

Figure 7.6 The regional trade share in Latin America, 1948–2008 (source: Data from the IMF *Direction of Trade Statistics* and *International Financial Statistics*).

Notes
The regional trade share is the proportion of total exports from nation states in the region that are directed to other nation states in the region. Trade is in constant U.S. dollars, with 1982–84 as the base year.

income distributions have grown more polarized and labour unions have grown weaker *within* national economies as European integration has deepened (Beckfield, 2006; Pinto and Beckfield, 2011), there is also evidence of convergence *among* European welfare states and economies (Beckfield, 2009; Caminada *et al.*, 2010). This arguably reflects the growing importance of the European level of policymaking and European institutionalization.

The consequences of regional integration outside Europe remain underexplored, and the degree to which regions can be compared systematically is an open empirical question, with some arguing for *sui generis* analysis of Europe. Without taking a side in this debate, what we can say from the analysis of trade regionalization presented above, and previously published analysis of the regionalization of international organizations (Beckfield, 2010), is that there is general evidence of a growing political-economic density in several world regions. That is, as political economists consider current configurations of state-economy relations, the regional political economy is becoming an increasingly prominent locus of such relations. Given that the increasing density of regional political economy in Europe has had wide-ranging social consequences, it seems natural to consider how attention to regional integration might change our thinking about embeddedness. Below, in the final section of our paper we outline three alternative courses for the future of embedding the European market, focusing on labour.

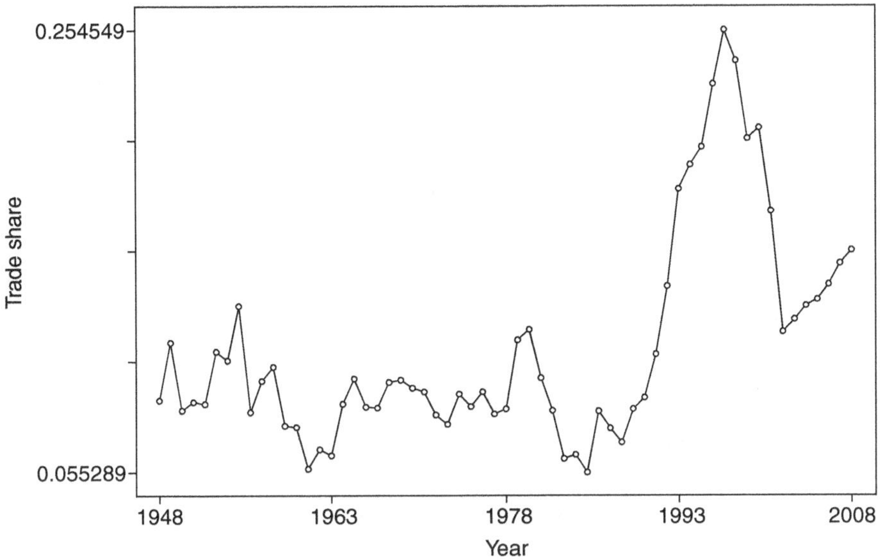

Figure 7.7 The regional trade share in the Southern Cone (MERCOSUR), 1948–2008 (source: Data from the IMF *Direction of Trade Statistics* and *International Financial Statistics*).

Notes
The regional trade share is the proportion of total exports from nation states in the region that are directed to other nation states in the region. Trade is in constant U.S. dollars, with 1982–84 as the base year.

One possibility, outlined by Caporaso and Tarrow (2009), is that the European Union itself re-embeds the market. Specifically, Caporaso and Tarrow identify a number of European Court of Justice cases wherein "social content" infuses the legal ruling; for instance, acknowledging the social needs of families in rulings on labour mobility. E.U. regulations in the areas of computing, genetically modified organisms, and food quality are also examples of the market-moderating countermovement that Caporaso and Tarrow see as operating at the transnational level. Caporaso and Tarrow note that the developing E.U. regulatory regime advances "social efficiency", and socially efficient regulations "narrow the gap between private costs and benefits and social costs and benefits". In this way, far from being a purely market-liberal movement, the European Union also advances a socially-progressive countermovement that proceeds in fits and starts. This identification of a countermovement resonates with Alter's (2000) argument that domestic policy produces a "backlash" against the market liberal bias of the European Court of Justice (ECJ). Specifically, the resonance is the idea that European integration, although generally moving in a market-liberal direction, is not a pure dis-embedding, but rather is a process that itself prompts countermovement politics – at either the national or the regional level. A central contribution of the Caporaso and Tarrow paper

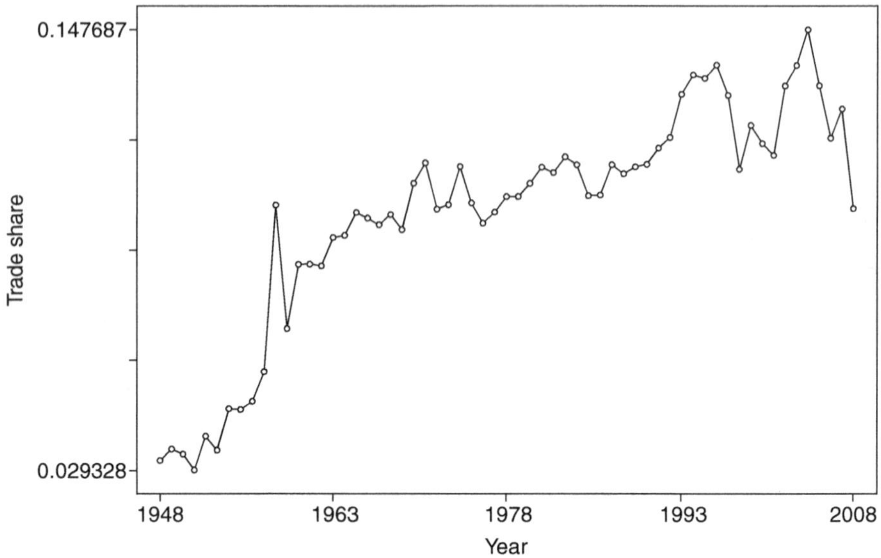

Figure 7.8 The regional trade share in Oceania, 1948–2008 (source: Data from the IMF *Direction of Trade Statistics* and *International Financial Statistics*).

Notes
The regional trade share is the proportion of total exports from nation states in the region that are directed to other nation states in the region. Trade is in constant U.S. dollars, with 1982–84 as the base year.

is to show that the countermovement is taking place in the political space between states and the regional polity; ECJ rulings are one of these spaces of articulation.

In response to Caporaso and Tarrow, Höpner and Schäfer (2010) argue that the general thrust of European integration as advanced by the E.U. is still more Hayekian than Polanyian, and they see evidence of a re-embedding countermovement as overstated. Focusing on labour, and setting aside for the moment regionalized policy in the many other domains touched by the E.U., we are persuaded by Höpner and Schäfer's argument that E.U. legislation and jurisprudence in the area of labour mobility and nondiscrimination is primarily aimed at commodifying labour. That is, even the nominally progressive gender-equality directives and rulings requiring the delivery of social benefits regardless of national origin are aimed at facilitating the creation of a Europe-wide labour market. Other European Court of Justice rulings limiting labour unions' rights to strike (namely, Viking and Laval in 2007) also facilitate this commodification of labour. The general point for positive analysis is that – regardless of whether the E.U. is seen as re-embedding or dis-embedding in some "ultimate" sense – regional social relations embed labour markets. At the same time, the general point for normative analysis is that the ongoing institutionalization of regional political economy creates winners and losers because it is a foundational shift in the rules of the game. Regional integration is implicated in the labour–capital balance of power; the question for analysts is how the balance is tilting.

A second possibility is that the European market will continue muddling toward a more classically liberal form, through the retrenchment of European welfare states, brought about in part through the pressures of jurisprudence by the ECJ. Scharpf (2009) outlines one potential way out of this bleak trajectory: he advocates the defence of national welfare states through the appeal of ECJ rulings to the Council of Ministers. Scharpf's idea is (very broadly) in line with that of Caporaso and Tarrow, insofar as an institution of the E.U. (for Scharpf, the Council; for Caporaso and Tarrow, the Court) is used to insulate national systems of market embedding against liberalization. The problem, apart from the unlikely politics of such a substantial revision to the institutions of the E.U., is that such a scenario might protect current embeddedness against further liberalization, but it is difficult to envision how a re-embedding of regional markets by regional-level institutions could be accomplished through the same mechanism. Scharpf is probably correct that "a European social market economy cannot come about, and social market economies at the national level will be destroyed, unless the politically uncontrolled dynamics of (negative) 'integration through law' can be contained" (2009: 34). However we propose that the mechanisms of containment should be pitched at the regional level, if the aim is to re-embed the regional market in a system of social relations more favourable to labour.

A third possibility takes the forceful arguments of Moravcsik (2002) and Moravcsik and Sangiovanni (2003) as a point of departure: a European *demos* does not exist, the public is rationally apathetic toward the E.U., and there is not a democratic demand for the progressive re-embedding of markets. In other words, there is no "public interest" in the embedding of markets, and the E.U. is not illegitimately biased toward neoliberalism because much of the European public (rationally) has no opinion toward the (technocratic) E.U. But, *pace* Moravcsik, there is growing evidence that the European Union – and the process of regional integration more broadly – does have an array of important consequences (Alter, 2000; Beckfield, 2006; Ferrera, 2005; Fligstein, 2008; Huber and Stephens, 2001; Höpner and Schäfer, 2010). This opens up possibilities for the formation of a European public (in the pragmatist sense), as something distinct from a European *demos* or a European society.

Such a possibility weaves together threads from Dewey's (1927) classic publication *The Public and Its Problems* and Offe's (2002) provocative essay, "Is There, Or Can There Be, a 'European Society'?" If problems form publics and spark social action aimed at solving them through combination of habit and creativity (Gross 2009), then regional integration pragmatically creates political opportunities. These opportunities are demanding, in that more habitual social practices (collective bargaining, social redistribution) face new challenges from the formation of regional political economy. The institutional boundaries have been redrawn (Ferrera, 2005). Still, it is the very redrawing of these boundaries that brings forth novel problems, creates an opportunity for the formation of a public, and calls for creativity. If the problems are income inequality, employment precarity, and the ongoing decline of collective bargaining institutions, what are the barriers to the formation of a European public?

Though a public is not equivalent to a society, Offe's essay on the challenges to the formation of a European society offers clues. He rightly notes that the E.U. lacks several fundamental capacities of the state: conscription, education, and taxation. The E.U. is also highly heterogeneous in terms of language, religion, economy, and institutional order. But Offe argues that the "core problem" preventing European social formation is the lack of an idea about what can be gained from Europe. He proposes the strengthening of regional political union through redistribution as a way to create self-conscious European citizens with a stake in a Europe that (pragmatically) addresses the challenges of the regional market. He concludes that "we can begin to speak of the reality of a European society only after European authorities set up bargaining tables" (Offe 2002: 187) for the discussion of what challenges need to be met and how they can be solved. This sounds remarkably like a regional public grappling with regional problems. There is hope for such a scenario from a recent analysis of European Social Survey data, which found that support for the European Social Model is strongest among those who report political *interest* in Europe (Koster and Kaminska, 2010).

Assuming for the sake of argument the formation of a European public interested in a reconfiguration of the labour–capital balance of power that favours labour (an assumption subject to both normative and positive analysis), what might the specific policy levers be? Consider the institutional arrangements that favoured labour organizing in the period of embedded liberalism in Europe: union-run unemployment insurance that helped to recruit workers on the margins to join labour unions, corporatist bargaining arrangements, and strong Left parties (Western, 1997). Of these institutional arrangements, union-run unemployment insurance and Left involvement in the European Parliament seem the most promising, as regional corporatism is undermined by the absence of employers' associations at the bargaining table (Streeck and Schmitter, 1991). It is difficult to imagine what would incentivize employers to engage in corporatist bargaining at the regional level in Europe, although international economic crises might be reminders that employers and employees can gain from corporatist arrangements (Kenworthy, 2002; Martin, 2010). Growing labour unions might also provide such incentives by capturing a larger proportion of the regional labour market.

In the policy context of labour market activation (Kenworthy, 2010), labour unions might adopt a larger role in the provision of activation, thereby guiding the direction of activation policy in a more pro-labour direction. This might have the added benefit of strengthening the recruiting positions of unions, in the same way that union-run insurance schemes in the Ghent system and works councils accomplished (Western, 1997). If employers' resistance could be overcome, it is possible that ECJ jurisprudence on freedom of movement and establishment might support rather than undercut the extension of such benefits to *European* labour, particularly as this could deepen integration of the European labour market.

Such is the most optimism we can muster toward the prospects of "re-embedding" the European market in a way that favours labour. As sociologists inclined toward positive analysis, we stress that we see the continuing liberalization of European labour markets as the most likely near-term course, and we doubt this movement will be limited to the European region. Indeed, we see regional integration and liberalization as trends that are at the heart of the "re-forming" of capitalism during the current historical period (Streeck, 2010). Nevertheless, we think there is substantial evidence from both normative and positive analysis that in many places around the world, the regional political economy is the appropriate locus of new problems – and new publics.

Note

1 The authors thank Sanjay Pinto and Neil Gross for helpful comments (and absolve them of any responsibility for remaining shortcomings). Please direct correspondence to Jason Beckfield, Department of Sociology, Harvard University, 33 Kirkland St., Cambridge MA 02138 (email: jbeckfie@wjh.harvard.edu).

8 Strengthening global economic governance

John Langmore and Shaun Fitzgerald

The evolution of international economic and social institutions lags well behind the deepening of global interdependence. Interest in reducing the global democratic deficit and improving the political effectiveness of international economic, financial and social institutions has not kept pace with globalization. Global economic fora are still too exclusive, unbalanced, slow, unaccountable or weak to enable formation of policies that facilitate improving with maximum effectiveness the wellbeing of most peoples. The upgrading of the Group of 20 (G20) to be the major international meeting for national leaders of large, economically influential, countries on economic and financial issues, is a substantial step forward. But the G20 is self-selected, exclusive, has a static membership, and lacks an independent secretariat. It is therefore only a step towards a more equitable and effective body. Other existing fora have even more serious inadequacies, so further extensive reform and innovation is imperative.

This chapter begins by reviewing the characteristics of the existing international macroeconomic fora, the significance of upgrading the G20 to the role of principal forum for global economic decision-making, and possible steps towards a more inclusive and accountable system of global economic governance. The chapter concludes with two examples of controversial issues which require international decisions to be resolved most effectively: improving international tax cooperation and the use of an international financial transactions levy to fund financial rescue packages.

Contemporary global economic fora

Just as a rule-based international system is vital for peace, so is it for economic and social development. But a necessary condition is that the rules be equitable. As Jeff Sachs (2008) writes, "until the poor are brought into the international financial system with real power, the global economy cannot be stable for long. There can be no harmonization without representation." Equitable, representative, open fora are needed to provide global economic governance aimed at improving the wellbeing of global citizenry.

A brief look at the existing global economic fora reveals severe imbalances: most developing, some developed and most transitional countries are under-represented in the global economic and financial institutions. The peoples of the developing countries account for more than 85 per cent of the world's population, yet decision-making on key global economic issues remains concentrated in the major industrial countries.

The UN Economic and Social Council (ECOSOC)

With the establishment of a new world order in 1945, ECOSOC was designed to be the principal international forum dealing, amongst other subjects, with global economic coordination. With every state privy to the Council's dealings, it is also the existing inter-governmental body with the greatest potential to link the isolating "silos" into which international economic, financial, trade, social and environmental organizations have tended to settle. Meetings of ECOSOC are held in public (though not of the executive), which means that it is more transparent and accountable than most other international economic and financial fora. Through being the most comprehensively representative global economic forum it is well placed to reflect global economic concerns. Because of these characteristics, as Durano notes in this volume, it has the greatest support from the poorer countries as a forum for international economic coordination.

Yet no one would claim that it is close to fulfilling its functions adequately. The Commission on Global Governance (1995) argued in the mid-1990s that "fifty years is long enough to know what works and what does not work. ECOSOC does not work." With 54 members it is too large to be swiftly decisive; its principal session is held once a year during July and so has not adequately addressed global crises as they have occurred in the past; the principal session of four weeks prevents high level participation for longer than a day or two; the world's major economies are only rarely engaged with its activities at senior levels; and it has few powers and no resources with which to implement its decisions.

There was even debate for some years about whether the project of reforming ECOSOC was worth the effort, given the unwieldy size of its membership and its failure to establish the kind of credibility and political importance needed to be effective. The Commission and some other analysts have proposed the establishment of an economic and social security council that would have similar status to the UN Security Council. Unfortunately, this attractive proposal remains elusive due to a lack of support in some quarters and outright opposition in others. For that reason a concerted attempt to improve ECOSOC's functioning should be pursued at least as an interim strategy. The effectiveness of ECOSOC has been improved somewhat in recent years by convening meetings twice a year with the heads of the International Monetary Fund (IMF), World Bank, World Trade Organization (WTO) and the United Nations Conference on Trade and Development, by having more freqent short meetings on high priority issues during the year and through improvements in procedures and preparation.

Following the 2004 report of the High-Level Panel on Threats, Challenges and Change, Secretary-General Kofi Annan made modest but valuable suggestions for upgrading the work of ECOSOC by holding annual ministerial assessments of progress towards such goals as the MDGs; convening timely meetings to address crises; and most important, by asserting leadership in driving a global development agenda to provide direction for the IMF, the World Bank and other agencies. His suggestions were accepted by the Global Summit in September 2005. These reforms could be further strengthened through the use of an ECOSOC executive committee with quick response capability, instituting an annual session on macroeconomic cooperation, regularly reviewing the provision of finance for development and by inviting other institutions of economic governance to contribute to sessions.

The small reforms already instigated have aided the development of ECOSOC, but the body remains problematic. While broadly representative, ineffective operation stymies its potential impact in sustaining democratic global economic governance.

The International Monetary Fund and World Bank

Established contemporaneously with ECOSOC, the problems with the IMF and World Bank (the Bretton Woods Institutions, BWIs) have been well documented (Buira, 2003; Lombardi, 2000). As the G24 (2009) has noted, "the imbalance in voice and representation in governance structure [of these institutions] impacts legitimacy and continued relevance". The governance of both institutions suffers from a lack of inclusiveness. In the case of the IMF this inadequacy can be identified in several areas. First, voting power grossly favours Western nations, especially Europe and America. The top 20 nations account for 71.2 per cent of IMF votes, leaving the remaining 166 nations with 28.8 per cent of voting power (IMF, 2009). This imbalance marginalizes the voices of large and smaller developing nations. This difficulty is further exacerbated by the unfair majority rules effectively requiring the affirmative vote of the U.S. to pass major decisions into effect. Without the significant input of developing nations, the BWI's policies are lopsided, favouring the wealthier countries of the global North rather than comprehensive strategies designed to benefit the world's range of economies.

The process for the election of BWI CEOs is contrary to modern notions of democratic legitimacy (Lombardi, 2000). Until now the Managing Director of the IMF has been a European appointed by a small group of European countries in consultation with the U.S., while the President of the World Bank has been an American. These organizational heads wield great power over the direction of economic policy. "Their actions are ostensibly supervised by an Executive Board which is ill-equipped to hold management to account. The result is that the countries who appoint [these organizational heads] … thereby skew the accountability of the whole organisation towards themselves" (Woods, 2008: 6). Without the participation of the broader global community in an *election* of these leaders, the BWIs will continue to be viewed as largely transatlantic institutions rather than truly global entities. By limiting the agency of developing nations, the rules of the BWIs continue to sustain the democratic deficit in global economic governance.

Accountability issues are exacerbated by a lack of openness. Many IMF and World Bank policies and procedures are not disclosed to the wider public. Even members have noted the difficulty with regard to securing executive board proceedings within a reasonable timeframe (Woods, 2008). BWI reform efforts have noted the need to redress the current system of board directors' representation. While certain board members represent one country (i.e., Germany or Japan), other members are tasked with representing as many as 23 diverse nations. The result of this situation is that "participants from smaller countries [feel] that there is no role for their authorities in actively contributing to the formulation of their constituency position" (Lombardi, 2009: 7). With so many countries clamouring for the attention of one director, it is inevitable that several divergent voices will be diminished, if not drowned out entirely. This reality further diminishes the leadership of BWIs.

The dominance of large economies in the development of BWI programmes has had three notable results reagrding the implementation of IMF and World Bank programmes in developing nations. The BWIs have shown a *bias towards macroeconomic contraction* with both the Fund and Bank often stymied by an excessively cautious and narrow financial approach. Policy is further undermined by *politically motivated loan decisions*, whereby donor nations' foreign policy preferences have been injected into loan decisions, violating the principle of political neutrality. Additionally, *intrusive conditions attached to loans* infringe unjustly on national sovereignty, subvert national democratic processes and ultimately lead to the ineffectual implementation of BWI programmes (You, 2002).

It is clear that there is a democratic deficit in the operation of these institutions. Yet the BWIs, especially the IMF, have been afforded an enhanced role by the G20 in response to the Global Financial Crisis. As Durano observes (in this volume), the financial crisis has done wonders to revive the role of the IMF and the World Bank after a period of declining legitimacy and relevance. Yet considerable concerns remain regarding the dispersion of funds by these bodies, which are linked to the issues of transparency and conditionalities (WWGFD, 2009). As Ross Buckley (n.d.) has noted:

> the IMF is the wrong organisation to set economic policy for nations in crisis and it should be removed from this role. These institutions, whose clients are the world's poorest countries, do the bidding of the richest countries. This is absurd. The principal clients of these institutions need a real voice in their governance.

Once again, democratic global economic governance is found wanting in these global bodies.

The Organisation for Economic Cooperation and Development (OECD)

Similar concerns may be raised with regard to the OECD. This body, constituted in 1961, possesses its own secretariat which works on the organization's stated concerns of economic coordination and growth. It has a membership of 32 nations, largely comprised of European and North American governments (although Turkey, South Korea and Mexico are also members). It therefore has a large spread of members, accounting for three-quarters of world trade and 60 per cent of global gross domestic product (GDP). The organization has gained a strong reputation for excellent technical work and reports. Yet its once strong position in international policymaking has been gradually diluted over the years as its membership has failed to take account of changes in the international financial landscape. "Many people see the OECD as little more than a nebulous group of wealthy countries", (OECD Observer, 2009) a group incapable of expressing a broad global consensus on financial matters. This democratic legitimacy issue is further complicated by the OECD's slow progress on key reform issues, such as its incapacity to successfully implement a multilateral agreement on investment (Elek, 2010). By relying on consensus amongst its members, the organization has proved ineffectual at affecting change. Combined with the exclusive characteristic of its membership, this policy inertia stymies the ability of the OECD to contribute to effective, democratic, global financial reform.

The Group of 20 (G20)

The road to the G20

Formed in 1975, the Group of Seven (or G8 following Russia's 1997 entry), is an informal annual meeting of powerful economies that has broadened in both scope of agenda and attendees in recent years. While this grouping of Western nations (Canada, France, Germany, Italy, Japan, Russia, the U.K. and the U.S.) was able to meet relatively exclusively for much of its existence, the development of an interdependent world economy has seen the diminishment not only of these nations' relative prestige, but also of their ability to steer the world economy. The G8 grouping is not only exclusive in its membership – one commentator deemed it "a European dinner club of the rich and decreasingly powerful" (Walker, 2009) – its constituent nations no longer have the influence to control the direction of international finances. Lacking the formal input of developing nations (including India, China and Brazil) has increasingly made the G8 outdated. As Lord Mandelson has noted, "however long it may persist as a grouping, as a steering committee for the global economy, the era of the G8 is over" (Luce, 2009).

As global economic interdependence has become a reality therefore, a broader informal grouping of powerful economies has emerged. The G20 was formed in 1999 as an international forum of finance ministers and central bank governors from 19 countries, and also includes the CEOs of the BWIs. Its purpose is to promote international financial and economic stability and to address the challenges posed by increasing globalization. At the September 2009 Pittsburgh Summit, the G20 was "locked in as the pre-eminent international economic body" (Thirwell, 2009), superseding the smaller, more exclusive groupings already mentioned (the G8, OECD), yet also diminishing the influence of groups with wider constituency (i.e., the UN) in this arena.

The G20: identity

The G20 includes in its membership emerging economies such as Argentina, Brazil, China, India, South Africa, Saudi Arabia and Turkey, as well as the powerful G8 nations.[1] One excited commentator noted that it "includes everyone who matters" (*Financial Times*, 2009). The grouping accounts for 85 per cent of global GDP, 80 per cent of international trade and two-thirds of the world's population. Unlike the OECD its constituent governments are diverse in their makeup: multi-party democracies, transitioning states, a monarchy, and a Communist one-party state are all members. They encompass a wide range of incomes and approaches to economics. Certainly when compared to its immediate predecessor (the G8), the G20 has a notable diversity and scope that has been widely applauded by politicians and commentators alike (Buckley n.d.; Foster, 2009; Mumford, 2009).

The G20: certain strengths

The elevation of the G20 to the level of heads of government has afforded greater prominence to developing nation issues. With the inclusion of nations as diverse as India, Mexico and Saudi Arabia in the international economic dialogue, the G20 is better positioned to take account of the concerns of the global South. For example, in 2005 China put on the agenda issues most relevant to developing countries – "demographic challenges, brain-drain, migration and innovative financing mechanisms for development" (Rubio-Marquez, 2009). This agenda expansion enhances the representativeness of the G20, affording the body the opportunity to contribute to a significant range of policies affecting a wide range of peoples globally.

The G20 has also made progress on certain economic reforms that had failed to lift off in the G8 or OECD. Work on tax havens and transparency "came through the G20 after a combined German/Australian initiative because the [other groups] were fundamentally incapable of breaking deadlocks" (Beeson and Bell, 2009). The former Governor of the Reserve Bank of India has commended the G20 for bringing nations together to coordinate responses to the global financial crisis (Bandyopadhyay, 2009). Recent G20 meetings have resulted in agreements to alter the voting structure of the BWIs (a matter essential for improved global economic governance, as discussed below). The engagement of a broader scope of nations in international financial cooperation has thus yielded certain commendable results.

The response of the G20 to the challenge of the Global Financial Crisis illustrated the strengths of the grouping. Faced with the most severe financial crisis in 70 years, the need for global economic policy coordination was paramount. Through its meetings in Washington, London and Pittsburgh, the G20 agreed upon "swift and decisive actions that helped to avert a global economic depression in the last year" (United Nations, 2010). This result strengthens the G20's position as the leading body for international economic policy development into the future.

The G20: apparent weaknesses

Despite the aforementioned successes, the G20 does not exist without substantial problems. Although there is widespread recognition that this body is an improvement on its G8 predecessor, the restricted membership and lack of transparency of the G20 undermines its ability to provide representative economic governance.

The *membership* of the G20 remains problematic. The 19 nations privileged to be members were chosen by the American and Canadian finance ministers in a largely secretive process (Martinez-Diaz, 2009). This method of appointment marks the G20 with a certain democratic deficit which is difficult to overcome. Additionally this membership is static – there is no provision for change over time. As the history of the G8 demonstrates, this negatively impacts the ability of a group to respond to alterations in the global dynamic. Ten years after its creation there is a strong argument to be made that the G20 is ill-constituted.

Indeed, famed economist Joseph Stiglitz has emphasized that the composition of the G20 "does not reflect the voice and priorities of the global community" (Muchhala, 2009). The interests of medium and smaller developing nations, especially low income economies, are not represented in the group's current make-up. The Heavily Indebted Poor Countries group has "deplored" the fact that no poor country is represented at the G20 and urged that this situation be "remedied" (AFP 2009a). The exclusion of 172 nations from critical financial governance decisions is a matter of great concern for G20 effectiveness. For global governance to be truly effective it needs to heed the input of a range of nations. By excluding many varied viewpoints the G20 risks sustaining the democratic deficit of existing economic fora.

Although it appears that the membership of the G20 is evolving as a result of national pressure and members' acquiescence (Spain and the Netherlands are invited to meetings, as are regional and international representatives), the grouping remains unrepresentative. It lacks key representatives from Nordic countries, the "stans" in West Asia, the non-Russian transitional countries or other African and Latin American nations. Developing country membership of the G20 has divided the G77 and is perceived by some as undermining the UN's work in the area, though the effects are still being assessed. Singapore has convened a group of about 30 members of the G77 to discuss how to react to the G20 and what can be done to improve cooperative activity between the G20 and the UN Undoubtedly, while the question of G20 membership is likely to remain under consideration, its present constitution raises critical question regarding the grouping's ability to adequately present a global response to critical questions.

Further questions have been raised regarding G8 *dominance* within the G20, with the organization effectively functioning as the G8 + 12 (Weisbrot, 2009). Besides the fact that developing nations have less substantive influence due to their limited resources and the tight bonds between the G8 countries, evidence suggests that the G20 has served as a vehicle for mobilizing support for G8 initiatives. Martinez-Diaz points out:

> The G7's position was reflected in G20 communiqués twice as frequently than [*sic*] the Group of 24 developing nations' [position]. The victories the G7 appear to have won at the G20 are not only more numerous,– they have been of much greater consequence than those won by developing countries.
>
> (Martinez-Diaz, 2009: 15)

Concern has been noted from not only developing countries but also certain European nations about the extent of U.S. and U.K. dictation of the G20 agenda (Bandyopadhyay, 2009). This problem is linked to larger concerns of G20 accountability. With the wealthiest nations dominating the agenda, the G20 cannot therefore be seen to provide representative economic governance aimed at ameliorating the wellbeing of all people.

It is notable that, unlike most international groupings, the G20 does not have a dedicated secretariat. Responsibility for the agenda and direction of the meeting lies with individual host nations. Delegates at these meetings then report back to their own governments. There is a distinct lack of accountability and transparency; in fact, many involved in the G20 summits laud their closed-door approach (Rubio-Marquez, 2009). This is especially significant, as a lack of transparency tends to favour the status quo, auguring against an approach to global financial governance that maximizes both efficiency and equity. With a secretive process shielded from global scrutiny, the G20 minimizes the opportunity for uninvited nations and global bodies to influence economic policy development.

These structural weaknesses in the G20 contribute to the questionable nature of some of its decisions. For example, Stiglitz has criticized its decision to give the big banks – those deemed "too big to fail" – carte blanche to continue with the kinds of activities that lead to the recent financial crisis (Muchhala, 2009). The G20 has failed to address the systemic causes of the crisis, instead preferring to authorize the socialization of private debt within countries (akin to the IMF's response to the East Asian financial crisis in nations such as Indonesia) (Buckley, n.d.). Indeed, "the G20's attempt to face the features of the monetary system that give rise to global imbalances can be predicted to lead to more of these imbalances" (Caliari, 2009). The reliance of the grouping on the IMF to carry out its financial decisions is additionally fraught with difficulty, given that latter organization's own issues of transparency and accountability. Accordingly, the policies pursued by the G20 thus far largely favour the existing economic power structure, significantly diminishing the role that developing nations play in global financial governance.

The emergence of the G20 as the pre-eminent international economic body is a step forward due to its enhanced membership, and the potential accompanying that broader scope. Enthusiasm about this should be tempered, however, as the static, unelected nature of the grouping diminishes its authority, and the lack of transparency further negates the potential of the G20 to ease the democratic deficit in global governance.

Where to now?

A gap continues to exist in the structure of international economic institutions through the absence of a representative, accountable, democratically legitimate forum for discussion of the principal issues of global political economy. The UN Secretary-General's 2001 high-level panel on finance for development, chaired by Ernesto Zedillo wrote that:

> Despite recent worthy efforts, the world has no fully satisfactory mechanism to anticipate and counter global economic shocks.... [G]lobal economic decision-making has become increasingly concentrated in a few countries. For a range of common problems, the world has no formal institutional mechanism to ensure that voices representing all relevant parts are heard in the discussion.
>
> (United Nations, 2001: 23)

The Panel proposed creation of a global council

> at the highest political level to provide leadership on issues of global governance.... [T]hrough its political leadership it would provide a long-term strategic policy framework to promote development, secure consistency in the policy goals of the major international organizations and promote consensus building among governments on possible solutions for issues of global economic and social governance.
>
> (United Nations 2001: 5)

More recently, the Report of the Commission of Experts for the 2009 UN Conference on the World Financial and Economic Crisis called for the creation of a Global Economic Coordination Council to "address areas of concern in the functioning of the global economy in a comprehensive and sustainable way" (United Nations, 2009).

Establishment of a permanent global council within the structure of the UN might involve changing the Charter, a difficult task. There are several less complicated measures that could be adopted, however, to enhance engagement between the G20 and the broader global community. The Global Governance Group (3G), a network of 23 diverse nations, has offered several valuable proposals to enhance the transparency and inclusivity of the G20 process.[2] Key among its proposals is an enhanced consultation period between G20 nations and the UN and its member states prior to G20 meetings. The G20 should then update the UN membership about its decisions following its meeting. With regard to the meetings themselves, the attendance of regional groupings (e.g., APEC, E.U., and ASEAN) and the UN Secretary-General should be formalized and fully integrated into G20 processes. Additionally, there should be "sufficient flexibility in the G-20 process to provide for the participation of non-G-20 members in discussions on specialized issues", for example through non-G20 state participation in Ministerial gatherings or working groups (United Nations, 2010). By adopting these relatively simple consultative measures, the G20 would enhance its inclusiveness and transparency, and therefore the authority of its economic governance measures.

A more substantial, longer-term alternative would be for the G20 leaders (who normally attend the beginning of the Assembly's annual session each September) to hold an annual summit meeting before the General Assembly starts at the UN The obvious next step would be to hold elections for the G20. States could select representatives to such a summit meeting in a number of ways, but one possible approach would be to mirror the structure of the General Committee of the General Assembly as it is regionally representative, each of the permanent five members of the Security Council is a member, and it has 28 members. It is therefore small enough to have decisive discussions, a crucial criterion for an effective leadership forum if it is to attract the serious political engagement of the powerful states. The President of ECOSOC could also be invited to attend. This Summit could be smaller still if there were agreement to two stage elections, first of regional representatives and then of summit members.

The principal value of such a summit could be in its articulation of goals, priorities and policies for the international system, in much the same way as was achieved in the Millennium Declaration agreed at the UN Millennium Assembly. That Declaration, and the Millennium Development Goals (MDGs) derived from it, is contributing to greater coherence of action by international agencies and amongst countries. Ultimately, such a meeting could emerge as a more legitimate and politically effective forum for global discussion and strategic decision-making than the static G20.

Two examples

The recent global financial crisis has vividly demonstrated the extent of global financial interdependence. It is thus worth using this discussion to illustrate the importance of improving international economic governance by considering disputed issues which due to their global dimension require international decision and action – international tax evasion, and the possibility of a currency transactions tax.

International tax evasion

Long recognized as an issue of global concern, this problem continues to plague economic governance systems. Despite some OECD progress, Raymond Baker estimates that mispricing and abusive transfer pricing alone are worth in the region of US$500–750 billion annually (Baker, 2005). The establishment of boundaries to minimize tax evasion and avoidance requires several steps. International transparency about cross-border financial flows has to be substantially improved. If secrecy is removed, and capital properly taxed, it would transform the economies and public finances of developing and developed nations. Linked with that must be the ready exchange of tax and other information between all countries. The E.U. has already established such a system. International rules are needed requiring multinationals to publish country-by-country reports, showing payments, profits and taxes paid in each country in which they operate. Such rules require global cooperation. The emergence of global economic governance bodies such as the G20 could provide a forum for such cooperation, although such cooperation might be limited by the concerns about the body's lack of representativeness (affecting the comprehensiveness of any agreement) and transparency (excluding key actors from the process of any decision-making).

Establishment of an international tax organization would be the most effective step. Such an organization would have an elected governing body representative of member states, responsible for drawing up broad objectives and major issues of policy; and a highly competent staff. This issue is already on the agenda of ECOSOC and it could also usefully be discussed by the G20. Agreement to strengthen international tax cooperation would be of value to every country, developing or developed, seeking to increase its revenue, reduce tax evasion and strengthen equity.

Currency transaction tax

James Tobin first proposed a related currency transaction tax (CTT) in 1972, and reiterated that suggestion in the mid-1990s (Tobin, 1996). Scholars have shown that a CTT could be imposed almost universally on the kinds of transaction it would target given only the active cooperation of the monetary authorities in the major vehicle currency countries, though ideally a few others would be ready to cooperate (Schmidt, 2007). This method was elaborated in 2010 by a Committee of Experts which recommends introduction of a global CTT at the point of global settlement (LGIFFD, 2010).[3] The Expert Committee recommends collecting a tiny tax of 0.005 per cent through a Global Solidarity Levy collected through the increasingly centralized foreign exchange trading system settlement bank.[4] A general CTT would be a source of funds for global provenance, which would require that they be allocated under global authority. The Expert Committee recommends establishment of a Global Solidarity Fund with a representative governing body to allocate funds for global public goods such as achievement of the Millennium Development Goals and climate change mitigation and adaptation.

In September 2009 the G20 at its summit in Pittsburgh charged the IMF with preparing a report ahead of the next G20 summit in June 2010 to consider "how the financial sector could make a fair and substantial contribution toward paying for any burdens associated with government interventions to repair the banking system" (IMF, 2011). The IMF reported in mid-2010, and recommended introduction of a financial activities tax set at 5 per cent annually, arguing that financial sectors are both too large and undertaxed. Partly because of opposition from the Canadian Government, which was chairing the meeting, the G20 meeting in Canada in June 2010 barely discussed these issues and referred them to its next meeting in Korea in November. Member governments have significantly different views about how to tax financial sectors: the U.S., U.K., France, Germany and most E.U. members want a levy on bank liabilities; France and Germany are also interested in a financial transactions tax.

To develop these ideas into the future, global economic leadership is required. The CTT is just one example of how integrated international financial governance could bring about needed reform. Given this emerging recognition of the need for better global coordination of taxation regulation and implementation, the strengthening of institutions of global economic governance should remain at the forefront of international debate.

Conclusion

It is often noted that the greatest reforms come at a time of crisis. As the world focuses its attention on recovery following the greatest financial crisis since the 1930s, it is only appropriate to consider how to strengthen global institutions of economic and social governance to better serve the global citizenry in the future. The G20 has emerged as an organization capable of enhanced global representation and effectiveness, yet is limited by its static membership, exclusivity and dominance by powerful states. Its performance in the future will depend on its ability to redress the problems caused by these features.

Potential for global leadership in this area of greater social and economic integration could be found within the UN system. As established, however, ECOSOC and the BWIs are flawed and in need of substantial overhaul before they could effectively act to facilitate with maximum effectiveness the improvement of the wellbeing of most peoples. Given the inadequacies of these bodies it is worth seriously considering the eventual development of a UN Global Economic Council akin to the existing Security Council of the UN In the meantime, further attention should be given to enhancing the channels via which the G20 can interact with the 172 nations outside its membership, in an effort to secure greater global financial cooperation. Such further reform would be valuable in an increasingly integrated world, as the example of cooperation on taxation matters has shown. As we move toward recovery following the financial crisis, it is imperative to strengthen institutions of global governance to facilitate the wellbeing of all people, everywhere.

Notes

1 The full membership officially consists of Argentina, Australia, Brazil, Canada, China, France, Germany, India, Indonesia, Italy, Japan, Mexico, Russia, Saudi Arabia, South Africa, South Korea, Turkey, the U.K., the U.S. and the European Union. See G20 (2011).

2 The 3G group comprises Commonwealth of the Bahamas, Kingdom of Bahrain, Barbados, Botswana, Brunei Darussalam, Chile, Costa Rica, Guatemala, Jamaica, Principality of Liechtenstein, Malaysia, Principality of Monaco, New Zealand, Panama, the Republic of the Philippines, the State of Qatar, the Republic of Rwanda, the Republic

of San Marino, the Republic of Senegal, the Republic of Singapore, Switzerland, the United Arab Emirates and Uruguay.

3 The Leading Group is an informal forum composed of 60 governments, the main international organizations and NGOs from every continent.

4 The Continuous Linked Settlement Bank (CLS) was established in 2002 by a consortia of central banks and global private banks. It provides an institutional framework for the world's 17 major currencies. "The CSL Bank's growing share of the foreign exchange settlement market suggests that it will have institutional dominance in the future over the management and collection of data related to the value and volume of foreign exchange transactions' (IGIFFD, 2010: 40).

9 From waning to emerging world order

Multipolarity, multilateralism and World Bank reform

Robert H. Wade[1]

Growth has gone South, debt has gone North.

(Quip about the current Great Recession)

Introduction

Multipolarity is the new catchphrase, used to herald the end of the "Truman era", when U.S. hegemony prevailed and the first world delivered development to the rest, and the start of a new era of "the rise of the rest" when some developing countries emerged as significant economic and political players on the global stage. The word is often used in a way which implies that rising multipolarity is being translated into stronger multilateral cooperation in economic governance. This paper examines trends in the World Bank to ask whether they substantiate the hypothesis that more multipolarity induces institutional change in the direction of multilateral cooperation.

The paper finds that developing countries have raised their presence in the Bank; but their bigger presence has resulted in only small changes in internal dynamics and external outputs so far, much less than the hoopla surrounding recent reforms would suggest. American and G7 operational dominance has not been much eroded, and to the extent that it has the new states' jealous guarding of their sovereignty results in "Westphalian assertion", or "every state for itself", which erodes a spirit of multilateral cooperation. On the assumption that this is a transitional period, the paper spells out steps for further reforms in the World Bank in order to boost its role and legitimacy as a multilateral organization.

In April 2010 Robert Zoellick, President of the World Bank, gave a speech hailed by some as the most important speech of a Bank president since Robert McNamara's in 1973, when McNamara set poverty reduction as the Bank's new mission. Zoellick's main point concerned the end of the Third World, the end of the distinction between developed and developing countries. He said:

> If 1989 saw the end of the "Second World" with Communism's demise, then 2009 saw the end of what was known as the "Third World". We are now in a new, fast-evolving multipolar world economy – in which some

> developing countries are emerging as economic powers; others are moving towards becoming additional poles of growth; and some are struggling to attain their potential within this new system.

Though he did not use the following words, Zoellick was in effect saying that the distribution of material power in the inter-state system has become more fluid over the past decade than at any time since the beginning of the Cold War; and that we are finally at the end of the Truman era, which began in the early post-war years when President Truman called on the West to take up the challenge of using "our" knowledge and resources to deliver development to the rest of the non-communist world. From a largely unipolar (non-communist) world, with the U.S. as hegemon, we have moved to "a new, fast-evolving multipolar world economy" as economic weight and political power has flowed away from the West towards East and South. Zoellick went on to indicate how this more multipolar world economy requires changes in the governance and operations of the World Bank to make it more multilateral, less dominated by the Western states.

Zoellick implied a hopeful answer to a basic question: will the international system be able to induce rule-bound cooperation between states, given the falling concentration of economic activity and political power in the West and the growing number and importance of "global problems" (including climate change, water shortages, regulation of international trade and finance, migration, criminal networks, nuclear proliferation and many more)? Will the aging post-World War II legacy organizations like the World Bank and International Monetary Fund (IMF) be able to reform themselves so as to reflect the new multipolarity, while also strengthening their ability to provide public goods to their borrowers and to the world economy at large? Will Southern states – on the other side of the Truman divide – become sources of initiatives in inter-state organizations, not just participants and takers?

While Zoellick implied a "yes", it is equally plausible that the growing number and diversity of states with enough weight in the world economy to exercise voice about international governance has a *centrifugal* effect, intensifying assertions of Westphalian sovereignty; and that Southern states show no more inclination to take on leadership roles than in the past, even as they claim a larger presence in global governance.

In other words, economic weight and influence in governance are different things. The "rise of (some of) the rest", combined with surging global problems, may not induce the established states to compromise with the newcomers and may not induce the newcomers to compromise with the established states or among themselves. All the more so for those economies in economic slump, with populations facing interrupted rising expectations, those whose governments may respond to accumulating social fury by blaming outsiders. And all the more so for fast-growing China, with hundreds of millions of people experiencing relative deprivation as millions become super-rich, whose authoritarian government tries to suppress news of domestic abuses of power and bristles at criticism from other states, interpreting it as infringement of sovereignty (see, for example: Wiles, 2010). The world system may experience "multipolarity without multilateralism", an outcome devoutly to be avoided. Multipolarity with only weak multilateralism is potentially destabilizing, as newly empowered states go their own way, because respect for the dissenting views of more numerous players shrinks the scope of cooperative solutions to global issues and tends towards stalemate.

The Bretton Woods organizations have their very identity rooted in inclusion of both Northern and Southern states. Enthusiasm greeted the governance reforms at the World Bank and IMF that were announced in 2010, which seemed to raise the influence of Southern states. How should we interpret the claims of a turning point?

First, a more general discussion of polarity and multilateralism; and then back to the organizations themselves.

The starting point: the U.S.-dominated unipolar system

For most of the second half of the twentieth-century the U.S. was by far the largest national economy in terms of gross domestic product (GDP), and one of the most prosperous in terms of average income. It also exercised primacy in the non-communist world, using its political position to promote a liberal, market-based economic order.

The Bretton Woods system of the post-war decades up to the early 1970s did impose some constraints on U.S. policy through the dollar–gold link, but since its breakdown the U.S. has been largely unconstrained in its monetary and fiscal policies by the need to take account of other states' interests. For example, leading up to Paul Volcker's decision to hike the Federal Reserve rate in 1979 (to curb U.S. inflation) the Federal Reserve did no analysis of the impact on the rest of the world and, specifically, none on the impact on Latin America – which, having loaded up on debt from U.S. banks, was plunged into a decade long debt-and-development crisis.[2]

Indeed, for the whole period from the 1940s to the 2000s, US monetary policy was set almost entirely for U.S. objectives even though it strongly affected global economic conditions. Thanks to its currency also being the main international reserve currency, the U.S. was able to run current account deficits every year from 1992 to 2010 (18 years), its deficit in 2008 being about the size of India's GDP. These deficits strongly affected financial stability and economic growth in the rest of the world, but the rest of the world had no say in U.S. policies which affected the size of those deficits. As a senior U.S. official remarked, "[t]he dollar is our currency but your problem".[3]

The U.S. exercised predominant power in the IMF and the World Bank – crystallized in its veto over decisions requiring a super-majority, the only state with such power. Conversely, the IMF has always been very weak in its ability to discipline the U.S. Joe Stiglitz tells how, when he was chair of the Council of Economic Advisors, he saw the U.S. Treasury ostentatiously toss the Fund's Article 4 consultation reports on the U.S. economy in the rubbish bin.[4]

This is the substance behind the *Financial Times* columnist Philip Stevens' (2010) summary remark, "[m]embership of the West once meant doing whatever Washington said".[5]

Rise of multipolarity

The rise of multipolarity (in the economic rather than bombs-and-rockets sense) means a fall in the concentration of economic activity in the international system; and within this, the rise of concentrations outside the previous core. The trend can be made more concrete by means of several indicators:

1. *Share of G7 (12 per cent of world population) in global gross domestic product:* in 2000 the G7's share was 72 per cent; by 2011 it will have fallen to 53 per cent, according to the IMF (measured at market exchange rates); and
2. *Share of developing and transitional countries (DTCs) in world output*: between 2000 and 2009 the share of DTCs in world output rose by 10 percentage points, from 23 per cent to 33 per cent measured at market exchange rates and from 40 per cent to 50 per cent measured in purchasing power parity dollars (see Table 9.1).
3. *South-South trade:* in 1997 the ten biggest Asian exporters (excluding Japan) sent 46 per cent of their exports to the U.S., European Union and Japan; in 2009, only 36 per cent, with the difference going to developing countries and oil exporters. China is now Brazil's biggest trading partner, displacing the U.S. from its long-held top position. Almost all of Brazil's Carnival costumes are now made in China; and most of its processed steel.
4. *Whose monetary policy matters to the rest of the world?* Ten years ago the world paid attention to U.S. and E.U. monetary policy and nobody outside China paid attention to China's monetary policy. Today, China's monetary policy is closely watched, especially in New York, Washington and London.
5. *The European Union and the euro:* the E.U., for all its recent travails, is slowly becoming more cohesive than it was; and the euro is slowly becoming the world's second main international reserve currency (the share of the euro in world foreign exchange reserves rose from 18 per cent in 1999 to 27 per cent in 2009). So the increasing economic cohesion in Europe – together with its sheer economic weight in the world economy – makes it a separate source of pressure on the international economic governance system.

Table 9.1 Share of developing and transitional countries in world output, 1980–2009 (%)

World output		*1980*	*1990*	*2000*	*2005*	*2009*
	MKT	26	18	23	26	33
	PPP	32	33	40	45	50

Source: data from the *World Bank Development Indicators*, 2011.

For convenience we can think of the new multipolarity in economic and financial affairs as involving three poles – the U.S., the E.U., and Brazil, Russia, India and China (the BRICs). This sets the context of the new Great Game, with two qualifications. First, the BRICs have little collective identity: the leaders of the four states met for the first time as a fraternity of rising powers as recently as 16 June 2009, in Russia (however, for the past couple of years the BRIC Executive Directors at the World Bank have met together once or twice a month, as have those at the IMF). Second, when thought as the third pole, "the BRICs" has permeable boundaries, and may include a larger number of states including middleweights like Korea, Mexico, Turkey and South Africa.

Stronger multilateralism?

Has the big increase in the relative economic size of the world's southern poles translated into stronger multilateralism in global economic governance?

Several indicators might be used. One is entry of new states to apex governing fora (such as the expansion of the G7 into the G20). Another is increases in voting power of Southern states in international organizations. A third might be new agreements on global issues subscribed to by many states of North and South.

We also have to distinguish modes of participation. One is "hegemonic incorporation", in which the organization becomes more inclusive, the larger body reaches agreements, but the agreements are scripted by the hegemon or hegemonic core (see Beeson and Bell). New members go along with what the dominant states want and use their participation to secure national advantage within this constraint. A second mode is "multilateral cooperation", when member states are willing to compromise in order to reach agreements, and when initiatives come from across the membership not just from the old hegemonic core. A third is Westphalian assertion, where states assert national sovereignties in the form of " 'no' votes" yielding a low level of cooperation – which may be masked by agreement on fine words.

How has rising multipolarity been translated into multilaterialism in the World Bank?[6]

The World Bank

The World Bank remains the world's premier development agency, especially as generator and sustainer of powerful beliefs about the best policies and institutions for development. The global economic crisis has been good for it, to the point where its lending commitments in the 2009 fiscal year were three times higher than two years previously. The middle income countries – the ones best placed to walk away from the Bank and borrow from private markets under their own name, or from regional development banks – have come out in strong support. The days of the early 1990s, when a powerful NGO movement with much influence in the U.S. Congress was campaigning to close down the World Bank and the IMF under the slogan "50 years is enough", and when a powerful right wing American constituency which disliked multilateralism and foreign aid was pushing for much the same, are long gone (Wade, 1997).

The package of reforms

The Spring Meetings of the Bretton Woods organizations in late April 2010 may be looked back on as a seminal event in the organizations' history. The governors of both – ministers from the member countries[7] – agreed on the outlines and some specifics of reforms hailed as equipping them for the new multipolar era (recall Zoellick's speech in the run up to the Spring Meetings).

The World Bank reform package includes five main components:

1. Voice: increase in shares and votes of Part II (borrower) countries;
2. Capital increase to support future lending;
3. Strategy, as laid out in a paper called "New World, New World Bank Group: (i) Post-Crisis Directions";
4. Internal organization: for example, further decentralization out of Washington;
5. Internal governance: for example, organization of the Board, relations between Board and president.

Causes of the reforms

The impetus for voice reform had been building for several years before the global economic crisis, focused on the fact that the Part I (high income, non-borrowing) countries had well over half of the voting shares. Moreover the U.S. on its own, and the Europeans acting as one, both wielded a veto on important ("super-majority") decisions. The Monterrey Consensus in 2002 stated that the Part IIs should have more voice in international organizations, in line with their rising weight in the world economy. But the Part I countries dragged their feet. Voice reform was not a priority for them, for much the same reason that Christmas is not a priority for turkeys.

The formation of the leaders' G20 in response to the global economic crisis in 2008, at the initiative of President Bush, gave impetus to voice reforms. Now the top political leaders were dealing face to face, and the developing country leaders put the voice demand firmly on the table. While disagreeing on much else they readily agreed to demand a shift in votes in favour of themselves. Moreover, the U.S. government came to see support for the change as a way to kill two birds with one stone – to cut Europe's over-representation and to strengthen its own alliances with the BRICs.

At this time the World Bank and the IMF both faced soaring demand for loans. As the Bank's lending commitments rose it became clear – at least to some senior World Bank officials and some member states – that it needed a big general capital increase (GCI) simply to avoid the necessity for sharp cutbacks to its future lending, let alone expansion of that lending.

But all the G7 states opposed a GCI, especially the U.S., U.K. and France. Right up to the summer of 2009 President Zoellick insisted that the Bank could boost its lending by making "efficiency savings". Only at the Annual Meetings in Istanbul in September did he finally lend support to a GCI. Why the G7 reluctance to support a GCI?

The G7 governors and executive directors, and many other Part I states, said they would have a hard time persuading their parliaments – especially the U.S. Congress – to increase funding for the World Bank at a time of fiscal stringency at home (even though the amounts of paid-in capital are tiny, only about 5 per cent of pledged or "callable" capital). The Europeans were doubly doubtful because they knew that they were going to lose voting shares in the voice reform, so they would be contributing more capital at the same time as they lost votes.[8]

During 2009 the World Bank management (with grudging permission of the president) worked intensively to demonstrate to doubtful Part I EDs that if the World Bank did not get a big general capital increase then it would have to substantially cut back its lending by 2014 to levels far below the rate before the global economic crisis just to keep within prudential limits. This evidence eventually persuaded many Part I executive directors (EDs) that the World Bank had to have a GCI.

So the Part I governments began to say: "We'll consider a GCI but first you have to carry out big reforms in internal organization." As U.S. Treasury Secretary Geithner said: "Donor countries are facing severe financial constraints at home; [so] we will be seeking critical institutional reforms in any consideration of additional resources." (quoted in BWI, 2009)

As the Board and the management worked on the reform package, the Part I governments reluctantly accepted that the GCI had to come *now*.[9]

So the main driver of the reform package at the World Bank was demands by external shareholders, led by the U.S., for reforms that looked bold and could be sold to parliaments as quid pro quo for additional capital at a time of fiscal stringency at home. This is the short answer to why the governors approved the reform package at the Spring Meetings in Washington in April 2010; and why the package was feted as a "New World Bank for a New Multipolar World".

What do the reforms amount to?

When the hoopla is stripped away the reforms look very modest. Most of the Part II EDs feel disappointed but not surprised, with the important exception of the Chinese ED who takes the view that they are a positive *first* step – in the spirit of crossing the river by feeling for the stones one at a time.

General capital increase

The agreed increase in the capital base is actually very small, probably only big enough to allow the Bank to sustain beyond 2014 the same level of lending in real terms as in the early 1980s.

Voice reform

The G20 leaders' meeting in September 2009 declared that the World Bank should raise the share of Part II votes by "at least 3 percentage points", and this statement, interpreted as "3.13 percentage points", constituted the Development Committee's and Executive Directors' marching orders. The shift would raise the Part IIs' share from about 44 per cent of the votes to about 47 per cent.

This fell well short of what Part IIs were demanding: parity, or 50 per cent. How was the 3 percentage points arrived at? By the ancient principle of split-the-difference. Three percentage points on the existing 44 per cent brought the Part II share up to half of the Part IIs' demand.[10]

Once the G20 had laid down the target the Board spent months of nearly 24/7 negotiations to allocate the change in shares among member countries. As one observer said, the process became a search for "compromises at the *third* decimal point" (as in bargaining whether country X would get 1.134 per cent or 1.135 per cent).[11]

The negotiations were guided by a formula, but the formula itself was highly contested (indeed, it was called a "framework" rather than a "formula", on grounds that "formula" sounded like something permanent which would set the starting point for the next round of negotiations. Words matter.) The U.S. said it should be based largely on "weight in world economy as measured by GDP at *market exchange rates*"; and, not coincidentally, the U.S. is underrepresented in the World Bank by this criterion. Europeans said that the formula should also include "contributions to the development mandate of the World Bank, as measured by IDA [International Development Association] contributions"; and, not coincidentally, Europe's are much bigger than the U.S.'s. Many Part II countries argued that the only criterion should be a country's share of world GDP in *purchasing power parity* terms – which would substantially raise the share of the Part IIs. Eventually a compromise was reached: the GDP metric should be weighted 60 per cent at market exchange rates and 40 per cent at purchasing power parity exchange rates, reflecting the continuing tilt of power towards the Part I countries.

In the end (including the entire change in voting shares since 2008):

- The headline jump in the Part II (developing and transitional) share from 44 per cent to 47 per cent was misleading. More than a dozen countries which by the Bank's criteria should have been counted as Part I ("high income") were counted as Part II. They include South Korea, Singapore, Saudi Arabia, Kuwait, Poland and Hungary. If added to the "high income" countries, the latter end up with a bit more than 60 per cent of the vote (60.95 per cent).[12]
- Within the Part I countries the West Europeans (combined) lost the most, Japan lost the most of any single country, the U.S. effectively stayed the same.
- The BRICs gained virtually the whole shift. The BRIC gain was concealed by being described as a Part II gain.

- The middle income countries (including the BRICs) now have about a third of the votes.
- None of the low income countries lost; but only a few gained, and these insignificantly.
- The low income countries have 4.46 per cent of the votes.
- China won respect by giving up about half of its entitled increase in shares (by share of world GDP) so as to allow this half to go to other Part IIs. (If China had not done so, it would have received the whole of the 3 percentage point shift.)
- Under the formula relating the capital increase to the change in shares, Russia and Saudi Arabia were destined to lose shares. They were very displeased, and Russian Prime Minister Putin and his Saudi counterpart informed the president in imperative tones that they would block the whole voice reform if they lost shares. So the architects of the voice reform changed the framework in such a way as to enable these states to gain back what they would have otherwise lost – by pledging an additional amount for the *next* IDA subscription (IDA16), and weighting these future contributions much more heavily than countries' past contributions (to the anger of the IDA-generous Nordics). Several other idiosyncratic arrangements were bolted on to accommodate the determined defence of existing voting shares by the top leaders of certain states.[13]
- The voting shares are due to be revised in 2015, not before.

Strategy

The focus on voice reforms at the third decimal point meant that other issues, especially the Bank's strategy for the new multipolar age, were eclipsed. This suited the Part I countries nicely.

The strategy document is short, vague and platitudinous, containing little to disagree with. It presents no new vision for a larger World Bank. Strip away the fluff and it reduces to something close to "business as usual" – to be done in a more decentralized way than before. However, the fact of its existence satisfied the demand of the Part I governments that the Bank show them what it was going to do with the additional resources made possible by a GCI.

The many drafts of the strategy paper, up to the last two (a couple of weeks before the April 2010 meetings), began with the sentence, "*The vision of the World Bank Group is to support an inclusive and sustainable globalization* – to overcome poverty, enhance growth with care for the environment, and create individual opportunity and hope" (emphasis added).

This reflected Zoellick's wish to pavilion "globalization" with praise. He has been supported by many middle income countries, who question the Bank's long-established primacy in matters concerning poverty reduction. They say that a World Bank focused on poverty reduction will go out of business, because the middle income countries want to borrow from it not for poverty-targeted projects but for general development projects, especially infrastructure.

The Nordics protested again and again at the draft strategy's prioritizing of globalization over poverty reduction. Finally, at the last minute, their efforts paid off. The strategy team revised the headline statement to read: "*The vision of the World Bank Group is to overcome poverty* – by supporting an inclusive and sustainable globalization, enhancing growth with care for the environment, and creating individual opportunity and hope" (emphasis added). The headline reaffirms the vision statement which has been displayed in the foyer of the main building of the World Bank since the days of Wolfenson's presidency in the mid-1990s. But in the intervening years several of the letters have lost their moorings and now droop at decrepit angles.

Conclusions

We have entered a much more turbulent period of global governance than for the past many decades. The turbulence reflects: (1) the increasing share of global economic activity outside the established Atlantic states plus Japan; (2) the associated growth of excess production capacity relative to effective demand (constrained by rising income concentration at the top of national distributions); and (3) the efforts by states to blame outsiders for their troubles and shift unemployment elsewhere by boosting exports as they contract domestic demand (Wade, 2009a; 2009b; 2011b).

This essay has discussed some of the institutional innovations made or proposed in response to the new international distribution of economic activity. It illustrates how the tension between the newcomers and the old G7 and the wider advanced-country elite is playing out. On the one hand, the advanced countries attempt to incorporate newcomers into their own beliefs and preferences for the global meta-agenda of economic policy ("globalization" in the sense of further privatization and liberalization plus social safety nets for the poorest, together with some tighter financial regulation post-2008). On the other hand, the newcomers demand more voice but without as yet much coordination of beliefs and preferences among themselves (but recall that the BRIC executive directors at the World Bank and at the IMF have started to meet once or twice a month).

The transition from the waning to the emerging global order is clearly proving tricky. It runs into the multipolar governance dilemma, whereby economic multipolarity, particularly at a time of economic slump, is generating more demands for inter-state cooperation; but the same multipolarity makes the supply response in the form of political multilateralism lag far behind. The G20 and the Bretton Woods organizations continue to show more "hegemonic incorporation" and "Westphalian assertion" than "multilateral cooperation".

The Americans and the Europeans are ambivalent about ceding some leadership to the DTCs, sometimes cooperating among themselves and sometimes falling out on what changes should and should not be made. At the World Bank the Part I countries as a group have dragged their feet on significantly increasing the Part II voting share, *and* on increasing the general capital base, *and* on opening the selection process for the heads of the World Bank and the IMF to global recruitment without nationality restrictions. And they cooperated to ensure that the real shift of votes to DTCs was much less than the headline shift.

The U.S. executive branch is fixated on a power play: first, to retain its veto in both organizations, and second, to retain the presidency of the World Bank. If it keeps these two things and does not have to pay in more capital, it is not too worried about the organization. The U.S. Congress is, if anything, even more concerned to protect U.S. dominance in both organizations, which it regards as arms of U.S. foreign policy. For example, the U.S. Senate demanded (March 2010) that the Obama administration maintain "United States voting shares and veto rights at the international financial institutions", and preserve "US leadership of the World Bank and senior level positions at the other international financial institutions" (quoted in BWI, 2010a). U.S. Westphalian pressure may well intensify in the wake of the November 2010 U.S. Congressional elections, which returned a Republican majority in the House of Representatives. U.S. foreign policy may become more unilaterally assertive, self-righteous and self-pitying than in the first two years of the Obama administration, because American conservatives unify around the belief in America's unique virtue and its corollary that the rules for others do not necessarily apply to America. Hence many conservatives are reluctant to adapt to the rise of new centres of power, and want to rely instead on "coalitions of the willing" or a "concert of democracies".

As for the DTCs, they wish to be *at* the top table, *in* global governance, but are wary of *more* global governance (which would curb their sovereignty) and wary of proposing initiatives which would put more responsibilities on their shoulders. This helps to explain the otherwise puzzling fact that at the World Bank, countries which should have been graduated to the Part I category according to the income per head criterion (like South Korea, Saudi Arabia and Kuwait) resist. One reason, noted earlier, is that the Part I countries wish them to continue to be classified as Part II, so that the shift in votes to "true" DTCs is less than it seems. But they themselves also wish to continue in Part II because once graduated they would be expected to: (1) contribute more capital; (2) give up voting share; and (3) share the burden of global responsibilities.

Meanwhile, China is becoming increasingly assertive, even swaggering, as the ruling Communist Party tries to show that it has made China a respected world power, not to be pushed around. It is drawing sharper distinctions between its own and others' national interests, as seen in its responses to rising tensions on the Korean peninsula and in the South China Sea.

To my knowledge there is no body of theory that might shape our expectations about the gap – large or small, increasing or diminishing – between economic globalization and multipolarity, on the one hand, and political globalization and multilateralism, on the other. It remains an open question whether the gap will reduce or widen over time. The optimistic answer is that surging global problems plus repeated interaction between the expanded body of leading states (in many international organizations, not just the Bretton Woods ones and the G20) will generate convergence in both solutions and enmeshed beliefs about causes (as repeated interaction among the Permanent Five of the

Security Council has helped to maintain the peace between them – with occasional exceptions – for more than 60 years, an epochal achievement); and that this convergence will generate expanded multilateral economic cooperation. The more pessimistic answer is that while bits and pieces of agreements (loosely coupled regulatory systems, or "regime complexes") may be forged by overcoming coordination problems of the prisoner's dilemma kind (where the parties agree on the nature of the problem), bigger advances in the form of strong, integrated regulatory systems ("comprehensive regimes") are blocked by differences in enmeshed beliefs, now combined with deep tensions resulting from the economic slump. Making enmeshed beliefs converge, especially when economic tensions run high, is more intractable than solving coordination problems.[14]

Clearly the repeated interaction between China and the U.S. in multilateral fora like the G20 and the Bretton Woods organizations has not been sufficient to generate convergence in their understanding of the root causes of global imbalances or complementarity in their policy responses. Yet think how much worse things would be in the absence of such fora, as in a pre-World War II type of order. In such a world the imbalances would be reduced through bilateral assertion, elephant against elephant, as the U.S. creates dollars without limit and China responds by creating Yuan without limit with which to buy the dollars and prevent Yuan appreciation. Innocent bystander states suffer, and the world would move from currency wars to even worse trade protection wars.

Whether this outcome can now be avoided will be a test of the diffuse value of global fora. Hopefully they will soften bilateral tensions between the giants by embedding them in cross-cutting ties which expose them to pressure from those sitting alongside whose economies suffer because of their actions. And hopefully they help the rising states to learn about open debate and superpower diplomacy. In this optimistic spirit let us consider how the role and governance of the World Bank might be improved.

Reform of the World Bank

The World Bank's future is assured because the BRICs and other middle income countries have come out strongly in support, even though they are better placed to borrow from other sources. Many are now more credit-worthy than some Part I countries such as the southern European Mediterranean states. However, some Part I governments – notably the U.S. government – are holding back its growth, as seen in their reluctance to support a GCI. These governments have no strong interest in allowing the Bank to grow much bigger and compete with their private financiers and consulting firms.

A big fight is likely within the next few years over the presidency of the World Bank and the managing directorship of the IMF, especially over whether the Americans can keep their monopoly on the Bank presidency and the Europeans their monopoly of the Fund. The reform packages for both organizations call for open selection of the heads, unrestricted by nationality. But many commentators immediately shrink back: what if former president of Brazil, Lula da Silva, decides that he wishes to be president of the World Bank? How does the organization hard-wire in a *merit* test? Worse, what happens if the Chinese government wishes to appoint a senior official or politician as managing director of the IMF? What would happen to the organizations' transparency and accountability? In the case of the Bank, should the positions of CEO and chair of the Board, which have always been held by the president, be separated so that a Lula could be chair with an effective manager as CEO?

The Europeans say that they and the Americans agree to give up the gentleman's agreement – but that it is up to the U.S. to make the first move by giving up the Bank. They worry about a U.S. strategy whereby it agrees to open up both jobs, then mobilizes an emerging market candidate as managing director of the IMF and deploys its veto to ensure his or her election, in return for which grateful emerging market states support an American as the next president of the World Bank – through "open" selection, of course.[15]

Another sensitive issue concerns the World Bank's role in servicing the emerging development agenda of the G20. Some non-G20 states strenuously object to the World Bank making itself into the "secretariate" for a self-appointed, non-representative body which includes no low income countries (India now officially being classed as a middle income country) and no premier aid donors except the U.K. Any World Bank help to the G20 only ratifies the G20's claims to be the global steering committee, they say (in this spirit they take a microscope to the Bank's budget in order to discover where the costs of servicing the G20 are being concealed). Other voices take a more pragmatic view that since the G20 exists and wants to talk about development, the World Bank had better lead the way in telling it what to say.

But in the larger scheme of things these are minor issues. What would be a bold vision for a new World Bank? It might start from the point that there is an obvious unmet global need for a financing mechanism to provide below commercial rate *long-term* loans on a much bigger scale than at present. First, for projects which provide "global public goods", where the investments are made in specific countries but the benefits spill over to many other countries (climate change investments are the obvious case in point). Second, for other kinds of investments where the benefits are mostly captured within the country but where costs are high and benefits accrue over a much longer period, such as some kinds of infrastructure and industrial loans.

The sum of both demands means that developing countries laying down production and distribution capacity in new activities need loans which – to be safe – mature in 15 to 20 years. Until developing countries develop a diversified production base they should be net importers of capital – *provided* that the capital imports are used to increase productive capacity rather than increase consumption and provided that the loans are long term (Bresson Periera, 2010). At present, with only a small supply of long term loans, developing countries have been borrowing abroad on much shorter terms and at commercial rates – setting themselves up for whiplash reversal of capital flows and ensuing financial crises (as in the East Asian/Russian/Brazil crisis of 1997–98 (see, for example: Wade,

2000)) and forcing them excessively into export production in order to repay the short term loans. In this way they helped to produce global imbalances and associated international financial fragility. This is the core argument for enabling one or more World Bank-like organizations to expand long term lending to middle income countries by ten times or more of its present level.

Organizationally, the International Bank for Reconstruction and Development (IBRD) and the IDA would probably have to be governed separately. The IBRD is the World Bank's lending arm for middle income countries, financed by the sale of bonds plus repayments of previous IBRD loans. The IDA is the lending arm for very low income countries, financed by grants plus repayments of previous IDA loans. The two arms are now governed by the same set of executive directors, and share the same staff.

The IBRD might be thought of as a credit union or cooperative bank, as distinct from a shareholder bank. In a cooperative bank shares and votes are allocated according to some combination of: (1) one member one vote; (2) financial contributions; and (3) borrowings. Since the Part Is now contribute very little paid-in capital and the bulk of the IBRD revenue comes from sale of IBRD bonds and from *borrowers'* repayments, the switch to the cooperative bank model would imply a big shift of votes away from the Part Is to the middle income countries, which would raise their shareholding to much more than parity.

The Part I countries say they provide the guarantees on IBRD bonds, and hence enable the IBRD to raise revenue at a cheap rate. But now that many Part II governments have a high credit rating, Part II governments could equally guarantee IBRD bonds. And some of those with large foreign exchange reserves would be happy to increase their capital subscriptions to the IBRD instead of using their reserves to finance the U.S.'s external deficits and overseas adventures.

The IBRD would then be run more by the middle income countries, and could lend ten and more times its present rate to meet the surging demand for infrastructure loans, heavy and chemical industry loans, climate change loans, and the like (based on a dynamic stages model of economic development distinct from the static comparative advantage and poverty-focused model which has dominated World Bank thinking for the past three decades) (Wade, 2010a). The IDA might then be governed separately, by a Board which continued to be dominated by Part Is as long as they gave most of the grants. Needless to say, this vision is completely rejected by all Part Is, and also (at least publicly) by most Part IIs.

Standing back from the specifics, the future over the next decade or so is likely to throw up repeated stalemates in global multilateral fora. Quests for global, top-down, everyone-in treaties may not be abandoned, but more progress is likely on more fragmentary regimes, comprised of narrow agreements on specific issues, and on diffusion of policy norms for shifting market incentives in globally sustainable directions (such as the norm of a tax on carbon emissions coupled with tax credits for energy efficient investments by households and firms, and likewise for a regulatory change to require investment banking to be carried out by unlimited liability partnerships).

Also, we can expect states to devote more effort to constructing regional economic governance regimes. Already several initiatives are under way in regions of the global South. The early Chiang Mai Initiative has more recently been joined by the South Summit (at heads of government level, held every five years since the first meeting in Havana in 2000), the Bank of the South (due to start lending in 2011), IBSA (annual meetings of the heads of government of India, Brazil and South Africa), UNASUR (ministerial meetings among Latin American countries to coordinate on matters of finance, social policy, defence and more). Brazil is taking a leading role in promoting South–South coordination; China is bringing African countries into common dialogues; India is more ambivalent, being less willing than Brazil and China to court U.S. disapproval.

The growth of fragmentary global and regional regimes will – hopefully – induce efforts in global fora to make the rules more consistent with each other (an analogy is "middleware", a type of software which enables different systems to communicate without the need for single unified systems). Many, including José Antonio Ocampo (in this volume) see great value in these regional governance regimes as the building blocks for international economic coordination. Much depends on what happens to China's foreign policy as the economy grows and closes the never-seen-before gap between its high ranking in terms of aggregate size (second largest GDP in the world) and low ranking in terms of average income (about 100th when measured at Gross National Income per head using the World Bank's Atlas method of adjusting market exchange rates); and as the polity slowly becomes more democratic. As these trends mature China is likely – hopefully – to cease playing the double game of a superpower in some contexts and an impoverished developing country in others and to assume more international responsibilities; and the West is likely to cease viewing China's international behaviour through the prism of scepticism and distrust.

Notes

1 Professor of Political Economy, London School of Economics. This paper builds on "The state of the World Bank" (Wade, 2010b); and on fieldwork inside the World Bank and the IMF in June and September 2010, conducted together with Jakob Vestergaard of the Danish Institute of International Studies (see Vestergaard, 2011). The author would like to thank Shelley Marshall and Sanjay Pinto for their helpful comments and editing.

2 This is according to Volcker at a private lunch with the author at Princeton University in 1990 (when we were both teaching at the Woodrow Wilson School).

3 Personal communication.

4 Personal communication.

5 One indicator of the extent of Western normative dominance is the voting coincidence score, which measures the amount of support a state receives from other states in the General Assembly. In the late 1990s, the E.U. and the U.S. received around 70 per cent support for their positions on human rights. By 2009–10, the score had fallen to only 40-42 per cent. China and Russia increased their score from around 40 per cent

and 60 per cent in the late 1990s, respectively, to around 70 per cent today (Gowan and Brantner, 2010).

6 In a longer version of this paper, I also consider the expanded G20 and reforms to the IMF: see *Politics and Society* for 2011, volume 39 (3).

7 In the World Bank, the 187 governors delegate their governance role to the "Development Committee" composed of finance or development ministers representing the countries and constituencies of countries which occupy the 24 seats on the board; and the latter delegate the day-to-day governance to the "Board of Executive Directors" (EDs), or Board for short, composed of civil service representatives of the same countries and constituencies, resident in Washington.

8 Some informants suggest a third reason, to do specifically with Zoellick's reluctance. He is a Bush government appointee (he and James Baker were the key figures who swung the Florida recount in favour of Bush), and is unlikely to be offered a second presidential term by the Obama government unless the failure to reappoint him jeopardizes the U.S. monopoly of the position. According to these informants, he has signalled that he may see his future lying outside multilateral development.

9 The work on the reform package built on ongoing work by a special Board subcommittee. After the inglorious end of the Wolfowitz presidency in 2007, the Board established an ad hoc committee to conduct an investigation into the Wolfowitz affair, which revealed flaws in management of the Board and the Bank that went far beyond the affair. So the Board established a standing committee to propose changes in the nuts and bolts of Board operations, Board–staff relations, and Board–president relations. But until the global financial crisis and the need for a CGI nobody was paying much attention to its work.

10 This discussion refers to voting shares in the IBRD, the near-commercial lending arm of the Bank, as distinct from IDA, the soft loan arm.

11 To make the voice shift within months was quick by the standards of Japan's rise from fifth biggest shareholder to second biggest (Wade, 1996).

12 In the IDA soft-loan lending arm, the high income countries, post-reform, have 61.18 per cent, in the International Finance Corporation, 66.24 per cent. The low income countries have 4.46 per cent in the IBRD, 11.31 per cent in the IDA, and 3.09 per cent in the IFC (BWI, 2010a; 2010b).

13 Such ad hoc-ery is hardly new. For an account of the same in the original allocation of IMF quotas see Mikesell (1994).

14 On fragmented and comprehensive regimes see Keohane and Victor (2011). On the belief–action relationship at different "levels" of learning see Spiro (1966).

15 The issue is complicated by rumours that Zoellick is playing a double game: keeping up pressure on Bank member countries for a second term at the World Bank under the banner of "the last American president", while also lobbying the Republican party to be appointed U.S. Treasury Secretary if a Republican wins the race to the White House in 2012.

10 Gender-equitable public policy

Challenges to policy design amidst contestations in a multi-polar world

Marina Durano

Possibilities and hopes from the global economic crisis

Many commentators see the current global economic and financial crisis as spawning opportunities for reform and transformation for a better world. Specifically reacting to the origins of the crisis, a "Bretton Woods moment" has been declared by those seeking structural changes in the international financial architecture. Others have declared the demise of the neoliberal consensus, which was headlined by policies promoting privatization, liberalization and deregulation, and the implementation of structural adjustment programs during the latter decades of the twentieth century.

Feminist activists have been among those voicing such hopes. At the same time, however, they acknowledge the complexity behind the contestations of power over global economic governance. These contestations define the parameters within which the promotion of gender equity and women's empowerment can be facilitated by the global development architecture. These contestations present challenges to the design of gender-equitable public policies at all levels of governance. Will the twenty-first century give birth to a better world like a phoenix rising from the ashes? This paper begins to outline the political atmosphere in which the struggles for change towards a gender-equitable world are being waged. The paper offers recommendations for initiating the first steps towards such a new direction.

This chapter deploys institutional analysis to map the challenges and future directions for gender equity and women's empowerment amidst ongoing political contestations at the global level. Section 2 demonstrates the importance of examining the interactions of market relations and gender relations when assessing the impact of economic policies and the global crisis. Section 3 notes that the combination of weak state capabilities and narrow policy space makes it difficult to pursue reforms, especially for developing countries. Section 4 offers tentative steps towards gender-equitable public policies, noting the asymmetries of power that currently characterize the global order. Section 5 concludes with a return to the role of institutions in development and the embeddedness of women's empowerment in these structures.

Rules of the game: market relations and gender relations

The importance of the role of institutions in economic development cannot be overstated, and is increasingly recognized by economists and economic policy-makers (Chang, 2007; Heilbroner and Milberg, 1995; North, 1990). The set of formal and informal rules that govern markets are meant to "create, regulate, stabilize and legitimize" (Rodrik, 2002: 3) these markets, whether domestic or global. The institutions that underpin markets, however, do not exist in isolation from social relations (Polanyi, 1944), including gender relations. According to Cagatay and Erturk (2004), "gender relations refer to the sum of social norms, conventions and practices which regulate the multifaceted relationships between men and women in a given society at a given time". The system of social relations and social structures that place men in positions of domination, oppression and exploitation over women has been termed as patriarchy (Walby, 1989). Beneria (2003) and Folbre (1999) add that patriarchal norms are also embedded in capitalist and other social orders:

> Patriarchal norms, gender inequality, and women's oppression can be intrinsically embedded in different forms of capitalist institutions, but they also exist in other economic and social formations. Gender-related hierarchies have often been reconstituted with institutional and systemic changes. This implies that any alternative analysis needs to incorporate the full range of factors that explain oppression, inequalities, and discriminatory practices tied to gender socialization and women's position in society. The same can be said for other hierarchical or class-based constructions/divisions such as those associated with race and ethnicity, colonial, and post-colonial tensions, and North–South divisions.
>
> (Beneria, 2003: 15)

Across societal structures, activities associated with provisioning[1] and care[2] have commonly been socially ascribed to women (Folbre and Bittman, 2004; Folbre, 1994; Picchio, 1992). The eventual distribution[3] of the work burden relating to provisioning within a household depends on the interaction between the norms of gender relations of the society in which the household belongs, and more specific features of intra-household bargaining and negotiations. Intra-household negotiations among household members involve decisions over the distribution of material and labour resources for survival, maintenance and flourishing. These decisions are never undertaken in a setting of equality among household members, so the outcomes of the decisions are not guaranteed to be fair.[4]

Social reproduction, however, is not only about what women and girls are expected to do in individual households; it is also about how a society organizes itself to provide care to its members. The ideal is often viewed as one in which provisioning for care is performed by both men and women, and is the combined work of the different social sectors, including states, markets or households (and non-profit sectors) (Razavi, 2007; UNIFEM, 2000).

Discussions of the consequences of the current global economic crisis – and associated policies for social response and economic recovery – are incomplete without recognition of the embeddedness described above. It is this interaction between institutions regulating markets and institutions regulating gender relations that defy the assumption of gender-neutrality in macroeconomics and in economic development. Elson and Cagatay (2000), Seguino and Grown (2006) and van Staveren *et al.* (2007), among others, have already integrated gender analysis into macroeconomic theories and policies, demonstrating how markets are structured in gendered ways. Sen (2010) reminds us of the variety of interactions that need to be taken into account as we try to determine the social impact of policies and programs.

Despite such analytical advances by heterodox and feminist economists, these kinds of concerns about market embeddedness have not yet carried forward into mainstream policy discourse. Certainly, in the Group of 20 (G20) Leaders' statements, there are some broad references to the negative social impacts of the global economic crisis and the need to respond to these concerns. In the G20's London statement, for example, there was mention of building a "fair and family friendly labor market for both women and men" (G20, 2009: 26). However, the concrete responses outlined in the communiqué have not specifically addressed these concerns. Elson (2009) and Horn (2009) are among a handful of writers who try to address how the global financial crisis might shift the boundaries of responsibilities among major social organizations, especially in terms of responding to adverse social impacts of the crisis. The impact on unpaid care work is especially important in their analysis.

Policy space in a multi-polar world: patriarchal states and global power structures

Given the constitutive powers that states wield over the market, the state must take into consideration the interactions between market relations and gender relations when it considers appropriate constitutive underpinnings for markets. It is not clear, however, what capacity the state possesses to design and implement reforms based on analysis of this kind. There are two main reasons for such doubt. The first is that the state has been criticized as patriarchal: this will be dealt with in Section 5. The second concern is that there are many "weak states" possessing low capacities for pursuing development goals and objectives. This section reviews some key reasons to doubt the capacity of developing country states to put in place effective public policy reforms that address entrenched gender inequalities within existing institutions of market embedding.

State capacity, particularly in developing countries, is often severely constrained.[5] Developing countries have been characterized as "predatory", "post-colonial", and "weak", implying, at best, that these states do not have the means to undertake reform and, at worst, that these states have no interest in reform. Yet the same governments face the pressure of delivering on various internationally agreed development goals (Mkandawire, 2001). Of particular importance to this paper, these governments are also charged with the responsibility of tackling interactions between market relations and gender relations.

But even when a "developmental" state attempts to assert policies consistent with such aspirations, its policy space may be limited by its international commitments. Limits to policy space have been discussed in relation to international trade agreements under the World Trade Organization (WTO) (Hamwey, 2005; Chang and Evans, 2000); macroeconomic policy options (Ocampo and Vos, 2008); and use of policy conditions by international financial institutions (UNCTAD, 2007; Kanbur, 2005). Much has already been written about the asymmetrical power relationships between donor and recipient, and these have not disappeared.[6] But geo-politics aside, the impact on macroeconomic policies resulting from shifts of official development assistance towards policy-based support and away from project assistance (Hjertholm and White, 1998; Gupta *et al.*, 2006) can also influence available policy space.

A comparison of economic stimulus packages in developed versus developing countries reveals important weaknesses in state capacity among the latter. Such inequalities are manifested in at least three ways. First, developed countries have managed to pull together massive resources for fiscal stimulus packages, particularly focusing on financial measures to save their banking systems (Khatiwada, 2009). In contrast, fiscal discipline combined with a view that their economies were only indirectly affected has tied the hands of many developing countries, especially those with large external liabilities, preventing them from responding on such a massive scale. Weisbrot *et al.* (2009) and Akyuz (2009) add that the International Monetary Fund (IMF) has put many of its client governments on a pro-cyclical path[7] by keeping monetary policy tight even as it takes a relatively less conservative stance with fiscal policy. Of course, such constraints have varied significantly across countries. For example, as Ocampo points out in this volume, China did not have a financial sector in crisis and had the foreign exchange and fiscal space to pursue aggressive Keynesian policies. Most Asian countries also adopted expansionary policies after the crisis.

Second, Baldwin and Evenett (2009) found protectionist policies were adopted by developed countries using trade subsidies, while developing countries tend to use import controls. Third, the G20 agreed for the IMF to execute a Special Drawing Rights allocation of approximately $500 billion that will be distributed according to each country's equity shares in the IMF, which means that most of this money will go to developed countries.[8] According to Woods (2009), the IMF approved SDR48.8 billion in new loans as of July 2009. About 82 per cent went to Romania, Ukraine, Hungary, Belarus, Latvia and Iceland. Only 1.6 per cent went to countries in Africa. Developing countries outside of the European neighborhood have not approached the IMF to borrow, except for middle-income country governments such as Ghana, Pakistan and Costa Rica.

Narrow policy space combined with weak state capabilities make it difficult for reform conditions to emerge within developing countries. Broader political battles over a globally coordinated response to the global economic crisis are encapsulated by the developing countries' demand for more policy space.[9] This demand for increased policy space may be interpreted as an implicit demand by developing country governments to secure sovereignty.[10] It is an assertion of political independence over the range of policies that these governments can pursue.

But these North–South divisions are never clear cut, especially when a realignment of states sees the increasing political influence of large, middle-income, and systemically significant countries. That there was already a trend towards greater regional integration was clear even in the early days of the WTO. Today, Brazil, China, India and South Africa have made themselves known as states with influence in the multilateral system. They have also increased efforts to work with other developing countries in terms of trade flows,[11] aid flows[12] and monetary arrangements (Vols and Caliari, 2010). Brazil has also held meetings with African leaders, seeking increased cooperation.[13]

Although the Group of 8 (G8) continues to function, with the onset of the global crisis the G20 became more prominent as a power structure defining the content and direction of multilateral political and economic relations.[14] The more influential multilateral institutions that are able to set the agenda for macroeconomic policies have been the World Bank, the IMF and the WTO.[15] The debates among diplomatic circles in New York at the United Nations reflect the preference of mostly developed countries to retain this configuration. The United Nations (UN), through the Review Conference of the Monterrey Consensus in December 2008 and the Conference on World Financial and Economic Crisis and its Impact on Development in June 2009, attempted to change the balance of power by becoming a legitimate space for discussions on global economic governance and the international financial architecture. Both conferences generated contentious intergovernmental debate, and consensus-building towards an outcome document proved difficult. The UN was already deep into its own reform process, seeking efficiency in its delivery mechanisms and operational activities. It was asserted by some of the developed countries that growth and development agendas were not appropriately under the UN's purview since expertise belonged elsewhere, such as the World Bank, the IMF and the WTO. Durano *et al.* (2009) argued that these reform processes have undermined the ability of the UN and its specialized agencies and programs to devise alternative proposals. Indeed, the G20 leaders chose to use the Bretton Woods Institutions (BWIs)[16] as the channels for implementing their global response to the crisis. This occurred despite the fact that the UN has the broadest membership of nation states, affording it greater political legitimacy than the G20.

As Wade shows with regard to the World Bank, Gallagher illustrates in relation to the WTO, and Buckley argues with regards to the IMF in this volume, these new poles of power have not yet produced significant changes in the policy prescriptions proposed by the World Bank, the IMF, the WTO or within UN negotiations. Indeed, despite reforms to governance structures in these organizations, especially the IMF, the status quo power structures remain in place (Woods, 2009). Gu *et al.* (2007), in attempting to analyze the impact of the rise of China, reaches indeterminate conclusions. Within the United Nations the follow-up to the New

York Conference on the crisis mentioned above has been held up or pushed aside. A report of the President of the Economic and Social Council revealed that country groupings have raised reservations regarding some of the aspects for follow-up (UNECOSOC, 2009). So while the UN may carry legitimacy through its broad membership and its normative ascendancy, its political relevance in global economic governance is least recognized by its own member states.

Overlapping capacity constraints of these kinds place important limits on the ability of developing country governments to implement reforms directed towards more gender-equitable public policies.

Tentative steps towards gender-equitable public policies

Against this global backdrop of intense power asymmetries, the pursuit of gender-equitable public policies is fraught with obstacles. This section can only offer tentative proposals to take us to closer to this goal. The central objective is to search for policy measures that create behavioral incentives to change the balance of responsibilities for social provisioning and care so that these are more evenly shared among the major social organizations – households, states, markets and non-profit sectors. Efforts at rebalancing require strengthened state capacities founded upon an economy that supports domestic resource mobilization. Strong domestic resource mobilization not only secures financing for state-led provisioning and care, but also pushes against the political influence of aid in global economic governance structures. Social welfare literature, particularly those segments concerned with feminist critique, has tended to favor provisioning by states, rather than other social organizations (Razavi, 2007).

There are three core elements of what we might refer to as gender-equitable public policy: (1) expanding policy space for the implementation of industrialization strategies that reduce gender-based segregation in employment generation; (2) designing automatic macroeconomic stabilizers that secure financing for social protection while reducing output volatility; and (3) a rebalancing of power among the Bretton Woods Institutions and the United Nations by confronting the politics of aid. The first two elements would help to contribute to the strengthening of domestic productive capacity that is inclusive of the roles and contributions of socially reproductive activities, especially those performed by women and girls, rather than taking advantage of these. Steps towards gender equity are taken when the planning for industrialization and economic development reduces the concentration of women's employment in a few occupations and industries or in export-oriented production. The second element also highlights the need for macroeconomic policy to secure financing support for publicly provided services in order for the state to effectively fulfill its obligations. At the same time, these stabilizers lower threats to unemployment and reductions in income through economic cycles. The last element would create more equitable global economic governance structures supportive of new and innovative policy directions so that the first two elements can be pursued vigorously. Each of these elements is discussed in turn below.

Expand policy space for industrialization strategies that generate gender-equitable employment

Alternatives to unhampered trade liberalization, such as those discussed in Chang and Grabel (2004), Lall (2001 and 2003), Chang (2003), Rodrik (2001) and Amsden (this volume), offer convincing approaches. However, these have yet to use any gender perspective in their formulations. Such analysis discusses upgrading of the technological content and skills content of production combined with appropriate incentive structures, clearly noting the role of institutions. However, the chosen industries may not equally benefit women, whether in terms of employment or products and services. For example, the choice of which industry to develop can have a gender bias in itself because the favored industries may not necessarily be crucial for social reproduction (such as the car industry as opposed to choosing the education sector or women's role in food production). Moreover, gender biases can exist in processes of skill formation and in the access and use of technology (Anker *et al.*, 2003). Alternative policies must be examined further in order to take gender concerns into account. For some time now feminists have been critical of the manner in which women have become incorporated into many export-oriented industries because of the employment trade-off with poor working conditions, as well as widespread neglect of the dynamic relationships among the genders within their respective households (especially in relation to the performance of unpaid care work) as women increase their labor force participation (Razavi, 1999). Others have criticized the exploitation of the gender wage gap as the basis for export competitiveness (Seguino, 2000a and 2000b). It is not only employment generation and the decent work agenda that needs to be pursued, as heterodox economists have argued strongly. We must also pay attention to gendered social structures that shape employment choices and employment access (Floro and Meurs, 2009; Heintz, 2006).

Strengthening automatic macroeconomic stabilizers to finance social protection while minimizing output volatility

Debates about the role of monetary and fiscal policy in growth and development continue to characterize approaches to crisis mitigation and resolution. Alternative approaches point to a reorientation towards output stability rather than price stability (Spiegel, 2007). Arguments have centred on counter-cyclical fiscal expansion and the use of capital controls.[17] Capital controls are argued to be beneficial to women by Singh and Zammit (2000) and Seguino and Grown (2006). It would be especially useful if these approaches were complemented by a broader structure of automatic macroeconomic stabilizers.

Automatic macroeconomic stabilizers strengthen the link between macroeconomic policy and social policy. These stabilizers are designed to raise more money as the economy grows, thus helping to finance social spending that is expected to expand during a downturn. Fatas and Mihov (2001) show international evidence of a reduction in output volatility due to an increase in government spending through automatic stabilizers. Automatic macroeconomic stabilizers can reduce the pressure for policies to have a "commodification bias", where public services are no longer tax-funded, resulting in a shift toward private market-sourced services (Elson and Cagatay, 2000). Funding for social programs becomes more secure under a setting of progressive tax measures, with revenues contributing to social stability funds. These funds could be tapped during recessions in a counter-cyclical manner, particularly if the public services that receive funding are labor-intensive. Output volatility would be further minimized. The availability and accessibility of stabilization funds might even reduce future debt burdens by reducing future borrowing needs.

Confronting the politics of donor countries and their aid programs

This section highlights two aspects in the politics of aid that are important for the promotion of gender equity and women's empowerment. The first consideration is in the contentious nature of intergovernmental negotiations within the United Nations, which makes it a challenging environment for political work on gender equity and women's empowerment. The second consideration has to do with upholding the normative standards set by the UN and valued by women.

Diplomats from European donor countries have been consistent allies in promoting gender equality and women's empowerment, while developing countries that make up the Group of 77, and China, are much less open to these ideals. Women's groups and networks, therefore, find themselves caught in this North-South trap, where one power paradigm, that is unequal state power, is asserted over another, which is unequal gender power structures. Some women's organizations lean towards strengthening alliances with Europe because of the shared goals on gender equity, but this means that progressive economic demands are prone to be set aside which then incurs the ire of developing country governments and bolsters their negative position against women's groups and networks. This approach to alliance work is not sustainable in light of discussions in Section 3. An examination of markets that takes into account market relations and gender relations is a step towards overcoming the adverse political position of women's groups and networks.

The realignments discussed in Section 3 have yet to create potential for opening up the political arena for feminist development alternatives. This trend raises risks in the political work necessary to advance gender equality and women's empowerment. Civil society organizations, including women's organizations and feminists, continue to engage with the UN as it still is the most representative, transparent and open of intergovernmental spaces (Durano *et al.*, 2009). This legitimacy is enhanced further when noting that normative standards for gender equality have been pursued under its auspices, most notably the Convention on the Elimination of all forms of Discrimination Against Women, the Fourth World Conference on Women's Platform for Action and the International

Conference on Population and Development Programme of Action. The risks are important in the face of the establishment of UN WOMEN – known formally as UN Entity for Gender Equality and the Empowerment of Women – in 2011.

How can this new entity navigate the political debates on macroeconomic policy directions and responses to global economic crisis in a multilateral system characterized by the politics of weak and patriarchal states against dominant donor countries?

Institution-building for gender-equitable development

The gender-equitable public policies that need to be pursued imply an institutional approach to development (Evans, 2005; 2007). This is not just about organizational structures and processes, as often discussed by those analyzing markets as institutions. It is also about culture and norms, as Evans (2005) argues. Therefore, the pursuit of gender-equitable public policies would require institution-building of the type that involves a reconstruction of market institutions and of culture and norms.

Reconstruction necessitates a discussion of power. As Evans argues: "the role of power in shaping both organizational structure and culture is central" (2005: 91). In pursuit of this argument, the notion of women's empowerment comes to the fore. Kabeer, in defining women's empowerment, refers to "the process by which those who have been denied the ability to make strategic life choices acquire such an ability" (2002: 437). Kabeer's discussion of women's empowerment raises the "interdependence of individual and structural change in processes of empowerment" (2002: 461).

> The studies here suggest a role for individual agency in challenging gender inequality but they also point to the importance of larger structural change. In a context where cultural values constrain women's ability to make strategic life choices, structural inequalities cannot be addressed by individuals alone. We have cited evidence that individual women can, and do, act against the norm, but their impact on the situation of women in general is likely to remain limited and they may have to pay a high price for their autonomy. The project of women's empowerment is dependent on collective solidarity in the public arena as well as individual assertiveness in the private. Women's organizations and social movements in particular have an important role to play in creating the conditions for change and in reducing the costs for the individual.
>
> (Kabeer, 2002: 457)

When feminists argue that states are patriarchal structures with implications for the notion and practice of citizenship (Pateman, 2000; Rai, 1996), this needs to be appreciated as a demand for institution-building that is aimed at creating enabling structures for the empowerment of peoples, especially of women and girls.

Evans (2005), citing Sen (1999), points out that it is only through deliberative democratic institutions that this identification of development goals can be "adequately defined". The arguments of Kabeer (2002) and Sen (1989) represent important qualifications to the notion of "adequacy" in light of the structural parameters that define women's choices. Evans further argues that "[t]he ability of communities and societies to define their goals is certainly the most basic kind of institutional technology. Without it, the acquisition of other institutional techniques is unlikely to bear fruit" (Evans, 2005: 97).

The tentative policy directions mentioned in Section 4 require a legitimation process attached to "messy and continuous deliberative involvement of the citizenry in the setting of economic priorities" (Evans, 2005: 102). Indeed, Razavi (2007) acknowledged the role of organized social forces in moving the boundaries of responsibilities among the major social organizations. There is, therefore, some institution-building that is additionally required, in which the focus is the establishment of "public mores that legitimate contestation and collective struggles" (Evans, 2005: 103), both within the nation state and, I argue, also in international political settings. The realignment of responsibilities for caring and provisioning in itself removes barriers to mobility and voice for those that carry these burdens, allowing for increased opportunities to practice citizenship and collective action. The social choice of gender equity and women's empowerment and the tentative policies that aim to contribute towards achieving these outcomes must arise from participatory processes. This broader role for institutions may also serve to strengthen state capacities for provisioning and care. By extension, it could take us closer to the end of the patriarchal state.

Notes

1 Feminist economists with critical perspectives on development thought have expanded definitions of the scope and purpose of an economy. According to this view, the purpose of an economy involves provisioning to benefit human lives rather than searching for the most efficient allocation of resources to maximize productive output (Cagatay and Erturk, 2004; Beneria, 2003). In the literature that views development as the guaranteeing of entitlements and capabilities, economics goes beyond the question of how best to produce, towards that of why there is production: that is, to provide for "the realization of fully human lives" (Nussbaum, 2004: 13). Provisioning for a lifetime across generations requires humans to spend at least part of their time in any of the three economic spheres of activity, which are production, finance, and social reproduction (Cagatay and Erturk, 2004). Thus, in this sense, production is only one aspect of provisioning.

2 This is sometimes referred to as socially reproductive activity.

3 There is variation in the intensity of care work done by men and women across different types of activities and across societies. Time use surveys indicate that women spend at least twice as much time in unpaid care work compared to men (Budlender, 2008).

4 Sen (1989) notes that perceptions of the value of one's well-being relative to other members of the household, and perceptions of the value of one's contributions to the household relative to other members, can define inequality within that household. Perceptions, he argues, are socially constructed so that women's ready acceptance of being of lesser value than men induces their cooperation even in a setting of inequality.

5 Feminists have criticized the trend toward marketization of governance following a period of structural adjustment programs. Taylor (2000), for example, argues that

budget deficits, corruption, and inefficiency have been used as justifications for the retreat of public service and resort to privatization.

6 See series of papers produced by the Oxford Global Economic Governance Programme that discusses this issue in the context of the implementation of the 2005 Paris Declaration on Aid Effectiveness. See also Woods (2007) for a discussion on the War on Terror and its influence on official development assistance.

7 Woods (2009) presents a less critical assessment, while the IMF (2009d, 2009e) actively defends these IMF policies. Weisbrot (2009) offers a reply to the IMF's defense.

8 Behind the policy conditionalities associated with multilateral financial institutions is a decision making structure based on equity shares controlled by developed countries. These undemocratic structures have become a symbol of the unequal global distribution of political power among nation states.

9 See Paragraph 18 of United Nations General Assembly Resolution 63/303.

10 Contrast this with the assertions of sovereignty in the context of political independence from colonial ties.

11 Hudson (2009) reported on a recent meeting of the Shanghai Cooperation Organization (membership includes Russia, China, Tajikistan, Kazakhstan, Kyrgystan, Uzbekistan with observer status for Iran, India, Pakistan, and Mongolia). One of this organization's recent decisions included meeting with Brazil to begin talks focused on the possibility of using each other's currencies, including the Chinese renminbi, for international trade in a clear attempt to move away from the U.S. dollar as the preferred currency for international payments.

12 Hogg (2011), in a report filed with BBC News, wrote that the China Development Bank and the China Export Import Bank have lent more than the World Bank to developing countries, citing a *Financial Times* report. China also openly sought a reform of the global reserve system (Helleiner, 2010) and this debate was prominently played out in a recent G20 Leaders' Meeting in South Korea.

13 See also www.ibsa-trilateral.org, a website that hosts a trilateral development initiatives among India, Brazil, and South Africa to promote South-South cooperation and exchange; it began in 2003.

14 Since the start of the new millennium, the G8 began to invite leaders from middle-income countries, such as South Africa and, later on, China, Brazil and India, among other countries. It has also invited more and more multilateral institutions and international organizations in recent years, adding to the United Nations, International Monetary Fund, World Bank and World Trade Organization, which attended since the late 1990s. Leaders of the G20 nations first met in Washington, D.C., in 2008 and met again in London in April and in Pittsburgh in September 2009 to outline and follow up on their responses to the crisis.

15 Recall debates around the Washington Consensus and the Augmented Washington Consensus.

16 Although, in effect, as Woods (2009) explains, it is the IMF that received the bulk of new resources through the SDR allocations. Meanwhile, the WB is fund-raising for its multi-donor trust funds and is using its most recent IBRD/IDA replenishment to fund its Vulnerability Financing Facility Framework, under which programs and projects in response to the crisis are financed.

17 See Epstein, Grabel and K.S. Jomo (2003) for an extensive discussion.

11 Developmental globalization and equity-enhancing multilateralism

Kevin P. Gallagher[1]

Introduction

By the turn of the century global trade talks seemed destined to raise the roof of low politics, where international political economy has long been relegated. Large street protests accompanied negotiations, heads of state and hopefuls discussed trade in public and on campaign trails at least as much as security, and the media followed it all in paparazzi-like fashion.

What a difference a decade makes. By 2011 global trade talks at the World Trade Organization (WTO) had come to a complete standstill. None of the major players – the United States, Europe, emerging markets or global justice protestors – had been willing to significantly engage since at best 2008.

For the first time in the history of global trade negotiations, rather than a clash among Western interests, deadlock among negotiators has been a function of a clash between industrialized countries and developing countries with new-found economic power. The seeds of this clash can be found in the Uruguay Round (1986 to 1994), where a deal was struck whereby the industrialized nations traded market access to their large and growing economies for domestic regulatory changes in the developing world in the areas of investment law, intellectual property, services and beyond (Narlikar, 2003).

To what extent is the global trading regime reducing the ability of nation states to pursue policies for financial stability and economic growth, and what political factors explain such changes in policy space over time, across different types of trade treaties, and across nations?

Interestingly, this chapter finds that there was a significant constraining of policy space under the Uruguay Round, but there is still a significant amount of room to maneuver for developing countries. However, many regional and bilateral deals, especially with the United States, severely restrict the ability of developing nations to amply deploy a range of development strategies for stability and growth.

In the latest round of WTO talks, many emerging market and developing economies saw the benefits of further global trade liberalization as relatively small, and the costs as being quite significant in terms of the loss of "policy space" they see as necessary to develop their economies or stay in office. The WTO's standstill can thus be seen as a relative success from a development standpoint. The WTO as an institution for settling disputes and monitoring remains intact, but it does not further impede regulatory changes at the domestic level that are politically and sometimes economically costly. And with respect to intellectual property rules and public health at least, the developing world has been able to gain back some policy space.

Such findings lead to a characterization of twenty-first century trade politics as a "clash of globalizations" whereby developed nations see it as in their interest to promote a global trade regime that helps solidify and expand their current (or static) comparative advantage in capital and knowledge-intensive goods and services. Many developing nations see it as in their interest to build upon their current comparative advantage in primary commodities and light manufacturing and expand into new, more value-added intensive areas where someday they *might* have a comparative advantage.

The key difference between the recent round of talks – referred to as the Doha Round – and past rounds, is that developing nations have had the economic and political power to refuse industrialized country proposals and to put forth an alternative set of negotiating demands that industrialized countries had to take seriously. As this chapter will sketch out, economic power of course isn't the only factor that explains the difference, but it is key among a confluence of factors that also include institutional structure, domestic politics, currency fluctuations, and ideas about globalization.

These two approaches to globalization can each be seen as rational. Each has been successful in maintaining or raising living standards for their respective citizens. This at least partly explains why the WTO is in deadlock, why the WTO in relative terms still grants developing nations relatively more policy space (than North-South bilateral investment treaties (BITs) and preferential trade agreements (PTAs)) to pursue their own development strategies, and why regional and bilateral trade treaties have proliferated to such a degree that they may threaten the global trade regime – a regime that has just started to generate more equal outcomes.

Varieties of globalization and the trade regime

This section of the chapter draws on the concepts of "embedded liberalism" and "varieties of capitalism" to develop a new framework titled "varieties of globalization" that may help us understand global trade negotiations.

During the post-war era many countries deployed a variant of what John Ruggie (1983) called "embedded liberalism" – global trade and investment liberalization "embedded" within national-level institutional frameworks to promote domestic economic growth and financial stability. As is the case in the industrialized world, where there are numerous "varieties" of industrial capitalism, there have been varying regimes of embeddedness across the developing world as well. The key difference between embedded liberalism in the industrialized countries and in the developing world is that, in the industrialized north, the interest was to *maintain* a high level of industrialization and stability, whereas, in the developing world, the goal was to *obtain* a satisfactory standard of living and stability for their populations. As countries seek to re-embed markets in the twenty-first century, these different goals persist. Such goals translate into different sets of interests and negotiation stances in trade politics.

Similar to the experiences of industrialized countries, embedded liberalism lost momentum in the developing world beginning in the 1980s (moreso in Latin American than in East Asia). For close to two decades the "Washington Consensus" approach characterized much of developing country economic policy – an approach that stresses the liberalization of trade and investment alongside the general reduction of the role of the state in economic affairs. Though many nations still espouse the Washington Consensus approach, some nations such as Brazil, South Africa, India, China, Malaysia and others began to re-embed markets with state activity to diversify economies and reach global markets with the goal of raising living standards. These nations represent a variety of globalization that has not received much attention in academic and policy circles. Indeed, some treatments of China and Brazil attribute the growth of those nations to "globalizing", although both nations have done so with a mix of industrial policy and state-facilitated macro-management for development.

There is an enormous literature in political economy circles known as the "varieties of capitalism" literature. The originators of this body of work, Peter Hall and David Soskice (2001), focused mainly on the West and keenly categorized industrial capitalism as having "liberal market economies" that are more market-based (U.S., U.K.) and "coordinated market economies" where the state plays a stronger role in coordinating markets activity (Scandanavia, Germany, Japan).

The core of the "varieties of capitalism" literature is largely focused on varieties of industrial capitalism in the West. However, a related discourse has been occurring among political economists of economic development, albeit under a different guise (standout exceptions are Schneider, 2009 and Breslin, 2007). In the 1980s and the 1990s there was significant attention paid by political economists on the role of the state in economic development (the classic summary volume is Woo-Cumings, 1999). This literature, which focused on East Asian nations beginning with Japan, as well some Latin American nations (especially Brazil and Mexico to the 1980s), suggested that:

> In states that were late to industrialize, the state itself led the industrialization drive, that is, it took on developmental functions. These two differing orientations toward private economic activities, the regulatory orientation and the developmental orientation, produced two different kinds of business-government relationships. The United States is a good example of a state in which the regulatory orientation predominates, whereas Japan is a good example of a state in which the developmental orientation predominates. A regulatory, or market-rational, state concerns itself with the forms and procedures – the rules, if you will – of economic competition, but it does not concern itself with substantive matters.
>
> (Johnson, 1982: 19)

The two literatures have never been neatly knitted together, but a global look at economies and the role of the state would put many developmental states into a separate "variety" of capitalism. In today's light, it should be stressed that globalization of trade, or at least export-orientation, was the key goal of the most successful developmental states in Asia. And the most significant emerging market players in the WTO and beyond are at least hybrid developmental states. While many of those nations that were developmental states in the past are not so today, such as South Korea, a new crop has arisen. Today, China is the exemplar developmental state, and Brazil, South Africa and India today are lesser variants as well. It should also be noted that developmentalism is not simply a state-centric "decision" but the outcome of a political process. In the case of Brazil, for instance, decision-makers in the government who subscribe to a more developmentalist perspective are bolstered by (or in office because of) a domestic industrial or service class that cannot yet compete with its industrialized country counterparts. The chapter by Amsden in this volume discusses the "new industrial policy" deployed by certain nations, both in terms of global trade policy and by securing the domestic market.

This "variety" of globalization – one where developing countries seek to integrate with the world economy in order to achieve a higher standard of living by having the state play a key role diversifying their product and export base – stands in contrast with the liberal market economy model and to some extent with the coordinated market economy models found in the West. In parallel to the description of embedded liberalism above, Western nations seek to maintain and expand global markets for those sectors where they enjoy an existing (or static) comparative advantage. Developing countries, at least some of them, seek to change the underlying structure of their economies over time and someday gain a comparative advantage in a broader set of sectors. The state may play a key role in such diversification.

What is clear is that liberal market economies pursue the most liberal trading arrangements, as do coordinated market economies from Europe, though to a lesser extent (see Gallagher and Thrasher, 2010). Western nations are seeking to consolidate and expand their current comparative advantages on a global level. Let us call them "consolidating globalizers". Meanwhile, poor and middle-income countries in other regions have a different variant of globalizing capitalism. They are "developmental globalizers" that are still working the right mix of markets and states in order to achieve higher standards of living.

Figure 11.1 shows that developing countries have been growing faster than their industrialized counterparts since the turn of the century. The developing world "took off" in terms of gross domestic product (GDP) per capita growth from 2000 to 2008, then dipped as the industrialized world did due to the financial crisis. Developing countries grew 4.7 per cent per annum in per capita terms, whereas the industrialized nations grew at 1.5 per cent. Since the trough in 2009, developing countries have grown 5.5 per cent versus 0.46 per cent in the north. This picture fits with the story told by Wade and others in this volume about rising multipolarity in the world economy.

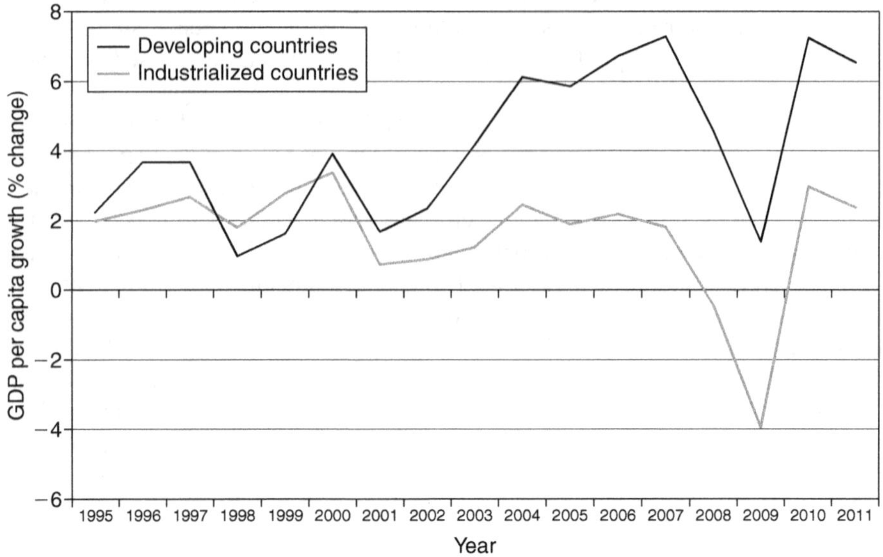

Figure 11.1 Developing country incomes grow and recover faster (source: *World Bank Development Indicators*, 2011).

A significant amount of this growth was due to China's emergence in the world economy and its subsequent demand for developing country goods, and the price effect that comes with such demand. China's growth is at least in part a function of developmental state policies, and other large emerging and developing nations such as India, Brazil, and South Africa – all the most significant WTO players – could be called neo-developmental states as well. We could call this variety "developmental globalization". All of these nations have been slow to open their capital accounts to foreign investment, and maintain capital controls to that end. All engage in industrial and state-led innovation policy to some degree. And together these nations form the heads of significant coalitions in global trade talks that have pushed back on industrialized country proposals aimed at making developing countries look more like industrialized liberal market economies. They have clout because these nations are fast growing markets to which firms and investors want greater access. They have clout because (in purchasing power parity terms) they lead an emerging market world that has a larger share of GDP in the world economy than Western nations (see Wade in this volume). Western nations want that market share.

Development success stories from the twentieth century all struck a unique blend between state and markets not because they just lifted certain policies off the shelf – they did so because they got the *political economy* of industrialization right. Indeed, the risks of trying to deploy capital controls and industrial policy can be at least as concerning as unbridled liberalization. Two key problems can be rent-seeking and picking winners (Krueger, 1996). The nations with the most success find a way to at least partly circumvent these problems. To circumvent the rent-seeking problem, political scientists have shown that successful industrializers have had states that were "embedded" in the private sector while maintaining "autonomy" from sectional elite interests seeking rents. State agencies that are charged with correcting market failures have to maintain constant communication and input with the private sector (Evans, 1995).

Perhaps most importantly, the problem of picking winners has been circumvented by having a good deal of discipline over private actors. Alice Amsden (2001) has referred to the need for "reciprocal control mechanisms". A control mechanism is "a set of institutions that disciplines economic behavior based on a feedback of information that has been sensed and assessed" (2003: 43). In other words, firms have performance requirements that, when they are not met, are no longer supported. The most successful industrializers were able to abandon projects that were not performing; in other countries, such projects were perpetuated because bureaucrats became hijacked by business interests that were dependent on the state.

These two varieties of globalization – a consolidating globalization in the north and a developmental globalization in the south – clash in global trade talks. The theoretical underpinning of the WTO is to aid nations in maximizing their static comparative advantage. This is solidified by the principles of non-discrimination and national treatment. Non-discrimination entails treating imports from a nation on the same basis as that given to the most favored other nation. National treatment means that foreign sellers and producers receive the same treatment in a host nation as domestic firms do. Until the last (Uruguay) Round of global trade talks, the WTO's predecessor, the General Agreement on Tariffs and Trade (GATT), largely pertained to Western countries and when developing countries took part there were a number of exceptions. All that changed with the establishment of the WTO in 1995, as did the political economy of trade policy.

More than market power at the WTO

Developing countries pursuing a more developmental variety of globalization were able to capitalize on their newfound economic power in the Doha Round. In previous trade rounds industrialized nations were able to use their market power to extract concessions by offering market access for regulatory change in the south. In a turnaround, beginning at the turn of the century, the developing nations were able to use their market power to exert bargaining power at the WTO. But there was more to it than having a different set of ideas about globalization and development and having new-found economic power. Developing country policies were backed by domestic political actors. Perhaps, most importantly, the institutional structure of the WTO worked to their benefit as well.

Many developing countries have sought to globalize in order to achieve a dynamic comparative advantage (Amsden, 2001 and Wade, 2004). As Amsden suggests in this volume, in many cases that entails favoring domestic firms or industries over foreign ones, and this at least in spirit would violate the principle of national treatment whereby one WTO nation cannot treat its domestic firms more favourably than those of other nations that are party to the WTO. Tariffs in the world economy are relatively low by historical standards and therefore this clash is often not seen to occur in discussions over goods tariffs. What has gone unrecognized by some is that trade treaties are no longer about trade in goods, but rather are about domestic regulations that could be seen as violating the two principles. Robert Lawrence (1996) has referred to this as "deep" integration, whereas trade talks of yesteryear were "shallow" integration arrangements that just dealt with tariffs and quotas at the economic borders of nations. New rules for services, investment, and intellectual property all constrain the ability to maintain financial stability and diversify the product base of a developing economy.

As China, India, Brazil, South Africa and others have continued to grow their economies at a significant pace since the turn of the century, they (and their domestic constituents) have fought hard to maintain at minimum the level of policy space they have at the WTO. Developed nations desperately want market access to these dynamically growing economies, as their own industrialized growth is lower and markets have become saturated. At the WTO this meant rejecting the proposals by the developed world to deepen international investment rules, intellectual property rules, government procurement, and financial services (the so-called "Singapore Issues" and others).

Moreover, the developing world turned the tables on the narrative of the talks. Whereas past rounds were pitched as the developing world being riddled with protections that are bad for growth and prosperity, the developing world flipped that on its head and accused the north of the same. Almost immediately into the negotiations the developing world made an issue of industrialized country subsidies and tariffs benefiting agricultural producers, and intellectual property rules that prevented developing countries from break patents to serve ailing and diseased populations. In effect this put the developing world on the moral high ground. Rather than the North getting agreement upon their Singapore issues at the 2003 WTO Cancun meetings, the North had to abandon those issues and also amend the WTO agreements on intellectual property rules to allow for public health exceptions – a key victory for developing countries. Turning away from a "deep integration" agenda, from 2003 on the negotiations were mostly about market access in agriculture, manufacturing goods, and some services. In addition, special attention was to be given to the poorest nations in the form of relieving cotton subsidies and "aid for trade" packages.

Starting in roughly 2005, the makings of a deal centered upon increased market access and "aid for trade" from the North in exchange for more cuts in manufacturing and liberalizing financial services in the South. A deal along those lines was close at the end of 2008: modest cuts in agricultural tariffs and subsidies by developed countries in return for modest cuts in manufacturing and services barriers in the developing world.

Table 11.1 Doha benefits, NAMA tariff losses, and declining terms of trade

	*WB "likely" scenario**	*NAMA tariff losses***	*Terms of trade****
	(billions of U.S. dollars)		*(percentage change)*
Developed	79.9	38.0	–0.12
Developing	16.1	63.4	–0.74
Selected developing regions			
Middle East and North Africa	–0.6	7.0	–1.32
Sub-Saharan Africa	0.4	1.7	–0.83
Latin America and the Caribbean	7.9	10.7	–1.12
Selected countries			
Brazil	3.6	3.1	–0.18
India	2.2	7.9	–1.62
Mexico	–0.9	0.4	–0.48
Bangladesh	–0.1	0.04	–0.58

Notes

* Anderson and Martin (2005). *Agricultural Trade Reform and the Doha Development Agenda.* Table 12.14; scenario 7. "WB" refers to World Bank.

** De Cordoba and Vanzetti (2005). *Coping with Trade Reforms.* UNCTAD. Table 11.

*** Polaski, Sandra (2006). *Winners and Losers: Impact of the Doha Round on Developing Countries.* Carnegie Endowment. Table 3.4. "NAMA refers to Non-Agricultural Market Access" vis-à-vis the WTO.

The problem was that, by all accounts, the gains from trade liberalization under the round were fairly small. What is more, the losses in terms of trade, lost policy space, and politics were seen as very high. Tariffs are at an all time low, and the world has reaped significant gains from that previous round of trade liberalization. By the time the Doha Round comes about there is little left on the table. The World Bank's model of the gains from a "likely" Doha deal is exhibited in the first column of Table 11.1. Under this scenario, global gains projected for 2015 are just $96 billion, with only $16 billion going to the developing world.

Of the benefits projected for developing countries, only a few see most of the gains. According to the World Bank half of all the benefits to developing countries are expected to flow to just eight countries: Argentina, Brazil (which stands to receive 23 per cent of the developing country benefit), China, India, Mexico, Thailand, Turkey, and Vietnam.

Total tariff losses for developing countries under the "non-agricultural market access" – or manufactured goods – aspect of the negotiations could be $63.4 billion, or almost four times the level of benefits (see Table 11.1, column 2). For many developing countries slashing tariffs will not only restrict the ability of these countries to foster new industries so that they may integrate into the world economy, but it will also limit government funds to support such infant industries and to maintain social programs for the poor. A majority of developing

Table 11.2 The shrinking of policy space in the global trade regime

Policy instrument	*WTO*	*LAC PTAs*
Goods trade		
Tariff sequencing tax drawbacks	*	X
Intellectual property		
Limiting patent scope	X	X
Short patent timelines with exceptions	X	X
Compulsory licenses		X
Subsidies		
Export	X	X
R&D	*	X
Distribution	*	X
Environment	*	X
Cost of capital		X
Foreign investment		
Local content	X	X
Trade balancing	X	X
Joint ventures		X
Technology transfer		X
R&D		X
Employment of local personnel		X
Tax concessions		X
Pre-establishment "screening"		X
Capital controls		X

Source: Gallagher 2008b.

countries rely on tariffs for more than one-quarter of their tax revenue. For smaller nations with little diversification in their economies, tariff revenues provide the core of government budgets.

In these models declining terms of trade for developing countries – the ratio of export to import prices – were also expected to occur in the developing world. This measure is considered a crucial estimate of the extent to which a developing country is moving up the value chain in the global economy, away from primary production and into manufacturing or knowledge-based economic activities. Since World War I many developing countries have seen their terms of trade deteriorate. Declining terms of trade can accentuate balance of payments problems and make the need to diversify into other export products ever more urgent (Ocampo and Parra, 2003). Under a likely deal, world prices for agricultural products increase and manufacturing prices decrease slightly or remain unchanged. According to the Carnegie Endowment for International Peace these price changes negatively effect the terms of trade for developing countries (Table 11.1, column 3). The report explains that, for many countries, the rise in world prices for imported food and agricultural goods is countered with a decline in world prices for their light manufactured exports, such as apparel. This partly explains the welfare losses for Bangladesh, East Africa and the rest of sub-Saharan Africa.

There was also significant concern about the economic and political cost of lost policy space. As noted earlier, to diversify, developing countries often look at the example of the U.S. and European economies, and more recently, the economies of South Korea and China. These countries diversified away from primary commodities and light manufacturing while slowly opening their economies. They moved into the world marketplace strategically, protecting their major export industries in order to nurture them to compete in world markets. The extent to which the WTO and regional PTAs restrict policy space for industrial diversification is examined later in the chapter. The first column of Table 11.2 lists many of the policies that developed and developing countries alike have deployed to diversify and globalize their economies. The second column places an "X" alongside a particular policy if it became actionable under the Uruguay Round and asterisk if developed countries had proposed further restricting a measure in the Doha Round.

Those small gains to begin with, alongside losses in terms of tariffs, terms of trade, and lost policy space, made the Doha Round difficult for developing countries from the start (Gallagher, 2008b). Still, a deal was close in 2008 – though it ended up being scuttled by a U.S. refusal to grant poorer nations exceptions to cuts that could have enabled them to build competitive national industries and protect their economies from unfair or unequal competition. Since 2008 there have been many false starts, but no movement. Despite the mammoth market power of the developed world, developing countries leveraged their new-found economic power to stop proposals they saw as harmful. Developing countries assumed the moral high ground in the talks by pointing to massive agricultural subsidies in the U.S. and Europe, and U.S. and E.U. proposal positions on intellectual property that were threatening the treatment of global health pandemics.

This leveraging on the part of developing countries would not have been able to occur if it was not for the way the WTO is structured. Institutions matter too. The WTO has a one-country-one-vote consensus voting system. Moreover, under a "single undertaking", every country had to agree on every letter of a deal with no individual amendments. Nations like Brazil, India, South Africa and China were all part of key coalitions on agricultural subsidies (G20), manufacturing (NAMA), food security (G33), and poverty (G90). By banding together they were able to mount a united front against developed country proposals and for their own proposals for market access and policy space.

From an institutional perspective it was also important that developing countries were preserving existing policy space rather than trying to carve out new space. Since its foundation by the industrial victors of World War II, and for almost 50 years afterwards, the GATT granted rich and poor countries a lot of flexibility. The GATT and other Bretton Woods institutions were founded on "embedded liberalism" and New Deal politics, and saw linking states and markets as a norm for economic and political stability (Rodrik, 2011; Helleiner, 1994). Although, beginning in the late 1980s under the Uruguay Round, some of this edifice began to be dismantled, a relatively large amount of policy space remained intact – not least because many industrialized nations still want the ability to nurture industry for social gain as well (Block, 2008).

Domestic politics within the developing countries also plays a role. China, India, Brazil, and South Africa all have formidable manufacturing classes, and, in the case of India and Brazil, significant financial services and health industries. In the early days of negotiations these interests were more willing to liberalize the WTO. Take Brazil, for example. Brazil has a large industrial class with segments that are globally competitive and in fact rely on world markets for inputs into their production process. Therefore it can be seen as in the interest of these globally competitive workers to allow more foreign access into their markets, as inputs will be cheaper with lower import tariffs. In addition, Brazil's soy and beef industries stood to gain significantly from a deal, and many manufacturing firms stood to gain in terms of providing machinery, transport and other inputs. Finally – and this is important – the Brazilian real was relatively undervalued during the first years of the Doha Round. A weak currency is implicitly import-substituting and a subsidy to exports. Thus, Brazilian industry was more open to negotiating. All this changed after the global financial crisis, with Brazil and many other emerging markets seeing their currencies appreciate by more than 40 per cent. Brazilian industrialists are now very averse to a deal at the WTO because they lack competitiveness and view more foreign market access as being out of the question (Amorim, 2011).

The paradoxical rise of regionalism

The good news for global trade is that, as the distribution of market power has become more dispersed among income classes at the WTO, the power of liberal and coordinated market economies in the developed world has waned. Thus, the WTO has become more equity-enhancing than during the Uruguay Round and relative to BITs and PTAs. There is more policy space for a variety of development strategies at the WTO because developing countries now have the power to leverage policy space (and maintain old space). If such strategies truly are more welfare-enhancing, then an equity-enhanced multilateralism at the WTO will be more optimal.

However, developed nations have become frustrated with their inability to push through a deal at the WTO, and the result is a proliferation of regional and bilateral preferential trade agreements (PTAs). Indeed, shortly after the 2003 Cancun meetings, the United States embarked on a stated policy of "competitive liberalization" whereby the U.S. has sought to sign smaller PTAs in order to surround the key nations at the WTO and make them succumb to U.S. proposals for deep cuts at the WTO level (Evenett, 2008).

Whether it be capital controls, sovereign debt restructuring, or industrial policy, the PTAs negotiated by the U.S. and to a lesser (but real) extent by the E.U. constrain the ability of developing nations to deploy policies for stability and growth in a manner much further than the WTO (Gallagher, 2008a; 2008b; Gallagher and Thrasher, 2010). This finding is generally depicted in the last column of Table 11.2. What is paradoxical is that some of those nations are core members of coalitions at the WTO where shallower versions of the same proposals are rejected.

In these cases lies the more traditional story. Most, if not all, of the countries with which the North signs PTAs are minuscule by relative economic size. Here, as Hirschman (1945) showed more than a generation ago, is where asymmetric bargaining power and influence can play such a big role – especially when the institutions are asymmetric. The average size of the U.S. economy relative to its negotiating partners is many times larger. Therefore, in large part the negotiation becomes the classic market-access-for-regulatory-reform equation (Gallagher, 2008b).

Hirschman noted that developing nations will be more likely to succumb to the negotiating positions of industrial countries when the industrialized nation has a large and growing economy relative to the developing nation, and if the developing nation has fewer export options (Hirschman, 1945: 18). This is exactly the case in U.S.–Latin American trade relations, and goes a long way towards explaining why Latin American nations abandon their WTO positions to sign PTAs with the U.S. Left over from the Cold War, the U.S. has a "generalized system of preferences" where developing countries get duty-free access to a number of markets in the U.S. These have been in place for some time and many nations' export orientation has become geared toward the U.S. These preferences have to be renewed on a regular basis in the U.S. Congress. As part of the competitive liberalization strategy, the U.S. offered permanent and expanded access that build on the GSP, in exchange for tough rules on intellectual property, investment, services, and so forth. Some nations had more than 40 per cent of all exports going to the U.S. It therefore became an offer that couldn't be refused if one wanted to stay in office (Gallagher, 2008a). Given that many Latin American nations have fewer opportunities to export those same products to other countries, Hirschman's framework is of particular relevance.

That is not the whole story, however. Domestic politics and collective action also play a role. It was just mentioned that many domestic interests become highly mobilized in support of a PTA with the U.S. because they would be "losers" without a treaty. What is more they will benefit from the reciprocity of a treaty because, being the more globalized sectors, they naturally import more inputs than domestic firms. Put another way, in a developing nation where there are few sectors that are export-ready, and those sectors that are export-ready stand to lose their market share, the short-term beneficiaries of a "deep" PTA with the U.S. are highly concentrated while the medium- and long-term losers – those who would benefit from a more diversified economy and more widely shared advances in economic welfare – are dispersed.

Unlike the Brazils of the world that already have significant sectors that will lobby for more policy space, many other developing countries, from Nicaragua to Peru, simply do not have a sector that will lobby for policy space that would enable diversification. By the very nature of the economy, a sector that would benefit from economic diversification and industrial policy does not exist and thus cannot have voice in the politics of the negotiation. The same is true for consumers who would benefit in the present or future if a more diversified and stable economy was achieved. According to common understanding of trade policy, static losers are concentrated and static winners are dissipated, and therefore good trade deals may not get through the politics because the losers are more politically organized. The reverse has been true on both sides of the U.S.–Latin America equation. The static winners are very concentrated and the medium- to long-term beneficiaries do not exist or are not competitive enough to exert enough political influence. This has played a key role in some Latin American cases.

Finally, ideology has really mattered in U.S.–Latin America trade relations. The nations that signed deals with the U.S. happened (at the time) to be dominated by right or center-right governments that were ideologically committed to the "Washington Consensus" and were indeed trying to out-liberalize one another. Those nations that are more to the centre or centre-left, such as Brazil, Argentina, Ecuador, Bolivia and Venezuela, have refused to negotiate bilaterally with the U.S. at all, and prefer the WTO.

Equity-enhancing multilateralism

The 2000s may have been a unique moment of "equity-enhancing multilateralism", whereby the WTO was able to yield pluralistic outcomes that allowed each member to pursue its own development policies within the existing set of rules at the WTO. This was due to the fact that the distribution of economic power was dispersed across income classes that had a variety of views of successful globalization, with many key and economically powerful emerging market nations using a one-country-one-vote consensus system to maintain the status quo. Given that we do not really know the exact recipe for growth and development, and indeed that history has shown that a wide variety of approaches can work, this could be seen in a normative sense as a positive outcome.

However parsimonious this model may seem, it is sure to be unstable. History has shown that domestic interests, regardless of the level of development, play a large part in setting the negotiating position of nations. Therefore, one cannot expect that nations which used a particular set of policies at one stage of development will be favorable to allowing other nations to have that same flexibility over time. Indeed, history points in the opposite direction. Europe, the U.S., and Japan all pushed for a very shallow GATT in its early years in order to expand domestic capabilities. When those capabilities became global and nations become capital exporters, their interests changed. South Korea is another example. South Korea was a quintessential developmental state but was a leader in pushing the Singapore Issues in Cancun. Now that South Korea is a capital exporter, its multinational firms do not want to be subject to capital controls and performance requirements, even if it was those very policies that played a role in bringing those firms to multinational status. We have begun to see this with China as well. While it has stayed in step with Brazil, India and South Africa for most of the WTO round, its bilateral investment treaties have increasingly begun to look more and more like developed world treaties.

From a policy perspective, then, when the larger emerging market and developing countries begin to become capital exporters, they, too, may have more in common with the West. Equal rules for unequal members may spell unequal rules in reality. It may just be that ideas, the WTO's institutional structure, and the international balance of market power, aligned in a unique way to provide policy space for developing countries during the Doha Round. In other words, it may not be replicable in the future. This particular mix of independent variables may be impossible to replicate over time, even if we could specifically quantify what the relative importance of each factor was. What is more likely is that those nations that have drawn a line in the sand now will want to erase that line as they export to poorer countries. This could be problematic in terms of the longer-run availability of policy space for the least-developed countries, because after the larger nations that have been discussed here, there are few large economies left – especially economies that have not already signed a PTA with the U.S. or E.U. As Amsden discusses in this volume, the least-developed nations are already having a difficult time developing the right developmental policies because of external constraints (being more apt to engage in BITs and PTAs) and domestic institutional and capacity constraints. So the beginning of the twenty-first century may have been a moment of victory for larger developmental globalizers, but it is not clear that such an era will be permanent. Where will that leave the smaller and still-less developed countries? How will they carve out the policy space that they need to propel their development?

Note

1 Kevin P. Gallagher is Associate Professor of International Relations at Boston University.

12 The "new" industrial policy

Securing the home market with subterfuge and SMEs

Alice Amsden

In recent decades industrial policies in the developing world have begun to be rediscovered as something "new", and re-examined from multiple angles. For many, what comes into view is "lite and lean" industrial policy – a delicate dance around the maypole of the market that frees it to be the propulsive force.[1] Past industrial policy allegedly careened out of control, resulting in too-high tariffs, distorted exchange rates and environmental decay. "Newness" lies in a swerve closer towards principles of openness, temporariness and non-preferential treatment. The dancers' steps are varied, but, generally, the tune is softer, involving *less* industrial policy and a vague emphasis on "institution building" and exporting. The transition from old to new is attributed to the maturation of industries which no longer need government support. Governments themselves have also grown richer, the argument runs, and needn't restrict their choice of industrial policies to those that are cheap (tariffs are cheap since consumers bear the cost). Instead of depending on protection, which also suffers from having no clear end (except from foreign political opposition), new industrial policies are supposedly temporary because they rely mainly on export tax-breaks, which impose a fiscal burden that can't be sustained.

If industrial policy in the developing world is, in fact, liter and leaner, as market mavens maintain, then this implies convergence towards the "American model", the acme of liberalism in theory.[2] Has such convergence occurred? We answer "No", that robust industrial policy continues to be used by developing and developed countries alike. The angle examined below is the use of industrial policy to "secure the home market", as seen through the lens of two successful role models from the era following decolonization; one for raw materials (OPEC), the other for manufacturing (the East Asian model). The securing of a home market, ultimately for expansion abroad, occurs when nationally owned firms predominate in two types of industry.[3] One type has high and rising productivity by world standards. The other has dense backward and forward linkages, such as the connections from spinning and weaving to cotton growing and garment making, both of which do business with machinery builders, and so on.[4] These two criteria, which tend to overlap with those of national security and monopoly pricing (also magnets for government intervention), were used by Japan to target new industries during its 1960s "growth-doubling plan".[5]

The East Asian and OPEC role models continue to exert a strong influence, but the argument here is not that today's developing countries hew to the paths they have forged. Rather than adhering to either the U.S. model or the Asian or OPEC models, the "rise of the rest" and the response of the West have led to something else. It might be described as the equivalent of a .45 caliber pistol on a .38 mm frame, or a set of *market-fleeing industrial policies* operating within a *free-market framework* (exchange rates and interest rates are set in deregulated capital markets). The focus on securing the home market remains. But, now, given a changed international institutional environment, industrial policy has gone underground. Emerged and emerging economies alike escape the intent of WTO law by forming "free" trade agreements. To secure the home market, they subsidize a broad range of industries under the headings of "defense", the environment, energy conservation, natural resource protection and regional development. And, faced with changed international economic conditions, industrial policy has gone small-scale. It remains a big part of the economic policy toolkit, but the attention has gravitated toward small- and medium-size firms (SMEs). Only in the poorest countries – customers of the World Bank, and hence a biased sample – is industrial policy lite and lean beyond mere appearances.

Securing the home market

Securing the home market became a top priority following decolonization. After struggling to secure its *political* independence, led by India in 1947, the decolonized generation turned to securing its *economic* independence, which started with the Far East's appropriation of Japan's overseas properties after its military defeat, and the Middle East's nationalization of local concessions of big oil multinationals in the 1950s.[6] Both ran parallel with policies to "localize" managerial positions in remaining foreign-owned firms.

Securing the home market in both East Asia and the Middle East took radical forms – forceful appropriation of foreign firms (after trying to "localize" managerial positions), which created the firm-level basis for further development. Only India achieved the same end – securing the home market through national enterprises – via acquisition, or the use of market forces. Indian enterprises bought out British companies at rock bottom prices as political independence approached and foreign investors fled (Tomlinson, 1981). By contrast, the state-owned national oil companies of OPEC members emerged from the outright nationalization of foreign concessions beginning with Mexico's pioneering success in 1938 and a failed attempt in Iran in 1953 (Penrose, 1971).

The biggest challenge to industrial policy and securitization came *after* the nationalization stage, when aggressive policies were introduced in favor of import substitution. The consensus became that import substitution was doomed without exporting; instead of measuring the success of securitization by market share, as business historian Alfred Chandler suggests, it should also be measured by export share. The point observers of trade and industry begin to make is not that developing countries start to export as prices become "right", but rather that they start to export once they accumulate sufficient scale and skills at home. Both came as a result of prior import substitution experience. In industries demanding capital and engineering capabilities, import substitution was the mother of exports, until the two activities became blurred. Securing the home market slowly extended as far as the international market.

This sequence, of exports emerging from import substitutes, also tended to typify the firm level in all but the most labor-intensive industries. The dominant form of big business in Asia, Latin America and the Middle East was the "diversified business group". Without proprietary technology, specialization in one area was risky, so firms diversified, widely and unrelatedly (see Amsden, 2001). Securing the home market at the firm level was the symbiosis of diversification at the industry level.

Around the late 1990s, the time finally had arrived when the distinction between industrial policies for import substitution and export promotion began to converge, as the two activities themselves became conflated. Whereas industrial policies to promote import substitution had typically included targeting, tariff protection, subsidies and entry restrictions, industrial policies to promote high-tech exports became similar minus tariffs (as market theorists correctly claim). In tightly contested electronics markets, tariffs were eschewed if only out of fear that they would raise production costs somewhere along the value chain. The similarity in other old and new policies is illustrated by the case of CD-ROMs, an optical storage device (Amsden and Chu, 2003).

Even before the rise of China (recognized by Korea in 1992) and the formation of the WTO (in 1995), the decolonized generation's industrial policies were moving into a second phase, from "securing the home market" to "securing the home market to secure the foreign market", and vice versa.

The gamut of industrial policies in the South's raw materials sector, originating in the OPEC development role model (as distinct from price cartel), is now diffusing from the Middle East and parts of Latin America to poor countries with newly discovered commercial oil reserves, many in West Africa. At its core is the state-owned national oil company (NOC). The manufacturing role model is spreading slowly to only a few countries with production capabilities (Vietnam and Nigeria), or skills enriched by émigré populations (Mauritius and Malaysia). Large countries such as Mexico and the BRICs (Brazil, Russia, India and China) straddle the two role models. Indeed, if the old industrial policy involved a race between East Asia and Latin America, the new industrial policy involves a symbiosis between manufacturers in the Far East and raw materials suppliers in the Middle East.

Both role models testify to one constant, even in the throes of change. The decolonized generation's industrial policy regimes over time have struggled with the weakness of the private sector. Import substitution and export diversification in both periods have been oriented towards creating efficient and sustainable, nationally owned enterprises (public and private). Chandler refers to securitization as the "functional and strategic competition" for market share, suggesting that the struggle over the home market is competitive, driven by both market forces and the visible hand of professional management (Chandler Jr., 1962). A firm's share in GNP is a good measure of its success or failure in securitization. Yet the market in which Chandler's competition occurs, late nineteenth-century America, engaged mostly American firms; the foreign challenge was minimal, making comparisons with decolonizing countries misleading (but see Chang, 2002). Big Business in the U.S. also preceded Big Government, whereas the reverse is true in the developing world (Chandler Jr., 1980). In developing countries, because of the private sector's weakness, industrial policies became as much a matter of forming national companies as fomenting new industries, and the job of securing the home market fell to newly independent states.

To secure the home market a corps of nationally owned firms, public or private, is more necessary than ever. Without it the new industrial policy is circumscribed in its scope. In the absence of national ownership it cannot promote outsourcing services to developed country assemblers; it cannot encourage outward FDI; it cannot circumvent local content restrictions under WTO law, and it cannot derive rents from brand-name products.[7] In the old days an electronics giant like the RCA Corporation would save labor costs by opening a wholly owned subsidiary in a low-wage country like Taiwan. Today the cost-savings of American and Japanese electronics companies include capital and logistics, by outsourcing to a *Taiwan-owned* firm in Taiwan; but one must exist for this to happen (Amsden and Chu, 2003). Hypothetically, if outward foreign direct investment (FDI) had been undertaken by RCA's Taiwan subsidiary, this would have done little to confer top corporate jobs, experience and entrepreneurial rents to Taiwanese. For Taiwan's economy to benefit most from outward FDI, a Taiwan-owned company must bear the risk. Finally, after the opening of the World Trade Organization in 1995, imposing local content requirements on *any* firm became prohibited. But this rule is a non-issue for state-owned enterprises, which do their own government's bidding, or even private, nationally owned enterprises with less power to resist their government's bidding and more incentive than a foreign subsidiary to invest voluntarily in their own local supply chain. Whereas in the past protection of an industry benefited both foreign and national companies, new industrial policies matter most in alliance with national companies only.

Despite globalization the home market remains a relatively profitable and comfortable market in which a firm can reach scale economies and learn to raise productivity because it is naturally protected by tastes, transport costs and government procurement practices (in the early phase of the cotton gin, even as great an innovator as Eli Whitney depended for his material existence on military contracts (Green, 1956)). But the home market isn't cheap if it exacts penalties in the form of low skills and poor infrastructure. It is prohibitively expensive if it "crowds out" national firms altogether, due to the entrenchment of foreign monopolies that enjoy first-mover advantage, tacit knowledge and brand names (Amsden, 2009). If costs outweigh benefits the local business elite has an incentive to cooperate with foreign firms rather than compete against them. This calculation, however, has a social and political dimension because a firm itself is a social and political construction. The top talent of any country may succeed in reaching the highest positions of pay and responsibility only in businesses that are nationally owned (Morris Chang, chief executive of Taiwan's premier semiconductor company, left a high executive position at Texas Instruments because he claimed he had hit the "yellow glass ceiling"; West African Unilever executives relate similar experiences with a "black glass ceiling").[8] Therefore, the business community may support industrial policies to discriminate in favor of national firms, and national firms can then attract top talent. If a firm does enjoy the natural protection and social benefits of the domestic market, it may be obliged politically to contribute to it in return, with a snowballing effect (the greater reciprocity, the easier to impose performance standards in exchange for subsidies (Amsden, 2001)).[9] But if national entrepreneurs are simply risk averse as a matter of history or culture, then the whole society suffers unless the government intervenes.

Industrial policy goes underground

The impulse to secure the home market has been an ongoing feature of industrial policy regimes, but, over time, this impulse has manifested itself differently. One key shift has to do with the relationship between national policy and international institutions. As the international institutional environment has become less accommodating to the use of industrial policy, national governments have resorted to the use of subterfuge. Thus, on the one hand, WTO members devise low tariffs and observe liberal and transparent rules (all is lean and lite, as market mavens maintain).[10] But, on the other, an obscure layer exists underground in the form of a "demi-monde", whereby WTO members act collectively or in pairs to deliberately undermine the intent of these rules, while honoring their letter. If at least three-quarters of WTO members agree not to "adjudicate" (take to court) a certain rule that is being violated, then for all practical purposes the rule is a paper tiger, as in subsidies for SMEs. The intent of WTO law has been diluted especially in industries with high global productivity growth rates and dense linkages related to:

1 defense and national security;
2 science and technology;
3 energy conservation;
4 environmental protection;
5 health and sanitation; and
6 regional development, which more or less covers all high-tech bases (Amsden and Hikino, 2000).[11]

The demi-monde even diminishes the effect of trade rules themselves. The WTO was founded on January 1, 1995, heralding a new era of free trade, but the North American Free Trade Agreement was finalized on January 1, 1994, heralding its compromise. NAFTA and other free trade agreements, which have been approved by at least three-quarters of WTO members, dilute the principle of free trade by countenancing preferential treatment (WTO, 2011). A product's duty-free access to a member's market typically depends on its local content ratio ("rule of origin"); that is, to qualify for free entry, a certain percentage of a product's value must be created *in a member's country* (Bhagwati *et al.*, 1998). If the ratio is too low, as agreed upon by members, then open markets don't apply and non-members' exports face a form of import substitution. By 2006 the number of custom unions or free trade agreements in effect had reached 200, covering roughly 75 percent of world imports.[12]

There are other subterfuges besides non-adjudication to evade the intent of WTO law (balance of payments crises, cultural safeguards), and a three-quarters majority is not always necessary. As just noted two countries can collude.[13] At one time American trade officials viewed China's export tax rebates as a form of protection, but, surprisingly, a court ruled otherwise: "tax rebates do not violate World Trade Organization provisions" (Landler, 2008). To avoid a clash both giants agreed to offer developing economies $20 billion in subsidized export credits to help them buy more Chinese and American goods, flagrantly violating the WTO equal treatment principle for other exporters (U.S. Treasury Department, 2008).

The new type of level playing field – *paved with subterfuges* – is evident in the rare earth elements industry, where China has positioned itself as the dominant player. Rare earths are "complicated and costly to extract", except in small quantities by renegade miners, and without such metals, "much of the world's modern technology would be vastly different and many applications would not be possible" – e.g., wind turbines, lasers, low-energy light bulbs, batteries for hybrid and electric cars, fiber-optic cables and cell phones (Hurst, 2010). China took an early lead with 97 percent of world exports by 2010, and the United States started to scramble for policies to catch up. As China was building its monopoly only one company in the U.S., privately held Molycorp Minerals, ran a rare earth mining operation. What little interest in rare earths had once existed in academia – after World War II the U.S. was ahead – had long since vanished. Molycorp went bankrupt during a Chinese price war, before resuming its role as the sole U.S.-based supplier.

The Chinese rare metals industry came out of the reformed planning period of the 1980s, when setting goals and mobilizing resources still obtained (as they do in Korea, as suggested by its SME policies). As first pointed out to an American audience in 2010 by Cindy Hurst, an analyst for the U.S. Army's Foreign Military Studies Office in Leavenworth, Kansas, three Chinese scientists jointly proposed a plan in 1986 to accelerate China's high-tech development, one that China's leader at the time, Deng Xiaoping, approved. According to China's Ministry of Science and Technology, which Hurst quotes, the objective of Program 863, the birth certificate of the rare earth metals industry, was to "gain a foothold in the world arena; to strive to achieve breakthroughs in key technical fields that concern the national economic lifeline and national security; and to achieve "leap-frog" development in key high-tech fields in which China enjoys relative advantages" – China's working definition of securing the home market.

Given China's massive reserves of rare earths (U.S. reserves are estimated at only 11–15 percent of the world total compared to China's estimated 50-plus percent), "a great deal of money" went into their research. This was led by one of China's most eminent chemists, Professor Xu Guangxian (an internee in a labor camp during the Cultural Revolution). The Bautou Research Institute of Rare Earths (located near rare earth reserves in Inner Mongolia) is the largest of its kind in the world, dating from 1963: it focuses on the exploitation and utilization of rare earth elements – their design and production. China began recovering rare earths during the process of producing iron and steel by the Baotou Iron and Steel Company. In 1992 Deng Xiaoping stated: "There is oil in the Middle East; there is rare earth in China", and the industry has been expanding at full throttle ever since in the form of the state-owned Baotou Rare Earth Hi-Tech Industrial Development Zone, out of which China has come to dominate the world magnet industry (Hurst, 2010).

Headaches for Chinese planners have come from illegal "49er-type" individual prospectors, who have caused a lowering of prices and created environmental havoc, precipitating the passage of a tighter law in 2010: "Once approved, the Ministry of Land and Resources will issue licenses and start allocating the resources to certain companies. Private enterprises can only collaborate with these designated firms through shareholding" (POSCO, Korea's steel giant, bought 60 percent of Yongxin Rare Metal Earth Company in Inner Mongolia for $8.8 million) (Yan, 2010).

James Bacchus, the former chairman of the World Trade Organization's appellate body, wrote in the *Wall Street Journal* (2010) that China was "hoarding rare elements and other raw materials". But the managing director of the China Society for World Trade Organization Studies, He Weiwen, told *China Daily*, "WTO rules stipulate that its members can take measures to protect their raw materials from being exhausted and China's measures are in line with them" (Yan, 2010). Bacchus also noted: "China is hardly the only country considering export restrictions" as domestic demand exceeds supply. "The sharp increase in restraints is happening world-wide, and raises fundamental questions about the rules and the resiliency of the World Trade Organization" (2010).

The response by the U.S. government has come mainly from states with mining interests: a Congressman from Colorado, Mike Coffman, and a Senator from Alaska, Lisa Murkowski, a ranking member on the U.S. Senate Energy & Natural Resources Committee. Both are Republicans, with strong voting records favoring free trade agreements and opposing big government and mining restrictions. Yet the legislation called for by Murkowski (almost identical to Coffman's Bill) would create a "*whole-of-government*" approach to creating a domestic supply chain in rare metals – one involving the U.S. Departments of Commerce, Energy, State, and Defense, Office of the U.S. Trade Representative (to challenge China's export monopoly in the WTO), and Office of Science and Technology Policy within the Executive Office of the President. The U.S. Magnets and Materials Association expressed support for the legislation, arguing that "urgent and collective action is needed by the federal government in order to head off the impending rare earth crisis" (USMMA, 2010). The CEO of the National Mining Association, Hal Quinn, stated in an American definition of securing the home market:

> Rare earths are merely one example of this nation's increasing reliance on outside sources to supply U.S. manufacturers and technology providers. America's drift away from greater self-sufficiency for the basic building blocks of our economy undermines our commitment to jobs creation and increased exports and ignores this country's rich reserves of metals and minerals.
>
> (Kosich, 2010)

In the House Bill (HR4866, Eleventh Congress, 2nd session),

> [L]egislation would also require the Secretary of Energy to establish REE industry loan guarantees [similar to those in effect in Korea's SME sector], while the Secretaries of Commerce, Defense, Energy and Interior would be required to provide R&D funding to academic, government labs, corporate R&D, not-for-profit research and development, and industry associations for REE projects.[14]
>
> (Kosich, 2010)

Thus, there is a level playing field between China and the U.S. with respect to rare earths, insofar as this industry in both countries will receive large subsidies from government, using subterfuges that are sanctioned by the WTO. Without these outlets and escape valves, WTO membership would probably approach nil. If liberalization is measured by tariffs only, then this entire level of market fleeing practices is obscured.

Where the new industrial policies of China and the U.S. differ is on another plane of government intervention, one that fares far from market behavior. To appreciate it China must be understood in the context of both the OPEC raw materials and Japanese manufacturing role models, where its affiliations lie. Unlike the U.S., China's industrial policy in rare earths is heavily involved in firm formation, investing in and strengthening the state and private companies that will mine, manufacture and market rare earth products, similar to the NOCs in OPEC countries. As we have tried to argue, firm formation in developing countries has been an integral part of industrial policy, old and new. Unlike the U.S., China's industrial policy, like Korea's policies towards SMEs, is also a product of long-term planning, even if central planning is dead.

Industrial policy goes small-scale

A second important change that has occurred in recent decades concerns the size of the firms being promoted by industrial policy. Earlier, upgrading was focused mostly on large-scale enterprise, to overtake the West's Rust Belts.[15] In the period now in progress, upgrading focuses on firms within the small- and medium-size range (up to 299 workers), to inch towards competing against its Silicon Valleys.

The weakness of the decolonized world's private sector has spanned the firm-size spectrum, but perhaps weakest of all is the small- and medium-size range. This size range tends to have fragmented markets, tacit technology and frail organizations, making it difficult to generalize about good performance and policy design.[16] Artisanal traditions within this size bracket enriched Europe and sustained colonial America, but emulation is difficult (McAllister, 1989).

Today, "embedded autonomy" is a key element in the relationship between OPEC countries and their NOCs, and is likely to be critical in the relationship between the Chinese government and its rare earth suppliers, to cite only one case. On the other hand, the new industrial policy is focused mainly on the small- and medium-size firm range, for purposes of "hollowing in". There are simply too many companies involved for embedded autonomy to function effectively; measurable standards in exchange for subsidies are more likely than political relationships to guide business–government collaboration, just as standards now typically come attached to the subsidies that public science and technology agencies extend to the private sector, including universities.

By 2000 the decolonized generation had come a long way in its ranking among the world's largest enterprises, as measured by revenue in *Fortune* magazine's top 500 international firms. The total went from four in 1962, to 33 in 1992, to 25 in 1999 (Amsden, 2001). The number stagnated under neo-liberalism but then jumped to 80 in 2008 as Chinese enterprises came aboard. Still, despite privatization (allegedly a marker between old and new industrial policy) more than 50 percent of the emerging economies' 80 ranking firms were state-owned, mostly in oil and banking. Although the press routinely calls China a "juggernaut", only 37 Chinese companies (30 of them state-owned) were on the 2008 *Fortune* list. The private sector still had a long way to go in joining the world's largest companies, which are noted not only for their scale economies but also for their knowledge accumulation (Chandler Jr. *et al.*, 1997). Securing the home market through large, national firm-formation did not cease altogether with the "new" industrial policy, but attention shifted to strengthening small- and medium-size firms with high technological capabilities that had to compete against the likes of Prada in shoes, Moët in champagne, Dansk in design, MAN in diesel engines, and Benz in cars – a catch up process even more difficult than taking on the "majors".

The private sector falls short in the small- and medium-size range, even in countries where early industrial policies excelled, such as Korea. Although much is made about differences between Korea and Taiwan in organizational structure, these differences exist mainly above the 299 employee firm-size mark (Korea's large firms are larger and more diversified than Taiwan's). While SMEs in Korea, Taiwan and Japan are defined slightly differently, in the mid 2000s all accounted for roughly the same share of total employment – around 75 percent. In all three cases SMEs have tended to advance fastest – in terms of quality, cost and technology – in concert with larger firms (in sub-contracting relationships that are either formal or informal). Thus, when we talk about Korea we are also thinking of one East Asian role model for SMEs, characterized by endless experimentation with scores of policies to improve the bottom 75 percent.

While most economists see SMEs in a consistently positive light, the development of SMEs tends to vary by stages, as do their industrial policies.[17] Korea's industrial policies from 1962–71 (first and second five-year plans) focused on promoting industries with scale economies by means of exports, so SMEs received only moderate support. Then from 1972–81 (third and fourth five-year plans) there was a shift toward promoting heavy and chemical industries. SMEs received strong support to help them supply parts and components to these industries – ironically, when the economy was becoming *more* capital intensive and concentrated, SMEs bloomed. From 1982–91 (fifth and sixth five-year plans), the government sought a balance between large and small firms, and to raise SMEs to the large firm level, support became more intense. From 1992–97, the year of the East Asian financial crash and the beginning of liberalization (seventh and new economy five-year plans), policy sought to strengthen SME competitiveness amidst market-opening. From 1997 to the present, during the "Government of the People" period and the "Participatory Government" period, SME policy has sought to nurture competition, innovation, and a social safety net, although, beginning in the 2000s, the growth rate of SMEs slowed.

Despite Korea's official policy in this time period being one of market liberalization (the Kookmin Bank, for example, was privatized in 1995, but with the government retaining a 24 percent share), these measures together involved almost the same number of infractions of market laws as past measures, with an end to reservation of special business sectors for SMEs, but with more central initiative and state ownership (of KOSDAQ and its parent, the Korea Stock Exchange). Whether old or new, there is little lite, lean or temporary about these policies.

The performance of Korea's SMEs (measured by indicators relative to those of big business) has differed by time period. Performance is difficult to measure due to SMEs' heterogeneity, but many suffered from the conditionality of the International Monetary Fund (IMF) after Korea's financial crash, and from the emergence of low-end Chinese competition. SMEs performed better the closer their relations were with big business. They also performed better or worse at different development stages – the most difficult stage involving securing the home market has been the most recent, when many Korean companies have been relocating their production to China to take advantage of lower wages (Yang, 2009; Cho, 2010). The challenge of industrial policy has become to "hollow in" by transforming the competitive basis of SMEs from one of exploiting low wages to one of exploiting advanced technologies. This ongoing challenge suggests that, in the near future, industrial policies towards SMEs will be anything but lite, lean and temporary.

The new industrial policy and the future of development

Which set of countries – emerging or emerged, China or the U.S. – will perform better with the new industrial policy? An industrial policy based on subterfuge requires skills, organizations, and political finesse to operate effectively, just as managing nationalized properties after World War II required first hand knowledge. And, while the emerged economies have more advanced technologies, the emerging economies have more experience in making subterfuges work. Moreover, emerging economies have become increasingly adept at promoting SMEs that are able to compete with those in emerged ones.

Of course one argument is that as countries emerge and their industries become more mature, industrial policies should be increasingly lite and lean. Positioned against this is the argument that industrial policies should be expanded in breadth and depth to exploit new nooks and crannies, and, as Gallagher suggests in this volume, there is plenty of evidence to suggest that this is precisely what many countries are doing.[18] But even assuming that lite policies are appropriate for mature industries, then shouldn't heavy policies at least be appropriate for immature (or "post-immature") industries in the poorest and least powerful developing countries? The World Bank makes a blanket argument for lite and lean regardless, presumably because "governance" is weak, or too much industrial policy is inherently bad.

Not surprisingly, the poorest and least powerful developing countries confront the biggest challenges in deploying the new industrial policy. They lack the state power and finesse that are required to promote large firms, let alone create an environment in which SMEs can flourish. They also are bound by World Bank and IMF conditionalities, and face difficulties carving out policy space within multilateral trade agreements, leaving little room for the use of subterfuge. Thus, while many countries make liberal use of the new industrial policy, the countries that most need to do so are largely shut out. Figuring out how to change these circumstances – endowing states in the least developed countries with greater capacity and finesse, and promoting both formal and informal changes in the international institutional environment – must be a top priority on the development agenda.

Notes

1 See Hausmann, Rodrik and Sabel (2008), Melo (2001), Melo and Rodriguez-Clare (2006), Schrank and Kurz (2005), World Bank (2005).
2 Which may not be as lite as theory suggests (see Block, 2008).
3 A firm's nationality depends on the majority of its shareholders and control of its corporate board. For a comparison of the advantages of private, nationally owned firms (POEs) over foreign-owned firms (FOEs), see Amsden (2009a).
4 The way the home market is secured depends on the time period. The first great nation states, France and England, allied with the middle class, which paid taxes and lent the state money to aggrandize territorially, thereby securing an expanding the home market (Tilly, 1990).
5 The economist who conceived these criteria for targeting industries in Japan is Miyohei Shinohara, who discusses them in an interview in 2000 (Amsden and Suzumura, 2001).

6 Property rights and securitization have had an unending relationship. In 2010, for example, Brazil stated plans to tighten restrictions on foreign ownership of farm lands. The Agrarian Development Ministry said under current law, large rural properties can only be purchased by Brazilian citizens or residents, but foreigners bypass that rule by setting up companies in Brazil, which are controlled abroad, to purchase land. The ministry said the restriction was necessary to ensure that Brazilians had secure access to food.

7 For the relationship between industrial policy and "branding" in Taiwan and China, see Chu (2009).

8 Interview, Morris Chang, Taipei, 2001. See Amsden and Chu (2003).

9 Performance standards and nationalism are discussed by Wan Wen Chu (2010) in the case of the Chinese automobile industry.

10 General Agreement on Tariffs and Trade, sometimes dubbed "General Agreement to Talk and Talk". Tariffs are still not low in some industries in poor countries, noted earlier, and in the North's agricultural sector.

11 For a comparison of subsidies to wind versus coal as energy sources, see Jacobson and Masters, 2001.

12 Statistics taken from the UNCTAD online database – see www.unctad.org for details.

13 In 1992 the United States and European Community reached a bilateral agreement on trade in civil aircraft. The maximum-allowed direct subsidy of development costs was agreed at 33 percent – not zero (Irwin and Pavcnik, 2001).

14 The World Bank notes that credit guarantees are being used in 85 countries, with great success in Japan, North America, the OECD and parts of East Asia. But the problem with this scheme is "obvious", to the Bank at least: "[I]f risk of the lender is removed, it sets up a moral hazard issue for the lender, and neither the borrower nor the lender has any incentive to repay the loan unless other conditions are enforced." Therefore the World Bank is lukewarm about credit guarantees for developing countries (PMIPSI, 2005).

15 Typical of a "new" first stage, China's Ministry of Industry and Information Technology announced a policy to consolidate 60 percent of China's total steel capacity by 2015 under the control of ten mills (up from 44 percent in 2010) in order to end exports of low-value added steel products, encourage greater efficiency and less pollution, and engender higher energy savings. Incentives will be given to large companies to invest in steel making facilities overseas and acquire stable sources of raw materials. Subsidies and tax breaks will be given on a regional basis to old and inefficient plants that shut down quickly, and more efficient plants will benefit from lower energy prices (Stanway, 2010).

16 According to a World Bank study by Asli Demirguc-Kunt and Thorstein Beck, there *is* a general empirical conclusion. Beck notes:

> In fact, there is no robust evidence that SMEs by themselves matter for growth or poverty alleviation.... More fundamental reforms must first be instituted to tackle the underlying reasons why firms do not fulfill their growth potential. These reforms should lead to a better business environment that promotes competition, protection of private property rights, and a sound contract environment. All of these are proven to boost economic growth.
>
> (World Bank, 2006)

But our discussion of property rights (above) suggests that getting them "wrong" may have a strong positive impact on growth.

17 This policy stage analysis rests heavily on the work of Yang (2009). For a cross-country analysis of SME policies, see Pacific Economic Cooperation Council (2007).

18 Consider, for example, the initiatives proposed by a Korean government think tank: expanding markets for dried noodles and fish snacks, investing in energy saving technologies, globalizing medical services, improving start-up firms, restructuring

shipbuilding, raising research and development expenditures in services, increasing testing labs for heavy electrical equipment, nurturing global media groups, establishing sovereign wealth funds for international expansion, off-shoring materials and services, exploring the implications of Russia's expanding gas industry, improving child care, outsourcing knowledge services, strategizing on regional industrial clusters, enhancing the role of export companies, investing in downstream expansion of the Middle East's petrochemical industry, linking the two Koreas, privatizing social services, unbundling the power industry, revamping digital broadcasting, shifting production towards micro-enterprises, gilding the NAND flash memory, deepening skills in the general machinery industry, implementing the five day working week in SMEs, utilizing aged manpower, reorienting the PC industry, and responding to steel price hikes.

13 Reframing labour market regulation after the financial crisis

The stimulus packages and new industrial policy

John Howe[1]

Introduction

In the wake of the collapse of global financial markets in 2008 one of the more contentious issues has been the merits of the various economic stimulus and rescue packages implemented by national governments around the world (see, for example, OECD, 2009). Governments in both developed and developing countries moved quickly to disburse public funds in order to prime economies and assist ailing businesses, especially in the financial sector. Two of the larger packages in terms of percentage of gross domestic product (GDP) were announced by Australia and the United States. In Australia the Rudd Labor Government announced an AUS$42 billion stimulus package in February 2009. The U.S. package of a total of US$787 billion commenced with the passage of the American Recovery and Reinvestment Act of 2009 (ARRA Act), on top of the various rescue packages under the Troubled Asset Relief Program (TARP). The U.S. Congress passed further, smaller-scale economic stimulus measures in 2010.

While the more general goal of these packages has been to arrest any decline in economic growth resulting from the crisis, a more specific objective of these packages has been to stimulate job creation and retention in order to minimize unemployment (see, for example, Jha, 2009). The extent of government expenditure has prompted debates over whether these packages represent a "re-regulation" of economies by the state after two decades of retreat in the face of neoliberal demands for smaller government, and over the likely effectiveness of such expenditure in stimulating the economy and rescuing jobs.

The use of government financial subsidies and incentives to foster and maintain private enterprise as a mechanism for stimulating employment is not a recent phenomenon. However, over the last two decades, these forms of government "intervention" have to some extent been driven underground as a result of sustained neoliberal economic critique. Although controversial, the stimulus packages were evidence of a new state willingness to shape markets with a view to broadening social and economic goals. In particular, the stated "job creation" objective behind the stimulus packages may enable closer attention to be given to a more coherent, strategic and transparent use of industrial policy – or "policies that stimulate economic activities and promote structural change" (Rodrik,

2008: 3) – as a mechanism of labour market regulation. Industrial policy is an avenue by which states in developed and developing economies can stimulate labour demand in a way that addresses economic and social priorities such as job quality and unemployment.

Not only does the extent of government priming of the economy open up a space to discuss industrial policy as an aspect of labour market regulation, debates over the Australian and U.S. rescue packages have explicitly questioned whether sufficient "strings" were attached to this expenditure by government (see, for example, Tingle and Rollins, 2009) – especially with regard to the risk of corporate siphoning of funds to pay excessive executive salaries and bonuses instead of deployment of funds for job creation and other activities with a public benefit. The debate around executive pay suggests that in the wake of the crisis there is normative space up for grabs around the appropriate use of company profits (for labour, for executives, for environmental purposes, for sustainable economic development?) and the mix of public/social and private purposes of companies more broadly in light of their dependence upon state bailouts.

Industrial policy, regulatory pluralism and labour market regulation

Markets, and labour markets in particular, are not natural mechanisms that are autonomous or self-ordering in the absence of the state and other institutions (Polanyi, 1944; Block, 2003a). They are constituted and regulated by the state and other cultural elements and social structures and institutions (Shearing, 1993). The term "labour market" is used here to describe the way work is offered and exchanged for reward as well as the demand for, and supply of, labour for hire (Howe *et al.*, 2006: 309). Taking this broad definition as a starting point we can say that labour market regulation encompasses a number of policy areas that impact on the operation of the labour market. This includes regulation, which affects the availability of employment (such as industrial policies) and which otherwise impacts on those who are dependent upon their labour for an income. In many industrialized countries the existence of industrial policy enabled the maintenance of labour law protection for workers by insulating domestic workers and businesses from global competition and alleviating the impact of economic restructuring (Chang, 2003).

This chapter adopts a pluralist conception of regulation, whereby a number of regulatory approaches might operate towards the achievement of substantive goals; including legislation, financial incentives and so on. Some of these regulatory approaches may be public and some may involve or be initiated by non-state actors, such as trades unions. While law is an important tool in the achievement of social policy objectives, there are other mechanisms that have been employed in the achievement of social goals, including the deployment of wealth (Howe, 2006; McCrudden, 2007).

Combining these perspectives on labour market regulation and regulatory pluralism presented here, there are elements of the stimulus and rescue packages that are essentially about the deployment of the fiscal power of the state to create and retain jobs. Many of the stimulus packages implemented by nation states around the world have included a combination of taxation and spending measures (OECD, 2009), while rescue packages have included loans and government investment in company shares. We might label these "industrial policies". Industrial policy has been one way that the state has constituted and regulated demand for labour in labour markets. There are a number of different definitions of industrial policy. Critics often define industrial policies as policies that provide subsidies to particular industries or sectors. However, I have adopted Dani Rodrik's broader definition set out in the introduction. Rodrik's definition is useful because it encompasses a number of state policies designed to foster economic growth, and it is not limited to outdated concepts of industry and industry assistance. Thus, tariff protection might be considered industrial policy, as might trade liberalization and adjustment assistance to alleviate the effects of trade liberalization, expenditure on infrastructure development, public procurement, and financial incentives to attract investment, business or to stimulate economic growth.

An aspect of regulatory pluralism that can be purposefully employed for the task of re-embedding markets is the meaningful involvement of non-state actors in regulation, such as business, worker and small producer representatives, as well as other representative bodies with a stake in a particular issue. Collaborative, tripartite approaches are perceived as enhancing the effectiveness and legitimacy of regulation. Further, accountability is enhanced where a system relies on multiple actors to secure compliance, thus avoiding a number of problems with state enforcement. These problems include the potential for "regulatory capture" of state agencies by industry, and insufficient resourcing of state agencies leaving gaps in supervision of a regulated sphere or community.

In the past, when there has been close cooperation between the state and industry groups – including capital and labour – in corporatist relations, this has often resulted in the drowning out of independent voices. Legitimate questions exist about the representational quality of corporatist institutions and the extent to which they function as instruments of co-optation rather than representation. However, this chapter proposes that by adopting new regulatory techniques, the potential for a form of deliberative democracy to inform both industrial policy development and implementation is significant. This potential is explored in light of the some of the experiences with the U.S. and Australian stimulus and rescue packages.

Lessons from stimulus and rescue packages

The stimulus and rescue packages represent an extremely visible deployment of public wealth for public policy purposes. This visibly creates a window for the pursuit of more coherent and sustainable industrial policies.

This is not to suggest that the stimulus packages represent a sudden government re-entry into industrial policy after years of absence. States in many jurisdictions have been engaged in economic activity that has been constitutive of labour markets. This is a feature of what John Braithwaite and others call "regulatory capitalism", where states may be more decentred, but the wealth capitalism generates means that states are regulating and providing more than ever before (2008). However, it is fair to say that state engagement in economic activity in the form of industrial policy or assistance has been relatively low key, though it has rarely gone by the label of industrial policy. Part of the reason for this low visibility strategy must lie in the dominance of neoliberal ideology and its calls for smaller government and freer markets, whatever the reality of regulatory capitalism.

Nevertheless, even the U.S. has been engaging in de facto industrial policy, albeit one that has involved ad hoc and industry specific interventions without a coherent overall strategy (Ketels, 2007; Block, 2008; Schrank and Whitford, 2009; Amsden, this volume). This supports Polanyi/Block's conception of markets as always embedded in the social, and that it is just a matter of degrees of embeddeness.

However, the stimulus and rescue packages render more visible the government and industrial policy's role in constituting and regulating markets, and in labour markets more specifically. This has the potential to lend previously hidden industrial policy greater democratic legitimacy than when obscured (Block, 2008: 195).

There is insufficient space here to describe these packages in detail, but, suffice to say, in both Australia and the U.S. the stimulus packages have involved significant expenditure, much of it with the express goal of supporting the creation or retention of jobs (in relation to the U.S., see Bernstein and Romer, 2009). While the packages have in reality encompassed a range of initiatives, what is of most interest to me are those elements of the packages designed to stimulate job creation, mostly through expenditure on infrastructure development. The U.S. ARRA Act requires 35 per cent of the stimulus package funds to be distributed as contracts, grants and loans, with the remaining funds to provide tax relief and entitlements. In the U.S. especially, the focus has been on so-called "shovel ready" projects, mostly in the nature of building and infrastructure construction. In Australia it has been the commitment to funding school building construction and refurbishment ("Building the Education Revolution") that has attracted the most attention. In both cases the idea was to find infrastructure projects that could be funded and commenced quickly. This led to criticism that longer-term projects of greater benefit to the economy were neglected, and some queried whether this strategy was the best and most efficient way to fund infrastructure and job creation. Accountability issues also arose. Government reviews of the U.S. and Australian packages have largely been positive, albeit with some caveats (see, for example, Council of Economic Advisers, 2010; BERIT, 2010). The packages were an urgent response to a crisis, and it is therefore understandable that many flaws can be identified.

My argument is that the stimulus and rescue packages – including their successes and flaws – have created some space to discuss a longer term and more coherent role for government in supporting industry. It is worth remembering that there are other, longer term aspects to the subsidy packages – the emphasis on green jobs being one example. $25 billion of the U.S. stimulus package was designated for projects which enhanced energy efficiency. The Australian package also included an Energy Efficient Homes Program. This was in addition to expenditure to "green" Australia's automobile industry (Banks, 2008), and the 2009–10 federal budget also provided for $3.6 billion in additional clean energy initiatives (SERC, 2009).

There have been at least two aspects to the debate over the packages that should inform any discussion about the extent to which they create room for a new push on industrial policy.

First is the debate about where public funds are best spent to stimulate economic growth and the effectiveness of the packages in creating and protecting sustainable jobs at various levels. One issue here has been a debate about what sort of jobs should be created or retained. Is any job enough, or should attention be given to the quality of jobs? Should the funds necessarily be directed toward "green jobs" on the basis that these jobs are more likely to be sustainable in the long term?

The second aspect, and the one with which this chapter is more concerned, is a question about whether, once a decision is made to deploy public funds, the money is getting to where it should go: was the money being used to create or retain jobs or to fund profits that had otherwise been sucked away by the financial crisis; were subsidies creating additional jobs or just subsidizing firms that would have employed people anyway?

Transparency and accountability are important goals whenever governments provide financial assistance and incentives to the private sector, and this has been an important theme in relation to both the U.S. and Australian stimulus and rescue packages. Law has played an important role in setting criteria and establishing mechanisms to ensure that monitoring of achievement of those criteria is carried out. For example, the legislation governing the U.S. stimulus package

> directs recipients and sub-recipients of Recovery funds, including state and local government agencies as well as contractors and other private entities, to report on their spending within 10 days of the close of each calendar quarter. Recipients are required to report almost 100 pieces of data, including the type of award, the date and amount, the project description and the number of jobs created or saved.
>
> (RATB, 2009: 14)

The fact that there has been a debate about executive compensation in the context of the disbursement of stimulus and rescue package funds is significant in that for the first time in many years there has been a mainstream public debate about inequality in income distribution and the ethics of business corporations.

The public outrage over AIG paying executive bonuses after receiving government bailout funds (and other events) resulted in attempts to use the terms of the packages in the U.S. to promote disclosure of executive compensation, and in the case of the AIG rescue package, some control over compensation. The ARRA Act requires disclosure of executive compensation by companies benefiting from rescue packages under TARP. The legislation also established a Recovery and Accountability Transparency Board to oversee the implementation of the stimulus package and assess its effectiveness.

This particular issue and the U.S. response might inform ongoing approaches to industry subsidies, as it highlights the importance of corporate accountability to social objectives of packages (thus extending the debate beyond criticism of government accountability). It is one thing to announce packages as having various social and economic goals. It is very much another thing to expect that the business recipients of subsidies will do their best to spend the money on jobs. It is here that regulatory pluralism becomes relevant, as business dependency on subsidies and other government support might trigger the better use of these subsidies as "meta-regulation": regulation that is used to leverage corporate responsibility (and internal self-regulation) to social goals (Parker, 2007).

Careful thought needs to be given as to how best to design industry policy to ensure that it is effective. And part of this design process may involve coming up with ways to ensure that industrial policy promotes economic growth that benefits those who most need it, and is not used to pad hip pockets of those who least need the money.

New industrial policy

The U.S. rescue packages and many aspects of the stimulus packages in Australia and the U.S. are essentially a form of industrial policy. Before the financial crisis there was a growing push by development economists for the pursuit of a "new" industrial policy (see Amsden in this volume). This push has been resisted by many economists and runs counter to the Washington consensus. The concept of new industrial policy is in part designed to overcome some of the objections to "old" industrial policy. The two main objections to industrial policy – aside from more general objection to government "intervention" in "free" markets – are as follows. The first is what Rodrik calls the "informational objection" (Rodrik, 2008), or in other words that governments are ill-equipped to identify firms, sectors or markets that are affected by market failure or imperfections (see, for example, Pack and Saggi, 2006). The second objection is that industrial policy encourages corruption and "rent-seeking" behaviour by firms. In other words, when government offers financial incentives to firms, the private sector will seek out those benefits even if they are not required for productive purposes.

It appears to me that the stimulus packages, and the collapse in support for pro-free market ideology, should add or restore some momentum to the push for new industrial policy. In other words, if this is a Polanyian "double movement" moment, then the stimulus packages may undermine the hegemony of opposition to government involvement in structuring the economy. As Rodrik argues, the two more specific objections outlined above can be addressed through appropriate policy design.

One issue to address is what sort of industrial policy should be pursued. I would not necessarily rule out an industry/sectoral approach in some circumstances, especially where the goal is to ease the adjustment difficulties for workers and communities in shrinking industries toward new and more sustainable industries, or in converting a particular sector or industry into a more sustainable industry. However, I also see the merits of encouraging innovation and assisting in the development of those new and more sustainable industries. It is also important that industrial policy be targeted toward the creation of quality jobs, not just job numbers, on the basis that decent work is more likely to be consistent with sustainable economic development (see, for example, Fields, 2003). Additionally, the focus on green jobs should inform new industrial policy. Jobs should be sustainable, and created through sustainable economic development, although this needs to be given careful consideration. Not all green initiatives create quality jobs. As one study found, "the fact that an employer is engaged in a business that benefits the environment does not necessarily mean that the employees of that enterprise are going to be treated well" (Good Jobs First, 2009: 34; see also Eren *et al.*, 2010).

Assuming that there is some consensus about the pursuit of industry policy as broadly conceived, the debates over executive compensation signal that it cannot be assumed that companies, or industry more broadly, will do the right thing, even with a willing government. Even the Left has objected to various forms of industry assistance on the basis that it is simply "corporate welfare". However, this does not mean that governments should not pursue industrial policy. It does mean that transparency and corporate accountability should be important elements in the development of industrial policy.

Rodrik and others have argued that industry policy should be seen as a process. In other words, as many of the criticisms of industry policy are largely about practical difficulties, these can be overcome by regulatory design. One of the design elements that Rodrik advocates is "embeddedness", based on Rodrik's understanding of Peter Evans' version of this concept (Evans, 1995). In other words the state must be embedded in the social, to some degree, for its policies to work. Rodrik argues that industrial policy has to be conducted as a system of discovery of all of the sources of uncertainty about what sort of industrial policy will work: "It requires mechanisms for eliciting information about the constraints markets face, and hence close collaboration between the government and the private sector" (Rodrik, 2008: 38). I suggest that to be properly embedded, this process will have to involve other participants as well: members of civil society with an interest in industrial development. This group could include trades unions, NGOs or other representative organizations or collectives with a stake in a particular initiative, industry, sector or activity.

The involvement of civil society in the form of unions and NGOs will enhance both the effectiveness and accountability of industry policy. This idea has overlaps with Joel Roger's "productive democracy", which would make deliberate use of democracy as a tool of wealth generation and government, not just representation and equity. Regulation is likely to be ineffective if those who are affected by it are not consulted and engaged in regulatory process. Moreover, these groups will also function to hold business and government accountable to policy goals in circumstances where the latter two institutions might stray from these objectives. Langmore has emphasized the importance of what the International Labour Organization calls "social dialogue" in the context of social development policies for these reasons (Langmore, 2004).

I provide an example of this from Australia. The federal Labor Government elected in late-2007 has cautiously pursued a more active and coherent industrial policy framework since coming to office (see Banks, 2008). This has involved consultation and policy development regarding the future of "old" manufacturing industries such as the automotive industry and the textile, clothing and footwear industry (TCF). The government has used this policy review process to support the development of a more "horizontal" industrial policy under the banner of "innovation" policy, including the restructuring of industries such as the TCF and promotion of green jobs in the automobile industry.

As part of its efforts to transform TCF industries in Australia, the Government has established a TCF Industries Innovation Council. The Innovation Council is an important initiative because it is based on a social dialogue model – the Council includes business, government and trade union representatives. The establishment of the Innovation Council was recommended by Professor Roy Green's Review of Australian TCF Industries, commissioned by the Australian Government. Australia's TCF industries have been in decline over a number of years because of a reduction in the previously high protective tariffs of the 1970s, exposing the sector to competition from cheaper overseas imports. The Green Report suggested that the Council would be an important component in a process of "mainstreaming" Australian TCF industries by adopting a broader policy framework of building innovation capacity (Green, 2008). To quote the federal Government:

> The TCF Industries Innovation Council provides strategic advice on innovation priorities for the sector to the Minister. It promotes and encourages innovation in the TCF industries and builds links with other organisations, including the Enterprise Connect network.
>
> The Council membership represents a wealth of TCF industries experience … [and] looks at a range of innovation issues and work[s] closely with businesses, unions, researchers and government in achieving its goals.
>
> (DIISR, 2011)

In late 2009 the Government announced that it was funding the establishment of a Textile, Clothing and Footwear Industry Innovation Network to strengthen collaboration on research and innovation in that industry (Dodson, 2009). This collaboration is between business and research institutions, but is subject to oversight by the Innovation Council.

The creation of both the TCF Innovation Council and the Innovation Network are important because they give labour a seat at the table in the development of future economic policy impacting on this particular industry sector. This engagement is not limited to discussing the impact of industry restructuring on workplaces and employees, as under some corporatist models, but provides representatives of TCF workers with an institutionalized, deliberative role in the development of a future economic strategy for the industry. Through their involvement in the Council, unions should have an opportunity to interpret research and shape the objectives of any restructuring of the industry. However, unions will presumably also have the capacity to influence the development of a process of implementing this change. In this way unions will not just have a voice in the development of the policy, but in the process of transforming that policy into outcomes. Their involvement will also lend legitimacy to the restructuring process, as workers in the industry will be more likely to accept the prospect of change in circumstances where their representatives have played a role.

Second, policies need to be implemented with the appropriate transparency and accountability mechanisms in place. This is where law can play a role. While the making available of public funds is the leverage the state uses to help persuade corporations create more jobs (or not reduce their workforces in difficult economic circumstances) this is unlikely to bring about internalization of social goals on its own. The regulatory framework of the U.S. stimulus and rescue package demonstrates that law can be used to set criteria which reflect industrial policy objectives, and to establish accountability and oversight mechanisms to ensure the achievement of those objectives.

For example, the first element of a legitimate and effective regulatory regime for industrial policy is a mechanism to ensure information disclosure by businesses or industries receiving financial assistance. The disclosure requirements in the ARRA Act concerning executive compensation practices are a good example of this. Disclosure of relevant information allows government and other stakeholders to determine whether industrial policy is, or is likely to, achieve its objective. For example, if the goal of industrial assistance is to achieve the creation of decent work, then the labour relations practices of firms seeking assistance will be of interest. Second, either legislation, or the terms of contracts entered into with the recipients of public largesse, must incorporate the goals of policy as legal criteria to be met by the beneficiaries of the policy. These might include mandating that the recipients of financial or other assistance comply with minimum employment standards under local labour and employment laws. In this way law can assist in ensuring that jobs created through industrial policy are decent to the extent that this is expressed in existing labour regulation.

Finally, I must emphasize that new industrial policy must be global in outlook. This article has focused on the potential for new industrial policies to be pursued by liberal market and mixed economies. In the debate over the financial crisis and the various responses to this in the U.S., there is great emphasis on protecting U.S. jobs, which is understandable. However, it is not just jobs in America or Australia that we should be thinking about. It is jobs all around the world, especially in developing countries with high rates of poverty and socio-economic disadvantage. The new industrial policy should be framed so as to achieve more quality jobs and a more equitable distribution of quality jobs around the world. This will require some coordination between nations in the development of industrial policies. It is possible that the UN Development agencies or the World Trade Organization are existing fora through which coordination could be carried out. Although more detailed consideration of these processes is beyond the scope of this chapter, the emergence of a more coordinated approach would enhance the potential of industrial policy at a domestic level.

Conclusion

In this chapter I have argued that the stimulus and rescue packages have rendered visible the extent to which governments play a role in stimulating economic activity through industrial policy. The stimulus and rescue packages were a crisis-led reaction to an old problem, the cyclical nature of capitalism. The careful adoption of new industrial policies, under a process driven approach as I have outlined in this chapter, may contribute to a more careful and considered re-embedding of labour markets in social policy goals. By adopting techniques of regulatory pluralism a broader range of social actors can become engaged in the process of industrial policy. In this way the "scope" of social re-embedding is increased. Industrial policy can therefore be used as a means by which state-led growth is embedded in plural social values *and* by which rent-seeking can be hindered by strong accountability and transparency mechanisms. I have suggested that industrial policy can also be used as a process for "regulatory learning" amongst all players involved, thereby enhancing not only the scope of social embedding, but also the depth.

Note

1 Centre for Employment and Labour Relations Law, University of Melbourne Law School and Visiting Scholar, University of Pennsylvania Law School.

14 Productive democracy

Joel Rogers[1]

Introduction

These are the best and worst of times for practical egalitarian democrats.[2] Globally, the number of peoples selecting their governments through free elections has rarely been higher, popular contempt for tyranny more evident, technical conditions for application of human knowledge to a host of pressing social problems more favourable, or local democratic innovation in that application more abundant. But also never, or at least in a very long while – especially in affluent capitalist democracies with rich social democratic traditions – has the corporate perversion and hollowing out of national democratic institutions, the weakness of worker and other popular organization in influencing public policy, the lack of citizen confidence in and engagement with governing institutions, or the amount of unnecessary harm elected leaders are prepared to inflict on their own citizens been greater. Over the past three years, the generally pre-1930s collective response of the world's major capitalist democracies to the global financial crisis and ensuing contraction (itself triggered by collapse of a seventeenth century-worthy debt-financed asset price bubble, studiously neglected by governments in hock to casino finance and intent on its deregulation) has offered a kaleidoscope of such democratic failure. That at the time of writing (September 2011) the main perpetrators of the calamity have emerged unscathed, or in some cases even better off, and the Right has gained more politically than the Left, suggests just how severely competent and egalitarian democratic politics has been diminished.

Many egalitarian democrats, again especially from those rich countries, fear that the combination of globalization,[3] the effective disintegration of social democracy's social base, and the incompetence of national government before these and a host of broader regulatory problems and citizen demands, effectively ends the practicality of their project. A recognizably modern as well as egalitarian democracy, a fortiori a world of many such democracies, peacefully trading and otherwise working together to advance their own and humanity's prospects, seems a fantasy. Most expect continued national decline into variants of "post-democracy" (Crouch, 2004; 2011) amid widening international disorder; at least until some even deeper crisis (of unknown dimensions but, given its antecedents, with no clear prospect of more favourable resolution) arrives. Egalitarian progress in the developed world will likely be halted or reversed for a generation or more, the time it will take for personal incomes in poor but technologically equipped nations to come close to those in currently rich ones. And by that time social collapse in the developed nations, a retreat from liberal democracy, mutating pandemic disease, militarized resource wars, climate change, other environmental catastrophes, or a variety of entirely unforeseen disasters are at least as likely as a peaceful resumption of egalitarian progress. Very few, certainly, are still confident in the current viability – meaning stable reproducibility, once achieved – of an egalitarian democratic project, locally rooted but globally cosmopolitan, able both to excite and organize a social base and govern efficiently, and sufficient in its collective international power to discipline and face down the mischief or malefaction of transnational corporate power and get back to the work of achieving humanity's promise.

I think that such a project, with a coherent public philosophy, is in fact available – both in the limited sense of not being foreclosed, and the bigger one of having a clear constituency and agent which, if organized, could put up a very good fight for its achievement. I don't think this project is defeated by globalization per se, but I do think its achievement requires that egalitarian democratic politics shed much of its traditional twentieth century social democratic form. Here I call this project and its associated public philosophy "productive democracy" (PD).[4]

Like social democracy, PD would premise the continued existence of private property, markets, complex economies, and international flows in ideas, labour, goods, and capital. And like social democracy it would provide a high "social wage" of public goods and individual services guaranteed to all citizens. But PD would, throughout, highlight the centrality of productivity growth in achieving egalitarian ends, and place a bigger and more visible bet on a well-ordered democracy's ability to elicit citizen contribution to creating social wealth and solving problems in governance. Its signature politics would entail efforts to develop and harness that contribution, not only assure fair representation and equity of outcomes. And it would define the general welfare not only by physical security and the promise of reasonably equal life chances, but by the capacity and incentive of all citizens to make such a contribution – to be meaningfully engaged in politics.

The table "Three Public Philosophies" offers a highly schematic contrast of neoliberalism, social democracy, and PD. It focuses on characteristic problems in policy and governance in any mass democracy. Since PD's contrasts with neoliberalism are obvious enough, in introducing the idea here I limit myself to its contrast with traditional social democracy, focusing on policy and governance.

In *policy*, PD would commit to an egalitarian "effective supply" of the necessary ingredients for environmentally sustainable egalitarian wealth generation, not just effective demand for market goods and services. It would adopt a defining goal of public power to be the creation, in places, of a "productive infrastructure" (of policy and institutions, along with physical infrastructure) that supported the use of democratic power/organization to foster both the maximally efficient, restorative, and value-generating use of all basic factors of production – i.e., natural (a.k.a. environmental), human, physical and financial capital – and equitable sharing of the benefits of that productivity.[5] PD would also focus redistributive efforts earlier in the life-course, include assets as well as income in redistribution, and seek directly to relieve household (e.g., gender-based inequalities in the division of labour) as well as class-based barriers to political participation. It would use taxes more deliberately to promote savings and investment, with steeply progressive taxation on waste, luxury consumption and non-reinvested profits. PD would also embrace "tax universalism" (progressive taxation of public income based on the recipient's private income). In international relations it would be more tolerant of national diversity in choice of sustainable development strategy, more resolute in eliminating speculative financial flows and corporate tax avoidance, and more ambitious in supplying non-military global public goods.

In *governing*, PD would focus central governments more squarely on deliberation about and declaration of desired outcomes, and the provision of the resources and enforcement needed to achieve them, rather than specification of the process by which they were achieved. Correlatively, it would more deliberately seek to develop and harness governing contributions from outside the nation state. This would include norms on intergovernmental and state–society relations both more indicative and accommodating of the use of sub-national units of government and extra-state institutions in meeting social goals. It would foster "progressive federalism" in managing relations between national government and sub-national units, with the latter supported in experiment consistent with benchmarked national outcome norms. It would in a variety of ways involve lower level managers and "street level bureaucrats" (i.e., the deliverers of services) in shaping public administration, with their management trading them greater autonomy and discretion in doing their jobs in exchange for their contribution to repeated cycles and reporting on: benchmarking, justification of departures from past practice, diagnostic peer review and performance assessment, and publicity of acquired learning. Outside the state, it would use whatever new technology and old-fashioned organizing it could muster to improve civic education, general engagement, self-organizing, and guided but essentially open-source systems of problem-solving and deliberative decision-making. Citizens would have work to do and reasons for doing it.

I will return below to these contrasts and PD's constitutive programme elements and claimed viability. But first, to clarify PD's motivation and general strategy, let me explicitly defend the two assertions above: that globalization per se doesn't defeat egalitarianism, but that promoting egalitarianism in the current environment requires something quite different from traditional social democracy.

Why globalization doesn't defeat egalitarianism

To be clear from the outset, I freely acknowledge that cross-border flows of goods, capital and labour have all increased the inequality or volatility of labour

Table 14.1 Three public philosophies

	Social democracy	*Neoliberalism*	*Productive democracy*
Economic strategy	Effective demand	Inequality/incentives	Effective supply (productive infrastructure)
Redistributive peak	Late	None	Early
Equality of opportunity	Thick	Thin	Deep (infancy, household, politics)
Social contribution	Enabled but not required	Required but not enabled	Strongly encouraged and enabled
State/civil society relation	Active/distinct	Passive/distinct	Active/integrated (*via* problem-solving)
Citizen engagement	Medium/structured	Low/structured	High/open
Privileged branch	Executive	Judiciary	Legislature and problem-solving public
National/'state' relation	Affirmative national	Limiting national	Progressive federalism
Public Administration	Executive delegation/rules	Incentives, privatization	"New governance", democratic experimentalism, deliberative polyarchy
Asset redistribution	No	No	Yes
Insurance	On labour income, health	None	Extended to assets and (*via* services) non-actuarial risk
Tax strategy	Progressive on private income/ profits	Regressive/flat on private income/ profits	Tax universalism, progressive on luxury consumption, pollution, non-reinvested profits
International Economic Strategy	Strategic protection	Forced integration	Managed diversity, curbed financial speculation, ended tax avoidance, global public goods

earnings in advanced industrial societies and constrained their governments' ability to tax globalization's winners to compensate its losers. In line with the arguments of Amsden and Gallagher in this volume, I also find many of the current rules on globalization often destructive to democracy, especially in their crowding out of space for difference and innovation in development strategies and their subjection of innocent publics to all sorts of unnecessary financial risk. These rules can and should be improved. So, for example, although I see more potential than he in non-state-based global institutions of justice, I happily endorse Rodrik's recent reform programme for globalization. Departing from seven simple and appealing principles for global economic governance, this recommends a "thin layer of simple, transparent, and commonsense traffic rules" for international economic dealings (Rodrik, 2011: 280), à la Bretton Woods, rather than the forced integration of national standards and strategies, à la neoliberal globalization.[6] Along with democratizing the governance of international institutions themselves, it would expand the Agreement on Safeguards to permit exemptions from WTO rules in cases of demonstrated threat to national development and social goals; enact a Tobin tax to curb volatile speculative capital flows; and pursue strong financial regulation and/or bank restructuring (e.g., increased capitalization requirements, punitive bars to certain sorts of transactions, breakup or restoration of limited purpose banking). Getting something like this programme "on the ballot" everywhere is an urgent political task. Again, I'd certainly vote for it.

This said, I think the most prominent basic argument for why globalization per se defeats egalitarianism is vastly overdrawn, and in central part simply wrong. The argument I have in mind is a political version of factor price equalization, with any public constraints on capital a costly factor. Greater economic integration of a world of gross inequality, mobile capital, and a vastly enlarged labour pool of technically equipped but very poor workers means that capital is able to shop among national regimes for its best deal, and can credibly threaten exit from any nation brave or foolish enough to limit its autonomy while adding to its costs. The inevitable result is a competitive race to the bottom, to a distinctly inegalitarian system of natural liberty. Any political resistance to this is powerless, since the world has essentially become a flat and frictionless surface where even the tiniest cost can prompt capital flight. The task of governing elites in rich countries is to assure their vulnerable populations of the inevitability of their fate, counsel their acceptance of it, and improve techniques of suppressing those who resist this sentencing.

This argument is overdrawn in a number of respects. It underestimates the share of the economy not touched by its assumptions (e.g., the large role of non-traded services and fixed infrastructure in national economies, or their still overwhelming level of self-supply in manufacturing and traded services); the continued importance of national institutions in determining living standards (as evidenced by continued high and effective welfare state spending, and resulting wide variation in unemployment, wage growth, and equality across nations with comparable gross incomes, industrial structure, and exposure to international competition); the evident capacity of welfare state institutions to adjust to competitive and budget constraints without abandoning their values (e.g., by providing "flexicurity" to promote labour market mobility with equity, or income-contingent social insurance and educational funding to reconcile public budgets with general security and opportunity); the continuing importance of sunk costs in economic activity; and, perhaps above all, the continued importance of *place* to economic activity – evident in everything from the close correlation of national savings and investment rates, to "home bias" consumption effect, to the mundane, but ever reliable, robustness of gravity models in mapping value flows, to, most striking and decisively, ongoing urbanization worldwide and the acknowledged "triumph of the city" as humanity's best source of environmentally sustainable practices, productivity, and innovation (Barhan *et al.*, 2006; Glaeser, 2011).

Put all this together, and it suggests considerable room for egalitarian politics.

But it's in considering what that politics might aim at that we can see where the view is actually wrong. Simply, there is no reason to believe, as this argument would have it, that any and all social constraints on capital generate net losses. Some measure of coercive public authority, of course, is needed even to make markets function. And "market fundamentalism", the idea/ideology/religion that markets not only provide the most efficient allocation of scarce resources but are able essentially to reproduce themselves without much outside assistance, hardly improves by elevation from village life to international spheres. But public authority's economic contribution hardly stops with assuring the possibility of markets. By helping to cure ubiquitous market failures and imperfections, by providing a range of public goods beyond the capacity of individual firms, and enlisting the diffused monitoring, enforcement, and problem-solving abilities of citizens, public power in well-organized democratic places can also, does also, immensely improve those places' productivity. In doing this it adds real value to the economy. And the places that do this better than others will naturally be rewarded by increased inflows of capital, a fortiori in a system where there are fewer barriers to them.

Democratic organizations can also ensure greater equity while increasing productivity. They can bargain directly with the capital attracted to their productive infrastructure, and make access to it conditional upon better behaviour by firms in the form of higher wages, higher taxes for public goods, and a greater share of profits reinvested.[7] They can shift from "taxing winners to compensate losers" to using that infrastructure to make "losers" into "winners" by increasing their human capital or access to credit. They can reassign property rights in more efficient ways that disproportionately benefit the poor, or promote alternative economic forms (e.g., worker cooperative or non-profit or public-benefit competitors to ordinary firms) to widen worker exit possibilities from oppressive employment relations (Bowles and Gintis, 1998). And, again, they can reduce waste throughout their systems and provide more efficient public goods and services.[8]

Indeed, such "high road" use of democratic organization for higher efficiency/productivity and egalitarian welfare – adding value, reducing waste, capturing and sharing the benefits of doing both – which is certainly possible under current conditions, would make sense even in the "nightmare" case of low sunk costs and frictionless capital markets. In this case capital would respond immediately to any change in expected after-tax rates of profit, making the rate of profit the same everywhere. No single nation (or place) could lower it, which would constrain the first equity strategy above. But equally, and typically less considered by troubled egalitarians, no place could *raise* its rate of profit. Any gain in productivity or efficiency would go to the local population, including all those immobile, unproductive "losers" (Bowles, 2006). And the losers in the best organized places, with the most robust productive infrastructure, would gain the most.

For all these reasons, then, I don't think globalization per se defeats egalitarianism.

Why something other than social democracy is needed

It's not enough, however, to make the case for the possibility of an egalitarian politics under globalization. That possibility needs to be realized in politics. People need to understand and be excited by what they can gain from this politics, to see where it's going and what's required of them to make that happen, to fight for its achievement against resistance, and to do that for however long it takes. It needs a social base and a programmatic mass politics. Today, however, both need to be created, since social democracy – the one successful egalitarian democratic political experiment under capitalism, the only time liberty and equality were married successfully and advanced in mass politics – no longer provides either.

The social democratic project ably satisfied for workers the two typical requirements of organization of any subordinated group. It offered member participants or potential participants something useful, and solved a problem for the broader society that elites have no interest or capacity to solve themselves, thereby gaining social cachet and political support. Under twentieth century "monopoly" capitalism, social democracy did this for the industrial working class by gaining income and power for them vis-à-vis capitalists and, through the alchemy of national Keynesianism, working as a motor for private accumulation and growth that increased the general welfare. It solved the problem of collapsed effective demand that capitalists couldn't solve on their own. Wage increases or state-led redistribution toward labour increased effective demand, which was captured by domestic firms supplying employment; stabilization of markets encouraged investment, which increased productivity, in turn lowering the real costs of consumption goods and further raising living standards. Social democracy also married particular and more universal interests in its organization. Strong industrial union movements made deals with individual firms, but, through centralized systems of wage-bargaining and state regulation, unions and union-based political parties also exchanged worker wage moderation for government and business commitments to increased social welfare spending and guarantees of full employment – a "social wage" not tied to particular employment contracts and paid for by all, in part through the greater stability and productivity it provided capitalists by taking wages out of competition.

This social democratic project, however, rested on several background conditions. The first was a nation state in effective control of the economy within its borders and capable of meeting broad citizen demands for security. This premised an economy sufficiently insulated from foreign competitors that the benefits of demand-stimulus were reliably captured by resident business, a monetary policy apparatus sufficiently insulated from worldwide financial flows to permit unilateral correctives to recession, and security demands essentially satisfied by employment, military defence, and broad social insurance. The second background condition was the organization of capital into large and sectorally-dominant firms with highly centralized operations, typically organized in Taylorist ways that suppressed natural differences within the workforce. The third was the popularity of a politics based in industrial unionism, centred on issues best organized through the lens of class and the worker–employer–state flow of money value and employment regulation.

None of these conditions hold today. Globalization has qualified demand-management policies, employment often rests on favourable microeconomic competitiveness, and many risks the state is asked to deal with are intrinsically individualized, unpredictable, and hence "non-actuarial" (i.e., not subject to ordinary insurance coverage). Asked to regulate and intervene more widely and locally, the state often lacks the local knowledge needed to determine appropriate standards or the most appropriate means to meet them under diverse circumstances; its monitoring and enforcement capacities, especially in areas requiring compliance across numerous, dispersed, heterogeneous, and usually volatile sites, is inadequate; so too is its ability to administer solutions that demand coordination across policy domains and communities of interest. As a result the nation state is commonly, and in considerable measure properly, perceived as incompetent.

Second, traditional mass production has collapsed, resulting in increased workforce heterogeneity. Greater decentralization and horizontal coordination within large firms, and more dynamism in (often loosely coordinated) small ones, has produced greater variation in the terms and conditions of work, the marketability of skills, and the structure of career paths. Along with complicating the state's task of economic regulation, this variation disrupts the commonalities of experience that provided the foundation of traditional industrial unionism. It unmakes the working class as a determinate transformative agent, since its heterogeneity now approximates the heterogeneity of the broader society.

Third, and related, political heterogeneity has increased. A variety of concerns not best addressed from class positions in the economy – e.g., for the environment, gender and racial justice, or respect for diverse ethnic and religious identities and sexual orientations, along with opposition to any of these things – are commonly expressed with a robustness and intensity exceeding that of class.

Not themselves reducible to concerns, they are often pursued through cross-class alliances. As a result a mass egalitarian politics limited to class concerns is likely doomed. But no new, more capacious, solidarity has thus far emerged out of this heterogeneity.

With its means of administration widely regarded as incompetent or worse, its social base fragmenting, and its political cohesion coming unstuck, social democracy has indeed fallen on hard times. We need a new institutional model that takes these disruptions of collective problem-solving capacities seriously, and helps generate the social base for a new, more inclusive and participatory egalitarian politics than social democracy was ever able to offer.

Productive democracy

Productive democracy offers itself as just such an alternative institutional model. It assumes the large task of building egalitarian productive infrastructure, prepares citizens for that task, and opens its governance to citizen contribution to problem-solving and de facto policy-generation outside the formal state. Consistent with these aims, it shifts current welfare state policy emphasis in a variety of areas to better reward citizen contribution while righting fiscal imbalances. The hope is that this better organized democracy will not just be a more productive and fairer one, but that the very demonstration of citizen participation in bringing it about will reassemble the sort of active social base that egalitarian politics has lost.

Before getting to the sorts of policies and institutional supports this likely requires, let me restate PD as a social project and clarify its basic normative and positive premises. The project is to use improvement in democratic organization to maximize social productivity and share the benefits of doing so, to highlight democracy's contribution to both in everyday projects, and to use public power to facilitate and harness that contribution. The normative premises of this project are: everyone deserves a chance at a healthy and productive life; the point of a democratic society is to marshal and manage resources to provide this chance, consistent with like chances for succeeding generations; all such societies should be free to make their own choices in how precisely to achieve that; and all members of those societies should contribute to their society's maintenance and health. The positive premises are that: knowledge and innovation in its productive application is the engine of social wealth, with each generation inheriting most of this engine's capacity from the previous one;[9] private competitive markets are an important tool of wealth creation, but not self-sustaining and often threatening the achievement of the normative goals just described; there is a fantastically large amount of difficult and interesting work to be done to achieve those goals – most fundamentally, reconciling shared prosperity with planetary survival – almost all of which requires effective engagement of citizens in democratic institutions outside the formal state; the kinds of relevant organization and engagement cannot be expected to arise naturally, but need to be aimed at to be achieved.

What are the broad sorts of institutions and policies this project would imply? By way of a brief answer, I refer again to the "Three Public Philosophies" table above and parse the elements on that list, again comparing PD to other dominant public philosophies to showing how those elements are coherent. The list itself is incomplete, and my parsing obviously lacks (to put it mildly) the detail needed to operationalize any of its elements (though references indicated provide at least some such detail). The point of the exercise, however, is only to give the reader a feel for PD's coherence and viability.

The institutions and policies of productive democracy

Economic strategy

Social democracy promoted an equity-oriented demand side strategy. Neoliberalism promotes the supply side, on distinctly inequitable terms. In the popular caricature of its programme: "pay the rich more to work harder, the less poor to do the same". PD doesn't forsake macroeconomic tools of demand management. But it concentrates heavily on effective supply of the "productive infrastructure" described above – a combination of constraints on firms that are consistent with basic human values (but with support mechanisms in place to allow those firms to meet such constraints under competitive conditions) and a series of complementary public goods (human capital systems, modernization systems, efficient physical infrastructure, planning facility, clean and learning government, etc.) designed to reduce waste, add value and capture and share the benefits of doing both. This place-specific infrastructure would be PD's principal source of wealth generation.[10]

Redistributive peak

Social democracy tends to redistribute income late in life. This is partly for the simple reason that adults have more power than children, but partly because redistribution is still seen as compensation, not investment. Neoliberalism is opposed to redistribution, except upward. PD would – more efficiently, and more in keeping with its stakeholder democracy, egalitarian, productivist culture – move redistribution earlier in the life course, with the aim of getting all children prepared for productive adulthood and reducing the claims they might otherwise make on the state during their adult lifetimes. As in social democracy there would also be transfers during the adult life course, but again guided by an interest in widening productive contribution.

Equality of opportunity

Traditional social democracy advanced equal opportunity primarily through education, labour market institutions promoting wage equality (e.g., unions, extension laws, minimum wage guarantees, training, etc.), and bars to invidious discrimination based on race, sex and other invariant and morally irrelevant predicates.

Neoliberalism is only committed to enough equal opportunity (in education and discrimination) to identify worthy successors in administering inequality. PD would keep social democracy's broad commitment to equal opportunity in labour markets but it would update it to include "flexicurity" policies aimed at speeding labour market transitions, themselves cushioned by a basic income guarantee, and promote wage compression as a general equity- and productivity-enhancing strategy. Consistent with its hostility toward excess consumption and interest in citizen engagement, it would also seek to reduce average work time.[11] And it would apply the idea of equal opportunity more directly to households and public life. In the household unit this is mostly about minimizing burdens on development and political participation created by the gendered division of labour within it (Gornick and Meyers, 2005), and gaining access to better welfare services for children (Esping-Andersen, 2009). In "politics" it would be about relieving all constraints on equal citizen participation via free and fair election financing, subsidized media, more intensive civic education in schools, time off for political activity and elections, and investment in local organization to make political action and discussion more accessible and inviting.

Social contribution

Social democracy at its worst was a claimant state, with citizen rights but no responsibility. Neoliberalism at its worst is Dickensian, with no real equality of opportunity or justice either in terms of reward or the punitive requirements of contribution. PD would, as already mentioned, rest on a social contract: "Society is going to prepare you to contribute, and celebrate and reward that contribution, but expects you to make it."

State/civil society relation

Like social democracy, though unlike neoliberalism, PD would support an affirmative state that directly supported elementary conditions of substantive political equality and equality of opportunity. But recognizing the current limits of state capacity, it would also support extra-state organizations and deliberative arenas that did these things and helped with problem-solving. More than either neoliberalism or social democracy, PD would seek to overcome the familiar pathologies of inequality and particularism that naturally arise in such organizations and arenas together with the many opportunities for constructive citizen contribution that are lost as a consequence. In accordance with Howe's discussion in this volume, it would underwrite a deliberate politics of association to address these issues (see also Cohen and Rogers, 1995).

Privileged government branch

As a practical matter, different governing regimes privilege or give more operational weight to different parts of government. The social democratic affirmative state was centred upon its executive, the famous headless "fourth branch" of government not contemplated by Montesquieu, and often deliberately insulated from democratic will-formation. Its rise substantially downgraded the relative importance of the legislature, while disrupting traditional market-liberal understandings of the rule of law. Neoliberalism returns to the latter (seeking to recover the "constitution in exile"), while limiting the active state largely to suppression and the defence of property rights. PD would rehabilitate the legislature as a privileged arena of democratic deliberation, without burdening it with detailed administration. The administrative state would continue but in substantially different form. Still privileged relative to private interests in asserting the public will, it would act in much closer relation to, and be self-consciously more dependent upon, the monitoring, enforcement and problem-solving capacities of a better organized democratic public.

National/state relation

Almost without exception, social democracy accreted power to the nation state at the expense of sub-national administration. It did this to force national unity on a basic platform of substantive right. Neoliberalism uses national power to limit democratic aspiration in sub-national arenas. PD would pursue a "progressive federalism". This means securing a floor of substantive rights, and some measure of fiscal federalism, while more deliberately encouraging experimentation consistent with nationally declared aims that promise achievement above that floor, as well as cross-site and national learning from such experimentation (Freeman and Rogers, 2008).

Public administration

Public confidence in government's ability to regulate and deliver public goods and services efficiently and accountably is a precondition of any affirmative state. Social democracy tried to inspire that confidence through "command and control" regulation, solving the efficiency problem by delegation to experts, and the accountability problem via rules limiting bureaucratic discretion. But very few have much confidence in command and control anymore. The distant experts lack local knowledge needed for most efficient solutions, the rules can't be updated fast enough to avoid over- or under-indicating action regarding changing facts on the ground, and those facts, given the heterogenity in life course and interests described above, are often individualized enough to prevent solution by any general rule. Neoliberalism of course welcomes all this, since it undermines support for an affirmative state. At its best, it favours a version of "new public management", applying market logic and the business sector's metrics revolution to government, measuring and incentivizing performance on known desired outcomes. While perfectly friendly to metrics and incentives, PD would recognize that, except at the more general level, desired outcomes – much less the means of achieving them – are not actually known in advance. It would favour a more interrogatory or diagnostic approach to designing solutions to problems, often requiring extra-state parties and expertise, and, within the state, pursue the sorts of "new governance" and "experimentalist governance" strategies described briefly in the introduction. These are particularly applicable to a more services-based welfare state that needs, at scale, to customize those services to different individuals (Noonan *et al.*, 2009; Sabel and Zeitlin, 2012; Sabel and Simon, 2012). And, again, it would mean encouraging a politics of association and the creation of more ad hoc discrete arenas of problem-solving appropriate to a "directly-deliberative polyarchy" (Cohen and Sabel, 1997).

Asset redistribution

Social democracy left initial property rights largely untouched. Neoliberalism again doesn't favour progressive redistribution. For reasons of equity and to increase an ownership sense of the economy, PD would encourage "alternative" property forms (coops, B-corps, non-profit producer or credit or service facilities, etc.) while awarding citizens a claim on the social surplus. Ideally this would not just be a one-time per capita grant or guaranteed income, though I favour both, but a guaranteed share of profits (Weitzman, 1984) or income-earning share of total assets to be drawn on through life and retired to the public weal at death. Whatever the precise form it takes (yet another thing to be experimented with by different publics), PD thus embraces the basic ideas and arguments for some version of a "property owning democracy" (Meade, 1964; Rawls, 1999; 2001; Roemer, 1994; O'Neill and Williamson, 2012).

Insurance

Social democracy limited social insurance to guard against loss of health or labour income, while neoliberalism is opposed to almost any social insurance. Retaining the labour income and healthcare guarantees of social democracy, PD would promote a range of finer grained and more targeted types of insurance, including protection against relative income losses and drops in asset prices (Shiller, 2003). It would also attend to non-actuarial risks, ubiquitous in human services, in part through the engagement of street-level bureaucrats and others (Noonan *et al.*, 2009).

Tax strategy

Social democracy is paid for chiefly by progressive taxes on private income and luxury consumption, neither of which neoliberalism wants to tax at all. The social wage of the social democratic state gains political support by its universality, but wastes money on rich people who don't need its assistance and strains immobile workers with heavier tax burdens, dividing them from the poor. Tax universalism is a way to square the circle of popular but often burdensomely expensive universalistic programmes and stingy means-tested ones. As basic tax principles recommend, it treats all income equally, including public income. It then implicitly targets general benefits on the poor and middle class by taxing them at steeply progressive rates, based on the recipient's private income. Done properly, this can lower taxes on private income while distributing more public income to the lower and working classes, re-establishing one sort of cross-class material solidarity that internationalization now threatens. Because it favours high levels of investment and savings over high and environmentally destructive consumption, PD would combine a progressive consumption tax with direct taxation of greenhouse gas and toxic emissions. (Frank, 2009).

International economic strategy

In general the point of PD would be to foster conditions, everywhere, that support its basic project: free choice by democratic organization to promote the widest possible contribution to social productivity consistent with the same or better possibilities for future generations. What that means in terms of programme is broadly familiar: less military spending and more cooperative security; more representative governance in international institutions, more technology transfer to poorer nations; and greater investment in a variety of public goods (climate, health, etc.) of obvious benefit to humankind. I take as utterly straightforward the need for international cooperation in solving a host of common security challenges (UN, 2004), clearer rules respecting national sovereignty while reaping the benefits of global exchange (Rodrik, 2011), the plenitude of suggestions on how to make that public goods investment highly efficient (Stiglitz, 2007; Sachs, 2008), and the technical and financial capacity to do all these things. Worthy of special note are the needless disruptions of democratic development introduced by financial speculation, regulatory arbitrage, and tax avoidance. But here too, the problem is not a lack of sensible ideas (Johnson and Kwak, 2010; Fleming *et al.*, 2001), but political will, especially from the great powers. PD would seek to assemble that will.

And so on... High real freedom, opportunity, responsibility, and ownership for all

Again, the above is certainly not comprehensive of egalitarian or other governance concerns, nor offered in anywhere near enough detail to be compelling, nor in ways immediately applicable to real world problems. All this admitted, I think it provides enough to at least give an intelligible sense of what PD is as a public philosophy, how it is different from traditional social democracy as well as neoliberalism, and why, in particular, it should be attractive not just to declared egalitarians but to the general public. PD requires citizens' contribution to social wealth creation, democracy, and efficient self-government. It proposes preparing citizens for that contribution, indeed expects it of them, but broadly shares the benefits of their contribution towards making it. It advances the equity interests of traditional social democratic egalitarianism while solving that system's fiscal problems and state failures. Based on a scaleable strategy for sustainable human development that is, at least conceptually, perfectly simple and plausible – reduce waste, add value, capture and share, and the benefits of doing both locally – it is applicable to any nation, with natural and benign implications for their mutual relation. It takes a realistic if hopeful view of human nature, recognizing the latter's famous crooked-timber quality (its frailty, fearfulness, confusion and worse) and susceptibility to dominance, but also its instinct for freedom and self-development. And it is coherent as a public philosophy, with all elements converging toward upholding the social contract it declares, with clearly defined gains and rewards for citizens who uphold their end of it. While it depends upon almost infinitely higher and more varied levels of citizen mobilization than at present, these things should give rational hope that, should PD be achieved, it would be capable of satisfying the sorts of interests that would be borne out of its rise – those associated with being an active and contributing citizen, one who is respected and rewarded in his community, country and the world. PD is viable.

Agency and achievement

Viability, of course, does not assure achievement, and no guarantees will be offered here. There are no laws of motion or bending historical arcs necessarily terminating in PD. As in any bid for greater justice, advancing it will inevitably be a long and contentious struggle, requiring the collective individual courage, street-smarts, cunning and guile of any good democratic movement. Also, and almost by definition, given the authority PD gives democracy to shape an open future, achievement will be as much process as event. Success will never be complete, nor any success completely secure. As in other democratic experiments the eternal vigilance of its supporters will be required.

Like any movement aiming at real lasting power in society, the struggle for PD will also need to build the independent institutions and coordinating routines that give it functional capacity to agitate, educate, organize, mobilize, learn, and govern. That means, inter alia: recognized and recognizably accountable leadership; reliable channels of communication among members and with the mass public; mechanisms for the recruitment and education of new members, naturally focused on the young; broadly shared message and programme, with short-term as well as intermediate and long-term policy and institutional goals; a consistency in messaging that permits public recognition in diverse arenas of collective action; an "inside-outside" game, both electoral and governing and not, in contending for public power in public power; and reliable sources of money to permit planning, experimentation, learning, and recovery from inevitable mistakes and reversals (through contribution, tithing, and revenue-generating PD-favouring market institutions effectively owned by the movement itself); and visible models of activity in this world that anticipate the freer one PD wishes to build (e.g., models of high road development, probably first best undertaken in urban areas with favourable background conditions, or models of how better organized democratic power outside formal government can improve government functioning, which can be undertaken almost anywhere).

PD, in short, will require deliberate and strategic organization. But beyond these generalizations about needed capacities and demonstration, I say no more about the organizational question here. This is not because it is unimportant, since nothing is more so. Nor is it because it is unsayable, since countless examples of all these elements exist. It is simply because the number of such examples is so great, and their particular form varies sufficiently by place, and the diverse practice producing them is itself evolving rapidly enough to defy any compact summary, or one of more than evanescent accuracy. A continually updated inventory of such work, a sort of Wikipedia of PD-inclined social innovation, would be very useful to have, but clearly beyond my capacity or essential purpose here. I'll simply stipulate that there are lots of vibrant models of the sorts of organization required.

But, returning to that purpose, I do not think it at all hard to find a constituency for that organization, which if undertaken at wider scale and denser scope would produce an effective agent for PD. In contrast with social democracy, that constituency-cum-agent is not so much "the working class" – though PD gives a clear role to it within the economy and beyond – but something like "the democratic public" of which that class is a central part. And such a public, I believe, can be found almost anywhere.

After all, interest in equity and social contribution and respect, all satisfied by PD, is almost universal among humanity. So, too, is the fear that unconstrained corporate power will soon obliterate these "basic humanities" from mass democracies, at peace with each other, on a habitable earth. And so too is the hope and technical capacity for a more equitable, cooperative, productive, and sustainable organization of human affairs. None of these things is obscure. Everybody in the world sees them. Everybody rightly knows them to be true.

So I think what is most needed now to advance egalitarian democratic ideals, apart from the work of fighting for them, is not another argument for the truth of these interests, fears and hopes, but a plausible picture of a political project that would enable that truth to be acted on in everyday, mostly national and varied subnational, public affairs. Satisfying this need means showing the plausibility of the project's general assumptions, strategy, institutional and policy supports, coherence, and viability – enough, in short, to allow its potential authors to explain its goals and rationale to themselves and others and to focus their joint efforts. That, and only that, is what I've tried to do here for PD.

Notes

1 Professor of Law, Political Science, Public Affairs, and Sociology, University of Wisconsin-Madison. My thanks to participants in "Beyond the Social-Civil Dialogue Dichotomy", Brussels, October 2009, and "Re-Embedding the Market: crisis and reinvention", Cambridge, MA/Melbourne/Cologne, December 2009, for helpful comments, and especially to Brad Barham, Isabelle Ferreras and Sanjay Pinto. Thanks too to Joshua Cohen, Charles Sabel and Wolfgang Streeck, co-authors of previous works

(Rogers and Sabel, 1993; Rogers and Streeck, 1994; Cohen and Rogers, 1995) that I draw on freely here. They are innocent of any errors I may have also introduced.

2 By "practical egalitarian democrats" I mean those who seek, starting from within the constraints on political deliberation and social investment typical of modern capitalist democracies, the best achievable "reconciliation of liberty and equality" (Rawls, 1999: 179). There are many views of the requirements of such reconciliation, but I will stipulate here to the view of the source just given, namely, universal civil rights and liberties and principles of substantive political equality, real equality of opportunity, and priority to improving the condition of the least well-off.

3 By "globalization" I mean, inclusively, reduced impediments to the flow of goods, capital, and at least some labour across national boundaries, the growing importance of transnational corporations with geographically dispersed production, and the recent addition (following collapse of the Soviet Union, India's turn from autarky, and China's embrace of market capitalism) of 1.5 billion plus (often very poor) workers to the world's active labour force. Other, less narrowly economic phenomena (e.g., cross-border cultural homogenization) are also associated with the term, but I limit myself to these because it is they which, according to the argument considered below, are said to have caused trouble for egalitarianism.

4 I don't wish to exaggerate the contrast with social democracy, whose Nordic variant in particular has long emphasized some of PD's suggested politics. Nor am I particularly attached to the PD name itself. Other suggestions are welcome. And if the reader prefers to think of PD as "social democracy 2.0" (one suggested name I've resisted, though as much from distaste with ubiquitous use of software industry notation to describe almost any social change as substantive objection) or "new egalitarianism" or "resilient democracy" (some other suggestions) or something else, that's fine with me.

5 Here and throughout, I take productivity not as output per hour but value per unit of input, a function of the value of the goods or services themselves and the efficiency (output per unit of input) with which they are produced. The inclusion of "natural capital" (Hawken *et al.*, 1999; Costanza *et al.*, 1997) among productive factors may be worth special emphasis. Maximizing its restorative and productive use implies sufficient decoupling of "growth" from permanent natural capital loss to fully accommodate increased population and/or *per capita* consumption. PD would be *very* green.

6 The principles are, according to Rodrik:

> 1. Markets must be deeply embedded in systems of governance .... 2. Democratic governance and political communities are organized largely within nation states, and are likely to remain so for the immediate future .... 3. There is no "one way" to prosperity .... 4. Countries have the right to protect their own social arrangement, regulations, and institutions .... 5. Countries do not have the right to impose their institutions on others .... 6. The purpose of international economic arrangements must be to lay down the traffic rules for managing the interface among national institutions .... 7. Non-democratic countries cannot count on the same rights and privileges in the international order as [democracies].
>
> (Rodrik 2011: 237–44)

7 The last alone would have enormous consequences for equity. As Przeworksi and Wallerstein (1985) remind, it is not the rate of profit per se that determines the rate of growth but the product of that rate and the rate of savings/reinvestment from profits. Consider two economies operating at identical 6 per cent rates of growth in output and capital stock, with identical net incremental capital-output ratios of 2, thus both requiring an investment/output rate of 12 per cent. One finances growth with a 30 per cent rate of savings out of profits, yielding a 40 per cent (12/30) share of profits in output, a complementary 60 percent share for wages and government, and a 28 per

cent (40–12) share of consumption out of profits. The other does so with a 60 per cent rate of savings out of profits, and thus a 20 per cent (12/60) share of profits in output, a complementary 80 percent share for wages and government, and permitting only an 8 per cent (20–12) share of consumption out of profits. Identical in output growth, the economies are quite different in distribution.

8 Equity is not the only reason to reduce waste (pride of place must go to the environment), but it's certainly an important one. A huge share of ordinary household income is spent on the necessities of housing, transportation, energy and healthcare. A more efficient supply of any of these disproportionately benefits the poor, both because these necessities take a larger share of their smaller incomes and because the poor often suffer from their least efficient supply.

9 This is one reason why, quite apart from a concern for fairness, we shouldn't overworry ourselves about sharing its fruits more equally. For a recent statement of this view, see Alperovitz and Daly (2008).

10 Here is as good a place to mention that, along with needing contribution from a vast number of other social groups, such productive infrastructure offers unions – understood as independent organizations of workers in the economy – a clear social role and route to political power. This time, however, the contribution would work less through their ability to demand wages and state spending than their potential breadth of presence in the economy and knowledge of the actual conditions of work. The same heterogeneity and decentralization of firm and work process that undermined centralized bargaining and union membership now limits efficient movement in the labour market and easy and often short-lived combinations of different firms (both of which employers want), while creating deep confusion and incapacities among workers about the skills they need to navigate it. Capital will not and cannot solve this problem, and the state lacks capacity. But unions might naturally articulate and mobilize around the general interest in getting better comparability across worksites (standards on compensation, and baseline worker rights) and counsel and train workers in the skills they need for successful careers, not just jobs. They could also give public regulation a localized presence and adaptability that it would otherwise lack. This would increase social productivity directly, not just via expected resulting investment.

11 Not for their endorsement of this package, but simply their usefulness in examining the effectiveness of different social democratic programmes of labour market regulation, see Kenworthy (2008; 2011) and Pontusson (2005; 2011); on the effects of basic income guarantees, see van Parijs (1998).

15 Always embedded neoliberalism and the global financial crisis

Damien Cahill[1]

The global financial crisis, precipitated by the collapse of the U.S. sub-prime housing market in 2007, has focussed both scholarly and popular attention on neoliberalism and its future. One common narrative to emerge in this context is that the crisis heralds the end of neoliberal hegemony. Commentators who make this argument typically contend that the crisis demonstrates fundamental flaws in the neoliberal economic model, and that the "return to regulation" in the wake of the crisis sounds the death knell for neoliberalism.

This chapter assesses the merits of such arguments. In doing so it puts forward the concept of "always embedded neoliberalism" as a way of thinking through the significance of the global financial crisis for the future of neoliberalism. First, the assumptions that underpin the argument that neoliberalism is dead are interrogated. Second, a parallel is drawn between such arguments and the conception of neoliberalism as a process of disembedding the economy from its social support structures. Third, drawing upon the work of Fred Block and Karl Polanyi, the concept of "always embedded neoliberalism" is developed as a useful alternative framework. Finally, some comments are made regarding the significance of recent regulatory responses for the future of neoliberalism.

Neoliberalism, "free markets" and the "disembedded economy"

The argument that the last three decades were characterized by a retreat of the state from the regulation of the economy is not new. It has been a feature of the literature on globalization, as exemplified by authors such as Susan Strange (1996), Thomas Friedman (1999), and Kenichi Ohmae (1991). Recently this view has been mobilized by prominent commentators to pronounce the death of neoliberalism in the wake of the global financial crisis.

For example, former Australian Prime Minister Kevin Rudd, in an essay published in the progressive *The Monthly* magazine that achieved international exposure when condensed and republished in the French newspaper *Le Monde*, argues that the current global financial crisis exposes the failings of neoliberalism, which he also refers to as "free-market fundamentalism, extreme capitalism and excessive greed" (2009: 20). "In the past year", writes Rudd, "we have seen how unchecked market forces have brought capitalism to the precipice" (2009: 22). As a consequence, the "ideological legitimacy" of neoliberalism is now destroyed (2009: 29). For Rudd, neoliberalism is understood as the triumph of the free market, or unregulated capitalism, underpinned by a slimmed-down version of the state. Therefore, he argues, "[w]ith the demise of neoliberalism, the role of the state has once more been recognized as fundamental" (2009: 25).

A similar argument is made by British intellectual Will Hutton (2008). Hutton contends that policy responses to the financial crisis mark a return to Keynesian-style "managed capitalism" – implying that in the previous neoliberal era the state had less of a role in managing capitalism. Such sentiments are echoed by French President Nicolas Sarkozy who is reported to have said that "Laissez faire is finished" (*The Economist*, 2008). These arguments reflect what seems to be a widely held perception that the global financial crisis heralds the end of neoliberalism. Such a perception is based upon the assumption that neoliberalism is constituted by a retreat of the state from regulation of the economy – hence laissez faire – and that the return of regulation, in the form of bank nationalizations, for example, induced by the global financial crisis, marks the end of neoliberalism.

Arguments such as these treat neoliberal theory, and the policy practices of neoliberal governments, as synonymous. That is, they tend to accept the normative vision of the state and economy, proffered by neoliberal polemicists such as Milton Friedman and Friedrich von Hayek, as the actual state of affairs that prevailed in most capitalist countries during the last two to three decades. Such a normative vision is expressed by Friedman as a government limited such that it only:

> maintained law and order, defined property rights, served as a means whereby we could modify property rights and other rules of the economic game, adjudicated disputes about the interpretation of the rules, enforced contracts, promoted competition, provided a monetary framework, engaged in activities to counter technical monopolies and to overcome neighborhood effects widely regarded as sufficiently important to justify government intervention, and … supplemented private charity and the private family in protecting the irresponsible, whether madman or child.
>
> (Friedman, 1982: 34)

This normative vision is also evident in Milton and Rose Friedman's *Free to Choose* (1980: 58):

> Our society is what we make it. We can shape our institutions. Physical and human characteristics limit the alternatives available to us. But none prevents us, if we will, from building a society that relies primarily upon voluntary cooperation to organize both economic and other activity, a society that preserves and expands human freedom, that keeps government in its place, keeping it our servant and not letting it become our master.

The conflation of the normative prescriptions of neoliberal theory with neoliberalism in practice is also evident in arguments that neoliberalism is a process of social disembedding (Best, 2003). Such arguments contrast neoliberalism with the "embedded liberalism" of the post-World War II era of capital accumulation, in which "market processes and entrepreneurial and corporate activities were surrounded by a web of social and political constraints and a regulatory environment that sometimes restrained but in other instances led the way in economic and industrial strategy" (Harvey, 2005: 11). Whereas the golden age of capitalism was a period in which the economy was embedded in social institutions, the neoliberal era, in contrast, is often presumed to have been characterized by the freeing of the economy from such socially imposed constraints, and thus disembedded from its social moorings. As David Harvey argues, "[t]he neoliberal project is to disembed capital from these constraints" (2005: 11).

Joseph Stiglitz seems, at least implicitly, to adopt a similar conceptual frame in *Freefall: America, Free Markets, and the Sinking of the World Economy* (2010: xii). He argues that:

> [e]conomies need a balance between the role of markets and the role of government – with important contributions by nonmarket and nongovernmental institutions. In the last twenty-five years, America lost that balance, and it pushed its unbalanced perspective on countries around the world

If the language of disembeddedness were to be superimposed upon this statement, then Stiglitz could be read to argue that during the last three decades, the global economy, in losing the balance between government and market, has become less embedded in society. Thus, those who understand neoliberalism as a form of disembedded capitalism, and those who understand neoliberalism as laissez faire, have substantially similar conceptions of the nature of neoliberalism and, as Panitch and Konings argue, tend "to analyse the … dynamics of the past decades within the terms of that era's hegemonic self-representation" (2009: 68).

Always embedded neoliberalism

However, such conceptions of neoliberalism would seem to be out of step with the reality of neoliberalism in practice. A close examination of neoliberalism reveals that it did not entail a retreat of the state from the economy, nor a disembedding of the economy from social institutions.

Numerous studies suggest that there has not been a general decline in the size of the state during the neoliberal era. Tanzi and Schuknecht (2000: 6–7) found that between 1980 and 1996, total government expenditure as a proportion of GDP in the 17 major industrial capitalist economies grew from 43.1 per cent to 45.6 per cent. Rodrik's study of OECD and non-OECD countries posits a "positive correlation between an economy's exposure to international trade and the size of its government" in the years from the 1960s to the 1990s (Rodrik, 1998).

While Geoffrey Garrett modifies this view somewhat by pointing out that "whereas levels of trade and levels of government expenditure are positively correlated, countries in which trade has increased more quickly in recent decades have experienced slower growth in government spending" (2001: 27), such evidence still points to an expansion of the absolute and relative economic size of government during the neoliberal era.

A similar phenomenon has been identified with respect to the regulatory scope of government. This is demonstrated in David Levi-Faur's study of the electricity and telecommunications industries in 171 countries between 1980 and 2002 (2005: 18–19). During this period the incidence of privatizations was outstripped by the creation of new regulatory authorities in these key industries. Levi-Faur therefore argues that "neoliberalism gave strong impetus to regulatory reform, including the creation of new instruments of regulation and the establishment of new regulatory authorities" (2005: 19). John Braithwaite makes a similar point when he argues that during the neoliberal era "the state grew and grew into a regulatory capitalism where the state both retained many of its provider functions and added many new regulatory ones" (2008: 24). Therefore, while the state may have been transformed and reshaped under neoliberalism it has certainly not withered away.

There thus appear to be significant discrepancies between the trajectory of capitalist states during the neoliberal era and both the normative policy prescriptions of neoliberal polemicists and the common understanding of neoliberalism as a system of laissez faire capitalism or as a process of disembedding the economy from its social context. Indeed, some scholars deploy the phrase "actually existing neoliberalism" to capture this discrepancy (Brenner and Theodore, 2002; Peck and Tickell, 2002) and to distinguish the normative ideals of neoliberalism from its concrete policy manifestations.

In this context, if neoliberalism in practice does not conform to the free market ideal, how then should we understand neoliberalism and how can the implications of the global financial crisis for its future be assessed? The strategy adopted here is to return to the concept of the socially disembedded economy, and by implication that of "free market capitalism" – both of which seem to underpin popular accounts of neoliberalism – and interrogate their utility for an understanding of the relationship between the economic and the social. The implications of this for an understanding of neoliberalism can then be examined.

The concepts of the socially embedded economy and the socially disembedded economy are most often associated with the work of Karl Polanyi, particularly *The Great Transformation* (1944). Here Polanyi described the transition from feudalism to capitalism – or, what he called a "market economy". Polanyi is often thought to have argued that this transition from feudalism to capitalism entailed the separation of the economy from its social foundations, its disembedding from the structures that gave it coherence under feudalism. Such a process of disembedding was disastrous for society as it became subjected to the economic logic of the "self-regulating market". This common account assumes that economies can be either embedded in – or disembedded from – society, and that the degree of institutionalized social protection reflects the degree of embeddedness. Kurtuluş Gemici (2008: 25) calls this the concept of "embeddedness as a historical variable". There is certainly some support for this position in Polanyi's work (Gemici, 2008). For example, Polanyi writes that "never before our own time were markets more than accessories of life" (1944: 71). He goes on to argue that "a self-regulating market demands nothing less than the institutional separation of society into an economic and political sphere" (1944: 74). One can readily see how the view of neoliberalism as a process of disembedding can be derived from this account.

However, as Block has argued, while Polanyi's work can be read in this way, another understanding of embeddedness can be inferred from *The Great Transformation*. Block argues that, during the writing of *The Great Transformation*, Polanyi began to move towards a conception of the economy as being "always embedded" in social institutions and processes. However, because of the time constraints he imposed upon himself in order to publish the book before the end of World War II, Polanyi was unable to formalise this conceptual shift and his book thus reflected "contradictions and conflicts" (Block, 2003b: 276) with respect to the embeddedness concept. Block argues that "Polanyi glimpsed the idea of the always embedded market economy, but he was not able to give that idea a name or develop it theoretically because it represented too great a divergence from his initial starting point" (276).

The concept of the "always embedded market economy" was expressed much more clearly by Polanyi in his later essay, "The economy as instituted process", in which he argued that the "substantive meaning of economic" (by which he essentially meant the conception of the economy as a system of material provisioning) is superior to the "formal meaning of economic" (by which he meant the study of choices made under conditions of scarcity, as conceived by neoclassical economics) because the substantive definition of the economic was universally applicable, whereas the formal definition was only relevant to understanding a "market economy", and even then it provided only a partial representation of it. According to Polanyi, the substantive definition of "economic" enables the recognition that human provisioning has been organized according to different logics – reciprocity, redistribution and exchange – in different places and at different times in history. Social institutions are always necessary to provide regularity and stability to these economic logics. Thus Polanyi argues that "[t]he human economy, then, is embedded and enmeshed in institutions, economic and noneconomic" (1957: 250).

Block argues that this concept of "the always embedded market economy", which Polanyi was able to articulate in later work, also "provides the most powerful and enduring way to make sense of Polanyi's core arguments in *The Great Transformation*" (2003b: 276). However, its utility goes beyond a coherent reading of *The Great Transformation*. Such a conception of embeddedness is akin to what Gemici describes as "embeddedness as a methodological principle" (2008: 25). The strength of this methodological conception of embeddedness is that it recognizes that markets and economic processes more generally are socially constructed. It is a qualitative rather than quantitative approach to understanding the social embeddedness of economic processes. As Gemici writes, it "invites the researcher to look for the social processes that structure and shape economic life" (2008: 27) and is therefore opposed to the artificial separation of the economic and social spheres of human activity (26). This conception of embeddedness recognizes that "the emergence of markets was almost always deliberately engineered by the state" (Chang, 2002: 547). Indeed, it invites the conclusion at the heart of the institutionalist tradition of political economy, that "the market is itself an institution" (Hodgson, 2007: 2), rather than conceiving of the market as simply a collection of atomized individuals. In terms of the relationship between the state and the economy, this conception of embeddedness accords with Levi-Faur's argument that "[r]egulation is a necessary condition for the functioning of the market, not only a compromise between economic imperatives and social values" (Levi-Faur, 2005: 19).

If the economy is "always embedded" in social institutions and processes, then it should not be surprising that the normative neoliberal ideal of free markets has not been realized in practice. Indeed, the "always embedded market economy" concept prompts recognition that neoliberalism is a utopian project, in that it posits not merely "the best place" (from the point of view of its advocates) but also "no such place". As Brenner and Theodore argue, "neoliberal doctrine represents states and markets as if they were diametrically opposed principles of social organization, rather than recognizing the politically constructed character of all economic relations" (2002: 353). Therefore "actually existing neoliberalism" was always likely to differ from the normative prescriptions of its proselytizers.

Moreover, just as capitalism, or the market economy, is "always embedded", so are historically specific manifestations of capitalism, such as "actually existing neoliberalism", always embedded. It is useful therefore to speak of "always embedded neoliberalism".

At least three mechanisms can be identified through which neoliberalism is "always embedded" in society. First, and perhaps most obviously, neoliberalism is embedded ideologically and discursively. It seems that this is the sense in which Cerny (2008) writes of an "embedded neoliberalism". Cerny argues that neoliberalism has become the new political "common sense for the 21st century" (2008: 39). The neoliberal conceptual framework has become embedded in the same way that liberalism became embedded as the dominant conceptual frame through which institutions were forged and policies crafted in the post-World War II period (2008: 2). Although neoliberalism has now become the dominant framework through which social and economic policies are made across the capitalist world, there is an unevenness to this. So while as Cerny argues, neoliberalism has become a "hegemonic concept" in a policy sense (2008: 3), it is also "highly internally differentiated ... made up of a range of linked but discrete subcategories and dimensions" (2008: 3). This recognizes that while there has been an ideological and policy convergence around a neoliberal core among both conservative and social democratic parties in most advanced capitalist nations, there remains, for example, differentiation between conservative and social democratic forms of neoliberal strategy and discourse.

Second, neoliberalism is embedded institutionally. The most important vehicle for this institutional embedding is the state. Not only has neoliberalism not resulted in a retreat of the state from the economy, the state has also been integral to the implementation, reproduction and extension of neoliberalism. As Peck and Tickell argue, while many of the key institutions, alliances and social truths that characterized the post-World War II capitalist order were dismantled, or "rolled back" through the process of neoliberalization, the implementation of neoliberalism entailed the "roll out" of new forms of regulation:

> In the course of this shift, the agenda gradually moved from one preoccupied with the active *destruction and discreditation* of Keynesian-welfarist and social-collectivist institutions (broadly defined) to one focused on the purposeful *construction and consolidation* of neoliberalized state forms, modes of governance and regulatory relations.
>
> (Peck and Tickell, 2002: 384)

New rules and their enforcement were required for ostensibly deregulated markets as well as for markets in which privatized entities operated. Thus market deregulation is better conceived of as a form of "re-regulation" (Anderson, 1999).

The marketization of social services has also often entailed an ongoing role for the state in subsidizing private providers – either through direct payments or through tax subsidies to either the providers or their users. Furthermore, the state has taken an active role in the suppression of organized labour in the neoliberal era. This active role of the state was evident from the very first instance of neoliberalism in practice: Chile under the Pinochet dictatorship. As Naomi Klein (2007: 75–97) demonstrates so powerfully in *The Shock Doctrine*, after deposing the elected President Salvador Allende following a coup in 1973, the new military government led by General Augusto Pinochet engaged in a process of privatization, the dismantling of protectionist barriers, and cuts to social expenditure. Concurrently, the coercive powers of the state were employed to suppress organized labour and other dissenters through the imprisonment, torture and murder of left-wing activists. Neoliberalism was enabled by state coercion.

While the case of Chile may be an extreme one, it draws attention to the centrality of the state to the project of neoliberalism and the contrast between neoliberal theory and practice (see Harvey, 2005: 64–86). Other path-breaking neoliberal governments have also used authoritarian political strategies to enforce market prerogatives. When federal air traffic controllers in the United States took strike action in 1981, the Reagan government confronted their union, the Professional Air Traffic Controllers Organization, sacking striking workers and gaoling its activists (Arnesen, 2007: 1123–6). In the mid-1980s the Thatcher Government in Britain used the coercive powers of the state, including the police and secret services, to undermine the powerful National Union of Miners

(NUM). Not only did this pave the way for the privatization of coal mines, but, by defeating the NUM, Thatcher also weakened the broader labour movement, paving the way for further neoliberal measures (Harvey, 2005: 59).

Third, and related to these latter examples, neoliberalism is embedded socio-relationally through class relations. As Albo argues, "[n]eoliberalism developed out of an important shift in the balance of class forces and the defeat of the left, and in particular social democracy" (2002: 48). Transformations to the regulatory apparatus of states (through privatization, deregulation and marketization) facilitated changes within processes of capital accumulation, which in turn led to a number of developments, including: a weakening of the power of organized labour and a strengthening of the power of capital at both the level of the firm and the level of state policy making; a freeing of capital from many of the restraints imposed upon it as a result of the post-World War II "class compromise" in many advanced capitalist economies; and an expansion of the sphere of commodification, by deregulation and the opening up of former state-monopolized services to profit making enterprises.

In combination with the state-supported assaults upon organized labour, this has led to an "historic victory of capital over labour" (Berger, 1999: 453), and a shift in the distribution of power from labour to capital. At least three aspects of this shift can be identified. First, various forms of labour market deregulation have strengthened capital in the employment relationship. Second, the organizational power of labour has diminished in most of the advanced capitalist countries as union density has fallen. Third, the "privileged position" of business (Lindblom, 1977: 170–88) with respect to policy making has been strengthened, albeit that some fractions of capital, such as manufacturing, have been subordinated to the interests of others, such as finance.

As a result, the trajectory of always embedded neoliberalism has been towards a diminution of democracy. This is reinforced by each of the mechanisms through which neoliberalism is socially embedded. The limits to democracy identified by Ellen Meiksins Wood (1995: 233–7) as constitutive of capitalism appear to be exacerbated by neoliberalism. The institutional facilitation of expanded commodification, combined with the strengthening of managerial prerogatives in the sphere of production, has narrowed the range of activities subject to democratic accountability. Instead, the power to determine the conditions of one's existence has shifted to the sphere of consumption, which in turn is buttressed by neoliberal ideology's claim that markets are democratic as they enable the diverse preferences of consumers to be registered and reconciled. As Wood noted in 1999, under this view:

> the "new democracies" of eastern Europe are "democratic" in proportion to their progress in "marketization", President Yeltsin's accretion of power to the presidency is 'democratic' because it is conducted in the name of privatization and "the market", or General Pinochet was more "democratic" than a freely elected Salvador Allende.
>
> (Wood 1995: 235)

It is certainly important to recognize the "uneven geographical development" (Harvey, 2005), as well as the uneven temporal development, of these features of neoliberalism. Nonetheless, the three mechanisms outlined here through which neoliberalism is embedded, when considered together, can be thought of as constituting a "metalogic" (Peck and Tickell, 2002) of neoliberalism globally. Locally mediated expressions of this metalogic form what Cerny calls "varieties of neoliberalism" (2008: 3, 40). Thus there exist regionally and historically specific manifestations of always embedded neoliberalism, and this again points toward differences between neoliberal theory and practice.

It is also important to recognize that neoliberalism has, in various locales, and at different times, been beset by crises during its period of dominance. Examples include the Asian Financial Crisis, the Savings and Loans Crisis, the dotcom crash and the collapse of the Long Term Capital Management fund. The responses by states and supranational bodies to these crises have often led to the further institutionalization of neoliberalism (for example in the case of the Asian Financial Crisis) or helped to rescue the legitimacy of neoliberalism. In doing so, such responses have also cemented or extended the power of large institutional forms of capital and of advanced capitalist states relative to developing states. As Peck, Theodore and Brenner argue, "neoliberalization has been repeatedly and cumulatively *remade* through crises" (2009: 105).

While neoliberalism is politically dominant, resistance to neoliberalism has been ongoing since the 1970s. Such resistance has taken both local and global forms. In some nation states this has led to a widespread roll back of neoliberalism, and the roll out of new social forms of production, most notably in Venezuela. On the whole, however, resistance to neoliberalism has produced only partial and localized roll backs of neoliberal forms of regulation and accumulation. Such roll backs have generally been sufficient to secure a practical legitimacy for neoliberalism – that is, to stave off widespread popular political mobilizations against neoliberalism – and this has enabled neoliberal forms of accumulation to continue.

The future of neoliberalism

It is now possible to address the issue of the future of neoliberalism in the wake of the global financial crisis. That neoliberalism is ideologically embedded means that a generation of policy makers have only known neoliberalism as the common sense frame for conducting and evaluating policy. The institutional embeddedness of neoliberalism affords it enormous inertia. The class-based nature of neoliberalism means that the accumulation strategies of the owners of capital are premised upon the maintenance of neoliberal forms of regulation, and, unless a significant shift in the balance of social forces occurs, have significant political power to prosecute these interests. The fact that, as Cerny argues, neoliberalism has become "overdetermined" (2008: 29), suggests it is so deeply embedded that it will be difficult to dislodge.

A brief consideration of recent events demonstrates this point. For example, while the nationalization of financial institutions in both the U.S. and the United Kingdom constituted a radical departure from the neoliberal policy common sense and from neoliberal institutional norms, they did not fundamentally challenge the power of capital. The nationalizations were designed to underwrite the viability of the system of capital accumulation itself, and did not have as their aim other social goals such as the provision of cheap credit for labour, or the use of the banks' funds to finance full employment. Furthermore, public assurances were given of the intention to return banks to private ownership as soon as practicable. Consider the example of healthcare reform in the U.S. What began ostensibly as an agenda by the Obama administration to overturn the neoliberal approach to healthcare, resulted in a policy which extends the public subsidization of private health insurance providers – a demonstration of the power of large private interests (the private healthcare lobby) to shape the political agenda. In the U.S. too, the once powerful United Auto Workers is party to a government funded bailout agreement with General Motors which, although handing formal control of the company to the Government, includes job and wage cuts and allows the company to use stocks, rather than cash, to meet half of its payment obligations to its employee health fund. As Albo, Gindin and Panitch note, the stated purpose of the government bail out was to restore GM to profitability, not "to convert GM to some larger social purpose" (2010: 78).

These examples suggest that the class relations in which neoliberalism is embedded have proven quite durable in the face of the crisis. While labour movements have mobilized in some nation states against further neoliberalization, these appear to have been mostly ineffective. Greece, for example, has been the site of perhaps the most widespread and militant movement against neoliberal responses to the "sovereign debt crisis". Despite this, the Greek government agreed to an IMF bailout package that was conditional on an austerity programme which includes widespread cuts to social services, public sector wages and extensive privatizations. As Buckley, in this volume, asserts, these austerity programmes amount to a net transfer of money from the populations in Southern nation states to creditors in the North.This indicates not only the labour movement's inability to stem the tide of neoliberalism, but also the continued institutional entrenchment of neoliberal logics, in this case within supra-national regulatory organizations which orchestrated the expansion of neoliberalism in many developing economies through the Structural Adjustment Programmes of the 1980s and 1990s.

The responses of other European states to the sovereign debt crisis suggest that neoliberalism continues to be the common sense framework for policy among political elites. Both the British and German governments, for example, have announced cuts to social services' expenditure. In Australia, where the economy has survived recession and official unemployment remains relatively low by contemporary global standards, the Labor Government introduced early in its first term a Minister for Deregulation.

The dominant picture that emerges is one of cutting expenditure to services which quarantine labour from the crisis and from market fluctuations, while capital has benefited from ongoing subsidies. While there have been some restrictions placed upon capital, these have, to date, been quite modest. Furthermore, the recent bank regulations proposed by the G20 may highlight the continuing influence of finance capital with respect to state policy, as lobbying from the financial sector is reported to have led to a compromise being struck by state negotiators regarding the discretionary timing for the implementation of the proposed regulations.

In a discussion of the movement against neoliberalism in Latin America, Emir Sader argues that "[t]o democratize means to de-marketize, to recuperate for the terrain of people's rights that which neoliberalism has delivered into the hands of the market" (2008: 15). Given the de-democratizing character of neoliberalism, it seems reasonable to suggest that the withering away of neoliberalism would require a programme of demarketization, and decommodification. By and large, however, in the wake of the crisis, states have not extended democratic control over economic processes. Rather they have regulated them so that such processes continue to be dominated by large private interests.

It might turn out, therefore, that the latest crisis will produce similar outcomes for neoliberalism as did its other crises. Responses to the global financial crisis by states and other powerful groups, including unions, might serve to re-embed neoliberal logics within a renovated institutional framework, while leaving its class basis and ideological dominance intact.

Conclusion

This chapter has proposed the concept of "always embedded neoliberalism" as a way to recognize that states and social processes have been integral to neoliberalism and therefore that the "return of regulation" (Helleiner, 2008) that has occurred since the onset of the financial crisis is not, in and of itself, sufficient to pronounce neoliberalism dead. This is not to suggest that neoliberalism has not been weakened, or that its days may not be numbered. Rather, it is to highlight that neoliberalism remains far more powerful and pervasive than is assumed by many of its critics.

Note

1 Damien Cahill is a Senior Lecturer in the Department of Political Economy, University of Sydney, Australia.

16 Re-embedding the market

Beyond Adam Smith's dinner

Charles Sampford

Introduction

Adam Smith (1976) famously said: "It is not from the benevolence of the butcher, the brewer, or the baker, that we expect our dinner, but from their regard to their own self-interest." Since late 2008, I have been suggesting that we might equally say that:

> It is not from the malevolence of the mortgage broker who writes the NINJA loan, or the ratings agency that anoints it AAA. It is not the malevolence of the arms manufacturer that invents the cluster bomb, or the polluter who steams the planet. It is, rather, from their regard to their own self-interest.

Self-interest is certainly an important motivation but there are some other critical variables or preconditions determining whether self-interest puts food on our plantation timber table, or cluster bombs in an overheated and flood-prone backyard that has been repossessed by a zombie bank. The key question is: what are those other variables, and why and how has their variation dealt so much damage so quickly? Or to rephrase this question in order to locate it within the central concerns of this book – in *what* might the market be "embedded" so as to deliver the former rather than the latter.

The first time I rhetorically counter-posed the alternative to Adam Smith's famously benign dinner, was in an address to a conference in the E.U. Parliament in November 2008, on the topic "Capitalism: Quo Vadis?" (Sampford, 2008). At the time, I apologized to the international audience that the question was posed in a dead European language because the answer is not going to be determined by the West alone. In seeking an alternative title, I looked first to the literal translation – "Whither capitalism?" A freer and more appropriate translation would be "Wither capitalism?" In answer to this question, which has been posed in many modern languages, three broad answers have been propounded over the last century. Some have said "nowhere"; some have said "everywhere"; and, others have suggested that capitalism has a vital but defined role within a larger ethical and social order. During the 1930s, statists of the right and anarchists of the left said that capitalism had nowhere to go. It was left to the American social democrats to save capitalism from itself. In the 1970s, the statists of the left said that capitalism had nowhere to go. However, the anarchists of the right saw it as going everywhere. From 1980 to 2008, the "everywhere" option seemed to be very popular. At the height of the global financial crisis (GFC), the nowhere (or at least "nowhere any good") alternative seemed a very possible one – though the resilience/chutzpah of those who now wanted state funding for failed market players, but who had previously wanted everything left to markets, was truly breathtaking.

This shifting back and forth reflects the interests of Polanyi scholars in recognizing periods in which there are attempts to "dis-embed" and "re-embed" markets. My own comments in this debate are profoundly influenced by my academic and business experiences over the last 40 years, starting at a time when it was still seriously and widely suggested that non-market economies and non-democratic polities might triumph, and attempts to control markets in the west reached a peacetime zenith. As I watched one extreme give way to the other (with less change in personnel than might be supposed), I have only occasionally stuck my nose into areas economists think to be their exclusive demesne.

One of the reasons is that I come to economics as someone fascinated by the vortex where law, politics and philosophy meet – an intellectual space where eighteenth-century theorists would have located economics but from which twentieth century economists seem to believe it has migrated (Sampford, 2010a). Accordingly, I recognize that what I would see as well-aimed broadsides from the legal, ethical and political corners of an integrated intellectual space, would be dismissed as irrelevant by most mainstream economists. The other reason is that I have had experience of real markets (for luxury imported goods, for currencies and interest rates) in operation through a smallish family company that few economic theorists can match. My practical experiences have stimulated my philosophical musings which have, in turn, affected the way I have understood my experiences. My philosopher's contempt for nonsense has been honed by practical understanding of the real phenomena that the nonsense claims to describe (see Winch, 1958).

In this essay, I will discuss some perspectives on Polanyi derived from my more academic encounters and then use these to reflect on some of my practical encounters with disembedded markets (both market economists and their followers) over the last 30 years. This will suggest that disembedding involves dissociation of market activities and their theorization from their foundations – not only from the societies the market is supposed to serve, but from its multidisciplinary base – leading to a disconnect with ethics, logic, and common sense. I will conclude by making some suggestions for "re-embedding" and reconnection to those forces. Not for the first time, I will repeat Hamlet's chiding of Horatio to neoliberal (and other) economists: "There are more things in heaven and earth … [t]han are dreamt of in your philosophy" (Shakespeare, 2006: 225). In this case, I will add that "there is more in the philosophy of Adam Smith whom you claim to follow" (see Sampford, 1998). They and their frequently self-interested adherents and opportunists have sleep walked us into the GFC. They can contribute to the team effort to get us out of it – but it is a team in which they play rather than lead and in which they must recognize the contributions of others.

Polanyi

I first encountered Polanyi's writing at the Royal Institute of Philosophy colloquium annual conference, hosted by the Centre for Philosophy and Public Affairs at the University of St Andrews in 1997. The take-home message from Polanyi was that the market should not be seen as separate and emerging without or in opposition to the state, but that its establishment involved a good deal of support from the state and the use of its coercive power. The market had emerged with more "royal" endorsement – and much more sovereign backing – than the past-times of Golf and Philosophy occurring on opposite corners of the intersection. As Polanyi puts it:

> Economic history reveals that the emergence of national markets was in no way the result of the gradual and spontaneous emancipation of the economic sphere from government control. On the contrary, the market has been the outcome of a conscious and often violent intervention on the part of government which imposed the market organization on society for noneconomic ends.
>
> (Polanyi, 1944)

Such insights from Polanyi helped to explain what might otherwise have been a puzzling phenomenon of the 1980s – that the high priestess of "free markets" and individual choice had been very active in building up the coercive power of the state and had first used it in a war that saved her premiership (see Crewe and King, 1995: 147) and then against unions in the 1984 Coal Miners' Strike and the 1986 Wapping dispute.

Different senses of embeddedness

Delving into a deeper exploration of the embeddedness of capitalism invites many jocular yet pointed analogies and questions. What kind of bed are we analogizing? If it is a human bed – is it the long term marital bed or that used for short term or one night stands with the wombat entrepreneur getting what he wants, moving to the next conquest and sending the money to the Bahamas? One might also ask how many are in the bed. Polanyi's point about the role of the polity suggests that it might be seen as a ménage a trois with the polity selling out society or forcing it into bed with the market. A better analogy is that of a "garden bed": it reminds us that how a plant grows depends on the soils in which it is planted and the other plants around it. One raises questions about the relevant roles of genetics and the environment in the success of a seedling. One might also raise questions of biodiversity versus monocultures. Finally, one wonders whether the capitalist seedling is a pest, a parasite or, for some continents, a kind of economic Triffid – a plant that does not take root but destroys and moves on.

In one sense the market is embedded within law, ideologies, various institutions and the power structures that support it. It is embedded in law, which determines who can trade, what can be traded, the rights and obligations of traders and the conditions under which the trade can be carried out. It is embedded in ideologies that affect market players and those in the institutions that operate within and support it. Polanyi emphasizes how reliant markets are on that support. This means that the market is embedded in at least some elements of society, but it also reminds us that society is not homogenous but differentiated, with the elements typically in tension and sometimes coming close to fracturing. At some points, elements of the society press for markets to enhance their power and secure the transfer of benefits to themselves. However, the market is never fully embedded, in that there will be some groups in society opposed, even if not completely coherently.

In another sense the market is consciously disembedded, in that market ideologies do not appear to recognize that they are dependent on the support of state power and the communities in which theory operate (needing tolerance in non-democratic states and majority support in democratic ones). That support may be promoted by the use of gunboats in the nineteenth-century (Polanyi, 1944: 307) or the IMF in the twentieth. But the most potent means of that support is the idea that there is no alternative. The most effective way in which the market might be embedded is by identifying the ways in which it is of benefit to the communities in which it operates and to ensure that those benefits are delivered.

Some close encounters with disembedded economics

Political debates surrounding market embedding have often been ferocious in countries such as Australia (where I am from). During the 1970s, for example, stark differences emerged concerning what should be provided by the market and what should be provided by government – generally focussing around proposals for greater government provision or greater government regulation of the market. However, the vast majority of politicians, voters and academics, clearly believed that there was a role for both. There was a small, and declining, number who still thought capitalism was going nowhere[1] and a very small, but increasing, number who believed that it should go everywhere.

The democracy of the dollar and the democracy of the vote

Around this time, I remember seeing Milton Friedman, the high priest of the latter group, arguing that markets are inherently superior to democracy. If you are a part of a 49 per cent minority, you got nothing while if you had 49 cents at least you could get something. I saw this as capturing part of the dynamic power of markets – in which you can trade what you have for what you would prefer. However, it also helped me see some of the limitations of this approach.

1 There is a big difference in the counting principle – one dollar, one vote, rather than one person, one vote (Sampford and Lui, 2004: 86–107).
2 This novel voting principle would naturally be attractive to those with more dollars as it would give them more power. It would be rational for those with more dollars to press for such an approach.

3 Where there is a large disparity of wealth, there will be a great temptation to use dollars to get votes (or the favourable exercise of power by those voted in) – as well as the long recognized temptation to use votes to get dollars.
4 The dollarized (or dolorized) version of utility was one that Bentham would have completely rejected. While numbers of dollars is easier to measure than the quantity of happiness, Bentham's principle of diminishing marginal utility (the first loaf of bread gives much more pleasure than the second and the third is not good for your health) renders such a shortcut untenable.
5 Most importantly of all, I started to see that those involved in the ferocious 1970s debates shared some important common ground.

   a There is a role for the market and a role for government provision.
   b What is covered by the former and by the latter is a matter of genuine debate in which the dividing line will ebb and flow.
   c The choice of which areas of activity will be governed by the democracy of one-vote-one-value, and which will be governed by the democracy of one-dollar-one-value, is determined by the former. Polities choose markets, not the other way around.
   d The extremism of the extreme left was that they found no room for the market and the extremism of the neoliberals was in finding no room for the state.
   e This kind of realization of common ground led to what some called "convergence" between 1970s opponents.

6 Many of the most profound governance problems are found at the interface between the two – election funding and political advertising (Sampford, 2010b; 2010d), media ownership (Sampford, 2010b) and corruption (Preston *et al.*, 2002). However, unless we are going to give up either markets or democracy, these are problems that must be managed rather than resolved, leaving a boundary line that needs constant policing. However, the management and policing cannot be done from the exclusive perspective of either market economics or democratic politics. Each has to understand the other – though, in the end, it is for the democratic institutions to decide where the boundary is drawn.

This latter point was driven home during the early 1990s, when some economists started to praise federalism, as it meant that states would compete with each other for business. This left traditional constitutional lawyers familiar with the history of the 1920s bemused. However, my fundamental point is that polities choose markets; not the other way around.

Economics as one governance discipline, not THE governance discipline

Given the importance of social and political choice over patterns of market embedding, it is useful to begin by trying to understand the role of ideas in shaping these choices.

I have always been attracted to that intellectual vortex where philosophy, politics, law and economics meet. My work has emphasized what each can learn from the others and the problems that emerge when they do not. This is particularly so in the field of governance, where these disciplinary specializations generate strongly theorized but limited conceptions of institutions, their problems and solutions. When lawyers look at institutions they tend to see formal norms: constitutions and contracts. Ethicists see informal norms, and the values a given institution claims to further. Economists see incentives and disincentives. Political scientists see governance as all about power: who gets what and how.

Consequently, lawyers see institutional problems in terms of deficiencies of existing laws or processes of drafting laws. Ethicists see institutional problems in terms of values insufficiently specified, articulated or communicated. Political scientists see the ineffective management of conflict and interests, while economists see perverse incentives. Their solutions to institutional problems are similarly limited to their own fields. Lawyers throw rules at problems; ethicists want to talk values; political scientists want to rationalize power structures and effectively allocate authority; while economists want to align incentives with behaviour to be encouraged. All these partial insights into institutions and their problems and solutions are important. Any solution that ignores them is likely to fail. However, solutions limited to the insights of a single discipline are also likely to fail, as a result of a disconnection between those disciplines, and a failure to recognize the insights and contributions of others (Sampford, 1994; 2010a).

Insights and ideologies

A related phenomenon is the tendency, often exacerbated by disciplinary isolation, for theorists to take an important insight into human beings and/or the relationships between them and to build on it a theoretical edifice that the insight cannot bear (Sampford, 1991: 37–70). An idea that provides an important insight into one part of human life and answers some questions about it does not ring true when applied to other areas or other questions. This is where a theory becomes an ideology. For example, advocates of unfettered free markets took important insights about the dynamism of markets to demand market-based solutions to every possible social issue, in a similar way to doctrinaire Marxists using class to explain everything. The doctrine of strident free-marketeers has been called "primitive" (Galbraith, 1990: 10), "infantile" or "vulgar" capitalism. In preferring the last mentioned term, I am not merely showing an aesthetic and moral distaste for the particular mixture of intellectual inadequacy and self-interest that characterizes the Anglo-Saxon conservative reaction of the 1980s. The term is primarily chosen to highlight the parallels between it and what we used to call "vulgar Marxism".

Vulgar Marxism was based on a superficial reading of Marx that he would have totally disavowed. Similarly, vulgar capitalism was based on a superficial understanding of Adam Smith with which he would have been equally horrified. Both make claims to be a science. Both claimed to have discovered laws governing behaviour and the operation of society – vulgar Marxists on the basis of class and economic determinism of the base, vulgar capitalists on the laws of the market. Both approach the world with a rigid set of assumptions and tend to blame the impurity of the real world when it does not behave as expected. Both find it easy to prove their conclusions within their own frame of reference because all their conclusions are already bound up in their assumptions. The Marxist pseudo-science went so far as to predict the imminent end of history; something that was outbid by the claim that history has already ended (Fukuyama, 1989: 15).

Both vulgar capitalism and vulgar Marxism tend to compare the idealized version of their own system with the actual and imagined workings of their opponents. Vulgar Marxists were notorious for comparing a highly overblown image of the West as a den of corruption in which money always won out over an ideal socialism, rather than the grim societies they had produced themselves. Similarly, vulgar capitalists are always talking about how an ideal market is superior to the defects of actual public institutions. Where vulgar Marxists might claim that the money–power will always win out in the West, vulgar capitalists would claim that public choice theory demonstrates that the interests of the majority will be frustrated by minorities. The Marxist ideal did not take into account the problem of the self-interest of those who were supposed to lead others for the benefit of all; vulgar capitalists ignore the influence of private power and ideology on the operation of markets. Vulgar Marxists and capitalists claimed a degree of rigour and coherence and consistency. The dogmatic repetition of simplistic nostrums is consistent but it is neither clever nor sophisticated. It is merely the dogmatic repetition of simplistic nostrums.

Vulgar Marxists and capitalists share even less attractive features. They tend to be brutal, intolerant of dissent, bellicose and adventurist. In less academic surroundings, politicians who are drawn to implement some of the recommendations of the more vulgar forms of socialism and capitalism often make statements that ignore what should be obvious to them. One example from the 1993 Australian election campaign was the argument that where "an individual worker negotiates with an individual company, the state should not interfere". Apart from the curious notion of linking the word "individual" to a massive collective enterprise, it ignored the issue of inequality of bargaining power that would have certainly been brought to this person's attention when he was a student at Sydney Law School. My response to my colleagues was to modify the old epithet by saying: "The man is either a knave or a fool. And I will not insult his intelligence." However, I realized that there is a third category – an ideologue – where ideology blinds people to the nonsensical overstatements in what they say. It disconnects them from what is obvious to others. Yet, the fact that ideologies take their insights too far and ignore the limitations of those insights does not mean that their insight is not important. Indeed, the willingness of adherents to adhere to their theories despite the strength of the criticisms is a testament to the power of the relevant insight. In rejecting the ideology, we should seek to recognize and preserve those insights and to integrate them with insights from other theories. This leads to a variation to Locke's concept of a philosopher as "underlabourer" (see Winch, 1958) – when cleaning out the rubbish of theoretical discourse, philosophers should also recognize the gems of insight that lie within it.

Vulgar capitalist ideologues as economic man

Adam Smith's writings on the theme of self-interest can help us account for this tendency of theorists to stretch and distort valuable theoretical insights in the service of vulgar ideologies of one kind or another. Statements by those who say that people are only motivated by self-interest are hardly credible as universal claims about others (especially as no attempt is made to demonstrate such claims by sociological, psychological or ethnographic means; they are based on assumption, assertion or anecdote). However, as statements about their *own* motivations, we should be happy to accept them. While the extrapolation of their own motivations to others is a remarkable overextension of induction, the statement "all people are driven by self-interest" entails "I am driven by self-interest". While they may not know the minds of others, they should know their own. However, if they are only motivated by self-interest, then why would they not be prepared to propagate an ideology that suits them rather than one that is true? Or, at least, skew their ideologies in ways that promote their self-interest?

This was not a trap that Adam Smith would set for himself. Smith did not see people as solely motivated by self-interest. Indeed, the pursuit of self-interest in a market economy could only work within a society with ethical underpinnings (the thrust of his first book, *A Theory of Moral Sentiments*). If anyone accepted his dinner invitation (like David Hume) or the broader and more current invitation to read his work, they would understand that he also recognized that self-interest linked to power and secrecy could be profoundly damaging. Smith (1976: Book 1, Ch. 10, para. 82) famously warned against meetings of those engaged in the same occupation in terms far tougher than any corporate regulator would countenance.

> People of the same trade seldom meet together, even for merriment and diversion, but the conversation ends in a conspiracy against the public, or in some contrivance to raise prices. It is impossible indeed to prevent such meetings, by any law which either could be executed, or would be consistent with liberty and justice. But though the law cannot hinder people of the same trade from sometimes assembling together, it ought to do nothing to facilitate such assemblies; much less to render them necessary.

I am sure that he would have warned even more vociferously against those who said that they were only motivated by self-interest devoid of "moral sentiments".[2] Where such men gathered together and emerged to claim that certain policies were in the public interest, he would probably have advised us to ignore them and be very careful of the economists who agreed with them.

Efficient markets apotheosis

Yet, there is no shortage of examples in which the disciples of vulgar capitalist ideology have sought to realize their vision of a social world built around unfettered free markets. The apotheosis of the efficient market hypothesis is one such example that has achieved particular notoriety in the wake of the GFC.

I remember my amusement when I first read about "efficient markets hypothesis" in 1984. The assumption of perfect knowledge and rationality of market participants was more than just an overstatement to make the mathematics work. It was a patent attempt to build in assumptions that would make government intervention by definition unnecessary and ineffective. It profoundly misunderstood a central part of the market dynamic. In my experience, the goal of most market players is to exploit differential knowledge to their advantage – and sometimes to create differential knowledge by conduct that borders on misleading and deceptive conduct and abuse of market power. It also ignored the huge swings in markets, the existence of market sentiment and the fact that greed and panic are not matters of random statistical variation but are highly infectious; indeed, they are probably more infectious for those whose only declared interest is in making money.

The extent to which this movement had penetrated and dulled the thinking of economists employed by the finance industry was brought home at a briefing provided by a senior economist at our company's bank. In 1988 I asked, semi-innocently, what his estimate was of the percentage by which currency markets were likely to overshoot and undershoot in the current climate. His response was that markets never undershoot or overshoot. I asked him how he could possibly adhere to that view given the previous decade. His incomprehension remained. Markets were, by definition, right. My taunting produced a more tangible result when our company sought to buy its headquarters from a Church Trust that owned it. The process was drawn out and we saw the valuation rise nearly fivefold between 1987 and 1990. After I pointed out this remarkable change and his inability to articulate a methodology, I pointed to the variation and asked: "Were you wrong then or are you wrong now?" He insisted that both figures were completely correct. I told him that the new figure beggared belief and that if the Church put it up for auction I would enjoy witnessing his humiliation, our savings and the fact that we would be fully justified in refusing to pay his fee. He dropped his valuation to a mere three and a half times his 1987 valuation which was, if a little on the high side, one we were prepared to wear.

The inefficiency of enforced speculation

Another example of vulgar capitalist ideology being pursued in practice was the deregulation of the Australian currency in 1984. At the time, Paul Keating, the then Australian Treasurer, announced that speculators would now speculate against each other rather than the government. Until then, governments had tried to move the exchange rate gradually to smooth and stabilize markets and reduce volatility, and currency traders sought to take advantage of this and profit. However, he was wrong to assume that they would henceforth profit from each other. If that were true then currency speculation would be a negative sum game. The trades would be neutral so that, on average, nobody would make a profit on the trades, but this would turn into an average loss because of the costs of staffing (egos do not come cheap in the finance industry), equipment and banking facilities. This would make the traders like punters on a horse race. The smart punters (or those with inside knowledge from the trainers or jockeys) do better than the less smart ones, but punters as a whole lose.

Currency traders did not turn on each other but sought profitability from those who were engaged in what I petulantly persisted in calling "real business" – those who innovate, manufacture, buy, sell and distribute goods and services – Adam Smith's butchers and bakers or, in our case, distributors of cookers to transform their products into hot dinners. The only time when I was really annoyed with a banker during the 1980s was when I was having a drink with some bankers selling hedging products (that is, providing protection against adverse currency movements). One told me, in what he thought was a compliment, that I was a speculator. "Everyone takes a position. If you hedge you are taking a position that the AUS$ will drop. If you do not, you are taking a position that it will not." My response was to say: "Our company is not 'taking a position'. We are trying to sell ovens. The volatility you create puts that at risk so that I have to buy your products but don't think it makes me a speculator like you." I made some mention of firebugs selling fire insurance, accepted another drink, reluctantly developed a currency strategy, and reflected.

The first reflection was that, in promoting volatility, traders benefited at the expense of those who needed to exchange currencies to conduct business, through a combination of asymmetric knowledge and outright manipulation. Although some risks could be hedged (generating major profits for the market players), long term risk was uninsurable (see Sampford, 2010c: 13–24). By increasing the risk of doing business, it discouraged what might otherwise be a profitable investment. For example, if a factory needed to secure a return of 20 per cent per annum to justify the investment, but there was a significant risk of a significant adverse change in the exchange rate (say a 50 per cent chance of a drop of 40 per cent over the payback period), then they would need a return of 40 per cent instead of 20 per cent. The second reflection is that there was a disconnection between the costs of hedging and the probability of a decline in the hedged currency. In fact the reverse is true. The cost of a hedging contract is equal to the difference in interest rates between the two currencies over the period plus a small margin (that is, if the interbank rate in the U.S. is 2 per cent and that in Australia is 6 per cent then a hedging contract to cover a payment in six months' time will cost just over half the difference, or 2 per cent). However, countries with declining currencies generally raise interest rates to reduce the likelihood or pace of decline – simultaneously leading to an increase in the cost of insuring against what is most likely to happen. This is, of course, an opportunity for speculation. Indeed, it is one of those areas where the deep flaws in some markets provide an opportunity for profit that is logically greater than the risk. However, those whose business lies elsewhere do not want to be speculators and want to reduce rather than increase risks. This is one area of growth in the "financial services" industry whose expansion does not serve either industry or community.

"Beware of merchant bankers bearing gifts"

Yet free market ideology continues to be vigorously pursued within much of the financial sector. One clear illustration of this is the establishment of a carbon market, as the creators and "market makers" for derivatives have attempted to work their magic on carbon trading. The more enthusiastic merchant bankers are about carbon trading the more we should be wary of it. I can see why believers in the efficient markets hypothesis, strengthened by the success of SO2 trading schemes, might have been enthusiastic about carbon trading schemes in the past. However, the experience of the GFC with complex financial instruments should make us very wary of trying to create a complex market for current and future carbon credits. While collateralized debt options, corporate development functions and exchange-traded funds once looked solid and now look virtual (sometimes in the sense of being non-existent), future carbon credits may seem just so much "hot air". The case for a steadily rising carbon price to drive innovation appears clear. Once again, industry needs predictability, while traders want volatility – volatility which they will promote and exploit. I have been making this argument for the last 11 years and continue to suggest that a steadily rising carbon tax is best (Sampford, 2000; 2009b; 2010c). For the last three years, I have been arguing for a "carbon added tax" that operates like a value added tax to be rebated on exports and imposed on imports. Such a tax could be offset by reductions in value added tax/goods and services tax making it inflation neutral, revenue neutral, and with the capacity to rise to about 6–10 per cent of GDP.

While I used the above insight in juggling various currency risks,[3] I was never tempted to make it my business or to set up a fund to exploit it. However, it might have been a better basis for making money than Long Term Capital Management. When I first heard about the algorithms they used, the flaw seemed obvious to me. They were relying on a sophisticated version of most betting systems which make a little bit of money under the vast majority of scenarios but in which the scale of losses on the remaining scenarios more than outweighs those profits when each is multiplied by their probability of occurrence.

The "privatization" of public power

While the practical pursuit of free market ideology has been particularly visible in the financial sector in recent times, this impulse has also been expressed in strong pressures to deregulate and privatize, particularly during the 1980s and

1990s. Deregulation is often sold on the idea that it is reducing the power of the state over people. However, it does not destroy power; it transfers it – from institutions ruled by democracy of the vote, to those ruled by democracy of the dollar.[4] Governments may find that such power, once transferred, will be used against the government. Privatization, however, does involve distinct benefits for some: certainly, to the stockbrokers, the underwriters and the lawyers. They are also certainly the most active and vocal in their advocacy of the advantages of privatization. I note that advocates of privatization tended to ignore:

- Transaction costs, including the costs of legislation, legal advice, due diligence, brokerage and underwriting fees (hardly irrelevant to the enthusiasm of the legal and stock broking industries – and the uncritical support they offer for it);
- The tendency to underprice the asset to ensure that the privatization is a "success" – something in which they will be aided and abetted by the underwriters who want to minimize their own risk; and
- The opportunities for corruption (which are much greater when the assets of government are at stake rather than "merely" its annual revenues).

Over the last decade there has been a strong push for "Private Public Partnerships" (PPPs) under which new infrastructure projects are built by corporations created for the purpose, highly geared, and with very large fees for those who set up the deals. Given the higher borrowing costs and the burden of fees, they are inherently more expensive to operate and suffer from most of the problems outlined above.

Many of the enterprises privatized were natural monopolies. One of Adam Smith's targets was the private monopolies granted to powerful individuals and corporations (created for that purpose). Just because a public company makes a profit from selling a service, does not necessarily make it a part of a "free market". Lada and Polski Fiat, communist state owned enterprises in the 1970s, were engaged in the European motor market. Sydney Airport was a monopoly before and after privatization. To deal with the obvious problems of price gouging and other monopolistic behaviour, the low priests of the ineffectiveness of regulation seemed to decide that regulation could fix such problems. I have argued that regulation is difficult but possible. However, having an organization supposedly dedicated to maximizing profit and another to regulating it for other purposes is not nearly as effective as having one organization required to secure multiple goals (the norm for most institutions) (Sampford, 1998).

Professionalization: getting financial services to serve the public?

The scandals in the financial services industry associated with the GFC have led to pushes in some circles to professionalize various groups within the financial services industry. Some are eager to clean up the profession; others seem keen for the prestige and the claim of self-regulation as an alternative to government regulation. Few seem to have focussed on the central element of a profession – service to the community whose delivery constitutes a public good.

A profession involves a body of knowledge, institutions for imparting it and a dedicated and identified group of experts who apply that knowledge for the benefit of the community they claim to serve. Many groups with a claimed expertise for sale have sought to be recognized as "professions" – with the associated prestige, autonomy, power and ability to charge higher fees. The great learned professions of medicine and law were joined by dentists, architects, accountants and engineers in the nineteenth-century and "allied health professions" (nurses, pharmacists, psychologists) in the twentieth-century. There have been moves to professionalize other areas (for example, journalism) and to re-professionalize the military.[5]

Professions are not charities, and professionals can charge fees for the service they render. Those who serve best may earn particularly high fees, in line with the service they perform and the public good they promote. But generating those fees can never be the central rationale or justification of the profession. A professional should never design or recommend services in order to maximize fees. A doctor must not recommend a procedure because he makes more money out of it. A lawyer must not recommend tactics to increase cost or delay – even if the client wants this to intimidate or bankrupt the opponent.

This addresses another vital point. Even though most professionals work for corporate or individual clients, they are not supposed to serve their clients at the cost of the public good to which the profession is dedicated. Even though many professionals work for large and often profit making corporations (engineering firms, private hospitals, corporatized legal practices), they are employed as professionals. Their employers should realize that they cannot be expected or required to compromise their professional standards and service to the public good which their profession claims to deliver for the sake of higher profits. Even if some professionals may breach these requirements and some professions develop a range of excuses for practices that might otherwise be seen to breach them, there is a genuine commitment to these principles by the profession and the vast bulk of relevant professionals. It would be very hard to say this about the "financial services industry" over the past 20–30 years, where the search for fees was paramount.

The other sharp distinction between professional bodies and the contemporary finance industry is in relation to the "body of knowledge" that should be at the core of the profession, and which it develops, communicates and applies. The best professions have multiple means for challenging that body of knowledge – through public contestation in the academy, in professional bodies and, in law, through the structure of adversarial court processes. Such challenges are critical to the development of that body of knowledge and its application in the service of the community. While no profession lives up to the above ideals in full, all acknowledge them and try. I see no evidence that this is true of the finance industry. Rather than being custodians of a body of knowledge they seem more like purveyors of self-serving ideological half-truths at best, and ideological nonsense in many other cases.

I referred above to the "efficient market hypothesis" (EMH) which so unimpressed me when I first read it. Professor Ian Harper was honest in saying that the members of the Wallis Inquiry into Australian financial services all believed in it and the collapse of the EMH meant we needed a new inquiry and a complete rethink (Quiggin, 2010a). A profession is always interrogating and challenging the ideas that form part of its knowledge and is particularly careful about those propositions that suit its own practitioners. If something appears to be too good to be true, it probably is too good to be true, and should be tested. Constant internal criticism means that major mistakes like EMH are avoided (can anyone point to a similar monumentally failed theory at the heart of medicine, engineering or law in the last 200 years?). When such failures unfold, it is incumbent on professionals to understand why they got it so wrong despite the criticisms of many who were proven right. They should then critically re-examine their theories and prescriptions. If they are not prepared to do so, it is not clear to me that they should have a job, let alone be listened to. This does not mean that they cannot play a leading role in new thinking. One can learn from error; and the larger the error the greater the possibility of learning.

Unfortunately, we still see nonsense like the suggestion that governments do not have enough money for infrastructure but they have enough for trillions of dollars of bailouts. In 1989 I was a post-doctoral research fellow at Monash University and the then Dean had appointed the first lecturer in banking law. I greeted him by enunciating a view of banking and banking law: "The first principle of banking is to ensure that as much money passes through your hands as many times as possible ensuring that a little bit sticks each time. The first principle of banking law is that what sticks is yours." A decade later, I added: "The first principle of banking ethics is that the transaction and the stickiness is justified as a service to the community to which banking claims to be a service industry."

Paul Krugman has pointed out that financial services now account for 8 per cent of the U.S. economy – up from 4 per cent half a century ago (Krugman, 2009). Does this mean that it is doing twice as much or does it mean that it is half as efficient – or just that a lot more clients' money is sticking to their hands – and in ways that do not serve the interests of the economy and the community? If law doubled as a proportion of GDP, it might be that we were getting twice as much justice: but it is more likely to mean that it is twice as expensive.

I would support the development of finance as a genuine profession recognizing that Finance is a service industry – like law and other real professions. However, its first task is to identify the public good it claims to deliver for the community it serves, and to set about ensuring that public good is delivered to the public rather than a private profit extracted.

Re-embedding and reconnecting markets

The above encounters with a small proportion of the intellectual excesses committed by triumphalist and/or rent-seeking proponents of free markets indicate a significant disconnection not just with "society" but with ethics, logic, common sense and the variety of disciplines which have a lot to say about the matters on which they claim expertise. The exposed nonsense of what has been said by the financial services industry might lead many to reject all they have to say out of hand. However, in line with the modified "underlabourer" view of philosophy and social science, it is important to pick out the gems from amidst the rubbish. We should no more reject liberal economists' insights into the power of market mechanisms than they should have rejected the insights into the deficiencies of those mechanisms pointed out by social democrats over the last 200 years. I would suggest that markets and market theory need to re-embed, reconnect and recognize some of the elements identified. These institutions, and the ideas that underpin them, should:

> ***Recognize***: Self-interest; Power.
> ***Reconnect*** with: Other disciplines; Critics; Logic and common sense.
> ***Re-embed*** with: Ethics and moral sentiments; Professions; Institutions.

Recognizing power and self-interest

The explicit recognition of power in the market economy should include recognizing:

1 Concentration of political and social power, people and resources within organizations.
2 The inevitabilities of asymmetries in knowledge and the fact that the exploitation of these is a feature of all market and political systems and the basis of much profit making.
3 The inevitability of agency problems that mean that markets cannot operate unregulated – and that those who have power and asymmetric knowledge may well propose unregulated markets to make it easier to exercise their power and asymmetric knowledge.

The recognition of ideology and of self-interest in public debates should include:

1 Recognition of the self-interest of financiers arguing that privatization and public private partnerships are necessary and desirable.
2 Recognizing the existence of ideology – political, economic, social, moral – within debates about governance of financial markets and the tendency to make self-serving comparisons between ideologies in which the ideal version of one's preferred ideology is compared with actualized versions of others.
3 Questioning how efficient markets theory ever got going and the ideological controls on appointments in so many economics faculties, including the role of thinktanks in pressing the interests of their donors.

Economists, especially, must recognize that their insights are partial and limited and can only be useful in conjunction with other disciplinary perspectives.

4 Repudiating the externalization of costs and risks onto others.
5 Ratings agencies should recognize and shed ideology – as well as recognizing the pro-American bias of ratings agencies based in New York.

Reconnection

Economists in particular must recognize that their discipline came out of an intellectual space shared by what is now ethics, politics, economics and philosophy. Contributions from all those disciplines need to be recognized and valued, while interdisciplinary methodologies must be developed and applied. The interaction of economics with other disciplines will generate critics from other disciplines. This should be welcomed. However, there should also be a strong tradition of self-criticism. This will help ensure that logic, common sense and the facts are not so easily ignored.

Embedding in ethics

Ethics is essential to the effective governance of any phenomenon – not least markets. The values of investors should be respected, and should flow through to their investments. More generally, for Smith, embeddedness is about embedding markets in an ethical framework. For me, it is about that, but also about relevant institutions. Indeed, the two are intimately related. In general, "embeddedness" is making the market and market institutions serve the community rather than the other way around.

Embedding in values and institutions

For the last 21 years, I have taken an institutionalist approach (Preston *et al.*, 2002; Sampford, 1990; 1992) in which I have argued that government agencies, corporations and professions need to justify themselves to the communities in which they operate for a number of reasons, including:

1 The various privileges they are accorded. For corporations, these include limited liability of joint stock companies. For banks, they include the ability to create credit, and access to central bank "lender of last resort" facilities. For professions, they include the right to practice in particular areas to the partial or full exclusion of others.
2 Various benefits that are provided – in particular, bank guarantees and, as we have seen, the bailing out of corporations that are "too big to fail", as well as a general expectation (for some an obligation) to use governmental powers to prevent some of the worst problems afflicting economies.
3 The legal protection of property rights that are backed up by state power.

The reasons why these privileges, benefits and protections are provided is not for the benefit of government agencies and corporations, but because doing so is believed to benefit the community as a whole. In general terms, we allow the creation of joint stock companies because they are seen as increasing the likelihood that we will have dinner on our table (as well as the many other things that people wanted then and the more things they want now). However, there is another, and in my opinion, decisive reason why governments, corporations, and indeed all institutions need to justify themselves to the communities in which they operate. All institutions concentrate power, people and resources to achieve certain publicly stated goals which are, or are seen to be, of benefit to the relevant community. However, that concentration of power, people and resources could be used for other purposes that might harm that same community. Police forces and the armed services are supposed to protect citizens but can use their coercive force to secure bribes, to terrorize inhabitants or even to seize state power. Banks and other financial institutions concentrate the resources of their shareholders, depositors and others who entrust them with their money. These resources are supposed to ensure liquidity for those who engage in the provisions of goods and services to others. Yet, those resources can be used in transactions that generate very high fees for the financial intermediaries at the same time as they create great risk for those who have entrusted their money to them.

For anarchists, the dangers are just too great, but most of us are prepared to take a risk. The American revolutionaries considered this very carefully. Governments are instituted to support the "inalienable rights to life, liberty and the pursuit of happiness", but they could turn against the people they were supposed to benefit, justifying revolution and the establishment of governments that could perform the relevant function (or in my terms, justify themselves). They did not decide to abandon the idea of government because government power had been abused. However, they wanted to reduce the risk of future abuse by creating a system of "checks and balances" that provided a form of "risk management".

While Adam Smith saw virtue in competition, he certainly recognized the dangers of the abuse of economic power in his warnings about combinations of merchants and large mercantilist corporations. Over the intervening two and a half centuries, we have seen many cases where governmental and corporate power have been abused and our "risk management systems" have been improved. The three responses typically tried are legal regulation, explicit ethical standard setting, and institutional reform. I have long argued that the three are relatively ineffective if tried on their own, but can be highly effective if used in combination and directed towards making it more likely that institutions will live up to the public justifications for the powers and privileges they exercise. I have argued that ethical standard setting provides the most effective means of integrating the three by encapsulating the core of explicit ethical standard setting, the principled basis of laws and the ultimate criteria for judging whether institutional reforms have been effective.

This "institutional" approach, which brings together ethical standard setting, legal regulation and institutional design, will need to be implemented at a number of levels – at the corporate level (with individual financial institutions, regulators and other players), and in coordinating regulators and oversight bodies into "integrity systems" at national, global and, in some cases, regional levels.[6] Providing details of how this may occur would be beyond the scope of this chapter, but some brief suggestions have been made elsewhere for corporate, national and global financial integrity systems (Sampford, 2010a; Sampford, 2010e).

A good night's sleep?

If markets are to be re-embedded in society, it should be as part of a long-term beneficial relationship rather than for short-term benefits. Re-embedding should be based on commitment, openness, transparency, mutual understanding and respect. The relationship should be of benefit to both, but the delivery of those benefits to society has to be more than promised – they need to be delivered. As argued in the essay, they cannot be delivered unless they are built into the way corporations are envisaged, structured and run. They need to be part of what a corporation is and does not just what they say.

Notes

1 For example, the Australian Labor Party still had "the socialisation of the means of production and exchange" in its platform, small numbers set up communes and the kibbutz drew a lot of interest. However, the so called "New Left" was generally not as concerned with economic issues and the inspiration for progressive socialists – the Dubcek led "Prague Spring" involved an increased role for the market as well as human rights.

2 Whether socially derived, as he would argue, or more driven by emotion, as Hume would argue.

3 We had higher DM debts than US$ debts so I adopted a simple strategy of swapping some of the former for the latter and covered approximately four months into each contract (which was generally just before the ship docked) – meaning that our debts on imports were about equal in DM, US$ and AUS$.

4 One of the many ironies of those who press for market solutions on the grounds of efficiency is that they do not produce results that are Pareto efficient.

5 Though I have argued that there is a long tradition of professionalism with "honour" playing the role of "ethics" in some militaries (see Sampford, 2009b).

6 Regional level financial integrity systems are important in Europe and their further development may be the key to solving the diverse problems of countries with financial systems in difficulty, like Ireland, Latvia, Iceland and countries with recessional problems like Germany.

A concluding note

Frances Stewart

> Our thesis is that the idea of a self-adjusting market implied a stark utopia. Such an institution could not exist for any length of time without annihilating the human and natural substance of society.... Inevitably, society took measures to protect itself, but whatever measures it took impaired the self-regulation of the market, disorganised industrial life, and thus endangered society in yet another way.
>
> (Polanyi, 1944: 3)

Karl Polanyi's brilliant analysis of the two-way movement towards and away from an unregulated market offers hope for those who live in a time when the pendulum has swung to one extreme. Today it is the harsh consequences of neo-liberalism for inequality, poverty and social cohesion that underlie the need for a swing back:

> to rehabilitate the lives of men and their environment, to give them some security of status, intervention necessarily aimed at reducing the flexibility of wages and the mobility of labour, giving stability to incomes, continuity to production, introducing public control of natural resources and the management of currencies in order to avoid the unsettling changes in the price level.
>
> (Polanyi, 1944: 225)

The apparent automacity of the Polanyian swings suggest that the present market extreme is temporary, although the Polanyian swings took a very long time – a century or so. Can we assume that the pendulum will (eventually) swing back?

The world has changed in important respects since Polanyi's *The Great Transformation* was published in 1944. First, his analysis was based primarily on the experience of just one country – Britain – and he did not take into account the possible different trajectories of different parts of the world, nor the interactions among countries, which is an essential aspect of any analysis in today's global economy. Second, increasing pressures on the environment have become overwhelmingly important in ways that require local, national and global collective action, yet to date such action has been blocked by particular interests. The environmental consequences of different models of development add an additional dimension to the Polanyian swings, giving further impetus to the need for a movement towards collective action.[1] Finally, the Polanyi swings were essentially the result of a *political* reaction to events. Yet arguably the nature of politics has changed since he wrote, posing obstacles to such political reactions. In this concluding note, I shall focus on the first and third of these issues, both of which form a recurring theme of this volume.

The movement of the Polanyian pendulum requires three types of development: first, changes in the economy and society in ways that provoke new thinking about development; second, political movements that take up this new thinking and press for policies that it advocates; and finally, actual changes in policy via the political system. Polanyi's focus was on a single model derived from the experience of Britain. When he was writing, what we today term "developing countries" were colonies subordinate to and exploited by the predominant model in developed countries without any independence of thought or action (although the Latin American countries which had gained independence in the nineteenth century were somewhat of an exception). Polanyi analysed the system of production and distribution of colonies briefly, on the basis of anthropologists' work, but this analysis was not incorporated into his main framework. Following World War II colonialism was gradually disbanded as countries gained their political independence. Yet, while there was political independence of a sort, for the first decades after World War II, there was very little independence of ideas or of policy-making. To start with colonialism had left low levels of education, while most of the developing countries' elite were educated in the advanced countries, imbibing and advocating their ideas. Second, heavy dependence on the advanced countries for investment, technology and loans limited independence of action. Consequently, most countries followed the patterns of development advocated by thinkers from advanced countries. In parallel with the Western Keynesian era, many countries adopted economic planning, import substitution, etc., until the late 1970s, while those in the socialist bloc broadly imitated socialist-style planning. When the pendulum swung towards neoliberalism (monetarism and markets) in the late 1970s in the West, pressure from the West, enforced by the International Monetary Fund (IMF) and the World Bank, ensured the same movement in the developing countries.[2] The absence of democracy in most developing countries facilitated this parallel pattern, since independent political movements that might have resisted some of these changes were generally absent. Thus a unified model of the world, implicit in Polanyi's analysis, continued to obtain despite huge differences in the actual conditions of countries.

Yet this situation is now changing as a result of both economic and political developments. Many so-called developing countries have achieved a considerable degree of economic independence through the transformation of their economies and their rising share of world markets, as well as due to the adoption of prudent fiscal and monetary policies aimed at avoiding dependence on loans from the IMF and World Bank. Consequently, during the financial crisis of

2008–09, far fewer countries borrowed from the IMF than in the crisis of the 1980s and many adopted their own stimulus packages (Stewart, 2012). Thus the West can no longer call the tune for many countries, especially in Asia and Latin America. In addition, a huge wave of democratization occurred in developing countries from the 1970s, so that by 1999, 25 out of 26 countries in Latin America and the Caribbean had multiparty electoral systems; and in Sub-Saharan Africa, 29 out of 42 countries had multiparty electoral systems (UNDP, 2002: 15). This provided the space for local political movements to fight for their own objectives, drawing increasingly on locally developed ideas and discourse. As a result of an increase in the real independence of action that these developments have facilitated, it is possible for Polanyi-type swings to differ across countries, and a unified model is no longer appropriate.

We can detect such an independent swing in a number of Latin American and some Asian countries. In Brazil, for example, the workers and peasants united to support the election of a more radical president, Lula de Silva, who introduced a number of progressive policies that limited the harsh consequences of the market – for example, a higher minimum wage, cash transfers to poor countries (the *bolsa familia*), and increased educational access. In Venezuela, Bolivia and Ecuador, similar political movements led to the election of presidents who challenged the pure market model in a variety of ways. These and other countries in Latin America have seen a reduction of inequality and poverty in the 2000s (Cornia and Martorano, 2011). India introduced the National Rural Employment Guarantee scheme in reaction to powerful political protest, and is now under similar pressure to provide everyone with the "right to food". All these are signs of an independent "swing back" against the pure market, independently of what is happening in developed countries.

Of course, constraints on independent action remain – and indeed now affect both developed as well as developing countries. While the actions of the countries cited modify the social consequences of the market, they rarely challenge the power of the market itself, with governments fearful of the consequences for investment and their currencies, and sensitive to political pressures from domestic capitalist interests. In developed countries the financial markets constrain action, as countries fear that the adoption of Keynesian fiscal policies will lead to capital flight. Without coordinated action – as advocated for example by Ocampo and Buckley in this volume – there is some reality to these fears. While market constraints on Keynesian policies are often argued by those with ideological and material interests in opposing Keynesian policies, the more the talk of the risks of losing market confidence, the more the fear is justified. As a result the potential Polanyian swing has become more complicated than in the era analysed by Polanyi, since it may require simultaneous action by multiple countries, if individual countries are not to suffer from "going-it-alone". This is one important constraint on the swing away from the extremes of the market model, and underlines the need for global coordination in ideas and action. If one takes into account the environmental issues noted above, global agreement becomes even more important.

Countries can take some action, however, to moderate some of the effects of market policies without global coordination. This includes some industrial policies, as analysed by Amsden and Howe in this volume, as well as some environmental policies. It also includes policies towards social protection, which, if extensive, can greatly moderate the harsh consequences of the market. Moreover, action in each of these areas of policy may actually *improve* market performance.

Both national and global action are dependent on political change, which itself frequently rests on mass movements favouring such change. Britain turned away from the extreme market in the twentieth century due to the growth of the trade union movement – itself a reaction to the abysmal working conditions of the nineteenth century – eventually leading to the electoral success of the Labour Party, which introduced many market-modifying policies. Yet there seem to be more constraints on the development of such mass movements than there were a hundred years ago. In developed countries the trade union movements are losing ground, partly because of differentiation in the labour market according to skill, changes in the regulatory environment that are hostile to labour (as discussed by Cahill in this volume), and perhaps also to rising wages that make such movements seem less important to many working people. In developing countries people are differentiated by sector (formal and informal, urban and rural), by ethnicity and by religion, all of which impede the development of mass movements and ideological politics. These impediments are particularly strong in Sub-Saharan Africa, where politics tends to be ethnic rather than class-based. In Latin America and Asia mass movements are emerging and are gaining some power, as noted above. When it comes to global politics, most global political movements are in an embryonic state, lacking unity or power. Movements with the most potential seem to be "green" ones (positively) and terrorist groups (negatively).

Not only has the basis for mass politics weakened, but new influences have emerged to distort "democratic" politics. In particular, large companies have acquired huge amounts of political influence, through their financial support for political parties, their influence on the media and their lobbying activities. They seem to be most powerful in the U.S. where their effects on Congress limits or prevents action to reduce environmental harms, to regulate the financial sector or to raise taxation. Spence has observed that while small- and medium-sized enterprises provide the most jobs in the U.S. it is global companies that most influence politics (Spence, 2011). They are powerful elsewhere too: in Australia, for example, attempts to tax carbon have undermined successive governments. In the U.K., heavy finance of the Conservative Party by property developers was probably responsible for proposals to reduce planning requirements greatly (Blake, 2011). The banking sector has succeeded in watering down proposals to separate deposit banking from investment banking, or to limit bonuses. The opposition of interest groups to reforms is alluded to in a number of the chapters in this volume, including Ross with respect to agricultural interests, and Quiggin with reference to the banking sector and financial reform.

Together the worsening conditions for mass politics and the increasing power of large companies are greatly limiting the possibilities for a truly new swing of the pendulum. Only if conditions become and remain really bad – as in the Great Depression – is a radical change likely. In conclusion, it seems the ideas for change are present, as evident in the contributions to this volume. What is lacking are the political conditions that would make them a reality.

Notes

1 Though Polanyi did argue that the unregulated market destroyed the environment and that a movement away from it was necessary for "[t]he protection of man, nature and productive organization … to rehabilitate the lives of men and their environment" (1944: 225).

2 This is analysed in much greater depth in Stewart (2007).

References

Abdelal, R. E. and Ruggie, J. G. (2009) "The principles of embedded liberalism: social legitimacy and global capitalism", in D. Moss and J. Cisternino (eds) *New Perspectives on Regulation*, Cambridge: The Tobin Project.

Adam, D. (2008) "Food price rises threaten global security – UN", *Guardian*, 9 April 2008. Online. Available at: www.commondreams.org/archive/2008/04/09/8192/ (accessed 8 June 2008).

Admati, A. R., DeMarzo, P. M., Hellwig, M. F. and Pfleiderer, P. (2010) "Fallacies, irrelevant facts, and myths in the discussion of capital regulation: why bank equity is not expensive", Rock Center for Corporate Governance at Stanford University Working Paper No. 86. Online. Available at: http://ssrn.com/abstract=1669704 (accessed 13 November 2011).

AFP (2009a) "African ministers demand G20 seat", *Global Policy Forum (Istanbul)*, 4 October 2009. Online. Available at: www.globalpolicy.org/social-and-economic-policy/the-three-sisters-and-other-institutions/global-governance-and-the-three-sisters-1–11/48259.html (accessed 7 October 2011).

AFP (2009b) "Richest countries ignore Hunger Summit", DW-world.de, 16 November 2009. Online. Available at: www.dw-world.de/dw/article/0,,4896301,00.html (accessed 13 November 2011).

AFP (2010) "Microfinance pioneer Yunus criticizes Indian lenders", *Economic Times* (India), 12 December 2010. Online. Available at: http://articles.economictimes.indiatimes.com/2010–12–12/news/27591863_1_sks-microfinance-vikram-akula-microfinance-pioneer (accessed 3 October 2011).

Aguiar, M. (2009) "Food speculation coalition letter to the Hon Barack Obama, President of the United States", *Grassroots International*, 24 March 2009. Online. Available at: www.grassrootsonline.org/news/articles/food-speculation-coalition-letter-president-obama (accessed 10 October 2011).

Aiginger, K. (2007) "Industrial policy: a dying breed or re-emerging phoenix?", *Journal of Industry, Competition and Trade*, 7: 297–323.

Akyuz, Y. (2010) *Policy Response to the Global Financial Crisis: key issues for developing countries*, South Centre Research Paper No. 24, Geneva: South Centre. Online. Available at: www.southcentre.org/index.php?option=com_content&view=article&id=1016:policy-response-to-the-global-financial-crisis-key-issues-for-developing-countries&catid=142:global-financial-and-economic-crisis&Itemid=67&lang=en (accessed 31 January 2011).

Albo, G. (2002) "Neoliberalism, the state and the left: a Canadian perspective", *Monthly Review*, 54 (1): 46–55.

Albo, G., Gindin, S. and Panitch, L. (2010) *In and Out of Crisis: the global financial meltdown and left alternatives*, Oakland: PM Press.

Alperovitz, G. and Daly, L. (2008) *Unjust Deserts: how the rich are taking our common inheritance*, New York: The New Press.

Alter, K. J. (2000) "The European Union's legal system and domestic policy: spillover or backlash?", *International Organization*, 54: 489–518.

Amorim, C. (2011) "Personal interview", Harvard University, June.

Amsden, A. H. (1989) *Asia's Next Giant: South Korea and late industrialization*, New York: Oxford University Press.

Amsden, A. H. (2001) *The Rise of "the Rest": challenges to the West from late-industrializing economies*, New York: Oxford University Press.

Amsden, A. H. (2003) "Industrialization under new WTO law", in J. Toye (ed.) *Trade and Development: directions for the 21st century*, Cheltenham: Edward Elgar: 82–99.

Amsden, A. H. (2009) "Nationality of firm ownership in developing countries: who should 'crowd out' whom in imperfect markets?", in M. Cimoli, G. Dosi and J. E. Stiglitz (eds) *Industrial Policy and Development: the political economy of capabilities accumulation*, Oxford: Oxford University Press.

Amsden, A. H. and Chu, W. W. (2003) *Beyond Late Development: Taiwan's upgrading policies*, Cambridge, MA: MIT Press.

Amsden, A. H. and Hikino, T. (2000) "The bark is worse than the bite: new WTO law and late industrialization", *Annals of the American Academy of Political and Social Science*, 570: 104–14.

Amsden, A. H. and Suzumura, K. (2001) "An interview with Miyohei Shinohara: non-conformism in Japanese economic thought", *Journal of the Japanese and International Economies*, 15: 341–60.

Anderson, T. (1999) "The meaning of deregulation", *Journal of Australian Political Economy*, 44: 5–21.

Anker, R., Malkas, H. and Korten, A. (2003) *Gender-based Occupational Segregation in the 1990s*, Declaration Working Paper 16, Geneva: International Labour Organization.

Ariosto, D. (2011) "Ohio voters repeal law limiting union rights, CNN projects", *CNN U.S.*, 8 November 2011. Online. Available at: http://articles.cnn.com/2011–11–08/us/us_ohio-collective-bargaining-vote_1_wisconsin-workers-ohio-voters-phil-neuenfeldt?_s=PM:US (accessed 13 November 2011).

Arner, D. W. and Buckley, R. P. (2010) "Redesigning the architecture of the global financial system", *Melbourne Journal of International Law*, 11 (2): 1–55.

Asian Development Bank (ADB) (2009) *Lessons from the Asian Development Bank's Response to Financial Crises*, Evaluation Information Brief 2009–02, Manila: Asian Development Bank.

Atkinson, A. and Leigh, A. (2007) "The distribution of top incomes in Australia", *Economic Record*, 83 (262): 247–61.

Azmi, A. (2009) "Microfinance investments make 2009 a watershed year", *Microfinance Focus*, 31 December 2009. Online. Available at: www.microfinancefocus.com/news/2009/12/31/microfinance-investments-make-2009-a-watershed-year/ (accessed 3 October 2011).

Bacchus, J. (2010) "Hoarding resources threatens free trade", *Wall Street Journal*, 19 May 2010. Online. Available at: http://online.wsj.com/article/SB10001424052748703957904575251813816207780.html (accessed 1 October 2011).

Baker, R. (2005) *Capitalism's Achilles Heel: how to renew the free-market system*, New York: Wiley.

Balakrishnan, R. (2009) "Soaring microfinance lures PE investors", *The Financial Express* (India), 6 November 2009. Online. Available at: www.financialexpress.com/news/soaring-microfinance-lures-pe-investors/537843/ (accessed 3 October 2011).

Baldwin, R. and Evenett, S. (eds) (2009) *The Collapse of Global Trade, Murky Protectionism, and the Crisis: recommendations for the G20*, London: VoxEU.org.

Bandyopadhyay, T. (2009) "US, UK are hijacking the G20 agenda", *Live Mint & The Wall Street Journal* (Mumbai), 14 September 2009. Online. Available at: www.livemint.com/2009/09/13233922/US-UK-are-hijacking-G20-agen.html (accessed 7 October 2011).

Banks, G. (2008) "Industry policy for a productive Australia", Colin Clark Memorial Lecture, Brisbane, 6 August 2008. Online. Available at: www.pc.gov.au/speeches/?a=82551 (accessed 13 October 2011).

Barhan, P., Bowles, S. and Wallerstein, M. (eds) (2006) *Globalization and Egalitarian Redistribution*, Princeton: Princeton University Press.

Bartik, T. (2005) "Solving the problem of economic development incentives", *Growth and Change*, 36: 139–66.

Basel Committee on Banking Supervision (2010) *Basel Committee for Banking Supervision: Microfinance Activities and the Core Principles for Effective Banking Supervision*, Consultative Document, Basel: Bank for International Settlements. Online. Available at: www.bis.org/publ/bcbs167.htm (accessed 9 February 2011).

BBC (2011) "EU austerity drive country by country", *BBC News Europe*, 11 November 2011. Online. Available at: www.bbc.co.uk/news/10162176 (accessed 13 November 2011).

Beckfield, J. (2005) "The consequences of regional political and economic integration for inequality and the welfare state in Western Europe", unpublished thesis, Indiana University.

Beckfield, J. (2006) "European integration and income inequality", *American Sociological Review*, 71: 964–85.

Beckfield, J. (2009) "Remapping inequality in Europe: the net effect of regional integration on total income inequality in the European Union", *International Journal of Comparative Sociology*, 50 (5–6): 486–509.

Beckfield, J. (2010) "The social structure of the world polity", *American Journal of Sociology*, 115: 1018–68.

Beeson, M. and Bell, S. (2009) "The G-20 and international economic governance: hegemony, collectivism, or both?", *Global Governance*, 15: 67–86.

Bell, S. and Quiggin, J. (2006) "Asset price instability and policy responses: the legacy of liberalization", *Journal of Economic Issues*, XL: 629–49.

Beneria, L. (2003) *Gender, Development, and Globalization: economics as if all people mattered*, New York and London: Routledge.

Berger, M. (1999) "Up from neoliberalism: free-market mythologies and the coming crisis of global capitalism", *Third World Quarterly*, 20: 453–63.

Bergsten, C. F. (2004) "G20 and the World Economy", speech presented to the Deputies of the G20, Leipzig, 4 March 2004. Online. Available at: www.iie.com/publications/papers/paper.cfm?ResearchID=196 (accessed 11 October 2011).

Bergsten, C. F. (2009) "We should listen to Beijing's currency idea", *Financial Times*, 8 April 2009. Online. Available at: www.ft.com/cms/s/0/7372bbd0–2470–11de-9a01–00144feabdc0,s01=1.html#axzz1aWgJGjgs (accessed 11 October 2011).

Bernanke, B. S. (2007) *The Community Reinvestment Act: its evolution and new challenges*, paper given at the Community Affairs Research Conference, Washington, DC,

30 March 2007. Online. Available at: www.federalreserve.gov/newsevents/speech/bernanke20070330a.htm (accessed 9 February 2011).

Bernstein, J. and Mishel, L. (2007) "Economy's gains fail to reach most workers' paychecks", EPI Briefing Paper No. 195, Washington, DC: Economic Policy Institute. Online. Available at: www.epi.org/publication/bp195/ (accessed 13 November 2011).

Bernstein, J. and Romer, C. (2009) "The job impact of the American Recovery and Reinvestment Plan", Washington, DC: Council of Economic Advisers and Office of the Vice President-Elect. Online. Available at: http://otrans.3cdn.net/45593e8ecbd339d074_l3m6bt1te.pdf (accessed 11 October 2011).

Bertini, C. and Glickman, D. (2009) *Renewing American Leadership in the Fight Against Global Hunger and Poverty*, Chicago: Chicago Council on Global Affairs.

Beshouri, C. P. and Gravråk, J. (2010) "Capturing the promise of mobile banking in emerging markets", *McKinsey Quarterly*, February 2010. Online. Available at: www.mckinseyquarterly.com/Telecommunications/Strategy_Analysis/Capturing_the_promise_of_mobile_banking_in_emerging_markets_2539 (accessed 3 October 2011).

Best, J. (2003) "From the top-down: the new financial architecture and the re-embedding of global finance", *New Political Economy*, 8 (3): 363–84.

Bhagwati, J., Greenaway, D. and Panagariya, A. (1998) "Trading preferentially: theory and policy", *Economic Journal*, 108: 1128–48.

Bittman, M. (2008) "Rethinking the meat-guzzler", *New York Times*, 27 January 2008. Online. Available at: www.nytimes.com/2008/01/27/weekinreview/27bittman.html (accessed 10 October 2011).

Blake, H. "Conservatives given millions by property developers", *The Telegraph*, 9 September 2011. Online. Available at: www.telegraph.co.uk/earth/hands-off-our-land/8754027/Conservatives-given-millions-by-property-developers.html (accessed 7 October 2011).

Blakely, R. (2008) "Microfinance raises fresh sub-prime fears", *Times Online*, 14 July 2008. Online. Available at: http://business.timesonline.co.uk/tol/business/economics/article4330593.ece (accessed 3 October 2011).

Blas, J. (2009) "Number of chronically hungry tops 1 billion", *Financial Times*, 27 March 2009. Online. Available at: www.commondreams.org/headline/2009/03/27–2 (accessed 30 March 2009).

Block, F. (2003a) "Introduction", in K. Polyani, *The Great Transformation: the political and economic origins of our time*, Boston: Beacon Press.

Block, F. (2003b) "Karl Polanyi and the writing of *The Great Transformation*", *Theory and Society*, 32: 275–306.

Block, F. (2008) "Swimming against the current: the rise of a hidden developmental state in the United States", *Politics & Society*, 36: 169–206.

Blyth, M. (2002) *Great Transformations: economic ideas and institutional change in the twentieth century*, Cambridge, New York: Cambridge University Press.

Bolton, P. and Jeanne, O. (2007) "Structuring and restructuring sovereign debt: the role of a bankruptcy regime", *Journal of Political Economy*, 115: 901–24.

Bowles, S. (2006) "Egalitarian redistribution in globally integrated economies", in P. Barhan, S. Bowles and M. Wallerstein (eds) *Globalization and Egalitarian Redistribution*, Princeton: Princeton University Press.

Bowles, S. and Gintis, H. (1998) *Recasting Egalitarianism: new rules for communities, states and markets*, New York: Verso.

Braithwaite, J. (2008) *Regulatory Capitalism: how it works, ideas for making it work better*, Cheltenham: Edward Elgar.

Brenner, N. and Theodore, N. (2002) "Cities and the geographies of 'actually existing neoliberalism'", *Antipode*, 34: 349–79.

Breslin, S. (2007) *China and the Global Political Economy*, Basingstoke: Palgrave Macmillan.

Bresser Periera, L. C. (2010) *Globalization and Competition: why some emergent countries succeed while others fall behind*, Cambridge, UK: Cambridge University Press.

Bretton Woods Project (BWI) (2009) "Expert panel calls for sweeping Bank governance reform", Bretton Woods Update 68. Online. Available at: www.brettonwoodsproject.org/art-565630 (accessed 13 October 2011).

Bretton Woods Project (BWI) (2010a) "Bank voting remains unbalanced", Bretton Woods Update 70. Online. Available at: www.brettonwoodsproject.org/art-566102 (accessed 13 October 2011).

Bretton Woods Project (BWI) (2010b) "IFI governance reforms freezing over?", Bretton Woods Update 71. Online. Available at: www.brettonwoodsproject.org/art-566349 (accessed 13 October 2011).

Bretton Woods Project (BWI) (2011) "World Bank deaf on food speculation, vocal on financial instruments", Bretton Woods Update 77. Online. Available at: www.brettonwoodsproject.org/art-568893 (accessed 13 November 2011).

Buckley, R. P. (n.d.) "Resilience and global financial government", unpublished paper.

Buckley, R. P. (1999) *Emerging Markets Debt*, London: Kluwer Law International.

Buckley, R. P. (2002) "The fatal flaw in international finance: the rich borrow and the poor repay, *World Policy Journal*, 19 (4): 59–64.

Buckley, R. P. (2009) "The bankruptcy of nations: an idea whose time has come", *The International Lawyer*, 43: 1189–216.

Buckley, R. P. and Dirou, P. (2006) "How to strengthen the international financial system by improving sovereign balance sheet structures", *Annals of Economics and Finance*, 2: 257–69.

Budlender, D. (2008) "The statistical evidence on care work and non-care work across six countries", Gender and Development Programme Paper No. 4, Geneva: United Nations Research Institute for Social Development.

Building the Education Revolution Implementation Taskforce (BERIT) (2010) *Interim Report*, Canberra: Commonwealth of Australia.

Buira, A. (2003) "The governance of the IMF in the global economy", in A. Buira (ed.) *Challenges to the World Bank and IMF: developing country perspectives*, London: Athenaeum Press.

Burgis, T. (2008) "Microfinance commercialisation warning", *Financial Times*, 29 July 2008. Online. Available at: www.ft.com/cms/s/0/6f05707e-5cc5–11dd-8d38–000077b07658.html#axzz1DQVn8HFu (accessed 9 February 2011).

Cagatay, N. and Erturk, K. (2004) *Gender and Globalisation: a macroeconomic perspective*, Policy Integration Department, World Commission on the Social Dimension Working Paper No. 19, Geneva: International Labour Organization. Online. Available at: www.ilo.org/public/english/bureau/integration/download/publicat/4_3_204_wcsdg-wp-19.pdf (accessed 5 November 2005).

Caliari, A. (2009) "Can the G20 have it both ways? Addressing global imbalances without reform of the world monetary system," Washington, DC: Center of Concern. Online. Available at: www.coc.org/node/6441 (accessed 7 October 2011).

Caminada, K., Goudswaard, K. and van Vliet, O. (2010) "Patterns of welfare state indicators in the EU: is there convergence?", *Journal of Common Market Studies*, 48: 529–56.

Caporaso, J. A. and Tarrow, S. (2009) "Polanyi in Brussels: supranational institutions and the transnational embedding of markets", *International Organization*, 63: 593–620.

Central Intelligence Agency (CIA) (2009) "The World Factbook – Indonesia". Online. Available at: https://www.cia.gov/library/publications/the-world-factbook/geos/id.html (accessed 11 October 2011).

Cerny, P. (2008) "Embedding neoliberalism: the evolution of a hegemonic paradigm", *Journal of International Trade and Diplomacy*, 2 (1): 1–46.

Chakravarty, S. (2008) "Microfinance institutions emerge as next asset class", *Economic Times* (India), 17 December 2008. Online. Available at: www.syminvest.com/market/news/microfinance/india-microfinance-institutions-emerge-as-next-asset-class/2008/12/17/1395 (accessed 9 February 2011).

Chandler Jr, A. D. (1962) *Strategy and Structure: chapters in the history of the American industrial enterprise*, Cambridge, MA: MIT Press.

Chandler Jr, A. D. (1980) "Government versus business: an American phenomenon", in J. T. Dunlop (ed.) *Business and Public Policy*, Cambridge, MA: Harvard University Press.

Chandler Jr., A. D., Amatori, F. and Hikino, T. (eds) (1997) *Big Business and the Wealth of Nations*, Cambridge, UK: Cambridge University Press.

Chang, H. (2002) "Breaking the mould: an institutionalist political economy alternative to the neo-liberal theory of the market and the state", *Cambridge Journal of Economics*, 26 (5): 539–60.

Chang, H. J. (2002) *Kicking Away the Ladder: development strategy in historical perspective*, London: Anthem.

Chang, H. J. (2003) "Kicking away the ladder: infant industry promotion in historical perspective", *Oxford Development Studies*, 31 (1): 21–32.

Chang, H. J. (ed.) (2003) *Rethinking Development Economics*, London: Anthem Press.

Chang, H. J. (ed.) (2007) *Institutional Change and Economic Development*, New York: United Nations University Press.

Chang, H. J. and Evans, P. "The role of institutions in economic change", paper prepared for the meeting of the "Other Canon" Group, Venice, Italy, 13–14 January 2000. Online. Available at: www.othercanon.net/uploads/CE4-The%20role%20of%20insitutions%20in%20economic%20change.doc (accessed 31 January 2011).

Chang, H. J. and Grabel, I. (2004) *Reclaiming Development: an alternative economic policy manual*, London: Zed Books.

Cho, D. H. (2010) *The Long-term Slowdown in the Growth of Small and Medium Enterprises and Its Implications*, KIET News Brief 478, Seoul: Korea Institute for Industrial Economics & Trade. Online. Available at: www.kiet.re.kr/kiet/eng/news/eng14.jsp (accessed 1 October 2011).

Chu, W. W. (2009) "How the Chinese government promoted a global automobile industry", *Industrial and Corporate Change*, 20: 1235–76.

Clapp, J. (2009a) "Responding to food price volatility and vulnerability: considering the global economic context", in J. Clapp and M. Cohen (eds) *The Global Food Crisis: governance challenges and opportunities*, Waterloo, ON: Wilfrid Laurier University Press.

Clapp, J. (2009b) "The global food crisis and international agricultural policy: which way forward?", *Global Governance*, 15: 299–313.

Clapp, J. and Fuchs, D. (2009) *Corporate Power in Global Agrifood Governance*, Cambridge, MA: MIT Press.

Cohen, J. and Rogers, J. (1995) *Associations and Democracy*, London: Verso.

Cohen, J. and Rogers, J. (1998) "Can egalitarianism survive internationalization?", in W. Streeck (ed.) *Internationale Wirtschaft, Nationale Demokrati*, Frankfurt: Campus Verlag.

Cohen, J. and Sabel, C. F. (1997) "Directly-deliberative polyarchy", *European Law Journal*, 3: 313–42.

Coleman, W., Grant, W. and Josling, T. (2004) *Agriculture in the New Global Economy*. Cheltenham, UK: Edward Elgar.

Collier, P. (2008) "The politics of hunger: how illusion and greed fan the food crisis", *Foreign Affairs*, 87 (6): 67–80.

Commission on Global Governance (1995) *Our Global Neighbourhood*, Oxford: Oxford University Press.

Committee on IMF Governance Reform (CIMFGR) (2009) *Final Report*, Washington, DC: International Monetary Fund. Online. Available at: www.imf.org/external/np/omd/2009/govref/032409.pdf (accessed 7 October 2011).

Consultative Group to Assist the Poor (CGAP) (2005) *The Market for Foreign Investment in Microfinance: opportunities and challenges*, Focus Note No. 30, Washington, DC: CGAP.

Consultative Group to Assist the Poor (CGAP) (2008) *Foreign Capital Investment in Microfinance: balancing social and financial returns*, Focus Note No. 44, Washington, DC: CGAP.

Consultative Group to Assist the Poor (CGAP) (2009) "Microfinance funding continued to grow in 2008". Online. Available at: www.cgap.org/p/site/c/template.rc/1.26.12206/ (accessed 3 October 2011).

Cornia, G. A. and Martorano, B. (2011) "External shocks, policy changes and income distribution: Latin America during the last decade", in V. Fitzgerald, J. Heyer and R. Thorp (eds) *Overcoming Persistent Inequality and Poverty. Papers in honour of Frances Stewart*, London: Palgrave.

Costanza, R., d'Arge, R., de Groot, R., Farber, S., Greasso, M., Hannon, B., Limburg, K., Naeem, S., O'Neil, R. V. and Paruelo, J. (1997) "The value of the world's ecosystem services and natural capital", *Nature*, 387: 253–60.

Cotula, L. and Vermeulen, S. (2009) "Deal or no deal: the outlook for agricultural land investment in Africa", *International Affairs*, 85: 1233–47.

Council of Economic Advisers (2010) *The Economic Impact of the American Recovery and Reinvestment Act of 2009*, Fourth Quarterly Report, Washington, DC: Executive Office of the President.

Crewe, I. and King, A. (1995) *SDP: the birth life and death of the Social Democratic Party*, Oxford: Oxford University Press.

Crouch, C. (2004) *Post-democracy*, Cambridge, UK: Polity Press.

Crouch, C. (2011) *The Strange Non-Death of Neoliberalism*, Cambridge, UK: Polity Press.

D'Arista, J. and Griffith-Jones, S. (2010) "Reforming financial regulation: what needs to be done?", in J. K. Sundaram (ed.) *Reforming the International Financial System for Development*, New York: Columbia University Press.

Dawe, D. (2009) *The Unimportance of "Low" World Grain Stocks for Recent World Price Increases*, ESA Working Paper No. 09–01. Rome: Food and Agriculture Organization.

Demeke, M., Pangrazio, G. and Maetz, M. (2008) *Country Responses to the Food Security Crisis: nature and preliminary implications of the policies pursued*, Rome: Food and Agriculture Organization. Online. Available at: www.globalbioenergy.org/uploads/

media/0812_FAO_-_Country_responses_to_the_crisis.pdf (accessed 10 October 2011).

Department of Innovation, Industry, Science and Research (DIISR) (2011) "TCF Industry Innovation Council", Canberra: Australian Government. Online. Available at: www.innovation.gov.au/INDUSTRY/TEXTILESCLOTHINGANDFOOTWEAR/TCFIIC/Pages/default.aspx (accessed 13 November 2011).

Dewey, J. (1927) *The Public and Its Problems*, New York: Henry Holt and Co.

Dodson, L. (2009) "Network to encourage fresh ideas", *Australian Financial Review*, 12 November 2009.

Doyle, L. (2008) "Starving Haitians riot as food prices soar", *The Independent*, 10 April 2008. Online. Available at: www.commondreams.org/archive/2008/04/10/8205/ (accessed 11 April 2008).

Drago, T. (2009) "Food Summit – concern yes, concrete steps no", *Inter Press Service News Agency*, 27 January 2008. Online. Available at: http://ipsnews.net/news.asp?idnews=45569 (accessed 11 October 2011).

Duina, F. (2006) *The Social Construction of Free Trade: the European Union, NAFTA, and Mercosur*, Princeton: Princeton University Press.

Durano, M., Francisco, G. and Sen, G. (2009) "Reclaiming institutional and policy space amidst crisis", *Development*, 52: 334–7.

Durbin, D. (2009) *Bill to Award Muhammad Yunus Congressional Gold Medal Unanimously Passes Senate*, Press Release. Online. Available at: http://durbin.senate.gov/public/index.cfm/pressreleases?ID=d50a0796–95ae-4e26-ac63–9a03ea21ea4f (accessed 9 February 2011).

Economist Intelligence Unit (2009) *Global Microscope on the Microfinance Business Environment*, London: The Economist. Online. Available at: www.eiu.com/site_info.asp?info_name=Global_Microscope_2009&page=noads&rf=0 (accessed 3 October 2011).

El-Din Haseeb, Khair (2011) "On the Arab 'Democratic Spring': lessons derived", *Contemporary Arab Affairs*, 4: 113–22.

Elek, A. "The G20: principles for meeting the global challenge of climate change", *East Asia Forum*, 7 January 2010. Online. Available at: www.eastasiaforum.org/2010/01/07/the-g20-principles-for-meeting-the-global-challenge-of-climate-change/ (accessed 7 October 2011).

Elliott, K. A. (2009) "US biofuels policy and the global food price crisis: a survey of the issues", in J. Clapp and M Cohen (eds) *The Global Food Crisis: governance challenges and opportunities*, Waterloo, ON: Wilfrid Laurier University Press.

Elson, D. (2009) "Social reproduction in the global crisis", paper presented at the United Nations Research Institute for Social Development (UNRISD) Conference on Social and Political Dimensions of the Global Crisis, Geneva, Switzerland, 12–13 December 2009.

Elson, D. and Cagatay, N. (2000) "The social content of macroeconomic policies", *World Development*, 28: 1347–64.

Environmental News Service (ENS) (2008) "UN: biofuel production 'criminal path' to global food crisis", 28 April 2008. Online. Available at: www.ens-newswire.com/ens/apr2008/2008–04–28–03.asp (accessed 10 October 2011).

Epstein, G., Grabel, I. and Jomo, K. S. (2003) *Capital Management Techniques in Developing Countries: an assessment of experiences from the 1990s and lessons for the future*, PERI Working Paper No. 56, Amherst, MA: Political Economy and Research Institute.

Eren, C., Richardson, D. and Denniss, R. (2010) *Green Jobs: what are they and do we need them?*, Policy Brief No. 15, Manuka: The Australia Institute.

Esping-Anderson, G. (1990) *The Three Worlds of Welfare Capitalism*, Princeton, NJ: Princeton University Press.

Esping-Anderson, G. (2009) *Incomplete Revolution: adapting welfare states to women's new roles*, London: Polity.

European Commission (2011) "Financial transaction tax: making the financial sector pay its fair share", Press Release No. IP/11/1085, 28 September 2011. Online. Available at: http://europa.eu/rapid/pressReleasesAction.do?reference=IP/11/1085&format=HTML&aged=0&language=EN&guiLanguage=en (accessed 13 November 2011).

Evans, P. B. (1995) *Embedded Autonomy: states and industrial transformation*, Princeton, NJ: Princeton University Press.

Evans, P. B. (2005) "The challenges of the 'institutional turn': interdisciplinary opportunities in development theory", in V. Nee and R. Swedberg (eds) *The Economic Sociology of Capitalist Institutions*, Princeton, NJ: Princeton University Press.

Evans, P. B. (2007) "Extending the 'institutional' turn: property, politics, and development trajectories", in H. J. Chang (ed.) *Institutional Change and Economic Development*, Helsinki: United Nations University Press.

Evans, P. B. (2008) "Is an alternative globalization possible?", *Politics & Society*, 36 (2): 271–305.

Evenett, S. J. and Meier, M. (2008) "An interim assessment of the US trade policy of 'competitive liberalization' ", *The World Economy*, 31:1.

Fatas, A. and Mihov, I. (2001) "Government size and automatic stabilizers: international and intranational evidence", *Journal of International Economics*, 55: 3–28.

Favell, A. and Guiraudon, V. (2010) *The Sociology of the European Union*, Basingstoke: Palgrave Macmillan.

Ferrera, M. (2005) *The Boundaries of Welfare: European integration and the new spatial politics of social protection*, Oxford: Oxford University Press.

Fields, G. (2003) "Decent work and development policies", *International Labour Review*, 142: 239–62.

Financial Times (2009) "G7 struggles to remain relevant", 4 October 2009. Online. Available at: www.ft.com/cms/s/0/e553e3ea-b111-11de-b06b-00144feabdc0.html (accessed 7 October 2011).

Fleming, J. C. Jr, Peroni, R. J. and Shay, S. E. (2001) "Fairness in international taxation: the ability-to-pay case for taxing worldwide income", *Florida Tax Review*, 5: 301–54.

Fligstein, N. (2008) *Euro-clash*, New York: Oxford University Press.

Fligstein, N. and Stone Sweet, A. (2002) "Constructing polities and markets: an institutionalist account of European integration", *American Journal of Sociology*, 107: 1206–43.

Floro, M. and Meurs, M. (2009) *Global trends in women's access to "Decent Work"*, Dialogue on Globalization Occasional Papers No. 43 (May 2009), Geneva: Friederich Ebert Stiftung.

Fogel, R. W. (2004) *The Escape from Hunger and Premature Death, 1700–2100: Europe, America, and the Third World*, Cambridge, UK: Cambridge University Press.

Folbre, N. (1994) *Who Pays for the Kids? Gender and the Structures of Constraint*, London and New York: Routledge.

Folbre, N. (1999) "Cleaning house: new perspectives on households and economic development", *Journal of Development Economics*, 22: 5–40.

Folbre, N. and Bittman, M. (eds) (2004) *Family Time: the social organization of care*, London and New York: Routledge.

Food and Agriculture Organization (FAO) (2010) "925 million in chronic hunger worldwide", Press release, 14 September 2010. Rome: Food and Agriculture Organization. Online. Available at: www.fao.org/news/story/en/item/45210/icode/ (accessed 23 January 2011).

Foster, J. (2009) "Pittsburgh: rally on the hill". Online. Available at: www.ifiwatchnet.org/?q=en/node/32823 (accessed 7 October 2011).

Fox, J. (2009) *The Myth of the Rational Market: a history of risk, reward, and delusion on Wall Street*, 1st ed., New York: Harper Business.

Frank, R. H. (2009) "Post-consumer prosperity", *American Prospect*, 20 (3): 12–15.

Fraser, N. (1997) *Justice Interruptus: critical reflections on the "postsocialist" condition*, London: Routlege.

Freeman, R. and Rogers, J. (2008) "The promise of progressive federalism", in J. Soss, Hacker, J. and Mettler S., (eds) *Remaking America: democracy and public policy in an age of inequality*, New York: Russell Sage Foundation.

Friedman, M. (1982) *Capitalism and Freedom*, Chicago: University of Chicago Press.

Friedman, M. and Friedman, R. (1980) *Free to Choose*, Harmondsworth: Penguin.

Friedman, T. (1999) *The Lexus and the Olive Tree: understanding globalization*, New York: Farrar Strauss Giroux.

Friedrich, B. (2009) "Solving the global food crisis: the case for a 'poverty czar' ", CommonDreams.org, 29 January 2009. Online. Available at: www.commondreams.org/view/2009/01/29–0 (accessed 15 February 2009).

Fukuyama, F. *Guardian Weekly*, 31 December 1989: 15.

G8 " 'L'Aquila' joint statement on global food security", statement presented at the G8 Summit in L'Aquila, 10 July 2009. Online. Available at: www.g8italia2009.it/static/G8_Allegato/LAquila_Joint_Statement_on_Global_Food_Security%5b1%5d%2c0.pdf (accessed 11 October 2011).

G20 "Leader's statement", statement presented at the Pittsburgh Summit, Pittsburgh, 24–25 September 2009. Online. Available at: www.g20.org/Documents/pittsburgh_summit_leaders_statement_250909.pdf (accessed 11 October 2011).

G20 "The Global Plan for Recovery and Reform", Leaders' statement presented at London, United Kingdom, 2 April 2009. Online. Available at: www.g20.org/pub_communiques.aspx (accessed 5 October 2011).

G20 (2011) "What is the G20?" Online. Available at: www.g20.org/about_what_is_g20.aspx (accessed 7 October 2011).

G24 (2009) "International Group of Twenty-Four on international monetary affairs and development communiqué", Washington, DC: International Monetary Fund. Online. Available at: www.imf.org/external/np/cm/2009/100309.htm (accessed 5 October 2009).

Galbraith, J. K. (1990) "Why the Right is wrong", *Manchester Guardian Weekly*, 4 February 1990: 10.

Gallagher, K. P. (2008a) "Trading away the ladder? Trade politics and economic development in the Americas", *New Political Economy*, 13: 37–59.

Gallagher, K. P. (2008b) "Understanding developing country resistance to the Doha Round", *Review of International Political Economy*, 15: 62–85.

Gallagher, K. P. and Thrasher, R. D. (2010) "21st century trade agreements: implications for development sovereignty", *Denver Journal of International Law and Policy*, 38: 313–50.

Garrett, G. (2001) "Globalization and government spending around the world", *Studies in Comparative International Development*, 35 (4): 3–29.

Gaudin, A. (2002) "Thirteen days that shook Argentina – and now what?" *North American Congress on Latin America Report on the Americas*, 35 (5): 6–10.

Gemici, K. (2007) "Karl Polanyi and the antinomies of embeddedness", *Socio-economic Review*, 6: 5–33.

Geminder, E. (2008) "The politics of food aid", *Diplomatic Courier*, 5 September 2008.

George, S. (1979) *Feeding the Few: corporate control of food*, Washington, DC: Institute for Policy Studies.

Gereffi, G. and Mayer, F. (2006) "Globalization and the Demand for Governance", in G. Gereffi (ed.) *The New Offshoring of Jobs and Global Development*, Geneva: International Institute for Labour Studies.

Ghosh, J. (2009) "The outcry is muted, but the food crisis is getting worse", *Guardian*, 9 January 2009. Online. Available at: www.guardian.co.uk/commentisfree/2009/jan/09/food-shortages-coverage-jayati-ghosh (accessed 17 January 2009).

Girroa, A. (2009) "Why Governance and Investment Matter for Development", *OECD Observer*, 275. Online. Available at: www.oecdobserver.org/news/fullstory.php/aid/3122 (accessed 7 October 2011).

Gokhale, K. (2009) "As microfinance grows in India, so do its rivals", *Wall Street Journal*, 16 December 2009. Online. Available at: http://online.wsj.com/article/SB126055117322287513.html (accessed 9 February 2011).

Goldstein, A. (2009) "Sharp rise in Americans going hungry". *The Age*, 18 November 2009.

Good Jobs First (2009) *High Road or Low Road: Job Quality in the New Green Economy*, Washington, DC: Good Jobs First.

Goodman, P. S. (2009) *Past Due: the end of easy money and the renewal of the American economy*, New York: Times Books.

Gornick, J. C. and Meyers, M. K. (2005), *Families that Work: policies for reconciling parenthood and employment*, New York: Russell Sage Foundation Publications.

Gowan, R. and Brantner, F. (2010) *The EU and Human Rights at the UN*, Policy Brief, London: European Council on Foreign Relations.

Green, C. M. (1956) *Eli Whitney and the Birth of American Technology*, Boston: Little, Brown and Company.

Green, J. (2010) "Magnet material industry leaders applaud Murkowski Leadership on rare earths. Alaska senator introduces Companion Bill to RESTART Act of 2010", *USMMA*, Press release, 23 June 2010. Online. Available at: www.usmagneticmaterials.com/press-releases.htm (accessed 1 October 2011).

Green, R. (2008) *Building Innovative Capability: review of the Australian textile, clothing and footwear industries*, Canberra: Commonwealth of Australia.

Gregory, P. "Food security in a changing climate", paper presented at the Selby Fellow Public Lecture, Canberra, Australia, 20 October 2009. Online. Available at: www.science.org.au/events/lectures-and-speeches/gregory.html (accessed 10 October 2011).

Gross, N. (2009) "A pragmatist theory of social mechanisms", *American Sociological Review*, 74: 358–79.

Gu, J., Humphrey, J. and Messner, D. (2007) "Global governance and developing countries: the implications of the rise of China", *World Development*, 36: 272–92.

Gupta, S., Pattillo, C. and Wagh, S. (2006) *Are Donor Countries Giving More or Less Aid?*, IMF Working Paper WP/06/01, Washington, DC: International Monetary Fund.

Hacker, J. S. and Pierson, P. (2010) "Winner-take-all politics: public policy, political organization, and the precipitous rise of top incomes in the United States", *Politics & Society*, 38 (2): 152–204.

Hall, P. A. and Soskice, D. (2001) "An introduction to varieties of capitalism", in P. Hall and D. Soskice (eds) *Varieties of Capitalism: the institutional foundations of comparative advantage*, Oxford: Oxford University Press.

Hamwey, R. M. (2005) *Expanding National Policy Space for Development: why the multilateral trading system must change*, T.R.A.D.E. Working Papers No. 25, Geneva: South Centre.

Haq, M. ul-, Kaul, I. and Grunberg, I. (1996) *The Tobin Tax: coping with financial volatility*, Oxford: Oxford University Press.

Harvey, D. (2005) *A Brief History of Neoliberalism*, Oxford: Oxford University Press.

Hausmann, R., Rodrik, D. and Sabel, C. (2008) *Reconfiguring Industrial Policy: a framework with an application to South Africa*, CID Working Paper No. 168, Cambridge, MA: Center for International Development at Harvard University.

Hawken, P., Lovins, A. and Lovins, H. (1999) *Natural Capitalism: creating the next industrial revolution*, Boston: Little, Brown and Company.

Headey, D. and Fan, S. (2008) "Anatomy of a crisis: the causes and consequences of surging food prices", *Agricultural Economics*, 39: 375–91.

Heilbroner, R. and Milberg, W. (1995) *The Crisis of Vision in Modern Economic Thought*, Cambridge: Cambridge University Press.

Heintz, J. (2006) *Globalization, Economic Policy and Employment: poverty and gender implications*, Employment Strategy Papers No. 2006/3, Geneva: International Labour Organization.

Helleiner, E. (1994) *States and the Reemergence of Global Finance: from Bretton Woods to the 1990s*, Ithaca, NY: Cornell University Press.

Helleiner, E. (2008) "The return of regulation and what a difference a decade makes", *The Globe and Mail*, 19 September 2008. Online. Available at: www.theglobeandmail.com/news/opinions/article710738.ece (accessed 31 May 2010).

Helleiner, E. (2010), "The new politics of global reserve reform", *Journal of Globalization and Development*, 1 (2): Article 12.

Helleiner, G. (2001) *Developing Countries, Global Financial Governance and the Group of Twenty: a note*, Washington, DC: Foreign Policy in Focus. Online. Available at: www.globaleconomicgovernance.org/wp-content/uploads/Helleiner%20on%20G20.PDF (accessed 11 October 2011).

Henriques, D. B. (2008) "Odd crop prices defy economics", *New York Times*, 28 March 2008. Online. Available at: www.nytimes.com/2008/03/28/business/28commodities.html?_r=1 (accessed 26 November 2009).

Hershberg, E. (2002) "Why Argentina Crashed and Is Still Crashing", *North American Congress on Latin America*, 36 (1): 30–5.

Hewitt, G. (2011) Greeks protest against austerity measures, *BBC News Europe*, 19 October 2011. Online. Available at: www.bbc.co.uk/news/world-europe-15372773 (accessed 13 November 2011).

Hirschman, A. O. (1945) *National Power and the Structure of Foreign Trade: Publications of the Bureau of Business and Economic Research, University of California*, Berkeley and Los Angeles: University of California Press.

Hjerholm, P. and White, H. (1998) *Survey of foreign aid: history, trends and allocation*, Discussion Paper 00–04, Copenhagen: Institute of Economics, University of Copenhagen.

Hodgson, G. (2007) "Introduction", in G. Hodgson (ed.) *The Evolution of Economic Institutions: a critical reader*, Cheltenham: Edward Elgar.

Hogg, C. (2011) "China lends more than World Bank – Report", BBC News Asia-Pacific,

18 January 2011. Online. Available at: www.bbc.co.uk/news/world-asia-pacific-12212936 (accessed 31 January 2011).

Holmes, S. A. (1999) "Fannie Mae Eases Credit to Aid Mortgage Lending", *New York Times*, 30 September 1999. Online. Available at: http://query.nytimes.com/gst/fullpage.html?res=9c0de7db153ef933a0575ac0a96f958260 (accessed 9 February 2011).

Höpner, M. and Schäfer, A. (2010) "Polanyi in Brussels? Embeddedness and the three dimensions of European economic and social integration", MPIfG Discussion Paper 10/8, Cologne: Max Planck Institute for the Study of Societies. Online. Available at: www.mpifg.de/pu/mpifg_dp/dp10–8.pdf (accessed 13 November 2011).

Horn, Z. E. (2009) *No Cushion to Fall Back on: the global economic crisis and informal workers: synthesis report*, Inclusive Cities Study. Online. Available at: www.wiego.org/gec_study/index.php (accessed 31 January 2011).

Horton, S. (2009) "The 1974 and 2008 food price crises: déjà vu?", in J. Clapp and M. Cohen (eds) *The Global Food Crisis: governance challenges and opportunities*, Waterloo, ON: Wilfrid Laurier University Press.

Howe, J. (2006) " 'Money and favours': government deployment of public wealth as an instrument of labour regulation", in Arup C., Gahan P., Howe J., Johnstone R., Mitchell R. and O'Donnell A. (eds), *Labour Law and Labour Market Regulation*, Sydney: Federation Press.

Howe, J., Johnstone, R. and Mitchell, R. (2006) "Constituting and regulating the labour market for social and economic purposes", in Arup C., Gahan P., Howe J., Johnstone R., Mitchell R. and O'Donnell A. (eds) *Labour Law and Labour Market Regulation: essays on the construction, constitution and regulation of labour markets and work relationships*, Sydney: Federation Press.

Huber, E. and Stephens, J. D. (2001), *Development and Crisis of the Welfare State*, Chicago: University of Chicago Press.

Hudson, M. (2009) "Appointment in Yekaterinburg: the ending of America's financial-military empire", Counterpunch.org, 15 June 2009. Online. Available at: www.counterpunch.org/hudson06152009.html (accessed 5 October 2011).

Hui, E. S. and Chen, C. K. (2011) "Workers struggles and labour regulations in post-crisis China", paper presented at the VII Global Labour University Conference, Johannesburg, 28–30 September 2011. Online. Available at: www.global-labour-university.org/274.html (accessed 12 November 2011).

Hurst, C. (2010) *China's Rare Earth Elements Industry: what can the West learn?*, Washington: Institute for the Analysis of Global Security.

Hutton, W. (2008) "A short history of capitalism's rise and fall", *The Observer*, 5 October 2008: 4. Online. Available at: www.guardian.co.uk/business/2008/oct/05/creditcrunch.marketturmoil (accessed 12 October 2011).

Independent Evaluation Office of the IMF (IEO) (2007) *The IMF and Aid to Sub-Saharan Africa*, Evaluation Report, Washington, DC: International Monetary Fund, Independent Evaluation Office. Online. Available at: www.imf.org/external/np/ieo/2007/ssa/eng/pdf/report.pdf (accessed 11 October 2011).

Institute for Agriculture and Trade Policy (IATP) (2009) "Call for U.S. Leadership at the World Summit on Food Security", open letter to Alonzo L. Fulgham, 13 November 2009. Online. Available at: www.iatp.org/files/451_2_106962.pdf (accessed 11 October 2011).

International Monetary Fund (2007) "Poverty Reduction Strategy Papers". Online. Available at: www.imf.org/external/np/prsp/prsp.asp (accessed 11 October 2011).

International Monetary Fund (2009a) "Communique of the international monetary and financial committee of the board of governors of the International Monetary Fund", Press release No. 09/347, Washington, DC: IMF. Online. Available at: www.imf.org/external/np/sec/pr/2009/pr09347.htm (accessed 11 October 2011).

International Monetary Fund (2009b) "IMF executive board's initial discussion on review of fund facilities – analytical basis for fund lending and reform options", Public Information Notice No. 09/41. Online. Available at: www.imf.org/external/np/sec/pn/2009/pn0941.htm (accessed 7 October 2011).

International Monetary Fund (2009c) "Questions and answers: IMF resources and the G20 Summit". Online. Available at: www.imf.org/external/np/exr/faq/sdrfaqs.htm (accessed 11 October 2011).

International Monetary Fund (2009d) *Creating Policy Space – Responsive Design and Streamlined Conditionality in Recent Low-income Country Programs*. Online. Available at: www.imf.org/external/np/pp/eng/2009/091009a.pdf (accessed 31 January 2011).

International Monetary Fund (2009e) *Review of Recent Crisis Programs*. Online. Available at: www.imf.org/external/np/pp/eng/2009/091409.pdf (accessed 31 January 2011).

International Monetary Fund (2010a) *Direction of Trade Statistics*, IMF Data Warehouse. Online. Available at: http://elibrary-data.imf.org/ (accessed 1 July 2010).

International Monetary Fund (2010b). *International Financial Statistics*, IMF Data Warehouse. Online. Available at: http://elibrary-data.imf.org/ (accessed 1 July 2010).

International Monetary Fund (2011) "Consultation on financial sector taxation: IMF seeks views on financial sector taxation". Online. Available at: www.imf.org/external/np/exr/consult/2009/index.htm (accessed 7 October 2011).

Irwin, D. A. and Pavcnik, N. (2001) "Airbus versus Boeing revisited: international competition in the aircraft market", *Journal of International Economics*, 64: 223–45.

Irwin, S. H., Garcia, P. and Good, D. L. (2007) "The performance of Chicago Board of Trade corn, soybean, and wheat futures contracts after recent changes in speculative limits". Online. Available at: www.farmdoc.illinois.edu/irwin/research/CBOTFutures-Performance.pdf (accessed 26 November 2009).

Jacobson, M. Z. and Masters, G. M. (2001) "Exploiting wind versus coal", *Science*, 293: 1438.

Jha, V. (2009) *The Effects of the Stimulus Packages on Employment*, Employment Working Paper No. 34, Geneva: International Labour Organization Employment Sector, Economic and Labour Analysis Department.

Johnson, C. (1982) *MITI and the Japanese Miracle: the growth of industrial policy, 1925–1975*, Stanford, CA: Stanford University Press.

Johnson, S. and Kwak, J. (2010) *13 Bankers: the Wall Street takeover and the next financial meltdown*, New York: Pantheon.

Jones, D and Kwiecinski, A. (2010) *Policy Responses in Emerging Economies to International Agricultural Commodity Price Surges*, OECD Food, Agriculture and Fisheries Working Paper No. 34, Paris: OECD Publishing.

Josling, T. (2009) "New trade issues in food, agriculture and natural resources", background paper prepared for Round Table 2 at the Conference for Thinking Ahead on International Trade (TAIT): Challenges Facing the World Trade System, Geneva, Switzerland, 17–18 September 2009.

Kabeer, N. (2002) "Resources, agency, achievements: reflections on the measurement of women's empowerment", *Development and Change*, 30 (3): 435–64.

Kanbur, R. (2005) *Reforming the Formula: a modest proposal for introducing develop-*

ment outcomes in IDA allocation procedures. Online. Available at: www.people.cornell.edu.pages.sk145 (accessed 9 April 2007).

Kenworthy, L. (2002) "Corporatism and unemployment in the 1980s and 1990s", *American Sociological Review*, 67: 367–88.

Kenworthy, L. (2008) *Jobs with Equality*, Oxford: Oxford University Press.

Kenworthy, L. (2010) "Labor market activation", in Obinger H., Pierson C., Castles F. G., Leibfried S. and Lewis J. (eds) *The Oxford Handbook of Comparative Welfare States*, Oxford: Oxford University Press.

Kenworthy, L. (2011) *Progress for the Poor*, Oxford, Oxford University Press.

Keohane, R. and Victor, D. (2011) "The regime complex for climate change", *Perspectives on Politics*, 9 (1): 1–31.

Ketels, C. H. M. (2007) "Industrial Policy in the United States", 7 *Journal of Industry, Competition and Trade*, 7: 147–67.

Khatiwada, S. (2009) *Stimulus Packages to Counter Global Economic Crisis: a review*, Discussion Paper DP/196/2009, Geneva: International Institute for Labour Studies.

Kindleberger, C. (2000) *Manias, Panics and Crashes: a history of financial crises*, New York: John Wiley and Sons.

Kirchner, S. (2008) "Beware political saviours", *The Australian*, 29 October 2008. Online. Available at: www.theaustralian.com.au/national-affairs/opinion/beware-political-saviours/story-e6frgd0x-1111117882095 (accessed 13 November 2011).

Kiviat, B. (2008) "The big trouble in small loans", *Time*, 5 June 2008. Online. Available at: www.time.com/time/magazine/article/0,9171,1812051,00.html (accessed 3 October 2011).

Klein, N. (2007) *The Shock Doctrine: the rise of disaster capitalism*, Camberwell: Penguin.

Kosich, D. (2010) "Sen. Murkowski introduces U.S. Rare Earth Minerals domestic program bill", Mineweb.com, 23 June 2010. Online., Available at: www.mineweb.com/mineweb/view/mineweb/en/page72068?oid=106715&sn=Detail (accessed 1 October 2011).

Koster, F. and Kaminska, M. E. "EU Citizens and the European Social Model, 2002–08: a multilevel investigation", paper presented at the World Congress of Sociology, Goteborg, Sweden, 11–17 July 2010.

Krasnolutska, D. and Martens, J. "Ukraine gets $16.5 billion loan from IMF; Hungary next in line", Bloomberg News, 26 October 2008.

Krueger, A. O. (1996) *The Political Economy of Trade Protection: a national bureau of economic tesearch project report*, Chicago, IL: University of Chicago Press.

Lall, S. (2001) *Competitiveness, Technology and Skills*, Cheltenham, UK: Edward Elgar.

Lall, S. (2003) *Reinventing Industrial Strategy: the role of government policy in building industrial competitiveness*, G24 Discussion Paper No. 28 (UNCTAD/GDS/MDPB/G24/2004/4), Geneva and New York: United Nations. Online. Available at: www.unctad.org/en/docs/gdsmdpbg2420044_en.pdf (accessed 23 October 2005).

Landler, M. (2008) "U.S. Treasury's lead role on China in doubt", *New York Times*, 2 December 2008.

Langmore, J. (2004) "International strategy for decent work", in E. Lee and Vivarelli, M. (eds) *Understanding Globalization, Employment and Poverty Reduction*, Basingstoke: Palgrave Macmillan.

Lawrence, R. Z. (1996) *Regionalism, Multilateralism, and Deeper Integration: Integrating National Economies*, Washington, DC: Brookings Institution.

Leading Group on Innovative Financing to Fund Development (IGIFFD) (2010)

Globalizing Solidarity: the case for financial levies, Report of the Committee of Experts to the Taskforce on International Financial Transactions and Development, Paris: Leading Group on Innovative Financing to Fund Development.

Leech, D. and Leech, R. (2009) *Reforming the IMF and World Bank Governance: in search of simplicity, transparency and democratic legitimacy in the voting rights*, Warwick Economic Research Paper No. 914, Warwick: University of Warwick.

Levi-Faur, D. (2005) "The global diffusion of regulatory capitalism", *ANNALS of the American Academy of Political and Social Science*, 598 (21): 12–32.

Levitsky, S. and Roberts, K. M. (2011) *The Resurgence of the Latin American Left*, Baltimore: Johns Hopkins University Press.

Lindblom, C. (1977) *Politics and Markets: the world's political-economic systems*, New York: Basic Books.

Lombardi, D. (2009) "Report on the civil society consultations with the IMF on reform of IMF governance", Washington, DC: International Monetary Fund. Online. Available at: http://api.ning.com/files/TYrIe*Afvd8Gp2qiDyQAttPBdV3VsV-PctGvhx6FAhvRRro2VcIv7iJoRluvvFdfR0syXbAPKntBYIhrnr8mtfAlgRxqPH3z/Report_IMFConsultationswithCivilSociety_Lombardi_FINAL.pdf (accessed 28 September 2009).

Luce, E. (2009) "New body takes on economic leadership", *Financial Times*, 25 September 2009. Online. Available at: www.ft.com/cms/s/0/99f5abc8-aa35–11de-a3ce-00144feabdc0.html (accessed 7 October 2011).

Luttwak, E. *Turbo Capitalism: winners and losers in the global economy*, New York: Harper Collins.

Luxembourg Income Study (LIS) (2010) *LIS Key Figures*. Online. Available at: www.lisproject.org/key-figures/key-figures.htm (accessed 1 July 2010).

Magnoni, B. and Powers, J. (2009) *Will the Bottom of the Pyramid Hit Bottom? The effects of the global credit crisis on the microfinance sector*, microREPORT no. 150, Washington, DC: USAID. Online. Available at: www.microlinks.org/ev_en.php?ID=36865_201&ID2=DO_TOPIC (accessed 3 October 2011).

Manning, A. (2011) "Wage inequality and job polarization show that it is time to be pursuing redistribution from the highest-earners to those with middle and lower incomes", *British Politics and Policy at LSE*, Blog Post. Online. Available at: http://eprints.lse.ac.uk/38319/ (accessed November 2011).

Marichal, C. (1989) *A Century of Debt Crises in Latin America*, Princeton, NJ: Princeton University Press.

Martin, C. J. (2010) "The revenge of coordinated capitalism? Reflections from the Presidential Plenary in Montreal", *Perspectives on Europe*, 40: 3–5.

Martinez-Diaz, L. (2007) *The G20 after Eight Years: how effective a vehicle for developing country influence?* Global Economy and Development Working Paper No. 12, Washington, DC: Brookings Institution, Online. Available at: www.brookings.edu/~/media/Files/rc/papers/2007/1017development/1017development.pdf (accessed 7 October 2011).

McAllister, J. (1989) "Colonial America, 1607–1776", *Economic History Review*, 2nd series, XLII (2), 245–59.

McCrudden, C. (2008) *Buying Social Justice*, Oxford: Oxford University Press.

McGovern, G. (2001) *The Third Freedom: ending hunger in our time*, New York: Simon and Schuster.

McIntyre, B. D., Herren, H. R., Wakhungu, J. and Watson, R. T. (eds) (2009) *Agriculture at a Crossroads: international assessment of agricultural science and technology development; global report*, Washington, DC: IAASTD.

Meade, J. (1964) *Efficiency, Equality, and the Ownership of Property*, London: Allen and Unwin.

Melo, A. (2001) *The Innovation Systems of Latin America and the Caribbean*, Research Department Working Paper Series 460, Washington, DC: Inter-American Development Bank.

Melo, A. and Rodriguez-Clare, Andrés (2006), *Productive Development Policies and Supporting Institutions in Latin America and the Caribbean*, Competitiveness Studies Series C-106, Washington, DC: Inter-American Development Bank.

Meltzer, A. (2000) *Report of the International Financial Institution Advisory Commission*, U.S. House of Representatives, Washington, DC: International Financial Institution Commission. Online. Available at: www.house.gov/jec/imf/meltzer.pdf (accessed 11 October 2011).

Mikesell, R. F. (1994) *The Bretton Woods Debates: a memoir*, Essays in International Finance No. 192, Princeton, NJ: International Finance Section, Department of Economics, Princeton University.

Mkandawire, T. (2001) "Thinking about developmental states in Africa", *Cambridge Journal of Economics*, 25 (3): 289–314.

Monbiot, G. (2009) "US car manufacturers plough a lonely furrow on biofuels", *Guardian*, 22 July 2009. Online. Available at: www.guardian.co.uk/environment/georgemonbiot/2009/jul/22/biofuels (accessed 10 October 2011).

Moravcsik, A. (2002) "In defense of the democratic deficit: reassessing legitimacy in the European Union", *Journal of Common Market Studies*, 40: 603–24.

Moravcsik, A. and Sangiovanni, A. (2003) "On democracy and ‚public interest' in the European Union", in R. Mayntz and Streeck, W. (eds), *Die Reformierbarkeit Der Demokratie: innovationen und blockaden*, Frankfurt/Main: Campus Verlag.

Muchhala, B. (2009) *Stiglitz Speaks Out on the Multiple Shortcomings of the G20 Agenda in Pittsburgh*, Penang: Third World Network. Online. Available at: www.twnside.org.sg/title2/resurgence/2009/228–229/cover04.doc (accessed 7 October 2011).

Mumford, G. (2009) "Inner circle calls the shots in G20", *Australian Financial Review*, 6 October 2009.

Narlikar, A. (2004) "Developing countries and the WTO", in B. Hocking and McGuire, S. (eds) *Trade Politics: international, domestic, and regional perspectives*, 2nd ed., London: Routledge.

Nesvetailova, A. and Palan, R. (2010) "The end of liberal finance? The changing paradigm of global financial governance". *Millennium* 38: 797–825.

Nobel Committee (2006) *The Nobel Peace Prize for 2006*, Press release. Online. Available at: http://nobelprize.org/nobel_prizes/peace/laureates/2006/press.html (accessed 8 February 2011).

Noonan, K. G., Sabel, C. F. and Simon, W. H. (2009) "Legal accountability in the service-based welfare state: lessons from child welfare reform", *Law & Social Inquiry*, 34: 523–68.

North, D. (1990), *Institutions, Institutional Change and Economic Performance*, Cambridge: Cambridge University Press.

Nussbaum, M. C. (2004) "Beyond the social contract: capabilities and global justice", *Oxford Development Studies*, 32: 3–18.

O'Neill, M. and Williamson, T. (2012) *Property-owning Democracy: Rawls and beyond*, New York: Wiley-Blackwell.

Obstfeld, M. and Rogoff, K. (2009) "Global imbalances and the financial crisis: products of common causes", CEPR Discussion Paper No. DP7606. Online. Available at: http://ssrn.com/abstract=1533211 (accessed 13 November 2011).

Ocampo, J. A. (2009) "A 7-point plan for development-friendly reform", in F. Ebert Stiftung (ed.) *Re-defining the Global Economy*, Dialogue on Globalization Occasional Paper No. 42, New York: Friedrich-Ebert-Stiftung.

Ocampo, J. A. (2010a) "Reforming the global reserve system", in S. Griffith-Jones, Ocampo, J. A. and Stiglitz, J. E., (eds) *Time for a Visible Hand: lessons from the 2008 world financial crisis*, New York: Oxford University Press.

Ocampo, J. A. (2010b) "Rethinking global economic and social governance", *Journal of Globalization and Development*, 1 (1): Article 6.

Ocampo, J. A. (2011) "A development-friendly reform of the international financial architecture", *Politics & Society*, 39: 315–30.

Ocampo, J. A. and Griffith-Jones, S. "G-20 and global financial governance", policy note to the workshop on "The G-20 in the post-crisis world", Seoul, South Korea, 15–16 July 2010.

Ocampo, J. A. and Parra, M. A. (2003) "The terms of trade for commodities in the 20th century", *CEPAL Review*, 79: 7–35.

Ocampo, J. A. and Vos, R. (2008) "Policy space and the changing paradigm in conducting macroeconomic policies in developing countries", in *BIS Papers No. 36: new financing trends in Latin America: a bumpy road towards stability*, Basel: Bank for International Settlements. Online. Available at: www.interbank.org/publ/bppdf/bispap36.pdf#page=38 (accessed 31 January 2011).

Offe, C. (2002) "Is there, or can there be, a 'European society'?", in I. Katenhusen and Lamping, W., (eds) *Demokratien in Europa. Euopäische Integration, Institutionenwandel und die Zukunft des Demokratischen Verfassungsstaates*, Opladen: Leske and Budrich.

Ohmae, K. (1991) *The Borderless World: power and strategy in the interlinked economy*, London: Fontana.

Organisation for Economic Co-operation and Development (OECD) (2009) *Fiscal Packages across OECD Countries: overview and country details*, Paris: OECD.

Organisation for Economic Co-operation and Development (OECD) (2010) *Benefits and Wages: OECD Indicators*. Online. Available at: www.oecd.org/document/3/0,3746,en_2649_34637_39617987_1_1_1_1,00.html (accessed 2 October 2011).

Ortiz, I., Chai, J. and Cummins, M. (2011) *Austerity Measures Threaten Children and Poor Households: recent evidence in public expenditures from 128 developing countries*, Social and Economic Policy Working Paper, New York: United Nations Children's Fund.

Oxfam International (2009) *Money for Nothing: three ways the G20 could deliver up to US$280 billion for poor countries*, Oxfam G20 media briefing, 4 September 2009. Online. Available at: www.oxfam.org.uk/resources/policy/debt_aid/downloads/money-for-nothing-g20.pdf (accessed 11 October 2011).

Pacific Economic Cooperation Council (ed.) (2007) *The Policy Environment for the Development of SMEs*, Taipei: Chinese Taipei Pacific Economic Cooperation Committee.

Pack, H. and Saggi, K. (2006) "Is there a case for industrial policy? A critical survey", *World Bank Research Observer*, 21 (2): 267–97.

Pakistan Ministry of Industries, Production and Special Initiatives (PMIPSI) (2005) *Towards a Prosperous Pakistan: a strategy for rapid industrial growth main report*, Islamabad: PMIPSI. Online. Available at: http://moip.gov.pk/strategy.htm (accessed 1 October 2011).

Panitch, L. and Konings, M. (2009) "Myths of neoliberal deregulation", *New Left Review*, 57: 67–83.

Parker, C. (2007) "Meta-regulation: legal accountability for corporate social responsibility", in D. McBarnet, Voiculescu, A. and Campbell T. (eds) *The New Corporate Accountability: corporate social responsibility and the law*, Cambridge, UK: Cambridge University Press.

Patel, R. (2007) *Stuffed and Starved: markets, power and the hidden battle for the world food system*. Melbourne: Black Inc.

Pateman, C. (2000) "The patriarchal welfare state", in K. Nash (ed.) *Readings in Contemporary Political Sociology*, Oxford: Blackwell.

Peck, J. and Tickell, A. (2002) "Neoliberalizing space", *Antipode*, 34: 380–404.

Peck, J., Theodore, N. and Brenner, N. (2009) "Postneoliberalism and its malcontents", *Antipode*, 41 (6): 94–116.

Penrose, E. T. (1971) *The Growth of Firms, Middle East Oil, and Other Essays*, London: Frank Cass.

Phillips, A. (1995) *The politics of presence*, Oxford; New York: Clarendon Press.

Picchio, A. (1992) *Social Reproduction: the political economy of the labour market*, Cambridge: Cambridge University Press.

Pierson, P. (1996) "The new politics of the welfare state", *World Politics*, 48: 143–79.

Piketty, T. and Saez, E. (2003) "Income inequality in the United States, 1913–1998*", *Quarterly Journal of Economics*, 118: 1–39.

Piketty, T. and Saez, E. (2003) (2006) "The evolution of top incomes: a historical and international perspective", *American Economic Review*, 96: 200–5.

Pinto, S. and Beckfield, J. (2011), "Organized labor in an evolving Europe", *Research in the Sociology of Work* 22: 153–79.

Polanyi, K. (1944) *The Great Transformation: the political and economic origins of our time*, Boston: Beacon Press.

Polanyi, K. (1957) "The economy as instituted process", in Polanyi, K., Arensberg, C. and Pearson, H. (eds) *Trade and Market in Early Empires: economics in history and theory*, Glencoe: Free Press.

Pontusson, J. (2005) *Inequality and Prosperity: social Europe vs. liberal America*, Ithaca: Cornell University Press.

Pontusson, J. (2011) "Once again a model: Nordic social democracy in a globalized world", in Cronin, J., Ross, G. and Shoch, J. (eds) *What's Left of the Left?*, Durham, NC: Duke University Press.

Preston, N., Sampford, C. and Connors, C. (2002) *Encouraging Ethics and Challenging Corruption: public sector ethics in theory and practice*, Sydney: Federation Press.

Przeworksi, A. and Wallerstein, M. (1985) "Democratic capitalism at a crossroads", in A. Przeworksi (ed.) *Capitalism and Social Democracy*, New York: Cambridge University Press.

Quiggin, J. (2010a) "Efficient markets hypothesis: a zombie idea", *Financial Review*, 14 January 2010.

Quiggin, J. (2010b) *Zombie Economics: how dead ideas still walk among us*, Princeton, NJ: Princeton University Press.

Rahman, K. S. (2011) "Conceptualizing the economic role of the state: laissez-faire, technocracy, and the democratic alternative", *Polity*, 43: 264–86.

Rai, S. (1996) "Women and the state in the third world: some issues for debate", in S. Rai and Lievesley, G. (eds) *Women and the State: international perspectives*, London: Taylor and Francis.

Rainsford, S. (2011) "Spain's 'indignants' lead international protest day", BBC News Europe, 15 October 2011. Online. Available at: www.bbc.co.uk/news/world-europe-15315270 (accessed 11 November 2011).

Rawls, J. (1999) *A Theory of Justice*, Cambridge, MA: Harvard University Press.

Rawls, J. (2001) *Justice as Fairness: a restatement*, Cambridge, MA: Harvard University Press.

Razavi, S. (1999) "Export-oriented employment, poverty and gender: contested accounts", *Development and Change*, 30: 653–83.

Razavi, S. (2007) *The Political and Social Economy of Care in a Development Context: Conceptual Issues, Research Questions, and Policy Options*, Gender and Development Programme Paper No. 3, Geneva: United Nations Research Institute for Social Development.

Recovery Accountability and Transparency Board (RATB) (2009) *Annual Report: breaking ground*, Washington, DC: Recovery Accountability and Transparency Board.

Rhyne, E. (2009) "Toward a distributed global banking grid", *New York Times*, 27 January 2009. Online. Available at: http://dealbook.blogs.nytimes.com/2009/01/27/another-view-a-local-fix-for-a-global-mess/ (accessed 3 October 2011).

Robinson, M. and Quiggin, J. (1985) "Retreat from social control: financial deregulation since World War II", *Journal of Australian Political Economy*, 18: 9–16.

Rodrik, D. (1998) "Why do more open economies have bigger governments?", *Journal of Political Economy*, 106: 997–1032.

Rodrik, D. (2001) *The Global Governance of Trade: as if development really mattered*, Background Paper, New York: UNDP. Online. Available at: www.undp.org/mainundp/propoor/docs/pov_globalgovernancetrade_pub.pdf (accessed 5 November 2005).

Rodrik, D. (2002) *Feasible Globalizations*, NBER Working Paper Series W9129, Cambridge, MA: National Bureau of Economic Research.

Rodrik, D. (2004) "Industrial policy for the twenty-first century", John F. Kennedy School of Government Faculty Research Working Paper RWP04–047, Cambridge, MA: Harvard University.

Rodrik, D. (2008) "Normalizing industrial policy", Working Paper No. 3, Commission on Growth and Development, Washington DC: World Bank.

Rodrik, D. (2011) *The Globalization Paradox: democracy and the future of the world economy*, New York: W. W. Norton & Co.

Roemer, J. (1994) *A Future for Socialism*, Cambridge, MA: Harvard University Press.

Rogers, J. and Sabel, C. (1993) "Imagining unions", *Boston Review*, 18 (5): 10–12.

Rogers, J. and Streeck, W. (1994) "Productive solidarities: economic strategy and left politics", in D. Miliband (ed.) *Reinventing the Left*, London: Polity Press.

Ross, S. (2011) *The World Food Programme in Global Politics*, Boulder, CO: First Forum Press.

Rozas, D. (2009) *Is There a Microfinance Bubble in South India?* Microfinance Focus, 1 November 2009. Online. Available at: www.microfinancefocus.com/news/2009/11/17/opinion-microfinance-bubble-south-india/ (accessed 3 October 2001).

Rozman, G. (2004) *Northeast Asia's Stunted Regionalism: bilateral distrust in the shadow of globalization*, New York: Cambridge University Press.

Rubio-Marquez, V. (2009) "The G20: a practitioner's perspective", in L. Martinez-Diaz and Woods, N. (eds) *Networks of Influence?: developing countries in a networked global order*, New York: Oxford University Press.

Rudd, K. (2009) "The global financial crisis", *The Monthly*, February 2009: 20–9.

Ruggie, J. G. (1983) "International regimes, transactions, and change: embedded liberalism in the postwar economic order", in S. D. Krasner (ed.) *International Regimes*, Ithaca: Cornell University Press.

S.D. (2010) "Big trouble for microfinance", *The Economist*, 2 December 2010. Online. Available at: www.economist.com/blogs/freeexchange/2010/12/microfinance (accessed 8 February 2011).

Sabel, C. F. and Simon, W. H. (2011) "Minimalism and experimentalism in the administrative state", *Georgetown Law Journal*, 100: 53–93.

Sabel, C. F. and Zeitlin, J. (2012) "Experimentalist governance", in D. Levi-Faur (ed.) *The Oxford Handbook of Governance*, New York: Oxford University Press.

Sachs, J. (1995) "Do we need an international lender of last resort?", paper presented for the Frank D. Graham Lecture at Princeton University, Princeton, NJ, 20 April 1995. Online. Available at: www.earth.columbia.edu/sitefiles/file/about/director/pubs/intllr.pdf (accessed 11 October 2011).

Sachs, J. (1997) "IMF is a power unto itself", *Financial Times*, 11 December 1997.

Sachs, J. (2008) *Common Wealth: economics for a crowded planet*, New York: Penguin Press.

Sader, E. (2008) "The weakest link? Neoliberalism in Latin America", *New Left Review*, 52: 5–31.

Sampford, C. (1989) *The Disorder of Law: critique of legal theory*, London: Blackwell.

Sampford, C. "Law, institutions and the public private divide", keynote address presented at the Australasian Law Teachers' Association Conference, Canberra, September 1990.

Sampford, C. (1991) "Dworkin's claim to a socialist inheritance", *Bulletin of the Australian Society of Legal Philosophy*, 16 (56): 37–70.

Sampford, C. (1992) "Law, institutions and the public private divide", *Federal Law Review*, 20: 185–222.

Sampford, C. (1994) "Law, ethics and institutional design: finding philosophy, displacing ideology", *Griffith Law Review*, 3: 1–38.

Sampford, C. (1998) "Cautionary reflections on corporatisation and privatisation", in J. Malbon (ed.), *Corporatisation and Privatisation: who benefits?*, London: Routledge.

Sampford, C. "Ethical standard setting for global incentives: towards an effective regulatory philosophy of global greenhouse response", open plenary to the World Council of Churches Colloquium on Carbon Trading, Saskatoon, Canada, May 2000.

Sampford, C. "Capitalism: Quo Vadis?", lecture presented at the International Association of Human Values conference, European Parliament, Brussels, 14 November 2008.

Sampford, C. (2009a) "Professions without borders: global ethics and the international rule of law", *Professions without Borders*, Brisbane: QUT.

Sampford, C. (2009b) "Re-conceiving the good life", paper presented at the Good Life Conference, Griffith Institute for Social and Behavioural Research, Brisbane, 12 February 2009.

Sampford, C. (2010a) "Adam's Smith dinner", in I. McNeil and J. O'Brien (eds) *The Future of Financial Regulation*, Oxford: Hart.

Sampford, C. (2010b) "Media ethics regimes and ethical risk management in Australia", *Journal of Mass Media Ethics*, 19 (2): 86–107.

Sampford, C. (2010c) "Re-conceiving the good life: the key to sustainable globalisation", *Australian Journal of Social Issues*, 41: 13–24.

Sampford, C. (2010d) "Submission on electoral funding and political advertising", Canberra: Senate Standing Committee on Finance and Public Administration Legislation Committee.

Sampford, C. (2010e) "Towards a global carbon integrity system: learning from the GFC and avoiding a GCC", paper presented at the 14th International Anti-corruption Conference, Bangkok, 10–13 November 2010.

Sampford, C. and Lui, R. (2004) "Australian media ethics regime and ethical risk management", *Journal of Mass Media Ethics*, 19 (2): 86–107.

Sanchez, D. and Cash, K. (2003) *Reducing Poverty or Repeating Mistakes? A civil society critique of Poverty Reduction Strategy Papers*, Church of Sweden Aid, Diakonia, Save the Children Sweden and The Swedish Jubilee Network. Online. Available at: www.diakonia.se/Documents/public/IN_FOCUS/Social_Economic_Justice/PRSP/PRSP_report_oct_04_eng.pdf (accessed 11 October 2011).

Scharpf, F. W. (2009) "The double asymmetry of European integration", MPIfG Working Paper 09/12, Cologne: Max Planck Institute for the Study of Societies.

Schmidt, R. (2007) *The Currency Transaction Tax: rate and revenue estimates*, Ottawa: North–South Institute. Online. Available at: www.nsi-ins.ca/english/pdf/CTT%20revenue.pdf (accessed 7 October 2011).

Schneider, B. R. (2009) "Hierarchical market economies and varieties of capitalism in Latin America", *Journal of Latin American Studies*, 41: 553–75.

Schrank, A. and Kurtz, M. J. (2005) "Credit where credit is due: open economy industrial policy and export diversification in Latin America and the Caribbean", *Politics & Society*, 33: 671–702.

Schrank, A. and Whitford, J. (2009) "Industrial policy in the United States: a neo-Polanyian interpretation", *Politics & Society*, 37: 521–33.

Seguino, S. (2000a) "Gender inequality and economic growth: a cross-country analysis", *World Development*, 28: 1211–30.

Seguino, S. (2000b) "The effects of structural change and economic liberalisation on gender wage differentials in South Korea and Taiwan", *Cambridge Journal of Economics*, 24: 437–59.

Seguino, S. and Grown, C. (2006) "Gender equity and globalization: macroeconomic policy for developing countries", *Journal of International Development*, 18: 1081–104.

Sen, A. (1989) "Cooperation, inequality, and the family", *Population and Development Review*, 15(Supplement): 61–76.

Sen, A. (1999) *Development as Freedom*, Oxford: Oxford University Press.

Sen, A. (2009) "Capitalism beyond the crisis", *New York Review of Books*, 26 March 2009. Online. Available at: www.nybooks.com/articles/archives/2009/mar/26/capitalism-beyond-the-crisis/ (accessed 13 November 2011).

Sen, G. (2010) "Poor households or poor women: Is there a difference?", in S. Chant (ed.), *International Handbook of Gender and Poverty: concepts, research and policy*, Cheltenham, UK: Edward Elgar.

Senate Economics Reference Committee (SERC) (2009) *Government's Economic Stimulus Initiatives*, Canberra: Commonwealth of Australia.

Shakespeare, W. (2006) *Hamlet*, A. Thompson and N. Taylor eds., London: Arden Shakespeare.

Shaw, D. J. (2001) *The UN World Food Programme and the Development of Food Aid*, Hampshire: Palgrave.

Shaw, D. J. (2008) *Global Food and Agricultural Institutions*, London: Routledge.

Shearing, C. (1993) "A constitutive conception of regulation", in P. Grabosky and Braithwaite, J. (eds) *Business Regulation and Australia's Future*, Canberra: Australian Institute of Criminology.

Shiller, R. J. (2003) *The New Financial Order: Risk in the 21st Century*, Princeton: Princeton University Press.

Shiva, V. (2000) *Stolen Harvest: the hijacking of the global food supply*, Cambridge, MA: South End Press.

Singh, A. and Zammit, A. (2000) "International capital flows: identifying the gender dimension", *World Development*, 28: 1249–68.

Smith, A. (1976, 1776) *An inquiry into the nature and causes of the wealth of nations*, Oxford: Oxford University Press.

Soesastro, H., Smith, A. L. and Han, M. L. (2003) *Governance in Indonesia: challenges facing the Megawati presidency*, Singapore: Institute of Southeast Asian Studies.

Soros, G. (2009) *The New Paradigm for Financial Markets: the credit crisis of 2008 and what it means*, Melbourne: Scribe Publications.

Spence, M. (2011) "Globalization and unemployment, the downside of integrating markets", *Foreign Affairs*, 2011 (July/August). Online. Available at: www.foreignaffairs.com/articles/67874/michael-spence/globalization-and-unemployment (accessed 7 October 2011).

Spiegel, S. (2006) "Macroeconomic and growth policies", UN DESA Guidance Note, New York: United Nations Department for Economic and Social Affairs.

Spiro, M. (1966) "Buddhism and economic action in Burma", *American Anthropologist*, 68: 1163–73.

Squires, N. (2009) "UN food summit 'fails before it begins'", *The Telegraph* (UK), 12 November 2009. Online. Available at: www.telegraph.co.uk/news/worldnews/europe/italy/6554952/UN-food-summit-fails-before-it-begins.html (accessed 11 October 2011).

Stanway, D. (2011) "China top 10 steel cos produce 48 pct of 2010 output-ministry", *Reuters*, 26 January 2011. Online. Available at: www.reuters.com/article/2011/01/27/china-steel-consolidation-idUSTOE70Q02B20110127 (accessed 12 November 2011).

Stephens, P. (2010) "The West must offer Turkey a proper seat at the table", *Financial Times*, 17 June 2010. Online. Available at: www.ft.com/cms/s/ 0/90750c70–7a45–11df-aa69–00144feabdc0.html#axzz1dXIPJKQO (accessed 12 November 2011).

Steward, F. and Wang, M. (2003) *Do PRSPs Empower Poor Countries and Disempower the World Band, or Is It the Other Way Round?*, QEH Working Paper No. 108, Oxford: Oxford Department of International Development.

Stewart, F. (2007) "Do we need a new 'great transformation'? Is one likely?", in G. Mavrotas and Shorrocks, A. (eds) *Advancing Development*, London: Palgrave Macmillan.

Stewart, F. (2012) "The impact of global economic crises on the poor: comparing the 1980s and 2000s", *Journal of Human Development and Capabilities*, 13.

Stiglitz, J. (2002) *Globalisation and Its Discontents*, New York: W. W. Norton & Co.

Stiglitz, J. (2007) *Making Globalization Work*, New York: W. W. Norton & Co.

Stiglitz, J. (2009) *Report of the Commission of Experts of the President of the United Nations General Assembly on Reforms of the International Monetary and Financial System*, New York: United Nations. Online. Available at: www.un.org/ga/econcrisissummit/docs/FinalReport_CoE.pdf (accessed 11 October 2011).

Stiglitz, J. (2010) *Freefall: America, free markets, and the sinking of the world economy*, New York: W. W. Norton & Co.

Strange, S. (1996) *The Retreat of the State: the diffusion of power in the world economy*, Cambridge, UK: Cambridge University Press.

Streeck, W. (2010) *Re-forming Capitalism: institutional change in the German political economy*, Oxford: Oxford University Press.

Streeck, W. and Schmitter, P. C. (1991) "From national corporatism to transnational pluralism: organized interests in the single European market", *Politics & Society*, 19: 133–64.

Stewart, H. (2011) "Robin Hood tax: 1,000 economists urge G20 to accept Tobin tax", *Guardian*, 13 April 2011. Online. Available at: www.guardian.co.uk/business/2011/apr/13/robin-hood-tax-economists-letter (accessed 13 November 2011).

Tanzi, V. and Schuknecht, L. (2000) *Public Spending in the 20th Century*, Cambridge, UK: Cambridge University Press.

Taylor, V. (2000) *The Marketisation of Governance: critical feminist perspectives from the South*, Cape Town: SADEP, University of Cape Town.

The Economist (2008) "Capitalism at Bay", 16 October 2008. Online. Available at: www.economist.com/opinion/displaystory.cfm?story_id=12429544 (accessed 11 October 2011).

The Economist (2011) "Basel 3: the banks battle back: a behind-the-scenes brawl over new capital and liquidity rules", 27 May 2011. Online. Available at: www.economist.com/node/16231434 (accessed 13 November 2011).

Thimann, C., Just, C. and Ritter, R. (2009) "Strengthening the governance of the International Monetary Fund: how a dual board structure could raise the effectiveness and legitimacy of a key global institution", *Global Governance*, 15: 187–93.

Thirwell, M. (2009) "One G to rule them all", *Lowy Institute for International Policy*, 28 September 2009. Online. Available at: www.lowyinterpreter.org/post/2009/09/28/One-G-to-rule-them-all.aspx (accessed 7 October 2011).

Tilly, C. (1992) *Coercion, Capital, and European States: AD 990–1992*, Oxford: Wiley-Blackwell.

Tingle, L. and Rollins, A. (2009) "Rudd throws $42 billion at economy", *Australian Financial Review*, 4 February 2009.

Tobin, J. (1988) "International monetary reform: sand in the wheels", *Neue Zurcher Zeitung (Zurich)*, 11 October 1988.

Tobin, J. (1996) "Prologue", in M. ul-Haq, I. Kaul and I. Grunberg (eds) *The Tobin Tax: coping with financial volatility*, New York: Oxford University Press.

Tomlinson, B. R. (1981) "Colonial firms and the decline of colonialism in Eastern India, 1914–47", *Modern Asian Studies*, 15: 455–86.

Toye, J. F. J. (1993) *Dilemmas of Development: reflections on the counter-revolution in development economics*, Cambridge, MA: Blackwell.

Treanor, J. (2011) "World food prices enter 'danger territory' to reach record high", *Guardian*, 5 January 2011. Online. Available at: www.commondreams.org/headline/2011/01/05–2 (accessed 6 January 2011).

Unger, R. M. (1998) *Democracy Realized: the progressive alternative*, New York: Verso.

United Nations (1999) *Towards a New International Financial Architecture*, Report of the Task Force of the Executive Committee of Economic and Social Affairs of the United Nations LC/G 2054. Online. Available at: www.un.org/esa/desa/ousg/articles/pdf/intlfinar.htm (accessed 12 November 2011).

United Nations (2001) *Recommendations of the High-Level Panel on Financing for Development*, 55th session of the U.N. General Assembly, A/55/1000, Geneva: United Nations.

United Nations (2004) *A More Secure World: our shared responsibility*, Report of the Secretary-General's High-level Panel on Threats, Challenges and Change, New York: United Nations.

United Nations (2009) *Report of the Commission of Experts of the President of the UN General Assembly on Reforms of the International Monetary and Financial System*,

New York: United Nations. Online. Available at: www.un.org/ga/econcrisissummit/docs/FinalReport_CoE.pdf (accessed 7 October 2011).

United Nations (2010) *Letter Dated 11 March 2010 from the Permanent Representative of Singapore to the United Nations Addressed to the Secretary-General*, A/64/706, New York: United Nations. Online. Available at: www.un.org/ga/search/view_doc.asp?symbol=A/64/706&Lang=E (accessed 7 October 2011).

United Nations Capital Development Fund (UNCDF) (2005) *The Blue Book: building inclusive financial sectors for development*, New York: United Nations. Online. Available at: www.uncdf.org/english/microfinance/pubs/bluebook/pub/index.php?get_page=contents (accessed 3 October 2011).

United Nations Conference on Trade and Development (UNCTAD) (2007) *Economic Development in Africa 2007*, Geneva: UNCTAD.

United Nations Development Fund for Women (UNIFEM) (2000) *World's Progress of Women 2000*, New York: United Nations Development Fund for Women.

United Nations Development Programme (UNDP) (2002) *Deepening Democracy in a Fragmented World*, Human Development Report 2002, New York: Oxford University Press.

United Nations Economic and Social Council (UNECOSOC) (2009) *Summary by the President of the Economic and Social Council on the Follow-up to Paragraph 56 of the Outcome of the Conference on the World Financial and Economic Crisis and Its Impact on Development*, E/2009/119, New York: UNECOSOC.

United Nations General Assembly (2009) *Resolution Adopted by the General Assembly 63/303. Outcome of the Conference on the Financial and Economic Crisis and Its Impact on Development*, A/3/303, New York: United Nations.

U.S. Treasury (2008) "United States and China announce $20 billion in finance facilities", Press release HP-1318. Online. Available at: www.treasury.gov/press-center/press-releases/pages/hp1318.aspx (accessed 17 November 2011).

van Parijs, P. (1998) *Real Freedom for All: what (if anything) justifies capitalism?*, New York: Oxford University Press.

van Staveren, I., Elson, D., Grown, C. and Cagatay, N. (2007) *The Feminist Economics of International Trade*, New York and London: Routledge.

Vestergaard, J. (2011) "The World Bank and the emerging world order: adjusting to multipolarity at the second decimal point", DIIS Report 2011:05, Copenhagen: Danish Institute for International Studies.

Vidal, J. (2009) "Millions will starve as rich nations cut food aid funding, warns UN", *Guardian*, 11 October 2009. Online. Available at: www.commondreams.org/headline/2009/10/11–0 (accessed 24 October 2009).

Vidal, J. (2011) "WikiLeaks: US targets EU over GM crops", *Guardian*, 3 January 2011. Online. Available at: www.commondreams.org/headline/2011/01/03–5 (accessed 4 January 2011).

Vines, S. and Gilbert, C. (2004) *The IMF and Its Critics: reform of global financial architecture*, Cambridge, UK: Cambridge University Press.

Vogel, R. C. (1984) "Savings mobilization: the forgotten half of rural finance", in D. W. Adams, Graham, D. and Von Pischke, J. D. (eds) *Undermining Rural Development with Cheap Credit*, Boulder, CO: Westview Press.

Vols, U. and Caliari, A. (eds) (2010) *Regional and Global Liquidity Arrangements*, Bonn: German Development Institute/Deutsches Institut für Entwicklungspolitik (DIE) and Center of Concern.

Vreeland, J. R. (2003) *The IMF and Economic Development*, Cambridge: Cambridge University Press.

Wade, R. (1996) "Japan, the World Bank, and the art of paradigm maintenance: *The East Asian Miracle* in political perspective", *New Left Review*, 217: 3–36.

Wade, R. (1997) "Greening the bank: the struggle over the environment, 1970–95", in D. Kapur, Lewis, J.P. and Webb, R. (eds) *The World Bank: its first half century*, Washington, DC: Brookings Institution Press.

Wade, R. (2000) "Wheels within wheels: rethinking the Asian crisis and the Asian model", *Annual Review of Political Science*, 3: 85–115.

Wade, R. (2004) *Governing the Market: economic theory and the role of government in East Asian industrialization*, Princeton, NJ: Princeton University Press.

Wade, R. (2009a) "From global imbalances to global reorganizations", *Cambridge Journal of Economics*, 33: 539–62.

Wade, R. (2009b) "The global slump: deeper causes and harder lessons", *Challenge*, 52 (5): 5–24.

Wade, R. (2010a) "After the crisis: industrial policy and the developmental state in low-income countries", *Global Policy*, 1 (2): 150–61.

Wade, R. (2010b) "The state of the World Bank", *Challenge*, 53 (4): 43–67.

Wade, R. (2011a) "Emerging world order? From multipolarity to multilateralism in the G20, the World Bank, and the IMF", *Politics & Society*, 39: 347–77.

Wade, R. (2011b) "The economy has not solved its problems", *Challenge*, 54 (2): 5–41.

Wagenhofer, E. (2005) *We Feed the World*, film, 96 mins, Austria: Allegro Film Productions – Helmut Grasser.

Walby, S. (1989) "Theorising patriarcy", *Sociology*, 23: 213–34.

Walker, T. (2009) "The significant other", *Australian Financial Review*, 2 October 2009.

Warwick Commission on International Financial Reform (Warwick Commission) (2009) *The Warwick Commission on International Finance Reform: in praise of uneven playing fields*, Report of the Second Warwick Commission, Warwick: University of Warwick.

Weisbrot, M. (2009) *CEPR Responds to the IMF's Reply and Defense of Its Policies During the World Recession*, CEPR Discussion Paper (October 2009), Washington, DC: Center for Economic and Policy Research. Online. Available at: www.cepr.net/documents/publications/imf-response-2009–10.pdf (accessed 31 January 2011).

Weisbrot, M. "The G20 fantasy", *Guardian Unlimited* (UK), 27 September 2009. Online. Available at: www.guardian.co.uk/commentisfree/cifamerica/2009/sep/26/g20-reform-pittsburgh (accessed 7 October 2011).

Weisbrot, M., Ray, R., Johnston, J., Cordero, J. A. and Montecino, J. A. (2009) *IMF-Supported Macroeconomic Policies and the World Recession: a look at forty-one borrowing countries*, Washington, DC: Center for Economic and Policy Research. Online. Available at: www.cepr.net/documents/publications/imf-2009–10.pdf (accessed 10 October 2011).

Weitzman, M. L. (1984) *The Share Economy*, Cambridge, MA: Harvard University Press.

Welsh, I. (2006) "The financial transactions of decline", *The Agonist*, 7 September 2006. Online. Available at: http://agonist.org/ian_welsh/20060907/financialization_and_the_transactions_of_decline?highlight=financialization (accessed 1 October 2011).

Western, B. (1997) *Between Class and Market: postwar unionization in capitalist democracies*, Princeton, NJ: Princeton University Press.

Wheatley, J. (2009) "Brazil and China in plan to axe dollar", *Financial Times*, 18 May 2011.Online.Availableat:www.ft.com/cms/s/0/996b1af8–43ce-11de-a9be-00144feabdc0.html#axzz1aWgJGjgs (accessed 11 October 2011).

Wiles, M. (2010) "China's censors misfire in abuse-of-power case", *New York Times*, 17

November 2010. Online. Available at: www.nytimes.com/2010/11/18/world/asia/18li.html (accessed 14 October 2011).

Winch, P. (1958) *The Idea of Social Science and Its Relationship to Philosophy*, London: Routledge.

Women's Working Group on Financing for Development (WWGFD) (2009) "G20 & IMF: peddling cosmetic changes while hounded by illegitimacy". Online. Available at: www.ffdngo.org/gender-financing-development (accessed 7 October 2011).

Woo-Cumings, M. (1999) *The Developmental State: Cornell studies in political economy*, Ithaca, NY: Cornell University Press.

Wood, E. (1995) *Democracy against Capitalism: renewing historical materialism*, Cambridge, UK: Cambridge University Press.

Woods, N. (2007) *The Shifting Politics of Foreign Aid*, GEG Working Paper No. 2007/36, Oxford: Global Economic Governance Programme.

Woods, N. (2008) *A Commonwealth Initiative to Support Reform of the IMF and the World Bank*, Commonwealth Heads of Government Meeting on Reform of International Institutions Report HGM-RII(08)3, London: Commonwealth Secretariat. Online. Available at: www.thecommonwealth.org/shared_asp_files/GFSR.asp?NodeID=179891 (accessed 7 October 2011).

Woods, N. (2009) *The International Response to the Global Crisis and the Reform of the International Financial Architecture*, Briefing Paper EXPO/B/DEVE/2009/21(PE410.200), Brussels: European Parliament.

World Bank (1989) *Strengthening Trade Policy Reform*, Washington, DC: World Bank.

World Bank (2006) "Strengthen access to finance for small & medium-size enterprises while improving business environment for all firms", Finance research feature. Online. Available at: http://go.worldbank.org/ZTC9BJ5VV0 (accessed 17 November 2011).

World Bank (2008) *Finance for all? Policies and pitfalls in expanding access*, Washington, DC: International Bank for Reconstruction and Development/World Bank.

World Bank (2009) "Development committee press conference: annual meetings 2009", Press release, 5 October 2009, Washington DC: World Bank. Online. Available at: http://go.worldbank.org/K3ITAT2UY0 (accessed 16 October 2011).

World Summit on Food Security (WSFS) (2009), *Declaration of the World Summit on Food Security*, WSFS 2009/2, Rome: World Summit on Food Security.

World Trade Organization (WTO) (2011) "Regional trade agreements: rules", *The WTO's Rules*. Online. Available at: www.wto.org/english/tratop_e/region_e/regrul_e.htm (accessed 1 October 2011).

Wright, E. O. (2010) *Envisioning Real Utopias*, New York: Verso.

Wroughton, L. (2011) "G20 fails to endorse financial transaction tax", *Reuters*, 4 November 2011. Online. Available at: www.reuters.com/article/2011/11/04/g20-tax-idUSN1E7A302520111104 (accessed 13 November 2011).

Xiaochaun, Z. (2009) "Reform the IMF". Online. Available at: www.china.org.cn/international/2009–03/26/content_17504019.htm (accessed 11 October 2011).

Yan, Z. (2010) "Government tightens control on rare earths", *China Daily*, 2 June 2010. Online. Available at: www.chinadaily.com.cn/china/2010–06/02/content_9919736.htm (accessed 1 October 2011).

Yang, H. B. (2009) *Development and Performance of Korean Policies for SMEs by Economic Development Stage, 1962–2007*, KIET Occasional Paper No. 76, Seoul: Korea Institute for Industrial & Economic Trade. Online. Available at: www.kiet.re.kr/kiet/eng/report/occasional.jsp?viewmode=read&serial=1718&keyWord=&keyField=&nowPage=0&numPerPage=10 (accessed 1 October 2011).

You, J. I. (2002) "The Bretton Woods Institutions", in D. Nayyar (ed.) *Governing Globalisation: issues and institutions*, New York: Oxford University Press.

Zerbe, N. (2009) "Setting the global dinner table: exploring the limits of the marketization of food security", in J. Clapp and Cohen, M. (eds) *The Global Food Crisis: governance challenges and opportunities*, Waterloo, ON: Wilfrid Laurier University Press.

Zhou, M. (2010) "Multidimensionality and gravity in global trade, 1950–2000", *Social Forces*, 88: 1619–43.

Zhou, X. (2009) "Reform the international monetary system", *People's Bank of China*, 23 March 2009. Online. Available at: www.pbc.gov.cn/publish/english/956/2009/2009 1229104425550619706/20091229104425550619706_.html (accessed 7 October 2011).

Zoellick, R. "The end of the Third World?", speech address to the Woodrow Wilson Center for International Scholars, Washington, DC, 14 April 2010.

Index

Page numbers in *italics* denote tables, those in **bold** denote figures.

For Product Safety Concerns and Information please contact our EU
representative GPSR@taylorandfrancis.com
Taylor & Francis Verlag GmbH, Kaufingerstraße 24, 80331 München, Germany

www.ingramcontent.com/pod-product-compliance
Lightning Source LLC
LaVergne TN
LVHW011119300926
849160LV00008B/443